C0-ALP-218

Sophocles Revisited

SIR HUGH LLOYD-JONES

Sophocles Revisited

Essays Presented to Sir Hugh Lloyd-Jones

Edited by
JASPER GRIFFIN

OXFORD
UNIVERSITY PRESS

OXFORD
UNIVERSITY PRESS

Great Clarendon Street, Oxford OX2 6DP

Oxford University Press is a department of the University of Oxford.
It furthers the University's objective of excellence in research, scholarship,
and education by publishing worldwide in

Oxford New York

Athens Auckland Bangkok Bogotá Bombay Buenos Aires Calcutta
Cape Town Chennai Dar es Salaam Delhi Florence Hong Kong Istanbul
Karachi Kuala Lumpur Madras Melbourne Mexico City Mumbai
Nairobi Paris São Paulo Singapore Taipei Tokyo Toronto Warsaw

and associated companies in Berlin Ibadan

Oxford is a registered trade mark of Oxford University Press

Published in the United States
by Oxford University Press Inc., New York

© Oxford University Press 1999

The moral rights of the author have been asserted
Database right Oxford University Press (maker)

First published 1999

All rights reserved. No part of this publication may be reproduced,
stored in a retrieval system, or transmitted, in any form or by any means,
without the prior permission in writing of Oxford University Press,
or as expressly permitted by law, or under terms agreed with the appropriate
reprographics rights organizations. Enquiries concerning reproduction
outside the scope of the above should be sent to the Rights Department,
Oxford University Press, at the address above

You must not circulate this book in any other binding or cover
and you must impose the same conditions on any acquirer

British Library Cataloguing in Publication Data

Data available

Library of Congress Cataloging in Publication Data

Sophocles revisited: essays presented to Sir Hugh Lloyd-Jones /
edited by Jasper Griffin.
p. cm.
Includes bibliographical references and index.
1. Sophocles—Criticism and interpretation. 2. Greek drama
(Tragedy)—History and criticism. 3. Mythology, Greek, in
literature. I. Lloyd-Jones, Hugh. II. Griffin, Jasper.
PA4417.S6916 1999
882'.01–dc21 99-21396

ISBN 0-19-813006-6

1 3 5 7 9 10 8 6 4 2

Typeset by Joshua Associates Ltd., Oxford
Printed in Great Britain
on acid-free paper by
Biddles Ltd., Guildford and King's Lynn

PA
4417
.S6916
1999

παιωνίζετ᾽, ἰή, φίλοι·
νοστῶν οἴκαδε πεντεχα-
βδομηκονταέτης ὁδὶ
τὴν γενέθλιον ἑςτιᾶι
  κωμαςτὴς φιλόμουςος.

ἑρμηνεύματι ποικίλωι
τὴν Δίκην Διὸς ἐκφράςας
καὶ Cοφοκλέα παγκάλως
ἐκδούς, ἀθανάτοις ῥόδοις
  Ἑλλάδ᾽ ἐςτεφάνωςεν.

"χαῖρε, cυμποςίου πάτερ,
χαῖρε, τρίςμακαρ" εὐςτομεῖ
χορὸς δώδεκ᾽ ἀηδόνων
ἑςτιάμαςί τ᾽ ἐμπρέπει
  θελξίφρων Διόνυςος.

        (Colin Austin)

Contents

The Contributors

COLIN AUSTIN is Reader in Greek Language and Literature in the University of Cambridge and a Fellow of Trinity Hall. He is one of the two editors of *Poetae Comici Graeci.*

P. E. EASTERLING is Regius Professor of Greek in the University of Cambridge and a Fellow of Newnham College. She was a pupil of Sir Hugh as an undergraduate. She is one of the General Editors of the series of Cambridge Greek and Latin Classics, in which she has published a commentary on Sophocles' *Trachiniae.*

ROBERT L. FOWLER is W. O. Wills Professor of Greek in the University of Bristol. He was supervised by Sir Hugh for his D.Phil. thesis, published as *The Nature of Early Greek Lyric: Three Preliminary Studies* (Toronto, 1987).

JASPER GRIFFIN is Professor of Classical Literature in Oxford University and a Fellow of Balliol College. His books include *Homer on Life and Death* (Oxford, 1980) and *Latin Poets and Roman Life* (London, 1987).

EDITH HALL is a Fellow and Tutor of Somerville College, Oxford, and joint Director of the Ancient Drama Archive. She was supervised by Sir Hugh for her D.Phil. thesis, published as *Inventing the Barbarian* (Oxford, 1993).

MALCOLM HEATH is Reader in Classics at the University of Leeds. He was supervised by Sir Hugh for his D.Phil. thesis, published as *The Poetics of Greek Tragedy* (London, 1987).

LEOFRANC HOLFORD-STREVENS works for the Oxford University Press, where he is active in the production of classical books. He is the author of *Aulus Gellius* (London, 1988).

GREGORY HUTCHINSON is Professor of Classical Literature at Oxford University and a Fellow of Exeter College. He was supervised by Sir Hugh for his D.Phil. thesis, published as *Aeschylus'*

Septem Contra Thebas, *edited with Introduction and Commentary* (Oxford, 1985).

BERNARD KNOX was for many years Director of the Center for Hellenic Studies, Washington, DC. His Sather Lectures were published as *The Heroic Temper: Studies in Sophoclean Tragedy* (California, 1966).

ROBERT PARKER is Wykeham Professor of Ancient History at Oxford University and a Fellow of New College. He was supervised by Sir Hugh for his D.Phil. thesis, published as *Miasma: Pollution and Purification in Early Greek Religion* (Oxford, 1983).

RICHARD STONEMAN is a Director of Routledge and responsible for a large classical list. He was supervised by Sir Hugh for his D.Phil. thesis, *A Commentary on Six Nemean Odes of Pindar*. Among his books are *A Literary Companion to Greece* (Harmondsworth, 1984), and *Alexander the Great* (London, 1997).

MARTIN WEST was Professor of Greek at Royal Holloway College, London, and is a Senior Research Fellow of All Souls College, Oxford. He was supervised by Sir Hugh for his D.Phil. thesis, published as *Hesiod's* Theogony, *edited with Prolegomena and Commentary* (Oxford, 1966).

STEPHANIE WEST is Fellow Librarian of Hertford College, Oxford. She was supervised by Sir Hugh for her D.Phil. thesis, published as *The Ptolemaic Papyri of Homer* (Papyrologica Coloniensia: Cologne, 1967).

NETTA ZAGAGI is Professor of Classics at the University of Tel-Aviv. She was supervised by Sir Hugh for her D.Phil. thesis, published as *Tradition and Originality in Plautus: Studies of the Amatory Motifs in Plautine Poetry* (*Hypomnemata* 62: Göttingen, 1980).

1

Introduction

BERNARD KNOX

Unlike the other contributors to this volume, I have never enjoyed the privilege of studying under the direction of the eminent scholar whose 75th birthday it celebrates. He began his undergraduate studies at Oxford in 1940 and resumed them in 1946 after military service in the Far East; I went down from Cambridge in 1936 and did not pursue further study of the classics until 1946, as a graduate student at Yale University in the USA. I did not meet him until some time in the 1960s, when he came to read a paper at the Center for Hellenic Studies in Washington, of which I was at that time Director. We became friends, so that although he is now Sir Hugh, I will adapt Falstaff's formula—Sir Hugh with all Europe but Hugh to his friends—and refer to him throughout as Hugh.

But long before that meeting I had become a fascinated student of his publications on Greek tragedy, the main field of concentration of my own study and teaching. I was delighted by the first article I read, which restored to Aeschylus' Iphigenia the clothes of which most modern commentators, following the lead of Fraenkel—'there she kneels, with upturned eyes, naked before men'—had deprived her. The next item, however, was a bombshell: the famous article in the *Journal of Hellenic Studies* that appeared in 1956, 'Zeus in Aeschylus'. It was one more attempt to deal with the problem posed by the *Prometheus Bound*: how to reconcile the vindictive Zeus tyrannos of that play with the majestic figure of Zeus presented in the *Supplices* and *Oresteia*—a stern but just, all-powerful god, whose decree that wisdom comes alone through suffering offered mankind a road to redemption. It was a notion epitomized in Fraenkel's comment on the closing lines of the *Oresteia*: 'all Homeric thought is here transcended in this notion of a unified and all-prevailing justice which in the wisdom of reconciliation triumphs in the end over the tangled fates and frightful misdeeds of mankind.' Such an exalted conception of the power and benevolence of Zeus is impossible to reconcile with the figure of the harsh tormentor of mankind's benefactor who in the *Prometheus Bound* sends his contemptible lackey Hermes to mock and deliver the threat of still more excruciating punishment to his victim spreadeagled on the rock.

One popular approach was to claim that in the succeeding plays of the trilogy Zeus 'evolves', that over the course of the long years of Prometheus' suffering, he becomes a more just, a more benevolent figure. Hugh's solution was to abolish the problem. His meticulous examination and analysis of the figure of Zeus in the *Supplices* and the *Oresteia* 'seems to lead to what many people will find the startling conclusion that Aeschylus' conception of Zeus contains nothing that is new, nothing that is sophisticated, nothing that is profound'. As he points out: 'No advanced theology of the kind Aeschylus is often credited with is found in any Greek author before Plato', who includes Aeschylus among the poets castigated for their misrepresentation of deity in the *Republic*. There is therefore no contradiction between the conception of Zeus in the *Oresteia* and that of the *Prometheia*. Prometheus is finally released from his agony in exchange for the secret that threatens the supremacy of Zeus and Orestes is spared by the Erinyes in exchange for a permanent home in Athens. In both cases Zeus, in the manner of many modern statesmen, is not involved in the deal; in both cases it is engineered through the action of subordinates, Athena and Heracles.

The harshness of the third item in the assessment of Aeschylus' theology—'nothing profound'—was modified in the later *Justice of Zeus* (1971) and in the end-note to the reprint of the original article in his *Academic Papers* (1990). He speaks there of his original reluctance to reprint the article and his final decision to do so 'because it played a part in the discussion of the time, and people may find it convenient to have a copy'. Though he still agrees with a good deal of its contents, he has 'grown to dislike its tone' ('Unlike Zeus, I have developed' he remarks elsewhere). He goes on to affirm that 'if Aeschylus' theology is comparatively simple, that does not mean that it is not profound'.

When I first read the article, in 1956, its tone was music to my ears. It gave eloquent expression to my own growing impatience with the doctrine, prevalent especially in American academic writing, that Aeschylus was a pioneering religious thinker whose tragedies (with the exception of the *Prometheus Bound*), offered a vision of Zeus and the Olympian gods far more exalted and refined than that of Homer, whose Zeus in the *Iliad* reluctantly yields his favourite city, Troy, to the destructive fury of Hera in exchange for his own future destruction of some great city that she happens to favour. (She offers him three: Argos, Sparta, and Mycenae.) What in fact had emerged from scholarly discussion of the *Supplices* and *Oresteia* was 'a new kind of monotheism pioneered by Aeschylus', a vision often backed up by comparison with suitable passages from the prophets of the Old Testament. Hugh's article came like a welcome cold wind to clear the air; Aeschylus was restored to his proper context, the Olympian religion, 'whose merits', as Hugh writes elsewhere, 'were perceived by Walter F. Otto . . . the insistence that the gods governed the universe for themselves and not for men, its reminder that the human condition imposed limitations that no action on the part of man could overcome, its teaching that human life was for the most part miserable but might by the favour of the gods and the supreme efforts of men themselves contain moments of felicity'. Otto is frequently cited in the text and notes of *The Justice of Zeus* which begins, in fact, with an epigraph from Otto in the original German, a passage that stresses emphatically the gulf between the laws that govern the existence of gods and those that prevail for men.

This appreciative understanding of archaic Greek religion, which Hugh obviously shares with Otto, also informs his many articles on Pindar, whose achievement he celebrated in one of the British Academy's lectures on a Master Mind delivered in 1982. In a survey of critical reactions to Pindar's poetry he spoke of 'the vast damage done by the fatal conjunction of nineteenth-century historicism with nineteenth-century Romanticism': the view that lyric poetry was 'the spontaneous outpouring of the poet's sincerest feelings' and the attempt to sound those depths by recourse to ancient biographies and commentaries, much of whose information 'has no securer base than jokes from comedy later taken seriously by owlish grammarians or frivolous speculations based on the poet's own work'. On the other hand, much as he respects Bundy's ground-breaking work on the conventions of the epinician genre which 'has placed new weapons in the hands of those who would defend the essential unity of the victory ode', he deplores the enthusiastic adoption of this approach by 'those humdrum scholars who are forever on the lookout for a mechanical recipe for getting results' and who 'have created a dreary scholasticism, treating an ode as a collection of commonplaces strung together by a few stock devices'. For him, much of the undeniable power of Pindar's poetry springs from the fact that 'Pindar is above all a religious poet, and much of the failure to understand him has been bound up with the failure to understand the Greek religion that pervades his poetry.' It is the same religion as that of Simonides and Bacchylides 'and, if we make allowances for the differences of genre and avoid the pervasive error of reading ideas into ancient tragedy that are not there, we can see that it is not very different from the religious outlook that we find in Aeschylus or Sophocles'. And Pindar is its most majestic spokesman. 'Presented by a poet whose imagination has grasped its tragic truth with utter honesty and clarity, the austere world of archaic Greek religion comes across to us in all its beauty and with all its hardness.'

Hugh spoke, in the sentence preceding this citation, of the need for awareness of how much Pindar has in common 'with other writers in the same genre, with Greek archaic poetry in general, and with all believers in archaic Greek religion'. In that last category one is inclined to list Otto for a start, and one is tempted at times to believe that Hugh, in his heart of hearts, has more respect for Zeus than for the organized Christianity to which he often makes slightly mischievous reference in his writings. In a brilliant review of Steiner's *After Babel* for example he remarks that 'in studying Japanese one is forced to recognize that what one had lazily assumed to be fundamental categories of human thought are merely local habits'. After citing some examples he goes on: 'Having learned some during the war, I set out in an essay for my tutor to refute St. Anselm's ontological argument for the existence of God by showing the difficulty of expressing it in that language'. He also records his hope that 'the Communist churches of Russia and China may prove Christian in their failure to be reconciled' and makes an affectionate reference to Oxford in 1848 as 'a somnolent beauty' which 'was slowly awakening from the clerical slumbers of the preceding century'. On the other hand he has no use at all for Romanticism in general and in particular for its precursor Rousseau. He complains of an educational system which suffers from a 'Rous-

seauite reluctance to make children work' and, true to his conservative bent—'I am a Conservative, with very little belief in the
intrinsic goodness of human nature'—he deplores 'the fatuous self-
complacency of Rousseauite utopian optimism'. This polemical
tone recurred often in reviews of work he considered misguided
or inadequate. 'The Greeks', he once wrote, 'were not tolerant of the
well-meaning idiot', and neither is he. He dismissed a book on
Greek tragedy by a well-known dramatic critic as 'tiresome' and
'silly' and a three-volume work on Greek culture that was highly
respected in America as 'pompous and pretentious'. He has been
especially eloquent on the subject of Freudian interpretations of
classical texts, often driving home his point by devastating quotations, as in his complaint that 'Freud's own occasional explanations
of individual myths are somewhat disappointing' followed up by the
sentence: 'His contention that the myth of Prometheus indicates
that "to gain control over fire man had to renounce the homo-
sexually-tinged desire to put it out with a stream of urine" is not
often mentioned even by his loyal adherents.'

Hugh was an enthusiastic auditor of some of the lectures I gave
on Greek myth as Nellie Wallace Lecturer in 1975, since I was
discussing Freudian psychological and Levi-Straussian anthropolo-
gical interpretations of Greek myth and literature and had come
armed with outrageously absurd quotations from transatlantic
scholars, including discussions of the relevance of the hilariously
scatological myths of the Bororos of the Brazilian rain forest. I felt
that the laughter provoked by some of the quotations was appropriate in view of the title of the lectureship; I was under the
mistaken impression that it was named in honour of the great
music-hall comedienne some of whose performances I had enjoyed
in my early years. (I was not, unfortunately, present at the famous
occasion when she came on stage as a cook seeking refuge from her
troubles in the garden and sang a ditty that began 'I sits among the
cabbages and peas . . .'. It is reported that when the Lord
Chamberlain objected to the wording she amended the text by
replacing peas with leeks). Some years later Hugh published a wide-
ranging and penetrating examination of psychoanalysis and the
study of the ancient world in which he gave a caustic verdict on the
value of this addition to the scholarly armoury: 'Since the last war,
to acquire a smattering of Freud, usually untainted by the smallest
admixture of more modern psychology, has been one way of solving

the perennial problem of how to publish work on Greek literature and not perish, without knowing any Greek.'

Sometimes, however, his targets were demolished with a lethally short phrase, swift and destructive as the thunderbolt of Zeus, like the sentence in his review of Mette's attempt to reconstruct the lost trilogies of Aeschylus—a recommendation that the author take to heart the first two lines of Catullus 8:

> Miser Catulle, desinas ineptire,
> et quod vides perisse perditum ducas.

I was one of several fascinated witnesses to a dramatic sequel to this onslaught. It took place at an international classical conference held at Bonn some time in the 1970s. The very full programme of papers was rounded off with a *Rheinfahrt*, a trip up river to Koblenz and back. As the ship moved slowly out into midstream, we saw the large group of German students who had acted as gofers for the conferees waving to us from the dock, and more than one of us, remembering our own days as the lowest of the low, read in their minds a fantasy that the ship, loaded with the bulk of the tenured classical professoriate of Europe and America, might sink in midstream and give everyone an upward move. As we went along, a voice on the loudspeaker drawing our attention to points of interest on the banks such as the rock on which Lorelei sat as she lured sailors to their deaths, my neighbours and I heard voices raised in anger on a deck immediately below us. Peering over the rails we saw Hugh and Mette shouting at each other. What was remarkable about the heated exchange was that Mette's harangue was delivered in very respectable English and Hugh's counter-attack in equally respectable German.

All non-German classical scholars have to learn German of course. Once in my days of graduate study at Yale I was seated in the classics department library, deep in Schmid-Staehlin's *Griechische Literatur-Geschichte* (Erster Teil, Zweiter Band), when a senior member of the department peeked over my shoulder in passing and said 'Good! You can get by in this profession without knowing too much Greek or Latin, but you *have* to know German.' Hugh not only knows it very well but has read widely in its literature and not just in its professional literature on the classics, as the essays on Goethe, Nietzsche, Humboldt, Wagner, and a surprisingly respectful assessment of Karl Marx bear witness. His admiration for the great German scholars, especially those who left Nazi Germany and found refuge at Oxford, finds affectionate expression in the splendid essays (many of them obituaries) on Reinhardt, Maas, Fraenkel, and Pfeiffer. He is also at home in Italian literature, as is clear from his essay on Leopardi, a poet whose vision of the world had some resemblances to his own view of the Greek religious mood—'a belief that the whole nature of the universe was necessarily adverse to human aspirations'. In the same essay and elsewhere he expresses great admiration for the work of Sebastiano Timpanaro 'at once the most distinguished classical scholar now working in Italy' (this was written in 1978), 'a leading authority on Leopardi, and a Marxist theorist of striking originality who can be read and admired even by the enemies of Marxism'.

When Hugh gave his inaugural lecture as Regius Professor in 1961, he spoke of the three different duties of the professional scholar: 'one to their subject, one to their pupils, and one to the general public'. As examples of scholars who had made an attempt to do their duty to the general public he cited his two predecessors, Murray and Dodds, adding 'and I shall do anything I can do to follow them'. In reviews and articles like those mentioned above, written in limpid and often witty expository prose for such periodicals as the *Times Literary Supplement*, the *New Statesman*, the *Spectator*, *Encounter*, the *London Review of Books*, and the *New York Review of Books*, he has more than lived up to his promise.

His first visit to the Center for Hellenic Studies in Washington was a memorable occasion. As we took sherry before lunch he questioned the fellows about their research projects, showering them with suggestions for articles they should consult, and discussing the merits and weaknesses of many contemporary scholars, to some of whom he would grant a certain importance, but qualify it with the statement, delivered with emphatic emphasis: 'But he doesn't know *Greek!*' Some of the fellows looked taken aback, but made no comment at the time; it was later, after Hugh's departure, that some of them came to me and asked how on earth the Professor could say *that* about So-and-so, who in one case turned out to be the Doktor-Vater of the young scholar asking the question.

I did my best to explain that Hugh was assessing knowledge of the ancient Greek language by standards so demanding that I, for one, could never meet them. He was the product, I told them, of a type of training in Greek and Latin which was uniquely characteristic of the best English schools, a programme of frequent translation from English to Latin and Greek from the earliest years, starting with prose and proceeding to verse composition in a variety of metres, a programme continued at a more intensive level at the university. Hugh himself took two terms of composition at Oxford under no less an authority than Denys Page, who would later become Regius Professor of Greek at Cambridge, as his pupil would later become Regius Professor at Oxford. Composition was a discipline that even in its heyday up to the end of the Second World War consumed what many scholars thought was an inordinate amount of the time of both tutor and student, yet, as Hugh points out, the great Wilamowitz, one of the champions of *Altertumswissenschaft*, 'insisted on its value and never ceased to try to persuade his countrymen to copy us in this respect'. It was a discipline that produced, in its most accomplished exponents, scholars uniquely equipped to deal with the complex problems—metrical, grammatical, linguistic—facing the editor of a classical text, particularly those that have come down to us as the tattered remnants of papyrus rolls.

Hugh's qualifications for such work are formidable but he also has an archaic Greek sense of the danger of excess, even in excellence. In his fascinating study of Gilbert Murray he cites some brilliant samples of Murray's talent for Greek verse composition, including one stunning three-line version of a Tennysonian pastoral in Theocritean verse, impeccable in every respect, including dialect. 'He was a subtle and ingenious textual critic,' Hugh remarks, but he goes on to add: 'indeed his main fault lies in an excess of those qualities.' He was too creative an editor.

I had to learn Greek in a school which offered only Latin, German, and French; with the aid of the smaller edition of Liddell and Scott and an occasional session with one of the Latin teachers who knew some Greek, I hacked my way through Murray's Oxford edition of Aeschylus, making what sense I could and in the process learning large chunks of it by heart, but never bothering with the apparatus—I had more than enough to deal with as it was. It was not until I went up to Cambridge that I learned how much of what I had struggled to understand and had learned by heart was pure Murray—πρὸς ἓν ῥέποις in *Agamemnon* 323 for example. (It appears in the second edition of 1955 only in the apparatus in the form *latet ut puto* πρὸς ἕν (ῥέποις, νέμοις?) and is nowhere to be found in Page's edition of 1972.) Hugh has the same expertise in the composition of Greek verse—I have seen him compose impromptu elegant Greek verses for the flyleaf of a book presented to him with a request for his signature—but he has also, unlike Murray, a reluctance to use his expertise for heroic textual surgery.

Quite apart from the many technical articles in the two-volume selection of his academic papers (Pindar, Aeschylus, Sophocles, Euripides, Aristophanes, and Callimachus the authors most frequently discussed) his talents as an editor are given full scope in his edition of the Aeschylean fragments in the Loeb volume, his text of Menander's *Dyscolus* in the OCT, in the monumental *Supplementum Hellenisticum*, on which he collaborated with his successor in the Regius Professorship, Peter Parsons, and, more recently, in the new Oxford text of Sophocles, followed by *Sophoclea* and *Sophocles, Second Thoughts*, on all three of which he collaborated with Nigel Wilson. Since then he has published a new Loeb edition of Sophocles, with a careful prose translation which 'has no literary pretensions, being intended as an aid to those who wish to understand the Greek text printed opposite'. It was a vast improvement over its predecessor, a version in professorial pentameters, which was of little help to the reader trying to understand the Greek and made Sophocles sound like a late-Victorian poetaster on one of his less inspired days. The third volume, which offers a text and translation of the Sophoclean fragments, is an invaluable supplement to Radt's edition as well as a new resource for the Greekless. The translation also offers interpretation in many places where the lack of context produces obscurity, and the text itself is improved and in the papyrus fragments often supplemented with excellent results. These Sophoclean editions are not the end of Hugh's scholarly production (reviews and articles continue to appear at a rate hard to keep up with) but they mark a climax in his distinguished career and provide a fitting theme for the essays which in this volume are offered as a tribute from his pupils in celebration of his 75th birthday. He has clearly done his duty to his subject as well as to the general public; the high quality of the essays in this volume is eloquent testimony to the fact that he has more than done his duty to his pupils.

2

Through a Glass Darkly: Sophocles and the Divine

ROBERT PARKER

Struggle against it though one may, it is hard in the end to talk about Sophocles without talking about his gods. In none of the surviving plays do the first twenty lines pass without a god or a religious practice being mentioned; in one a goddess makes the opening speech. Yet, saturated with the divine though the plays are, the Sophoclean gods remain distant and elusive. What follows will be an attempt to approach these familiar issues by a side path. The initial question will not be about the conceptions of the gods that may emerge from the plays but about the ways in which they emerge. Where and how in the tragedies do theological issues arise? How is the audience's understanding of them shaped, and how insistently? What is the spectator told about divine involvement in human affairs that can count as certainty, what as possibility, what possibilities or even certainties present themselves without being spoken of directly?

The most obvious and incontestable way in which the gods' involvement in the action of a play is revealed is their physical appearance on stage. The total of certain or highly probable cases of such epiphany in Sophocles now stands at six. To four long known—those of Athena in *Ajax*, Heracles at the end of *Philoctetes*, Demeter in *Triptolemos*, Thetis in *Syndeipnoi* (which may be a

I offer this θρεπτήριον in warm gratitude to an inspiring teacher who has also been to me a profound intellectual influence and a most steadfast friend.

I am most grateful to participants in the birthday colloquium for Hugh Lloyd-Jones for their comments, and most particularly to Richard Rutherford and Jasper Griffin for written responses to a draft of this chapter.

satyr-play)—two have been added from papyri published in 1971
and 1976 respectively. In *Niobe*, Apollo eggs on Artemis to shoot
the children of the boastful Niobe, in *Locrian Ajax* Athena
expresses furious anger to the Greek army over the rape of
Cassandra.[1] Through the new discoveries we have a more varied
picture of the ways in which tragedians present gods on stage. It is
now too simple to distinguish merely between the participatory
gods of early tragedy (such as Apollo and Athena in *Eumenides*),
who take part in the main action of the play, and the framing gods
so familiar from Euripides, who forecast events in prologues or
direct them to an end in final speeches 'from the machine'. At least
one and perhaps both of the new Sophoclean epiphanies seem to
represent dramatic interventions by an angry god in mid-play (to
add in fact to one or two such instances already known, such as
that of Iris and Lyssa in Euripides' *Heracles*[2]). Almost equivalent in
effect to an epiphany is the messenger's report in *Oedipus at
Colonus* of the divine voice which so ennobles Oedipus by
associating him with itself in a first person plural: 'Hey there,
Oedipus, Oedipus, why are we delaying?' (1627–8). The reactions
of the various characters to this and other signs[3] create just as
palpable a sense of divine presence as if a god had appeared on the
stage.

[1] *Ajax* 1–90; *Phil.* 1409–44; frs. 598; 562; 441a; 10c. I relegate this 'dark stranger'
of *Inachus* to a note, given the majority view that the play is satyric (see West (1984:
292–302) who dissents). For further possibilities in Sophocles see Mueller (1910:
47–61). v. Blumenthal (1929) postulates *dei ex machina* for *Epigoni*, *Tereus*, *Tyro*,
very questionably.

[2] Itself reminiscent of that of Lyssa in Aesch. *Xantriai* fr. 169 Radt. Other misfits
are Athena in Soph. *Ajax*, who is part framing (she opens the play), part
participatory (she engages in dialogue with the characters), and Athena in [Eur.]
Rhesus, who makes an epiphany in mid-play but then participates for about 80 lines.
A further traditional type is the disguised god (Dionysus plays of Aeschylus and
Euripides; Aeschylus' Hera, in a Dionysiac play, fr. 168 R.: cf. Oranje (1984: 124–
30)). Other divine characters certainly attested in tragedies of Aeschylus are:
Aphrodite in *Danaides*, fr. 44; Hermes in Φρύγες ἢ Λύτρα, p. 365 Radt; Boreas in
Oreithyia, fr. 281; Zeus in *Psychostasia*, p. 375 Radt (doubted by Taplin (1977: 431–
5)—but there are two independent testimonia); Dike in fr. 281a (satyric?); Thetis in
Ὅπλων κρίσις, cf. fr. 174, and various in the *Prometheus* plays. See further Mueller
(1910: 1–46). The possibilities among lost plays of Euripides are very numerous (cf.
Oranje (1984: 118)), and on Zeus in *Alcmene* West (1984: 294–5): divine speeches
survive from *Antiope*, p. 68 Page *GLP*; *Erechtheus*, frs. 39, 65, 55 ff. Austin.

[3] Beginning with the thunder of 1447 ff. Note esp. Theseus' reported reaction to
what he saw, and we did not, in 1649 ff.

Within the world of the play, the actions, directly experienced, and the remarks of the gods surely have unique authority as revelations of divine will. But in the admittedly small sample the gods prove very economical as to how much they will or can reveal. Athena's dealings with Ajax have a prehistory, but we learn of her two complaints against Ajax not from her own mouth but from the seer Calchas later in the play (756–77): she herself takes Ajax's guilt for granted, and all her emphasis lies on the moral lesson to be drawn from it (127–33). In *Philoctetes* Heracles appears in order to convey the plans of Zeus (Διὸς βουλεύματα, 1415)—the only reference in extant Sophocles to such plans[4]—but what he reveals of them is rather limited. He tells his listeners what is destined to happen at Troy and what they must do; he hints that the moral balance will be restored, with death for Paris and glory for Philoctetes; but he does not attempt to explain to Philoctetes in any detail how or why his long sufferings were necessary within Zeus' plan. 'Never apologize, never explain' might seem to be the divine motto. Instead Heracles gives his listeners a solemn warning against committing impiety at the time of the sack of Troy[5]—a warning which we know that one of them, the good young Neoptolemus, will fail to observe.[6] The unnamed, invisible god of *Oedipus at Colonus* reveals nothing at all about the meaning of the summons to Oedipus that he bears. We are left only with the view of characters in the play that it might represent a form of compensation offered to the all-suffering man by a 'just god'.[7]

---

[4] Note, however, the oracle from Zeus in *Tr.* 1157 ff.

[5] Cf. Pl. *Clit.* 407a on Socrates ἐπιτιμῶν τοῖς ἀνθρώποις ὥσπερ ἐπὶ μηχανῆς τραγικῆς θεός. The grim austerity and moralism of Sophocles' gods in epiphany, in contrast to those of Homer, is stressed by Pucci (1994: 15–46). For a similar tone in Euripides see *El.* 1354–6, *Tro.* 85–6, *Hipp.* 1339–41; and on the things said by *dei ex machina* in general Mikalson (1991: 64–8).

[6] There may be a similar effect in Plato's *Charmides*, where that evil politician (as many judged him) appears as an attractive young man, whose moral choices are still to be made.

[7] 1565–7 (with the note ad loc. of J. C. Kamerbeek, whose criticism of Linforth's minimizing interpretation I accept); cf. 385–95. Oedipus himself initially reacts caustically to Ismene's optimism (395); but that is not his last word, or the play's. Blundell (1989: 254) points out that mutability (including change for the better) is often seen in Sophocles as a kind of natural, amoral cycle; but the direct divine involvement surely makes a difference here. Winnington-Ingram (1965: 43) comments that the gods by honouring Oedipus endorse his 'vindictive justice'. But would we like them better if they abandoned him?

A second window on the divine is a very obvious one, that opened
by divination and oracles. Here too we have evidence that is beyond
question. All Sophoclean characters are temperamentally disposed
to accept the validity of divination,[8] highly controversial at the time.
Particular circumstances may push one or two into sceptical
positions, but their doubts are immediately confuted by events.
And it is central to the effect of *Oedipus Tyrannus* that the
confutation, which establishes that it is not, after all, best to 'live
at random' as Jocasta suggests (979), brings with it a grim relief,
even though it is achieved at the expense of the largely innocent
Oedipus.[9] The authority of prophecy seems to extend to the
interpretations that characters occasionally offer of prophecies
concerning themselves—Heracles in *Trachiniae*, Oedipus in *Oedipus
at Colonus*, and perhaps Neoptolemus in *Philoctetes* all seem in the
world of the play to enjoy a kind of vicarious inspiration.[10]

But there are strict limits to what is actually revealed even through
the especially authoritative medium of prophecy. You will kill your
father and marry your mother, Oedipus is warned; neither he nor
we learn why. No more is Heracles in *Trachiniae* told why at the end
of fifteen months he will either die or find release from his labours.
Backward-facing divination, that which identifies past causes of
present afflictions, can be more revealing in pinpointing particular
causes of divine anger. We learn in this way why Thebes is plague-
ridden at the start of *Oedipus Tyrannus*, what Athena's ground of
anger is against Ajax, what Creon's offence is in *Antigone* and what it
will lead to.[11] The longest causal chain is that which can be put

---

[8] On Jocasta, the apparent counter case, see Perrotta (1965: 249) or Reinhardt
(1947: 130 = 1979: 120).

[9] See esp. Burkert (1991). One critic has even described Sophocles' masterpiece
as 'a powerful paradigm of theocratic and prophetic rhetoric in need of exposure':
Peradotto (1992: 12–13).

[10] See *Trach.* 1174–229; *OC* 576–82, 616–23, 787–93, 1518–37, also 1370–96
(where prophecy is blended with curse) and other characters' allusions to Oedipus
'prophesying' ($\mu\alpha\nu\tau\epsilon\acute{u}\mu\alpha\tau\alpha$, $\theta\epsilon\sigma\pi\acute{\iota}\zeta\omega$, 1425, 1516); *Phil.* 839–42 (in 'prophetic'
hexameters). In these passages it is often unclear, but scarcely important, whether
the speakers are merely revealing, or also elaborating and extending, past prophecies
concerning themselves. Richard Rutherford reminds me of what he calls 'Oedipus'
memorable though enigmatic lines' in *OT* 1455–9.

[11] *OT* 96–107; *Ajax* 756–77; *Ant.* 998–1032, 1064–83. Professor Easterling (in
conversation) queries whether the second-hand report of Calchas' views which is all
we have in *Ajax* deserves the trust I put in it. But it seems to square with Athena's
own hints in 127–33.

together from the various partial revelations in *Philoctetes*. Philoctetes' illness is his own fault, a punishment for trespassing on the sacred precinct guarded by the sacred snake that bit him, but also a retarding device to prevent Troy being sacked once again with weapons of Heracles before its destined time.[12] But even this explanation, in its way quite full, makes appeal to certain crucial propositions—the time at which Troy must be sacked, the necessary role of the weapons of Heracles—that are not explained but presented as unquestionable facts of the situation.

A third context where the purposes of gods are sometimes explicitly mentioned is the speech of characters who neither are prophets nor have access to prophecy. It is necessary to speak in this clumsy way of 'a context where the purposes of the gods are sometimes explicitly mentioned', rather than of a third mode of access to the divine, because all interpretations of divine motive by characters are in principle unreliable, and in practice may demonstrably be products of anger or passion or incomprehension. When, for instance, Tecmessa blames the suicide of Ajax on an intervention of the 'terrible daughter of Zeus, Pallas' made 'for the sake of Odysseus' (*Ajax* 953–4) we can recognize it for an embittered distortion: Athena was indeed at work, but unless we are to disbelieve Calchas (756–77) mere favouritism for Odysseus was not her motive.

Interesting instances falling under this rubric are not in fact very numerous. Confident statements about the attitudes of the gods in general, or about their presumptive attitude to particular situations, are, of course, common. Characters in Sophocles regularly make much more optimistic assumptions about the gods' concern for justice than do Sophoclean critics, and 'I am just, the gods are aiding/will aid me' is a proposition to which almost all parties to a dispute will normally subscribe.[13] The whole debate between Creon and Antigone is conducted in these terms, and Antigone displays a certitude (at least at this point, face to face with an antagonist) that contrasts sharply with the tentative way in which, as we shall see, characters often speak of the divine world. But she is not claiming that she can explain the interaction of god and man throughout the

---

[12] 191–200, 1326–42, 1421–40.

[13] For various forms of such speech see e.g. *El.* 459–60, 1379–83; *Phil.* 601–2, 1035–9; *OC* 279–81, 1380–2. For recognition of divine aid or favour see *Tr.* 200–1, cf. *OT* 38.

history of the house of Labdacus. All she knows is that, since the
gods uphold the just, they must most certainly in the present case be
on her side.

Various other rather unremarkable forms of divine involvement
are also recognized by characters: that of Eros in love affairs (*Trach.*
354),[14] for instance; of Zeus Agonios in contests (*Trach.* 26); of 'one
of the gods' in events that are peculiarly extraordinary, catastrophic
or (by contrast) propitious.[15] Such cases aside, it is not common for
characters to speak of the involvement of a specific god in a
particular situation, present or past. Where such claims do occur,
they are often products of extreme emotion, usually anguish: this is
true of Tecmessa's exclamation about Athena just mentioned, of
Oedipus' declaration that 'it was Apollo, friends, Apollo' who
brought about his blinding, and of the several statements by the
penitent Creon that '(a) god' or (a) deity' has leapt upon his head.[16]
In calmer moments, we normally find language that is much vaguer
and more tentative. 'I was born of a free man, the richest of the
Phrygians, but am now a slave: such I suppose was the gods' will
(θεοῖς γὰρ ὧδ' ἔδοξέ που)', says Tecmessa (487–90), softening her
claim by a use of the indefinite adverb που, 'I suppose', that was long
ago identified as a characteristic feature of Greek statements about
the divine.[17] Similarly Oedipus in *Oedipus at Colonus* (964–5) says
of his abominable past actions: 'such was the will of the gods, who
were perhaps angry against my race from long ago.' Later in the play
Polyneices goes no further than to identify his father's Erinys as the
'chief cause' of his afflictions.[18] Electra merely 'believes', though
with great vehemence, that the ill-omened dreams afflicting Clytaemnestra have come from Agamemnon (*El.* 459–60).

Even the more specific claims mentioned earlier are not stabs in

[14] More commonly it is the chorus that detects Eros: *Trach.* 497–530, 860–1; *Ant.*
781–800.

[15] *OT* 1258; *Ant.* 376, 421; *OC* 371, 1505–6. Antigone's ascription of the troubles
of the house of Oedipus to Zeus (*Ant.* 2) is a little more specific.

[16] *OT* 1329 (for similar language of divine attack around here see 1301, 1311,
with Mikalson (1991: 28–9)); *Ant.* 1273–5, 1345–6. These last are indefinite, but
much less so than 'some god'. Note too the emphatic claim made by Odysseus, in a
state of feigned passion, that he is fulfilling the will of Zeus (whose name he repeats
three times): *Phil.* 989–90.

[17] See the citation of Wackernagel (1895: 22 = 1979: i. 700) in Fraenkel's note
(1950) on Aesch. *Ag.* 182 f.

[18] 1298–9; cf. 1434.

the dark but are based on what in the world of the play are realities. Athena's involvement with Ajax is for Ajax and his circle a fact, grounded in the hero's direct experience of contact with the goddess;[19] so Tecmessa is going beyond what she knows only in ascribing to Athena a motive. The main reason why 'it was Apollo' for Oedipus is simply that, as no one could deny, what Apollo had decreed had come to pass. Creon speaks more vaguely of 'god' or 'deity' because he knows from Tiresias' speech of divine anger, not of a specific offended deity.

There are two clear exceptions to this account, instances of characters who make concrete and confident claims about divine motivation neither in passion nor on the basis of facts already presented in other ways within the world of the play. When Electra defends to her mother Agamemnon's decision to sacrifice Iphigeneia, she tells of the king's offence against Artemis and Artemis' subsequent anger against him, but gives as the basis for her knowledge a vague 'as I hear'(Electra 566–72). In Trachiniae, the messenger Lichas declares confidently that Heracles' enslavement by Omphale was a punishment imposed by Zeus for the treacherous murder of Iphitus (274–9). But neither case proves at all difficult to explain. In other accounts of the same events, it is said explicitly in both cases that the divine element in the situation was diagnosed by an oracle or prophet.[20] The natural assumption of any hearer who worried about the matter at all would surely have been that the ultimate if undeclared basis for the confident claims of the Sophoclean characters was prophecy. Unaided by divination, we conclude, humans in Sophocles neither know nor claim to know anything much about the divine world except in general terms.[21]

There remains the chorus. If one turns to the sung parts of the plays with these questions in mind, a first impression must be of the omnipresence of the gods. The chorus, it seems, never stop invoking gods or singing about them. This is one manifestation of the way in which the chorus in tragedy is not just a collective voice within a play but also, precisely, a Greek chorus, a relative of all those

---

[19] 401–3, 450–2: contrast the vaguer earlier language of Tecmessa and the chorus, 172–86, 243–4, 278, still used by Menelaus in 1057, cf. 1128.

[20] See Proclus' summary of Cypria, EGF p. 32. 58–9 Davies; Pherecydes FGrH 3 F 82 and e.g. Apollod. 2. 6. 1–3. The role of Apollo in the death of Achilles (Phil. 334–5) was presumably visible to all.

[21] Cf. the excellent remarks (apropos of OT) of Buxton (1996: 42–3).

choruses that hymn the gods in numerous extra-dramatic contexts.[22] They speak therefore of certain general theological truths such as the powers of Zeus Morios or of Poseidon[23] with a freedom and confidence untypical of individual characters. They are also in different degrees involved in the action of the play, and where their sympathies are engaged they claim divine favour for their own side just as we have seen characters to do: the chorus of *Electra* is particularly clamorous in this regard.[24] When less involved emotionally, they may celebrate the values of piety in more general terms.[25]

What they are chary of doing is to assume the stance of commentators with the authority to trace the workings of divine will in any precise way.[26] The kind of weaving of the particular action of the play into a long pattern of divine purpose so characteristic of Aeschylean choruses is far less common in Sophocles, and where it does occur far less insistent. In *Electra*, the chorus once look back briefly to the origins of sufferings for the house of Atreus: ever since Myrtilus, Oenomaus' charioteer, was hurled into the sea by Pelops, trouble and affliction have never left the house (502–515). No moral conclusion or interpretation is offered; Pelops' treatment of Myrtilus is, it is true, presented as an outrageous act, but emphasis lies not on the idea of crime and punishment but simply on the continuity of trouble since that time. The case is similar on a larger scale with the famous meditation in *Antigone* on the sufferings of the Labdacid house (582–603). Though the disasters of the Labdacids in successive generations are indeed ascribed to divine agency, no specific god is named—only 'one of the gods'—and the matter at issue between gods and Labdacids is never made explicit.[27] Later in the play in a sung exchange the chorus allude again to the burden of the past upon Antigone: 'You are paying for some crime of your forebears' (πατρῷον δ' ἐκτίνεις τιν' ἆθλον, 856). Here the idea of inherited guilt is for once explicitly present, but still in the vaguest terms. In regard to ancestral

---

[22] See Henrichs (1995) and (1996).

[23] *OC* 704–19: cf. e.g. *Phil.* 726–9, on the divinization of Heracles.

[24] *El.* 174–83, 472–501, 823–5, cf. *Ant.* 127–33.

[25] e.g. *Ant.* 368–75; 1103–4; *OT* 863–910.

[26] I approach here, with a different emphasis, matters treated in Lloyd-Jones (1983: 111–28).

[27] Cf. Easterling (1978: 142).

affliction the chorus are as it were plain persons, observers of symptoms, not specialists skilled in diagnosing causes.[28] In *Seven against Thebes* Aeschylus had used the chorus to recall both Apollo's original prophecy to Laius and Oedipus' subsequent curse on his sons.[29] Sophocles never gives his chorus this vicarious authority as a mouthpiece for inspired utterance. In *Philoctetes* Neoptolemus, not the chorus, is the repository of Helenus' crucial prophecy about the final sack of Troy.[30] There is anyway a question about the authority to be allowed to the voice of the Sophoclean chorus, that sometimes fallible organ;[31] but the question is less urgent than one might expect, because that voice says so little.

It may seem that the argument thus far can be summed up as 'cherchez le *mantis*': real insight into the will of the gods in Sophocles comes only from the interpretation by oracles and seers embedded in the plays. But there is one further way for the spectator not exactly to learn particular divine purposes but to learn about the divine. This is what one might call, inelegantly, the mechanism of triggered responses: necessary reactions by the audience, sometimes involving its prior knowledge of myth, to structural features of the plays, or to words spoken, or to both. By eliciting such responses the text irresistibly suggests certain ideas about the divine, even if these are never made explicit in words. We will approach this issue too by way of what may seem a side path. A few words must be said first about 'complaints against the gods' and even theodicy.

The word 'theodicy' was apparently coined by Leibniz, who used it in the title of a work published in 1710, *Essais de Théodicée sur la bonté de Dieu, la liberté de l'homme et l'origine du mal;*[32] and

---

[28] When the Labdacids speak of themselves, it is often in a similarly pragmatic way, as a family in which trouble and rash anger are hereditary: *Ant.* 2–6, 49–60; *OC* 369–70.

[29] 720–91, 822–47; note too e.g. *Ag.* 126–55, where the chorus repeat a prophecy of Calchas at length. Jasper Griffin reminds me how hard it is to separate these issues of theology from issues of literary form. Sophocles' single-standing plays with reduced choral role lack space for the Aeschylean presentation of the legacy of generation to generation.

[30] 1326–42; cf. 839–42. The chorus do not go beyond hints, 176 and 1116.

[31] See Müller (1967: 212–38). On the question whether choruses in general are to be interpreted as embodying a 'civic voice' see the interchange of Gould (1996) and Goldhill (1996: 217–56), and the comments of Taplin (1996: 193–4) and Gredley (1996: 211–12).

[32] Leibniz (171), available in Gerhardt (1885), trans. Huggard (1985).

theodicy as we know it is a product of a Christian and a scholastic tradition to which Sophocles unquestionably did not belong.[33] Zeus did not create the world and so is not answerable for its imperfections as is the Christian (or indeed the Stoic) god. None the less, he controls it, and when things go wrong in it they can be blamed on him, however little direct involvement in the unfortunate events he may seem to have had. The mere existence of the scorpion is, perhaps, not a reproach to Zeus. But as soon as a just man dies of a scorpion's bite, Zeus has a case to answer.[34] He is blamed too for the consequences of the actions of unjust men, and does not have the Christian argument about the necessary hazards of free will to shelter behind. As a result there is ample scope for a kind of theodicy. Not as a word but as a practice, it goes back to the earliest Greek literature, and its first practitioner is the Zeus who defends himself against mortal complaints in the divine council at the start of the *Odyssey*: 'How mortals blame gods! They say that evils come to them from us; but they themselves by their own follies incur suffering beyond their lot.'[35]

Both things—complaints and rebuttals—continue to occur for most of antiquity. One of Plato's objections to tragedy is that tragic man blames the gods when he should rather blame himself, or simply endure.[36] Paul Veyne has argued that god-faulting remained popular religion's characteristic response to blows of fortune until the rise of a 'new paganism' in the second century AD: thenceforth the approved response to blows of fortune was to be one not of protest but of submission and wonder. That interested hypothesis perhaps underestimates the extent to which moralists, the Stoics in particular, had always spoken up in the gods' defence—or rather in denunciation of the weakness of man.[37] And it has often been recognized that Plato is grossly

---

[33] For a historical account see Hick (1966), and for the recent debate, e.g. Swinburne (1991: 200–24); McNaughton (1994: 329–51).

[34] As one example out of many, take Hyllos' complaints against Zeus in *Trachiniai*, discussed below.

[35] *Od.* 1. 32–4. This is a central text in *Justice of Zeus*, that classic exercise in *théodicée à la grecque*.

[36] *Resp.* 379d–380c, 603e–606b, with the enlightening study of Halliwell (1996: 332–49).

[37] Veyne (1991: 281–310), which builds on Versnel (1981: 37–42). On Stoic and other moralizing protests (many in fact mentioned by Veyne himself) see Rutherford (1989: 213 n. 96).

unfair in presenting tragedy as simply a vehicle for τὸ ἀγανακτη-
τικόν, whingeing.

On the contrary, complaints against the gods in tragedy are
normally products of what turns out to be ignorance, and, it can be
argued, such a complaint when uttered in the tragic theatre is not a
thing that can pass away unregarded. It creates an expectation that
the god will be in some way vindicated, even if that vindication
brings only cool comfort to the humans involved; it is a sore spot
that looks for a salve. (The effect of a complaint left genuinely
unanswered, as apparently in Troades,[38] is rare and extremely
powerful.) We owe to Plato the preservation of a lovely fragment
of Aeschylus that he wished to suppress: 'We shall not praise
Aeschylus when his Thetis tells how Apollo sang at her wedding
and dwelt on her fair offspring "free from disease and long in life . . .
and I thought that Apollo's sacred mouth, full of prophetic skill, was
infallible. But he who sung this himself, he who was present at the
feast himself, who said all this himself, is himself the one who killed
my child".' Apollo's guilt appears so blatant that a later poet
pointedly excluded him from the wedding feast.[39] But did Apollo
have the capacity to speak untruth, even if he had the will? It is more
likely that Thetis had misunderstood the god's riddling words (in
which, certainly, she deserves all our sympathy).[40]

The pattern is one that is seen several times among the so-called
tragi-comedies of Euripides (Iphigeneia in Tauris, Helen, and Ion),
where in the early part of the play mortals with their deficient
knowledge heap upon a god reproaches which the conclusion

[38] On this see the references given in Pelling (1997: 154–5). Other problematic
cases: the criticisms of Apollo's oracle in Eur. El., which are even endorsed by Castor
speaking ex machina at the conclusion (1245–6); of Hera's jealous malice in Eur. HF
(1308–10, cf. 822–73, 1127, 1189, 1253, 1263–5, 1392–3: Yunis (1988: 150–1)); of
Apollo's vindictiveness in Eur. Andr. 1161–5 (cf. 51–5, 1147–9, and, for other
doubts about Apollo's conduct, 1009–36: cf. Yunis (1988: 88–93)). In these last
three cases, the fault is said to lie not with 'the gods' in general but with an
individual Olympian other than Zeus. In Euripides, polytheism lacks, it seems, any
mechanisms to control the excesses of rogue deities (whence indirect blame can fall
on Zeus: HF 1087–8, 1127, 1263–5).

[39] Aeschylus fr. 350 R. ap. Plat. Resp. 383a: Catullus 64. 299–302. On the part of
Catullus, more a conundrum for the reader, no doubt, than a symptom of
theological anxiety.

[40] See Gantz (1981: 18–32), who suggests that Achilles' 'long life' was post
mortem. Apollo's white lie in Eur. Ion 69–73 is scarcely a sufficient parallel for the
supposed deception in Aeschylus.

proves to be misguided.[41] Plays of Sophocles never reach happy
endings in that way, but the mortal impulse to 'blame the gods' is
none the less often deprived of its foundation. Early in *Philoctetes*,
for instance, Philoctetes questions Neoptolemus about affairs at
Troy, and on learning that Ajax and Antilochus are dead, but
Odysseus and Thersites and the Atreidai alive and flourishing,
concludes: 'Of course! Nothing bad ever perishes, but the gods
take good care of it . . . how can I explain these things, how praise
them, when I look at the gods' doings and find the gods evil?' (446–
52). But near the end of the play the interaction of the three human
characters leads to impasse, and Philoctetes in spite of the oracles
which promise him health and glory at Troy is about to sail home to
Malis, unbowed indeed but inglorious and unhealed. Only the
intervention of Heracles, dispatched by Zeus, allows the action to
reach the ending which the audience, if it wishes the well-being of
Philoctetes, must strongly desire.[42] This easy loosing by a god of the
knot which the mortals have inadvertently tied so tight is sometimes
seen by critics as obtrusively artificial, almost a brief moment of
theatre of the absurd.[43] But from a different perspective one might

---

[41] See *IT* 143–235, 475–7, and esp. 560, 570–5, 711–15; *Helen* 357, 609–10, 674–
83, 711–19, 1093–106, 1137–50 (but for reservations about 'theodicy' in *Helen* see
Matthiessen (1964: 181–3)); *Ion* 232–4, 384–91, above all 436–51 and 859–922,
952, 960, etc. The surface movement in *Ion* is certainly as described; whether there is
any residual inadequacy in Apollo's conduct is disputed: see the doxography in
Yunis (1988: 137 n. 69), and for a brisk theodicy Heath (1987: 55 f.). On similar
issues in 17th-cent. drama see Gethner (1983: 39–51). The apparent optimism of
many Euripidean endings is regularly interpreted, often with particular reference to
the role of the *deus ex machina*, as irony: v. Fritz (1956: 64–7 = 1962: 312–16);
Romilly (1961: 108 n. 2, 137 n. 2); Reinhardt (1960: 233, 256); Schmidt (1963);
Rohdich (1969: 42–3). For a non-ironic view of the optimism of *IT*, *Helen*, and *Ion*
see Whitman (1974: 138); and of the *deus ex machina* in general, Spira (1960) (cf.
Lloyd-Jones (1983: 155)). Sourvinou-Inwood will present a full non-ironic
interpretation in her forthcoming Jackson lectures. Cf. n. 43 below.

[42] So Easterling (1983: 217–28) at p. 225; cf. Winnington-Ingram (1980: 295).
Critics have rightly stressed that Heracles appears as an old comrade of Philoctetes,
and that he offers no general theodicy (Winnington-Ingram (1980: 299–301);
Blundell (1989: 222)); but he is also a representative of Zeus (1415), and the
absence of a general theodicy does not devalue the particular restitution made to
Philoctetes. For positive views of the role of the divine in the play see Segal (1977:
133–58); Gill (1980: 137–46).

[43] For such views see Easterling (1983: 224–5) (who dissents), and the nuanced
position of Pucci (1994: 43–4). Such an argument is regularly applied to the
Euripidean *deus ex machina* (see the works cited in n. 41 above, esp. Schmidt

apply to this passage, as perhaps to no other in Greek tragedy, the words, 'There's a divinity that shapes our ends I Rough hew them how we will.' This turn of events picks up and more than cancels Philoctetes' earlier denunciation. Much remains unexplained—we do not in fact learn, for instance, why Achilles is dead and not Thersites[44]—but the impression of divine indifference to human desert has been effaced.[45] What is not wiped out but underlined, through Heracles' warning against impieties at the sack of Troy, is the tragic potential for badness inherent even in good men. The plays of Sophocles, it is often supposed, exalt heroic individuals who surmount the worst that can be put upon them by gods indifferent or cruel.[46] But there is much to be said for a more Aristotelo-Bradleian view, whereby Sophocles' world is one marred, above all, by the disastrous flaws endemic in human personality.

The most conspicuous complaints against the gods in Sophocles are those relating to the death of Heracles in *Trachiniai*. Seized with hideous pains in the very act of consecrating a new altar to his own father, Heracles complains bitterly of the 'favour' (χάρις) he has got in return for his offerings (994–9). The point is a serious one for a religion based on the exchange of favours between man, with his sacrifices and dedications, and the gods, the 'givers of good things'.[47] At the end of the play Hyllus makes a direct charge of great heartlessness (ἀγνωμοσύνη) against the gods, they who 'beget offspring and are called fathers, but look on at sufferings such as this' (1266–9). This contrasts with and apparently overthrows an earlier assurance by the chorus to Deianeira that she should be of good heart, since Zeus always stands by his children (139–40). But Hyllus goes on at once to say that 'the future none can see', and it

(1963)), with some plausibility in regard to the bizarre reversal engineered by Apollo at the end of *Orestes*, but none at all in the case of patriotic plays such as *Supplices* or *Erechtheus* (whence the view of Patzer (1983: 31–3) that the device only becomes ironic in late Euripides).

[44] Possibly Neoptolemus' tentative statement that Thersites was still alive is not true; it certainly runs counter to the tradition that Thersites was killed by Achilles, as the Σ on *Phil.* 445 notes.

[45] Jasper Griffin comments, however: 'But the substance of the earlier criticism still stands; I'd take a cooler view—some of the divine purpose looks explicable to us; some doesn't (like what happened to Oedipus).'

[46] See e.g. v. Fritz (1962: 18–19, 254) with excellent remarks on the 'schonungslose Härte' of Sophocles; Reinhardt (1947: 10 = 1979: 2).

[47] See Parker (1998: 105–25).

has been argued with irresistible force in recent years that the future for Heracles is apotheosis and that certain features of the text act as triggers to evoke the audience's knowledge of the relevant myth—a myth that is no obscure variant but the foundation of a large part of everyday religious reality in Attica, with its innumerable cults of Heracles.[48] The complaints against Zeus' apparent injustice are themselves among the triggers that work in this way. The characters in the play, ignorant, rub at a sore point; but, since a salve exists, the audience are encouraged to apply it.

The question remains why Heracles had to attain immortality by such an anguished route, and it may be that no answer is available other than that the favour of Zeus can indeed be violent. But a serious and otherwise unpunished crime by Heracles is mentioned in the play: he sacked Oechalia out of lust for Iole, 'having fabricated a trivial complaint and excuse' (359–65). 'May I not be a city-sacker' and 'the gods observe those who kill many', sing the chorus in *Agamemnon* (472, 461–2), magnificently. The idea that Zeus might punish Heracles for misdirected violence was explicitly raised earlier in the play, when Lichas declared that the hero's enslavement to Omphale was punishment for the murder of Iphitus (274–9). So there is perhaps another item of implicit theodicy to be noted here.[49]

The stricken Oedipus barely complains against the gods, much though moderns have complained on his behalf.[50] The emphasis of *Oedipus Tyrannus* would be very different, the problem of theodicy much more urgent, if he had repeated after the final revelation (or in *Oedipus at Colonus*) the kind of complaint that he raised, hypothetically, before it: if I turn out to be the victim of my own curse, 'would not anyone who judged this the work of a cruel destiny against me be right?' (828–9). The final speech of Antigone, by contrast, ends with a magnificent complaint—which is also, since the real culprit is Creon, an excellent example of the way in which gods can be held co-responsible for injustice inflicted by mortals. What god can she look to now for aid, she asks, when it is her piety that has brought her to disaster (921–8)?

---

[48] See Lloyd-Jones (1983: 126–8) and, for the subsequent debate (especially the important contributions, on opposite sides, by Easterling (1983) and Stinton (1986)), Holt (1989: 69–80).

[49] So Lloyd-Jones (1994: 1–2).

[50] Nor does Ajax, though he does declare that he 'owes nothing to the gods' (589–90).

Critics sometimes speak as if these complaints go unanswered; thus it has been said that Antigone's fate poses the acutest problem of theodicy in all Sophocles.[51] If we believe the chorus—and this is the main case where it matters theologically whether we do nor not—she has brought her troubles on herself, and is also the luckless heir to inherited guilt.[52] But the main answer to Antigone's complaints surely lies in neither of these factors but in the immediate punishment, which fulfils her final curse, of her persecutor Creon.[53] The punishment occurs not by direct divine intervention, but via a credible chain of human responses, but we know from Tiresias—know therefore for sure—that the human mechanism is also a divine one.[54] The downfall of Creon does not mitigate the pathos of Antigone's own destiny one jot; but it shows that her cosmic despair, as if the gods had forgotten their own rules, is misplaced.

We have luxuriated in theodicy for long enough, and must now revert to the original theme of ways of knowing the will of the gods. It was stressed earlier how few and weak these were, how little is in fact revealed or explained, and the subsequent discussion of theodicy has not been intended to alter those conclusions. What vindication of the gods amounts to in Sophocles is very far from a Leibnizian demonstration that we live in the best, or even the justest, of all possible worlds, with all that such an argument implies about the possibility of a full and rational understanding of the purposes of the gods and of the workings of the world. On the contrary, the logical structure of theodicy in Sophocles frequently seems to be of a restricted and negative form: in *Trachiniai* 'it is not the case that Zeus abandoned his son for no reason to a horrible death', or in *Oedipus at Colonus* 'it is not the case that the gods let Oedipus die unregarded', and so on. What is adduced, in a way found in the other tragedians too,[55] is a mitigation or limitation of

---

[51] See Winnington-Ingram (1980: 148–9), who cites (149 n. 89) but rejects what seems an appropriate response by Kitto (1956: 170).

[52] 853–6: cf. Lloyd-Jones (1983: 117); Burton (1980: 120–3); Sourvinou-Inwood (1989: 139–40).

[53] For a similar restoration of balance through τίσις in Herodotus, see e.g. 1. 13. 2, 3. 109. 2, 3. 126. 1. For the Erinyes avenging wrongs in Sophocles, see *Aj.* 835–44, *El.* 110–17.

[54] 1064–86; cf. already the suggestion of 278–9.

[55] See e.g. Aesch. *Suppl.* 571–89, 1064–7; Eur. *Hipp.* 1416–30 (cf. Yunis (1988: 120)); *El.* 1291, 1340–2; *Andr.* 1231 ff., esp. 1250–2 (contrast 1010–27); *Bacch.* 1339

suffering or a compensation for it, and these mitigations and compensations serve to blunt the sharpest of men's complaints of divine cruelty and neglect. But too much remains unexplained and unknowable for strong positive claims about divine justice, still less about divine benevolence,[56] to be possible.

Sensitive critics have always been struck by these silences of Sophocles' text, of which the most famous is doubtless the apparent silence in *Oedipus Tyrannus* about the ultimate motivation for the destiny prophesied for Laius and Oedipus.[57] In a sense the central problem for any study of Sophocles' presentation of the divine is that of responding to these silences: at all events, it is at this point that the paths of even the best critics diverge. Does Sophocles leave the divine will unexplained because to reason about it would be a distraction from the true human centre of the plays?[58] Or is the point rather the ultimate incomprehensibility to mortals of the divine world? And if so, if the ways of the gods are incomprehensible, is that because those ways are good, but human comprehension weak?[59] Or because mortals seek justice where none is to be found?[60] This is a maze where criticism may well wander bewildered. 'I will call no being good, who is not what I mean when I apply that epithet to my fellow creatures,' said John Stuart Mill in protest against the God of Hell.[61] But do we know enough about the Sophoclean gods to determine whether to call them good, by Mill's standard or any other? Language, modern theoreticians never weary of insisting,

(which Winnington-Ingram (1948: 145, 147) discounts too readily); fr. 446 N. (from the first Hippolytus); [Eur.] Rhes. 962–79.

[56] Note that, unlike Aeschylus (*Septem, Eumenides*), Sophocles seems never to look beyond individual suffering to future collective well-being (there is very little well-being at all in Sophocles, though as in the *Aeneid* there are brief deluded hopes). The forward vision even of *OC* is not of Athenian felicity but of Theban suffering.

[57] On this contrast Lloyd-Jones (1983: 119–23) and Stinton (1986: 72–4 = 1990: 461–4). Winnington-Ingram (1980: 173–8) sees Apollo cruelly at work in the play; even were he right, we would still be unsure of the god's motive.

[58] So Reinhardt (1947: 144 = 1979: 134). Contrast Halliwell (1990), an admirable essay which emphasizes the 'inconclusiveness' of the tragic presentation of the divine but also the religious power of this very inconclusiveness.

[59] So Lloyd-Jones (1983: 128); though note his slightly different emphasis: 'In Sophocles, the difference between gods whose ways are inscrutable to men and gods who deal with men in an arbitrary fashion often appears minimal' (1991: 47).

[60] So Dodds (1973: 64–77) and many predecessors cited in Lloyd-Jones (1983: 108–9).

[61] See Rowell (1974), 3.

defies stable interpretation. But how much more inscrutable is silence! As mortals we see the Sophoclean gods through a glass darkly, and we shall never see them face to face.

REFERENCES

BLUMENTHAL, A. V. (1929), in *RE* v. 'Sophokles (aus Athen)' (Stuttgart).

BLUNDELL, M. W. (1989), *Helping Friends and Harming Enemies* (Cambridge).

BURKERT, W. (1991), 'Oedipus, Oracles and Meaning', *The Samuel James Stubbs Lecture Series* (University College, Toronto).

BURTON, R. W. B. (1980), *The Chorus in Sophocles' Tragedies* (Oxford).

BUXTON, R. (1996), 'What can you rely on in *Oedipus Rex*? Response to Calame', in Silk (1996): 38–48.

CROPP, M. J., FANTHAM, E., and SCULLY, S. E. (1986) (eds.), *Greek Tragedy and its Legacy: Essays presented to D. Conacher* (Calgary).

DILLER, H. (1967) (ed.), *Sophokles* (Wege der Forschung 95, Darmstadt).

DODDS, E. R. (1973), 'On Misunderstanding the Oedipus Rex', in E. R. Dodds, *The Ancient Concept of Progress and other Essays* (Oxford), 64–77.

EASTERLING, P. E. (1978), 'The second Stasimon of *Antigone*', in R. D. Dawe, J. Diggle, and P. E. Easterling (eds.), *Dionysiaca: Nine Studies presented to Sir Denys Page* (Cambridge).

——(1983), 'Philoctetes and Modern Criticism', *Illinois Classical Studies* 3 (1978): 27–39 (repr. in Segal (1983), 217–28).

FRAENKEL, E. (1950) (ed.), *Aeschylus*, Agamemnon, 3 vols. (Oxford).

FRITZ, K. V. (1956), 'Euripides' Alkestis und ihre modernen Nachahmer und Kritiker', *Antike und Abendland* 5: 27–69 (repr. in v. Fritz (1962): 256–321)).

——(1962), *Antike und Moderne Tragödie* (Berlin).

GANTZ, T. (1981), 'Divine Guilt in Aischylos', *CQ* 31: 18–32.

GERHARDT, C. L. (1885) (ed.), *Die philosophischen Schriften von Gottfried Wilhelm Leibniz*, vi (Berlin).

GETHNER, P. (1983), 'Providence by Indirection in Seventeenth-Century Tragicomedy', in J. Redmond (ed.), *Drama and Religion* (Themes in Drama 5, Cambridge), 39–51.

GILL, C. (1980), 'Bow, Oracle, and Epiphany in Sophocles' *Philoctetes*', *GR* 27: 137–46.

GOLDHILL, S. (1996), 'Collectivity and Otherness—The Authority of the Tragic Chorus: Response to Gould', in Silk (1996), 244–56.

GOULD, J. (1996), 'Tragedy and Collective Experience', in Silk (1996), 217–43.

GREDLEY, B. (1996), 'Comedy and Tragedy—Inevitable Distinctions. Response to Taplin', in Silk (1996), 203–16.

HALLIWELL, S. (1990), 'Human Limits and the Religion of Greek Tragedy', *Journal of Literature and Theology* 4(2): 169–80.

——(1996), 'Plato's Repudiation of the Tragic', in Silk (1996), 332–49.

HEATH, M. (1987), *The Poetics of Greek Tragedy* (London).

HENRICHS, A. (1995), '"Why Should I Dance?" Choric Self-Referentiality in Greek Tragedy', *Arion* 3(1): 56–111.

——(1996), *Warum soll ich denn tanzen?* (Lectio Teuberiana 4, Stuttgart and Leipzig).

HICK, J. (1966), *Evil and the God of Love* (London).

HOLT, P. (1989), 'The End of the *Trachiniai* and the Fate of Herakles', *JHS* 109: 69–80.

KITTO, H. D. F. (1956), *Form and Meaning in Drama* (London).

LEIBNIZ, G. W. (1710), *Essais de Theodicée sur la bonté de Dieu, la liberté de l'homme et l'origine du mal* (Amsterdam).

LINFORTH, J. M. (1951), 'Religion and Drama in *Oedipus at Colonus*', *University of California Publications in Classical Philology* 14 (Berkeley).

LLOYD-JONES, P. H. J. (1983), *The Justice of Zeus* (Berkeley; 1st edn. 1971).

——(1991), *Greek in a Cold Climate* (London).

——(1994) (ed. and tr.), *Sophocles* (Cambridge, Mass.).

McNAUGHTON, D. (1994), 'The Problem of Evil: A Deontological Perspective', in A. G. Padgett (ed.), *Reason and the Christian Religion: Essays in Honour of Richard Swinburne* (Oxford), 329–51.

MATTHIESSEN, K. (1964), *Elektra, Taurische Iphigenie und Helena* (Göttingen).

MIKALSON, J. D. (1991), *Honor thy Gods: Popular Religion in Greek Tragedy* (Chapel Hill).

MUELLER, E. (1910), *De deorum graecorum partibus tragicis* (Gießen).

MÜLLER, G. (1967), 'Chor und Handlung bei den griechischen Tragikern', in Diller (1967), 212–38.

ORANJE, H. P. (1984), *Euripides' Bacchae: Play and Audience* (Leiden).

PARKER, R. (1998), 'Pleasing Thighs: Reciprocity in Greek Religion', in C. Gill, N. Postlethwaite, and R. Seaford (eds.), *Reciprocity in Ancient Greece* (Oxford), 105–25.

PATZER, H. (1983), 'Methodische Grundsätze der Sophoklesinterpretation', *Poetica* 15: 1–33.

PELLING, C. B. R. (1997) (ed.), *Greek Tragedy and the Historian* (Oxford).

PERADOTTO, J. J. (1992), 'Disauthorizing Prophecy: The Ideological Mapping of *Oedipus Tyrannus*', *TAPA* 122: 1–15.

PERROTTA, G. (1965), *Sofocle* (Florence; 1st edn. Messina 1935).

PUCCI, P. (1994), 'Gods' Intervention and Epiphany in Sophocles', *AJP* 115: 15–46.

REINHARDT, K. (1947), *Sophokles* (3rd edn.; Frankfort am Main).

——(1960), *Tradition und Geist* (Göttingen).

——(1979), trans. of Reinhardt (1947) by D. and H. Harvey (Oxford).

ROHDICH, H. (1969), *Die Euripideische Tragödie* (Heidelberg).

ROMILLY, J. DE (1961), *L'Évolution du pathétique d'Eschyle à Euripide* (Paris).

ROWELL, G. (1974), *Hell and the Victorians* (Oxford).

RUTHERFORD, R. B. (1989), *The Meditations of Marcus Aurelius: A Study* (Oxford).

SCHMIDT, W. (1963), *Der Deus ex Machina bei Euripides* (diss. Tübingen).

SEGAL, C. (1977), 'Philoctetes and the Imperishable Piety', *Hermes* 105: 133–58.

——(1983) (ed.), *Oxford Readings in Greek Tragedy* (Oxford).

SILK, M. S. (1996) (ed.), *Tragedy and the Tragic: Greek Theatre and Beyond* (Oxford).

SOURVINOU-INWOOD, C. (1989), 'Assumptions and the Creation of Meaning: Reading Sophocles' *Antigone*', *JHS* 109: 134–48.

SPIRA, A. (1960), *Untersuchungen zum Deus ex Machina bei Sophokles und Euripides* (Kallmünz).

STINTON, T. C. W. (1986), 'The Scope and Limits of Allusion in Greek Tragedy', in Cropp, Fantham, and Scully (1986), 67–102 (repr. in Stinton (1990), 454–92).

——(1990), *Collected Papers on Greek Tragedy* (Oxford).

SWINBURNE, R. (1991), *The Existence of God* (Oxford, rev. edn.).

TAPLIN, O. P. (1977), *The Stagecraft of Aeschylus* (Oxford).

——(1996), 'Comedy and the Tragic', in Silk (1996), 188–202.

VERSNEL, H. S. (1981), 'Religious Mentality in Ancient Prayer', in H. S. Versnel (ed.), *Faith, Hope and Worship* (Leiden), 1–64.

VEYNE, P. (1986), 'Une évolution du paganisme gréco-romain: injustice ou piété des dieux, leurs ordres et "oracles"', *Latomus*: 259–83 (repr. in Veyne (1991), 281–310).

——(1991), *La société romaine* (Paris).

WACKERNAGEL, J. (1895), 'Miszellen zur griechischen Grammatik', *Kuhns Zeitschrift* 33: 22 (repr. in Wackernagel (1979), i. 700).

——(1979), *Kleine Schriften* (Göttingen).

WEST, S. (1984), 'Io and the Dark Stranger (Sophocles, *Inachus* F 269a)', *CQ* 34: 292–30.

WHITMAN, C. (1974), *Euripides and the Full Circle of Myth* (Harvard).

WINNINGTON-INGRAM, R. P. (1948), *Euripides and Dionysus: An Interpretation of the Bacchae* (Cambridge; 2nd edn. 1997).

——(1965), 'Tragedy and Greek Archaic Thought', in M. J. Anderson (ed.), *Classical Drama and its Influence: Essays presented to H. D. F. Kitto* (London), 31–50.

—— (1980), *Sophocles: An Interpretation* (Cambridge).

YUNIS, H. (1988), *A New Creed: Fundamental Religious Beliefs in the Athenian Polis and Euripidean Drama* (*Hypomnemata* 91, Göttingen).

3

Ancestral Curses

MARTIN WEST

The Greek word for 'curse' is ἀρά or ἐπαρά or κατάρα. This suggests that a curse is a sort of prayer, ἀρή being one of the ordinary Homeric words for a prayer. It is still found with that general sense in Pindar and Herodotus, though in the fifth century it has mostly become specialized in the sense of 'curse'. A curse is a prayer that harm may befall someone.

But it is not as simple as that. Already in Homer we can see a distinction between a simple prayer for someone's harm and the curse proper. When, at the outset of the *Iliad*, Chryses prays to Apollo that the Danaans may pay the price for the distress they have caused him by taking his daughter, we cite this as a fine illustration of Greek prayer form, and we do not at all think of it as a curse. It stands in clear contrast to the two parental cursings recalled in book 9: the one where Phoenix's father Amyntor invoked the Erinyes to see to it that Phoenix should never have a son, and his prayers were answered by Zeus of the Underworld and Persephone;[1] and the other where Meleager's mother prayed to the gods for his death, crouching and sobbing and beating the earth with her hands as she called upon Hades and Persephone, and the pitiless Erinys heard her prayer from Erebos.[2] In both these cases the Erinyes, the powers of vengeance, and the gods of the Underworld are involved.

[1] *Il.* 9. 454–7, πολλὰ κατηρᾶτο, στυγερὰς δ᾽ ἐπεκέκλετ᾽ Ἐρινῦς, | μή ποτε γούνασιν οἷσιν ἐφέσσεσθαι φίλον υἱόν | ἐξ ἐμέθεν γεγαῶτα· θεοὶ δ᾽ ἐτέλειον ἐπαράς, | Ζεύς τε καταχθόνιος καὶ ἐπαινὴ Περσεφόνεια.

[2] *Il.* 9. 566–72, ἐξ ἀρέων μητρὸς κεχολωμένος, ἥ ῥα θεοῖσιν | πόλλ᾽ ἀχέουσ᾽ ἠρᾶτο κασιγνήτοιο φόνοιο, | πολλὰ δὲ καὶ γαῖαν πολυφόρβην χερσὶν ἀλοία | κικλήσκουσ᾽ Ἀΐδην καὶ ἐπαινὴν Περσεφόνειαν | πρόχνυ καθεζομένη, δεύοντο δὲ δάκρυσι κόλποι, | παιδὶ δόμεν θάνατον· τῆς δ᾽ ἠεροφοῖτις Ἐρινύς | ἔκλυεν ἐξ Ἐρέβεσφιν ἀμείλιχον ἦτορ ἔχουσα. Cf. also *Od.* 2. 135, where Telemachus fears his mother's curse if he sends her away against her will.

The connection between curses and Erinyes is easy to understand. Most curses are uttered by someone who has been wronged and who has no immediate means of redress. The Erinys is the divine agent of vengeance who can be summoned in aid, or who is automatically called into life by the wrong, while the curse is the direct evocation of punishment for the wrongdoer. The two concepts are readily combined, so that the Erinys is thought of as the agent who brings the curse to fulfilment. When Antinoos hurls a footstool at the beggar who is Odysseus, Odysseus says, 'if beggars have gods and Erinyes, may death catch Antinoos before he marries'.[3] The curse itself may be conceived as a supernatural force which operates independently of other agencies, taking on the function of the avenger. Hence the Erinyes in Aeschylus can say to Athena, 'We are age-long children of Night, and in our home below the earth we are called Curses.'[4]

Gods of the upper world can also be invoked in curses. In the episode of the *Odyssey* which I have just quoted, Penelope hears what has happened and exclaims, addressing Antinoos though out of his earshot, 'Would that Apollo the archer would hit you likewise!' There is a fragment of Hipponax in which two people, probably a young man and a girl, are furious with each other. He says, 'Artemis destroy you!', and she retorts, 'And Apollo you!' ἀπό σ' ὀλέσειεν Ἄρτεμις.—σὲ δὲ κὠπόλλων.[5] Very often such imprecations do not specify a divine agent at all: one simply says ἀπόλοιο. There is still an analogy here with a prayer, because that too can take the form of a simple declaration of what one wishes for, without any god being addressed, as when Hipponax says εἴ μοι γένοιτο παρθένος καλή τε καὶ τέρεινα.[6] At the same time the idea of the curse as a self-sufficient, quasi-magical procedure is not far away, as if the act of pronouncing the proper formula may set in motion the process that will lead to the effect desired.

People who uttered curses or wrote *defixiones* must often have

---

[3] *Od.* 17. 475 f.
[4] Aesch. *Eum.* 416 f., ἡμεῖς γάρ ἐσμεν Νυκτὸς αἰανῆ τέκνα, | Ἀραὶ δ' ἐν οἴκοις γῆς ὑπαὶ κεκλήμεθα. Cf. *Sept.* 70, Ἀρά τ' Ἐρινὺς πατρὸς ἡ μεγασθενής; *Cho.* 406, where Orestes calls on the powerful Ἀραί of the dead (i.e. of Agamemnon) to take note of the present dismal situation of Atreus' line; ibid. 692, ὦ δυσπάλαιστε τῶνδε δωμάτων Ἀρά; Parker (1983: 196).
[5] *Od.* 17. 494; Hipponax fr. 25 West = 35 Degani.
[6] Hipponax fr. 119 W. = 120 Deg.

been disappointed. Here we must take note of an important difference between the prayers or curses of real life (or realistic fiction) and those of myth. In real life the Greeks are well aware that the fulfilment of a prayer of any kind is entirely at the discretion of the divinity. Man proposes, God disposes. This is reflected in Homeric narrative. When Chryses prays that the Greeks may suffer, Apollo hearkens to his prayer and takes prompt action. But when Theano prays to Athena on behalf of the Trojans, 'Lady Athens, guardian of the city, smash Diomedes' spear, and grant that he falls dead before the Skaian Gates', Athena nods backwards, meaning 'No'.[7] In myth, on the other hand—and we must be clear that those Homeric prayers are not part of the myth of the Trojan War, but inorganic elements in a poetic narrative constructed over the myth—in myth prayers and curses, like oracles and prophecies, are invariably fulfilled, because they are parts of a working mechanism, and they have to work. When Apollo pursues Daphne, and she flees to avoid a fate worse than being turned into a tree, she prays to Zeus for deliverance, and the merciful god administers a metamorphosis that does not extinguish Apollo's love but transmutes it from the carnal mode to the horticultural. Daphne's prayer is a functional element in the myth, and it can only be functional if it is answered; a prayer that was not answered would have been pointless. So too with curses. It was part of the myth of the sons of Oedipus, at least as early as the epic *Thebaid*, that their father was angry with them and cursed them, to the effect that they should not divide their patrimony in amity but by the sword. And so it had to be; the curse was inexorable.

I say it was part of the myth 'at least as early as the epic *Thebaid*', because myths develop and can be remodelled with an altered mechanism. There might have been an earlier form of the myth in which it was simply related that Polynices and Eteocles quarrelled over the division of their inheritance and fought and killed one another. The motif that they were doomed to do so by their father's curse enhances the story but is not essential to it, and may well have been a secondary elaboration. We shall see how such developments can occur.

Let us now consider inherited or ancestral curses. These have played an important role in the interpretation of tragedy, but the

[7] *Il.* 1. 35–43; 6. 304–11.

discussion has been bedevilled by looseness of conception, or at any rate of terminology. Critics have often spoken of an inherited curse when what they mean is inherited guilt, or some kind of genetic corruption, or persistent but unexplained adversity. Let us keep these things distinct.

What do we mean by an inherited curse? We mean a curse, pronounced by somebody, whose effects continue to afflict not only the immediate victim but also his descendants. Why should it? There are two possibilities in myth. One is that the original victim has the status of a prototype: he is the eponym of a people, or in some other way he stands as the representative of all who will follow him, so that his destiny determines theirs. When God discovered that Adam and Eve had been beguiled by the serpent into eating of the forbidden fruit, he pronounced curses on the lot of them. 'Because you have done this,' said God to the serpent,

> cursed are you above all cattle,
> and above all wild animals;
> upon your belly you shall go,
> and dust you shall eat
> all the days of your life.

To the woman he said,

> I will greatly multiply your pain in childbearing;
> in pain you shall bring forth children.

And to Adam he said,

> Cursed is the ground because of you;
> in toil you shall eat of it all the days of your life;
> thorns and thistles it shall bring forth to you;
> and you shall eat the plants of the field.[8]

All serpents, all women, and all men consequently suffer these inconveniences, inherited from their prototypes. When Noah lay drunk and dishevelled in his tent, and then discovered that his youngest son, Ham the father of Canaan, had observed his nakedness and gigglingly reported it to Shem and Japheth, he said

> Cursed be Canaan;
> a slave of slaves shall he be to his brothers.[9]

[8] Genesis 3: 14–18 (quoted after the Revised Standard Version).
[9] Genesis 9: 20–5.

Because of Noah's curse the peoples of Canaan were doomed to be subjected to the people descended from Shem and Japheth.

The other reason why a curse may affect the victim's descendants as well as himself is that the curser may specify so explicitly. In a world where a major concern was for sons to maintain and enhance their family's wealth and status, and thus their own fame, the infliction of hardship on one's enemy's descendants, or the prevention of his having any, was a cruel blow. And in a world where sons were expected to avenge wrongs done to their fathers, it was in the curser's interests to guard against danger from his victim's sons.

Let me quote an example from the eighteenth century BC. Hammurabi, king of Babylon, concludes the epilogue to his great Law Code with a lengthy series of curses on any future king or official who alters his statutes or effaces Hammurabi's name. Here is one of them:

> May the great gods of heaven and earth,
> the Annunakku in their totality,
> the Guardian Spirit of the temple, the Brickwork of Ebabbar,
> curse him, his descendants, his land, his soldiers,
> his people, and his army, with a morbid curse![10]

Similarly in the treaty between the Hittite king Mursili II and Duppi-Teššub of Amurru:

Should Duppi-Teššub not honour these words of the treaty and the oath, may these gods of the oath destroy Duppi-Teššub together with his person, his wife, his son, his grandson, his house, his land and together with everything that he owns.[11]

Such provisions are typical of Near Eastern treaty oaths. The parties to a treaty, in swearing their oaths, lay conditional curses upon themselves, to take effect in the event of their failing to uphold the terms. The extension of the curses to cover the oath-taker's descendants is matched in the Greek oath κατ' ἐξώλειαν. Inscriptions and the orators provide many examples of such oaths, in which one had to pray for destruction for oneself and one's whole family and house in case of violation.[12]

Apart from oaths and treaties, other curses too often included the

---

[10] Code of Hammurabi, li. 70 ff.
[11] Friedrich (1926: 24 § 21); trans. A. Goetze in *ANET* 205.
[12] References in Parker (1983: 186 n. 234; 201); cf. my notes on Hes. *Op.* 284.

victim's family in their scope. So, for example, in the public imprecations pronounced annually by magistrates at Teos and recorded in an inscription of perhaps *c.*470 BC: they are directed against anyone who uses φάρμακα δηλητήρια against the Teians, interferes with the import of corn, resists the authorities, betrays the city, practises piracy or highway robbery, or conspires with Greek or barbarian against Teos. The curse on each of these categories of malefactor is that he may perish, himself and his γένος. The motif can be followed down to the late Jewish tomb inscription which stipulates that any grave-violator shall be afflicted, together with his children, his descendants, and his whole family, by 'all the curses in the Book of Deuteronomy'.[13]

What is the role of the inherited curse in myth? In the case of the first of the two types I distinguished, the type where the victim of the curse is a prototype figure, its role is aetiological. It serves to account for permanent affliction or diminished status affecting a tribe, a sex, or a zoological species. In the case of the other type, it serves to make a link between the disasters which, according to tradition, affected a particular family in successive generations.

The paradigm case is that of the house of Atreus. In the generation of Atreus and Thyestes there arose a pernicious quarrel between the two brothers over the kingship. Atreus claimed it after a golden lamb was discovered in his flocks. Thyestes seduced Atreus' wife and got possession of the animal. He announced that the throne was now his, and vowed that he would never surrender it so long as the sun continued to rise in the west and set in the east. Zeus upset his calculations by reversing the sun's course. Atreus seized power again, murdered Thyestes' children, and tricked him into eating portions of them. One child survived, however. Aegisthus.

Atreus' son Agamemnon succeeded to the throne. He led the Achaeans against Troy, and in the process found it necessary to put his daughter Iphigeneia to death. While he was abroad, Aegisthus, having now become a man and put away childish things, seduced Clytaemestra, Agamemnon's wife, and they conspired to murder him. The royal power thus reverted for some years to Thyestes' line. But then Agamemnon's son Orestes appeared on the scene and, in

---

[13] Meiggs and Lewis (1988: no. 30); *MAMA* 6. 335 (Lattimore (1962: 114)); further references in Parker, loc. cit.

concert with his sister Electra, assassinated Aegisthus and Clytaemestra. Atreus' line thus finally triumphed.

Here is a dynastic saga of murders and other atrocities extending
over three generations. Was there a thread linking them all together?
One answer might be 'revenge'. In real life the vendetta can sustain a
series of murders and counter-murders over generations. Orestes is
certainly motivated by the urge to avenge his father, and Aeschylus
represents Aegisthus as a conscious avenger of the wrong done to
his father by Atreus.[14] However, in our earliest source, the *Odyssey*,
there is no reference to this: Aegisthus appears to kill Agamemnon
simply because he wants him out of the way so that he can keep
Clytaemestra. The story was told more fully in the epic *Nostoi*, but
the action of that poem was set at the end of the Trojan War: the
tale of Atreus and Thyestes had no place in it, and we have no right
to assume that any back-reference was made to it.

The fact is that it is not typical of epic to move across generations,
and even less to make connections between events in different
generations. So long as epic was the principal vehicle of the myths,
we should not particularly expect the story of Atreus and Thyestes
to be seen as belonging in a chain with the story of Agamemnon, or
a causal link to be made. Such a linkage was more likely to appear
with the more synoptic approach to mythology that we find in fifth-
century lyric, tragedy, and the logographers. In particular we may
think of the Aeschylean connected trilogy, in which successive plays
dealt with a set of events which could be regarded as forming a
series. The process of constructing a trilogy from these events
naturally favoured the drawing and tightening of links between
them. In certain cases the trilogy might cover successive generations,
as in Aeschylus' *Oedipodeia*. We do not know that anyone ever dealt
with the Thyestes story, the murder of Agamemnon, and Orestes'
revenge within one trilogy, but the thing is at least conceivable.

At any rate it is in Aeschylus that we first meet the motif of the
inherited curse linking these events. Aegisthus relates in the
Agamemnon how Thyestes, on realizing that his children were in
the stew, got into a stew himself, kicked the table over, and voiced a
crisp curse to the effect that the whole race of Pleisthenes should be
overthrown likewise.[15] Earlier in the play Cassandra has seen visions

[14] Aesch. *Ag.* 1223, 1582–611.
[15] Aesch. *Ag.* 1600–2, μόρον δ' ἄφερτον Πελοπίδαις ἐπεύχεται, | λάκτισμα δείπνου
ξυνδίκως τιθεὶς ἀρᾷ, | οὕτως ὀλέσθαι πᾶν τὸ Πλεισθένους γένος.

of the Thyestean banquet, which gives the house the character of a charnel-house. But she has also detected the presence of a permanently resident band of Erinyes, drunk on blood, who cleave to the house and sing of Thyestes' adultery with his brother's wife as the πρώταρχος ἄτη.[16] This suggests that the curse at the banquet was not after all of unique importance as the link holding the saga together: the Erinyes, the spirits of the vendetta, were already established from the moment when Thyestes bedded Atreus' wife. The curse is introduced subsequently as an auxiliary unifying motif.

Aeschylus twice refers to the family as Pelopids (and once as Tantalids), but he does not trace its troubles back to Pelops' time. By the end of the fifth century, however, the motif of the inherited curse had been taken back to Pelops. The story went that Pelops, to win Hippodameia, defeated her father Oenomaus in a chariot-race with the help of Oenomaus' mechanic, Myrtilus, who sabotaged his master's vehicle so that it crashed. Pelops made off with the girl and Myrtilus, but presently disposed of the latter by throwing him out of the chariot into the sea. As he disappeared into the wine-dark waves, Myrtilus cried a curse on Pelops' family. We know that the drowning was related by the mythographer Pherecydes, who may also have been the source for the curse. In any case Euripides refers to it in the *Orestes* and makes it the origin of the family's troubles. Sophocles too traces them back to the drowning of Myrtilus, and although he does not speak explicitly of a curse uttered by Myrtilus, it is surely what he had in mind.[17]

Hellanicus had a different story of a Pelopid curse. According to him, when Pelops married Hippodameia he already had a son by a previous wife. The son's name was Chrysippus, and Pelops was very fond of him. Atreus and Thyestes, Hippodameia's eldest sons, were jealous of Chrysippus and murdered him. Pelops found out that they were the culprits and banished the pair of them with a curse to the effect that they and their descendants should perish at each other's hands. Thucydides also knows Atreus as a killer of Chrysippus.[18]

---

[16] Aesch. *Ag.* 1087–97, 1186–93.

[17] Pherec. *FGrHist* 3 F 37; Eur. *Or.* 988–1012, cf. 1548 (conjectural at *IT* 192); Soph. *El.* 504–15.

[18] Hellanicus *FGrHist* 4 F 157; cf. Thuc. 1. 9. 2. Praxilla (*PMG* 751) had yet another version of Chrysippus' end: he was abducted by Zeus (cf. Wilamowitz 1880: 611). What is common to the different stories about him is that he was beautiful and

Comparison of these different versions makes it clear that the inherited curse was not a fixed, primary element in this mythical complex but an accessory motif that could be fitted in at various points, according to the changing horizons of individual authors.

Let us turn now from the Pelopids to the Labdacids, that other family that suffered a train of sensational disasters extending over three generations: 'das unheilbeladene Labdakidengeschlecht'. Again no epic covered the whole saga: the first part of it was the subject matter of the *Oidipodeia*, the second part that of the *Thebaid*. The first time they were brought together within a single frame, so far as we know, was in Aeschylus' prize-winning trilogy of 467 BC, consisting of the *Laios*, the *Oedipus*, and the *Septem*, followed by the Satyr-play *Sphinx*. The first play, the *Laios*, presumably centred on the killing of Laios by his unrecognized son Oedipus in the earliest reported instance of what is nowadays called 'road rage'. One of the fragments alludes to the exposure of a baby in a jar, and another to a homicide. From references in the *Septem* we gather that Apollo had warned Laios, not once but three times, that if he wanted Thebes to be secure from danger he should be sure to die childless; but Laios had allowed sensibility to prevail over sense, and fathered a son. The second play, *Oedipus*, will have dealt with Oedipus' discovery that he had killed his father and married his mother. The *Septem* portrays the fatal conflict between Oedipus' sons, whose mutual slaughter signifies the final extinction of the family.

Was there a single thread linking all these events? Were Laios and his descendants doomed by an ancestral curse? There is certainly one curse involved in the story: the one laid by Oedipus upon his sons. As I have mentioned, this goes back to the epic *Thebaid*. In fact it is rather embarrassing that two of the six verbatim fragments from that poem describe Oedipus cursing his sons on different occasions. In one he explodes because Polynices gives him wine in a gold cup that had been Laios', on a silver table that was also a family heirloom. His curse is that the two brothers should not divide their inheritance in friendship but fight continually. In the other fragment he takes offence at their sending him a leg of beef instead of

died (or disappeared) before marrying. One may guess that he was originally a figure of Peloponnesian local cult, similar to Hippolytus (and with the same horse in his name).

their customary shoulder, and he prays to Zeus and the other gods that they may die at each other's hands.[19]

In Aeschylus' version the occasion of the curse fell in the interval between the second and third plays, but the Chorus of the *Septem* supply the information, in terms recalling the epic, that Oedipus' anger was aroused by the way his sons were providing for him.[20] There is much emphasis in the play on this paternal curse as the force that drives Eteocles and Polynices to their deaths.[21] But as to the earlier misfortunes of Laios and Oedipus, there is no hint that these had anything to do with a curse. Aeschylus does indeed endeavour to present the whole saga as flowing from one original ἀρχὴ κακῶν, but when the women of the Chorus look back to it— 'for I tell of an ancient transgression, soon punished, but abiding to the third generation' (742)—they tell us that it was Laios' disregard of Apollo's repeated warnings not to father a son, a disregard due to foolish fondness (κρατηθεὶς ἐκ φίλων ἀβουλιᾶν, 750). They go on to emphasize Oedipus' misguidedness in marrying Jocasta, and in cursing his sons; they have previously pointed out to Eteocles that he is in the grip of irrational urges. So what is highlighted as the common factor in the whole story is ill-judged, deluded behaviour, not an ancestral curse. When a Messenger brings the news that the brothers have slain one another, his verdict is that Apollo has brought Laios' old imprudence to its conclusion; and in the following ode the Chorus first sing of Oedipus' curse having done its work, but then they add, 'and Laios' disobedient choice has persisted throughout'.[22]

What does Sophocles make of the story? He did not treat it in a connected trilogy, so he was under less pressure to represent it as a connected tale. Nevertheless, in the earliest of his three Theban plays, the *Antigone*, he was still sufficiently under the influence of Aeschylus to include a choral retrospect similar to the one in the *Septem*.

---

[19] *Thebaid* frs. 2–3 Bernabé = Davies. Cf. Welcker (1849: 333–40); Bethe (1891): 102 f.); Davies (1989: 25 f.).

[20] Aesch. *Sept.* 785–90, τέκνοις δ' †ἀραίας† ἐφῆκεν ἐπίκοτος τροφᾶς, αἰαῖ, πικρογλώσσους ἀράς, καί σφε σιδαρονόμωι διὰ χερί ποτε λαχεῖν κτήματα.

[21] Ibid. 70, 655, 695–701, 709, 720–33, 766, 819, 832, 840, 886, 894, 898, 946, 955, 977 = 988.

[22] Ibid. 801 f., ἄναξ Ἀπόλλων . . . Οἰδίπου γένει | κραίνων παλαιὰς Λαΐου δυσβουλίας; 842 βουλαὶ δ' ἄπιστοι Λαΐου διήρκεσαν.

Happy are they whose life has never tasted ills,
for when a house is shaken by the gods,
ruin unfailing advances through generations . . .

Ancient are the woes of the Labdacid house
I see breaking on woes of the dead,
nor does generation relieve generation: some god
batters away, and they have no escape.
So now the light beamed over the last shoot
in Oedipus's house,
but down again it is mown
by the bloody sickle of the gods of death,
and folly, and the Furies of the heart.

ἀρχαῖα τὰ Λαβδακιδᾶν οἴκων ὁρῶμαι
πήματα φθιτῶν ἐπὶ πήμασι πίπτοντ᾽,
οὐδ᾽ ἀπαλλάσσει γενεὰν γένος, ἀλλ᾽ ἐρείπει
θεῶν τις, οὐδ᾽ ἔχει λύσιν.
νῦν γὰρ ἐσχάτας ὑπὲρ
ῥίζας ἐτέτατο φάος ἐν Οἰδίπου δόμοις·
κατ᾽ αὖ νιν φοινία
θεῶν τῶν νερτέρων ἀμᾷ κοπίς
λόγου τ᾽ ἄνοια καὶ φρενῶν Ἐρινύς.[23]

Later the Chorus suggest to Antigone that she is paying for some trial of her father's—πατρῷον δ᾽ ἐκτίνεις τιν᾽ ἆθλον—and she replies, 'you have touched on my most painful concern—the thrice-ploughed furrow of my father's doom and the fate of our whole Labdacid family'.[24] Neither she nor they know anything of a curse. They only know that the family has suffered a catalogue of disasters, and they can only speculate that 'some god' is set on its destruction.

In *Oedipus Tyrannus* the story begins with the oracle given to Laios, not warning him not to have a son, as in Aeschylus, but informing him that it was his destiny to be killed by his son. Nothing precedes the oracle. The only curse is the one laid by Oedipus on Laios' murderer and on anyone who shelters him; when Teiresias tells Oedipus that 'you will presently be driven out of this land by the double-edged curse of your father and mother', this is vatic language and does not refer to a literal curse uttered by Laios or Jocasta.[25]

---

[23] Soph. *Ant.* 582–603.   [24] Ibid. 856–62.
[25] *OT* 417 f. Similarly at Eur. *Phoen.* 1610 f., παῖδάς τ᾽ ἀδελφοὺς ἔτεκον, οὓς

In *Oedipus at Colonus*, as in *Antigone*, the tribulations of the house are contemplated with baffled despair. Oedipus protests that his actions were unintentional errors; he does not see himself as the victim of any curse, but of the gods, who led him into trouble, perhaps (he surmises) because they had some long-standing grudge against the family. Again, the oracle given to Laios is treated as the start of the whole matter, and nothing prior to it is mentioned.[26]

Sophocles, then, is consistent. There is no question of a family curse going back to Laios. From the high incidence of calamities people infer some divine enmity, but they have no explanation to offer for it; they are unaware of any incident that could have provoked it.

Some modern interpreters know better. They aver that both for Aeschylus and for Sophocles Laios and his descendants laboured under an ancestral curse, whether in the proper sense of a curse or in the sense of a divine μῆνις; and that the reason for it was Laios' abduction and rape of Pelops' son Chrysippus, who committed suicide. According to certain ancient sources, this did in fact lead Pelops to pronounce a curse on Laios.

How old is the story? A line of scholars going back to Welcker has held that it appeared in the epic *Oidipodeia*, on the basis of an account found in a scholium on the *Phoenissae* and ascribed to one Pisander. Welcker took this Pisander to stand for a Cyclic poet, and Bethe and Wilamowitz claimed the account to be basically a summary of the contents of the *Oidipodeia*. Carl Robert took a much more sceptical view of it as a late piece of mythography drawn from various sources. Jacoby put it with other scholiastic citations of 'Pisander' to the credit of a Hellenistic prose author, and his view is now widely accepted.[27] That text certainly cannot be used as evidence for the presence of the Chrysippus story in the epic *Oidipodeia*.

As we have seen, there is no hint of it in the surviving dramas of

ἀπώλεσα, | ἀρὰς παραλαβὼν Λαΐου καὶ παισὶ δούς, there is no reference to an actual curse by Laios.

[26] OC 265–74, 521–48, 960–99, esp. 964 f. θεοῖς γὰρ ἦν οὕτω φίλον, | τάχ' ἄν τι μηνίουσιν ἐς γένος πάλαι, 969 f. (the oracle to Laios), 997 f. τοιαῦτα μέντοι καὐτὸς εἰσέβην κακά, | θεῶν ἀγόντων.

[27] Welcker (1865: 91–5); Bethe (1891: 4–12); Wilamowitz (1898: 499; 1899: 209); cf. id. (1900: 66 n. 1); Robert (1915: i. 149–67); F. Jacoby, *FGrHist* 16 F 10 with commentary and Nachträge (i.² 544–7); Mastronarde (1994: 31–8).

Aeschylus or Sophocles either. The idea that it formed the subject of Aeschylus' *Laios*[28] is hard to reconcile with the allusion in that play to an exposed child, who must be Oedipus; in any case it does not fit the references to Laios in the *Septem*. The earliest known source for the myth is Euripides' *Chrysippus*. For all we know, Euripides may have invented it. He might have taken his cue from some earlier source, but if so it does not seem to have been much noticed before him. Hellanicus and Thucydides, as we have seen, knew a quite different account of Chrysippus' fate.

It is sometimes thought that Euripides' *Oenomaus* and *Chrysippus* formed a connected trilogy with his *Phoenissae*. They might go well together, but the combination is speculative.[29] In the prologue of the *Phoenissae* Jocasta recites the history of the Labdacids, going right back to Cadmus. When she comes to Laios, the story is just as in Aeschylus. Being childless, he went to consult the oracle, which warned him not to beget a son, because if he did, that son would kill him. But Laios got drunk and yielded to desire. Chrysippus plays no part in her account.

We do not know whether Euripides' *Chrysippus* contained the detail that Pelops laid a curse on Laios following the boy's death.[30] Pelops was a character in the play, so it is quite possible. If so, Euripides might have been supplying *suo Marte* what the Labdacid saga had hitherto lacked, a real hereditary curse analogous to the one that Myrtilus laid on Pelops. However, we should note that only one of the late sources which refer to the curse suggests that Pelops cursed Laios and his descendants. According to the others, the curse was that he should not have a son, or that if he did, he would be slain by him.[31] In that case the curse merely served to connect the

---

[28] Lloyd-Jones (1971: 121) after Welcker and others. Criticized by Hutchinson (1985: p. xxiii); West (1991: 231); Mastronarde (1994: 35 f.).

[29] See Mastronarde (1994: 36–8).

[30] See Mastronarde (1994: 33 f.). Hartung's view that a hypothesis of the play is preserved in [Plut.] *Parall. min.* 33 (313de = Dositheus, *FGrHist* 290 F 6) is very attractive; see Wilamowitz (1893: 179–85). (*Contra*: Robert (1915: i. 410–12); Jacoby (as n. 27).) There Chrysippus is killed (not very efficiently) by Hippodameia, who frames Laios. Pelops is convinced that he is the murderer. But Chrysippus takes some time to die and is able to denounce Hippodameia and exculpate Laios. However, Pelops might have laid his curse on him before the disclosure, and it would then have been too late to revoke it.

[31] Hypotheses to *Septem* and *Phoenissae*: Smith (1972: 3. 16, 7. 2), Mastronarde (1988: 6. 5, 9. 2, 12. 25). The one that suggests an inherited curse is sch. *Phoen.* 60,

Chrysippus episode up with the better-known story about Laios. It
was fulfilled by Laios' death, and there was no sense in which
Oedipus could inherit it.

The idea of the ancestral curse exercises a dangerous fascination. It
found its way by stages into myths where it did not originally
belong; and interpreters of tragedy have persistently introduced it
where it is not present. It has become, so to speak, one of the
inherited curses of scholarship.

REFERENCES

ANET = J. B. Pritchard (ed.), *Ancient Near Eastern Texts Relating to the Old
Testament* (3rd edn., Princeton 1969).
FGrHist = F. Jacoby (ed.), *Die Fragmente der griechischen Historiker* (Berlin
and Leiden 1923–58).

BETHE, E. (1891), *Thebanische Heldenlieder* (Leipzig).
DAVIES, M. (1989), *The Epic Cycle* (Bristol).
FRIEDRICH, J. (1926), *Staatsverträge des Hatti-Reiches in hethitischer Sprache*
(*Mitteilungen der Vorderasiatischen Gesellschaft* 31/1).
HUTCHINSON, G. O. (1985) (ed.), *Aeschylus, Septem contra Thebas*
(Oxford).
LATTIMORE, R. (1962), *Themes in Greek and Latin Epitaphs* (Urbana).
LLOYD-JONES, H. (1971), *The Justice of Zeus* (Berkeley and Los Angeles).
MASTRONARDE, D. J. (1988) (ed.), *Euripides, Phoenissae* (Leipzig).
——(1994), *Euripides, Phoenissae, ed. with Introd. and Commentary* (Cam-
bridge).
MEIGGS, R., and LEWIS, D. M. (1988), *Greek Historical Inscriptions* (2nd
edn. Oxford).
PARKER, R. C. T. (1983), *Miasma* (Oxford).
ROBERT, C. (1915), *Oidipus* (Berlin).
SMITH, O. L. (1976/1982) (ed.), *Scholia in Aeschylum* i, ii(2) (Leipzig).
WELCKER, F. G. (1865/1849), *Der epische Cyclus*, i (2nd edn.), ii (Bonn).
WEST, M. L. (1991), 'The Religious Interpretation of Myth in Aeschylus', in

φασὶν ὅτι Πέλοψ Χρυσίππου ἁρπαγέντος κατηράσατο μέχρι παίδων εἶναι τὸ κακόν.
The curious formulation looks like a distortion; it is used to explain Euripides'
reference to ὁ πάντ' ἀνατλὰς Οἰδίπους παθήματα, although there is no mention there
of inherited evil.

Mito, Religião e Sociedade. Atas do II Congresso Nacional de Estudos Clássicos (São Paulo), 226–38.

WILAMOWITZ, U. VON (1880), *Commentariolum grammaticum* ii (Greifswald); cited from *Kleine Schriften* iv (Berlin, 1962), 597–618.

——(1893), *De tragicorum graecorum fragmentis commentatio* (Göttingen); cited from *Kleine Schriften* i (Berlin, 1971), 176–208.

——(1898), 'Über griechische illustrierte Volksbücher', *Archäologischer Anzeiger* 1898: 228–30; cited from *Kleine Schriften* v(1) (Berlin, 1937), 497–501.

——(1899), 'Exkurse zum Oedipus des Sophokles', *Hermes* 34: 55–80; cited from *Kleine Schriften* vi (Berlin, 1972), 209–33.

——(1900), *Textgeschichte der griechischen Lyriker* (Berlin).

4

Sophocles and Time

G. O. HUTCHINSON

This paper is not directly concerned with Sophocles' views on time. It is interested rather in considering how structures of time are used in the plays to shape the experiences they depict and provide. In a literary work time is, among other things, a way of organizing material, articulating its meaning, intensifying its force. The sequence of past, present, and future is a framework fundamental to most criticism of drama; but the area of time that will primarily concern us here is the opposition, little explored for drama, between imperfective and perfective. This may sound like an eccentric move from a grammar of drama to a drama of grammar; but what is envisaged is not principally a matter of the forms of verbs, and not at all a matter of linking the grammar of a language to the frame of mind in its users. The grammatical structure of Greek, or Russian, offers essentially only a metaphor for the kind of thing that interests us; and it is not an authority but a stimulus. Can we sharpen our understanding of the tragedies by considering a contrast between (roughly) single, decisive, final events, and continuous states or repeated attempts, which fall short of, or look towards, completion and fulfilment?

Like other basic categories, this apparently elemental division can force us to look more closely and freshly at the shaping and meaning of the plays. It does not limit the interest of the topic that the categories are not fixed and absolute, or that their

Contributing to a volume in Hugh's honour is a delight. It was an incalculable privilege to be taught by him. He was so wonderfully encouraging, and demanding; and for all the passion of his intellectual convictions, he was so extraordinarily tolerant of his pupils' wild ideas. His energy and enthusiasm, his judgement and finesse, the breadth of his scholarship and culture inspired and continue to inspire. The present offering is unworthy of him, of course; but it is at least well meant.

application varies with the stance of the speaker, and with the development of the play. We shall in fact be positively interested by the way that happenings which are looked forward to as perfective can come to acquire a more complex and imperfective appearance as they come closer and the play subjects them to scrutiny. We shall also be interested by the role of the individual's viewpoint in the perception of time, something much stressed in some modern studies of linguistic aspect. The literary kind of 'aspect' that concerns us will be referred to as 'aspect', in inverted commas. It is not implied that Sophocles would have made so abstracted an analysis; but such an approach draws us to things that are important in the plays.[1]

Particularly important in several plays of Sophocles is the portrayal of imperfective suffering. We shall start by considering the *Trachiniae*. In the restricted space of a tragedy, this play continues the depiction of female waiting on which the *Odyssey* had lavished the length and accumulation of epic. Deianira's experience is not imperfective simply in its long duration; it is dominated by emotion towards a possible event in the future, by fear of her husband's death.[2]

Some points in the first part of the play may be considered for their presentation of Deianira's existence. In the narrative of her opening speech, the time before her marriage appears as a miniature

---

[1] The literature on verbal aspect is huge; for an introduction to it see Fanning (1990: ch. 1); note esp. Galton (1976); add notably Mellet (1988), Tobin (1993). I have not yet been able to see Giorgi and Pianesi (1998). For our purposes, the disputes on the nature of linguistic aspect can be set on one side; in any case, the relation to subjectivity becomes less pressing when one is dealing with drama, precisely because it is formally nothing but a collection of subjectivities, without even a narrator. Some writing on Sophocles makes passing use of 'aspectual' time: I have noticed Winnington-Ingram (1980: 233–4); Segal (1995: 146–7). But I am not aware of attempts to apply such conceptions more sustainedly to ancient or modern drama. Naturally the matter has aroused more interest in narrated genres like the novel or history, especially with references to narrative tenses, see e.g. Reid (1993); Bakker (1997). Note also e.g. Mann, *Der Zauberberg*, beginning of ch. 5. Some interesting remarks which bear, by extension, on the significance of the imperfective: Hamon (1981: 95–8).

[2] These footnotes do not attempt any comprehensive reference to the literature on Sophocles; they are mostly confined to relatively recent work. It follows from what is said above that we should not regard Deianira's suffering as self-contained circularity (Segal (1981: 105–6); for the approach cf. 262–7 on the *Electra*). It is also important that Deianira's fear is for somebody else; cf. Heiden (1989: 28–9).

version of the later suffering which supersedes it (note the sequence
in 4–8). Her fear that she will have to marry the unalluring Achelous
(φόβωι, 24) is ended by Heracles' victory, but this perfective event
leads her, ironically, into a perpetual sequence of fears.

> τέλος δ' ἔθηκε Ζεὺς ἀγώνιος καλῶς,
> εἰ δὴ καλῶς. λέχος γὰρ Ἡρακλεῖ κριτὸν
> ξυστᾶς' ἀεί τιν' ἐκ φόβου φόβον τρέφω,
> κείνου προκηραίνουςα. νὺξ γὰρ εἰςάγει
> καὶ νὺξ ἀπωθεῖ διαδεδεγμένη πόνον. (26–30)

The irony is marked by the development of the first sentence. The
language of what follows (27–30) expressively conveys the restless
continuum of what she endures. The repetitions bring out colour-
fully both the multitude of her anxieties and how it feels to
experience them in time. νύξ itself contains a grim imperfectivity:
the night-time of worry, powerfully described by Penelope.[3]

The first antistrophe of the parodos portrays the same anguish
with lyrical richness, and from a third-person perspective. There is a
more sensuous element in the depiction of Deianira's longing for
Heracles' return; there also appears the idea of much weeping,
which the Nurse had introduced (50–1): οὔποτ' εὐνάζειν ἀδάκρυ- |
τον βλεφάρων πόθον (106–7). The comparison with a bird, and the
potent verb τρύχεσθαι, further intensify the portrayal of her continuous pain. The ode sets against Deianira's unchanging lot the
tumultuously varied and dynamic existence of Heracles; this too is
imperfective, from Deianira's perspective, but plainly in a different
fashion. The contrast recalls the *Odyssey*.[4]

Deianira's speech after the parodos brings in a further contrast,
with the maidens of the chorus. Deianira's imperfective state, we
have seen, is related to a future beyond itself; the sequestered
existence of the unmarried girl is unaffected by anything outside.
The very sentence that describes that existence moves on, in forceful
opposition, to the nocturnal worries of the married woman (144–
50). It is interesting that Deianira's plight is connected to the
general experience of wives; the passage will also inform the

---

[3] Hom. *Od.* 19. 515–29; but her worries are more active than Deianira's. (Active
and passive make another interesting category . . .)

[4] What follows 106–7 suggests that those lines mean Deianira spends every night
weeping. ἀδάκρυτον should in my view be taken as proleptic; Lloyd-Jones's Loeb
translation seems to indicate a happy change of mind on this point (cf. Lloyd-Jones
and Wilson 1990: 153).

complex scene where Deianira encounters the supposed maiden and fellow-sufferer Iole. Deianira's speech proceeds (153) to her particular reasons for worry now, already indicated in the prologue (79–81). An oracle limits the future which will follow the present state to two possibilities, perfective or imperfective: the event of Heracles' death or the new situation of an untroubled life for him. Fifteen months is both the length of Heracles' latest absence and the time after which things will change (44–5, 164–5): the emphasis on the figure sharpens consciousness both of Deianira's extended misery and of the impending catastrophe.[5]

That brings us to Heracles. When the catastrophe is actually upon us, it wears a more complicated appearance than it had in advance. Heracles' agonized death in some ways continues to be seen as a perfective moment: the ironic end of his labours (ἀναδοχὰν τελεῖν πόνων, 825; μόχθων . . . λύςιν τελεῖςθαι, 1170–1), the deed of destruction which Deianira, terribly turned from passive to active, has unwittingly performed (1063, etc.). But Heracles' agonies are also presented on the stage, and become an imperfective state of suffering which only the actual moment of death (or apotheosis) will end, outside the borders of the play (1208–9, etc.). The play, the stage, and time are handled with great audacity as Heracles' roaring pain and rage engross the scene. Inventive language and strong death-bed drama give force and extension to the depiction of physical anguish. Thus the unconsciousness into which Heracles has fallen when he appears (974–92) and the attack that breaks in on Heracles' iambic speech (1081–9, cf. 1242, 1253–4, 1259–60) give change and dimension to the time of his torture. The very abundance of verbs used with the disease or the like as subject give a horrible richness to the torment: so ἐδαίνυτο (771), αἰκίζει (838), βρύκει (987), ἧπται . . . ἕρπει (1010), θρώιςκει (1028), βέβρωκε . . . ῥοφεῖ ξυνοικοῦν . . . πέπωκεν (1054–6), ἔθαλψε . . . διῆιξε (1082–3), δαίνυται . . . ἤνθηκεν, ἐξώρμηκεν (1088–9). The magnifying-glass of poetry makes us see the experience in a closer, and different, way.[6]

---

[5] The perpetual weeping alleged of Iole (325–7) is a particularly interesting element; note further on those lines Dumanoir (1996: 60).

[6] The inventiveness of Sophocles' writing here and in the *Philoctetes* is shown by comparison with the medical writing of the time, vigorous as that can be; cf. e.g. Hipp. *Vet. Med.* 19. 1 for violent verbs, *Morb.* 3. 7 for graphic imagery. On the course of Heracles' suffering Zielinski (1896: 609–16) remains of interest, though curiously literal-minded. It is notable that the chorus think the unconsciousness

It seems hard to think that we should not contrast the sufferings of Heracles and Deianira, the physical with the mental, the violent with the loving, emotion centred on the self with emotion related to another. One cannot fail to compare the two figures, and in doing so one surely must compare what they both endure, and in what manner. In a passage full of ironies and pathos, Heracles presents himself as made womanish in his girlish weeping, while Deianira has done a deed unlike a woman's (1062–3, 1070–5). The reversal of categories makes us connect the two characters in their pain; it does not obscure the difference in feeling of Heracles' weeping from Deianira's. Important too is the suggested opposition between the earlier life of Heracles, who was ἀстένακτος αἰέν (1074, cf. 1199–201), and that of Deianira, whose nightly longing was never ἀδάκρυτον (106–7). From that perspective Heracles' present suffering appears more as a single moment than as an extended period. The last we are shown of both characters is notable: Deianira ends her life with a tearful speech and a heroic act (917–26), Heracles with superhuman endurance ceases his cries and awaits the end (1259–63).[7]

The play, then, illustrates Sophocles' depiction of imperfective suffering, the changes in our conception of events when they come closer, and the relation of 'aspect' in time to the structure and meaning of the work. Sophocles' other play of prolonged female suffering will be considered at rather greater length.

The *Electra* explores the waiting of a woman in a more intense and challenging fashion than the *Trachiniae*. Electra's waiting has a more active and heroic quality than Deianira's. Deianira's suffering is presented more as imposed on her by circumstance. It is seen more emphatically as Electra's own choice to continue her unceasing lamentation of Agamemnon and waiting for Orestes, amid

might be death (969–70; cf. 806); that marks the length and handling of this death, unusual in tragedy.

[7] Note also Deianira's imagined weeping at 846–8. The choruses at 821–61 and 947–70 emphatically connect the present sufferings of Deianira and Heracles. Heracles' previous heroic abstention from crying is of course akin to Ajax's from laments (*Aj.* 317–22); cf. also Hom. *Od.* 11. 528–30, and esp. Balzac, *La Cousine Bette*, ch. 95, of *le maréchal Hulot*, 'Et, pour la première fois de sa vie peut-être, deux larmes roulèrent de ses yeux et sillonnèrent ses joues' (the specific point there is that he did not dry the tears before they fell). The contrast Deianira has drawn between maiden and woman is of no importance to Heracles (παρθένος 1071 merely sounds even worse). The reversal of the sexes here is discussed by Rehm (1994: 78–9).

persecution from without and disappointment from within. The relation of this unbearably protracted experience to single events is both starker and more complicated than in the less extraordinary experience of Deianira.[8]

Electra's life is first presented in the parodos (86–250). This long lyric sequence brings in a great many elements to depict Electra's imperfective state.[9] As in the *Trachiniae*, the heroine's perpetual weeping is stressed (e.g. ἀεί *El.* 122, *Trach.* 104). As there, the pattern of day and night is exploited (86–94, cf. 259), comparisons are made with birds that continually lament (107, 147–8). The relation of the period to the woman's life is different. For Deianira the 'natural' sequence of marriage after maidenhood has taken a shape of suffering presented in part as normal. Electra's decision to suffer has given her an 'unnatural' life, a permanent deprivation of womanly fulfilment (164–5).

The relation of the period to perfective time is also different, though connected. Deianira's suffering is connected to the future, Electra's to the future and the past. Electra's suffering begins from one terrible past event, the murder of Agamemnon, to which she looks back unceasingly. It is graphically described at 95–9 and 193–206. At 207–8 the relative clauses proceed to connect boldly the killing of Agamemnon with the blighting of Electra's life; it was a single event whose effects endure: χειροῖν, | αἳ τὸν ἐμὸν εἷλον βίον | πρόδοτον, αἵ μ' ἀπώλεσαν.[10] There are two ways in which Electra's life of grief might be ended, before her death: she might choose to end it, or Orestes might come. The coming of Orestes has actually occurred; but for Electra that coming is the future event for which she waits, half in despair (186). The relation of present and future is more fully brought out in the spoken continuation of the dialogue with the chorus, where she talks (303–6) of her hopeless waiting for Orestes to come, Ὀρέστην τῶνδε προσμένουσ' ἀεὶ | παυστῆρ' ἐφήξειν. The idea of perfective 'stopping' is important to the play, as will be seen. In the earlier passage the 'always' of her waiting is bitterly

[8] Electra would have concurred with Medea (as reported by Christa Wolf): 'Auch Warten sei eine Tätigkeit, der eine Entscheidung vorausgehen müsse, eben die, daß man warten wolle und nicht abbrechen' (*Medea. Stimmen. Roman* (1996: 171).

[9] It is one of the longest lyric sequences in extant Sophocles; the longest, if one includes the anapaests.

[10] Cf. *Phil.* 1356.

rhymed with the 'always' of his supposed intention to come (165, 171, cf. 303, 305); at 171–2 ἀεὶ μὲν γὰρ ποθεῖ, | ποθῶν δ' οὐκ ἀξιοῖ φανῆναι the imperfective intention is forcefully set against the closing perfective (and aorist) verb (cf. 1273–4). The chorus have ended their half of the stanza with an exalted presentation of Orestes' arrival, culminating in his name (160–3, cf. 180–2). Father principally in the past and brother principally in the future: these are the points to which Electra's emotion is directed (cf. e.g. 115–18).

The second possible perfective end to Electra's imperfective condition, her giving the grief up herself, is much exploited in the parodos; it is used to stress that her condition is chosen. It appears on her own lips only in negation: she will never stop. The continual recurrence of the declaration is itself expressive; but the different instances are different coloured. At first Electra presents the negation in sublime language: ἀλλ' οὐ μὲν δὴ | λήξω θρήνων ςτυγερῶν τε γόων, | ἔςτ' ἂν παμφεγγεῖς ἄςτρων | ῥιπὰς λεύςςω δὲ τόδ' ἧμαρ (103–6). Even at the end of these anapaests, however, she shows the difficulty of this act of will: she can 'no longer' sustain this burden alone (119–20). In response to the chorus's urgings to desist, she seems partly to acknowledge their criticism of her extremity (131, 135), but bluntly insists οὐδ' ἐθέλω προλιπεῖν τόδε (132). However, she shows graceful manners here, and there seems to be a reasonable quality in her very profession of unreasonableness; she is not simply a raucous zealot (cf. 254–7, 616–21). In the next stanza she more lyrically and loftily appeals to the examples of perpetual lament supplied by the nightingale and by Niobe: Electra holds Niobe a god, for her unending tears. Later she is again allowing a point to the chorus, the dangers she is incurring by her ferocious attitude; but the language of dissuasion is nobly turned into defiant assertion: ἀλλ' ἐν γὰρ δεινοῖς οὐ ςχήςω | ταύτας ἄτας, | ὄφρα με βίος ἔχηι (223–5, cf. 215). The end of the stanza presents the same thought with more pathos: οὐδέ ποτ' ἐκ καμάτων ἀποπαύςομαι | ἀνάριθμος ὧδε θρήνων (231–2). Here and elsewhere she stresses the generalizable moral foundation for her stance. The parodos, in my opinion, cannot fairly be seen as leaving a negative impression of Electra; but we see this willed imperfectivity in many lights.[11]

[11] At 135 ἀλύειν may suggest a viewpoint not fully shared by Electra, cf. e.g. Virg. *Aen.* 12. 680. Niobe is called a god at *Ant.* 834 (contr. Philem. fr. 102. 3 KA); but here the statement sounds more controversial and paradoxical (cf. 151–2, with

The parodos, then, creates a diverse and powerful vision of Electra's experience. It should not be seen merely as establishing a necessary premiss for the play; its themes are sharpened and intensified in what follows, and the vision is enlarged and modified. Particularly significant is the concrete detail of Electra's coexistence with her family. Her speech after the parodos already introduces her life with Clytemnestra and Aegisthus, its recurring but varying encounters, the restrictions (285–6) it imposes on her wish to lament: these complicate the picture of seamless uniformity in her imperfective existence. Her scenes with Chrysothemis and with Clytemnestra strengthen the idea of continual dissension (note e.g. 372–3, 556–7). This is not the first time there have been arguments in this unhappy family.[12] The scene with Chrysothemis gives new force to the theme of Electra's ceasing to lament. That theme has appeared in the scene already (cf. τῶνδε ληξάcηι γόων, 353), when Chrysothemis in turn has sought to dissuade Electra and Electra has declined. But Chrysothemis then reveals a plan by Aegisthus and Clytemnestra to imprison her in a cave, εἰ τῶνδε μὴ λήξεις γόων (379, cf. 375 ὃ ταύτην τῶν μακρῶν cχήcει γόων). Electra faces this extreme pressure with nonchalant bravado (387). The threat is in turn linked (386–9) with another perfective event important in the play: the expected return of Aegisthus.

Electra's continuous way of life and frame of mind is actually ended (she supposes) by an event that lies outside her previous thoughts: the death of Orestes. A brutal exchange (795–8) stresses the stem παυ-: Κλ. οὔκουν Ὀρέcτηc καὶ cὺ παύcετον τάδε; | Ηλ. πεπαύμεθ' ἡμεῖc, οὐχ ὅπωc cε παύcομεν, κτλ. With moving insight, Sophocles now has Electra saying once again that Orestes has destroyed her hopes, her hopes that he would come; but now it is completely true (809–12, 854–7, al.; cf. 305–6, al.). Orestes has now joined Agamemnon among the dead (813–14, cf. 968–9). Rather than resume her life but without hope, she bleakly imagines remaining exactly where she is, outside the palace, until perhaps she is killed (817–22).

The next scene produces turns of a Baroque ingenuity and extremity. Chrysothemis proclaims that she has proof of Orestes' return; the return is indeed the true end of Electra's woes

αἰαῖ). For the tone of ἄραρεν cf. Cic. Att. 9. 10. 3 init. On the chorus in the parodos, note Paulsen (1989: 35–6).

[12] Assuredly unhappy, as Tolstoy asserts, in its own particular manner, po-svoemu.

(Chrysothemis restrainedly speaks of a respite, κἀνάπαυλαν ὧν | πάροιθεν εἶχες καὶ κατέστενες κακῶν, 873–4). Electra harshly destroys this supposed illusion of joy with her own illusion of misery. And yet when Chrysothemis has reached Electra's own point of despair, Electra surprises her (she is always surprising her family). Electra has constructed her own way of ending their woes: παῦσον ἐκ κακῶν ἐμέ, | παῦσον δὲ cαυτήν (986–7, cf. λύcειc 939). She urges Chrysothemis to help her undertake the killing of Aegisthus, and, when she declines, declares she will undertake it alone. In attempting to persuade Chrysothemis, she fluently sketches the imperfective consequences of this perfective act: some of the points are calculated to appeal to her sister, but the Homeric vision of their future glory reflects her own mentality. The sensationally audacious plan, which almost undercuts the situation of the play (note 1021–2), displays Electra transcending the boundaries of gender. It is no improvisation of the moment (1049, with Hom. *Il.* 9. 527; 1319–21); yet events will make irrelevant this desperate scheme of ending too.[13]

We may pause to consider Electra's great lament over Orestes' ashes, which shows the poet's poignantly imaginative handling of 'aspect'. Thus the terrible power of the destructive moment is conveyed with a drastic metaphor: πάντα γὰρ cυναρπάcαc, | θύελλ' ὅπωc, βέβηκαc (1150–1). The πάντα gains especial depth from the lines before, which refer to the remote past, and a new and moving element; Electra's care for Orestes in childhood, presented as repeated and continuous, has now been annulled in one day (1149–50). After βέβηκαc come staccato clauses which depict Electra's present situation in its totality: the present state resulting from the separation of the family in death (οἴχεται πατήρ· | τέθνηκ' ἐγὼ cοί· φροῦδοc αὐτὸc εἶ θανών), and the present exultation of her enemies.

The speech is largely built around perfective moments of sending and receiving. The starting point is the vital event of Electra's sending Orestes forth from the house to rescue him when Agamemnon was killed (ἐκπέμπειν, 1128, 1130, 1132–3; cf. e.g. 12, 321). This sending is set against the return of the dead Orestes, sent

---

[13] For the Homeric use of speech in 975–85, cf. *Aj.* 500–4. The movement of τάλαινα in the first part of the scene is noteworthy. Electra uses it several times of her sister (cf. Chrysothemis at 388). Chrysothemis finally (926, 930) applies the word to herself in the present (cf. 902), just after Electra's 924, and with the exclamation that Electra has used (883, cf. 674, and 1108, 1115, 1143).

on a terrible journey (πεμφθείς, 1163), sent by their δαίμων (προὔπεμψεν, 1158), and received by Electra (εἰcεδεξάμην, 1128). The original sending is essentially presented perfectively; but in the initial ὥc ⟨c᾽⟩ ἀπ᾽ ἐλπίδων | οὐχ ὧνπερ ἐξέπεμπον εἰcεδεξάμην (1127 f.) the imperfect regards the act from the perspective of her hopes at the time, and also suggests its futility. Electra's perfective act of sending Orestes out is also set against all the imperfective, repeated sending of messages by Orestes to say, in vain, that he would appear as avenger. προὔπεμπεc (1155), picked up by προὔπεμψεν (1158) threads this sending into the verbal sequence; the opposition with the original act has been felt in the play already (320–1, al.). At the end of the speech, the idea of receiving acquires a bold and stirring development: Electra asks Orestes to receive her into his urn (δέξαι, 1165). The thought expresses her wish, which transcends actuality, to overcome through death their separation by death; it also shows how she can envisage, in the world of the living, no bearable future. The speech shows how the detail of Sophocles' poetry can exploit literary 'aspect' with the greatest richness.[14]

At last Orestes reveals himself, and we might seem to have the desired end; but things prove more complicated as they draw closer. For Electra the decisive event has now occurred, and her life of waiting and misery is over; for Orestes, who naturally has a different perspective, the most decisive event has still to happen. Clytemnestra and Aegisthus have yet to be killed, the enemy have yet to be 'stopped' from laughing (ὅπου . . . γελῶντας ἐχθροὺς παύcομεν, 1294–5). The Paidagogos strongly reinforces this view. Electra displays her own vision as she dwells on the supreme event of the return, so starkly discontinuous with the despair she had felt before it (1262–3, 1281–7, cf. 1362–3).

The dialogue on the stage itself exploits the contrast between Electra and Orestes, through a further opposition between imperfective and perfective time, as Electra gives rein to her feelings, while Orestes urges silence and action.[15] Orestes and the Paidagogos again

[14] Note too, for example, how 1131–42 juxtapose unrealized perfective events in regard to the moments both of Orestes' rescue and of his death. The negative depiction in 1138–40 has a Homeric potency, cf. e.g. Il. 21. 123–5, 24. 743–5.

[15] The idea of action as inherently perfective, emotion as inherently imperfective finds notable connections with Wittgenstein, Philosophische Untersuchungen, §620 'Tun scheint selbst kein Volumen der Erfahrung zu haben. Es scheint wie ein ausdehnungsloser Punkt, die Spitze einer Nadel', §638, etc.

and again disapprove of speaking 'at length' now, when action is required; such abundant speech must be saved for the future (e.g. 1259 μὴ μακρὰν βούλου λέγειν, 1288–92, 1335 τῶν μακρῶν λόγων, 1363–72, 1372). Electra's emotion can hardly be confined: she asks with vigorous rhetorical questions how anyone could respond to Orestes' return with silence (1260–1), how she could cease from weeping with joy (1313–15). Her declaration οὔ ποτ' ἐκλήξω χαρᾶι | δακρυρροοῦσα (1312–13) movingly and pointedly reverses her earlier οὐ μὲν δὴ | λήξω θρήνων (102–3) and the whole theme of ceasing to lament. This is the more striking in that her tears are meant to be taken by Clytemnestra for tears of grief.

The treatment of time in this scene brings out how the decisive event awaited by Electra is less atomic than it appeared in advance. It contains at least two events (return and killing), and various aspects. The spectator's reaction also starts to split, or does so more definitely than before. The joy of Electra in finding her brother and her freedom must engage every responsive person; her remorseless zeal for the killing contains more to disturb.

The final scene with Aegisthus, an extraordinary way to close a Greek tragedy, exploits time both on stage and more widely. Aegisthus' return is itself a crucial event in the play, which has now acquired an altered significance. He believes that a decisive event has occurred for Electra, Orestes' death: this has brought an end to her resistance and her hopes (1445–6, 1464–5, cf. 1460–3). The passage displays with sharp irony the alternative endings to imperfective periods which the plot has deployed; the political dimension Aegisthus adds to the imagined ending makes him the more disagreeable (1458–63). In fact his death is to be the crucial ending for Electra: her last words chillingly make Aegisthus' death and loss of burial the only release from the period of her woes, ὡς ἐμοὶ τόδ' ἂν κακῶν | μόνον γένοιτο τῶν πάλαι λυτήριον (1489–90). She now has in mind not the fact of deliverance but the emotional satisfaction of revenge.

The opposition on stage of lengthy speaking and swift action appears again with Aegisthus. His talking defers or could defer the crucial moment (μηδὲ (ἔα)μηκύνειν λόγους, 1484; πόλλ' ἀντιφωνεῖς, ἡ δ' ὁδὸς βραδύνεται, 1501; cf. 1491–2). It is Electra who breaks in on his dialogue with Orestes and first urges speed (1483–4, 1487–90). One feels the difference from her lavishly emotional manner at the reunion; now she is as practical and intent on speed as Orestes is, or more. But this intentness is the disquieting expression of fierce desire. The velocity of the ending to the play sharpens rather than overrides our uneasiness.[16]

The *Electra* has shown a treatment of an extended period of suffering related to that of the *Trachiniae*, but different in nature and significance. The play has developed in the most elaborate and probing fashion the idea of a perfective cessation to the imperfective period. We have seen again how events which look perfective from a distance appear more complex in 'aspect' when they appear; we have seen also how they look different to different characters. The complication of 'aspect' has proved to be bound up with the moral complication of the last part of the play; consideration of time heightens our consideration of meaning.

Two of the plays with male central figures are similarly founded on the long period of suffering which the foremost character has endured: the *Philoctetes* and the *OC*. The exigencies of space allow only a discussion of the latter, and that a brief one. The *OC* is chosen because it is particularly rich and intricate in its use of 'aspect', as of time in general; it should be evident enough that the kind of analysis applied above to the *Electra* and the *Trachiniae* can fruitfully be applied to the *Philoctetes*.

The *OC*, like the other three plays, is built around an extended, imperfective experience which leads up to the present; what is built around it is particularly elaborate. The experience is that of Oedipus' life of exile as a wandering beggar. The idea of wandering is much stressed, though little is said of particular places Oedipus has passed through (compare Walcott's *Omeros!*). By contrast with the fixity of Philoctetes or Electra, Oedipus' experience is defined by unresting motion. The present place as well as the present time are set against this incessant movement. Oedipus will here be received, fixed, and will not move; his wanderings and his life will end. Oedipus announces himself in the first lines of the play as τὸν πλανήτην Οἰδίπουν (3, cf. 50 etc.). With that conception are swiftly associated repeated begging, poverty, acceptance, heroic endurance, prolonged life; the idea of extended time is soon explicitly added (22). Ironically Oedipus sees in ἡμέραν | τὴν νῦν (3–4) mere

---

[16] Through 1416 Electra's last speech is emphatically linked with her earlier appalling imperative to Orestes (1415, on which see Lloyd-Jones and Wilson (1990: 74); note 1407–8, 1413–14). More straightforwardly positive views of Electra have been offered recently by Harder (1995), and March (1996).

repetition of a routine, varied in place but not substance; in fact the present day will provide the perfective end to that routine. The visual side of the opening is no less important: the slow movement, guided by Antigone, which embodies the wandering, and their squalid appearance, which embodies his degraded exile.[17]

Later, when Oedipus speaks of Antigone's life, he conveys in an expressively long sentence the extension of what she has undergone, and the poverty.

> ἣ μὲν ἐξ ὅτου νέας
> τροφῆς ἔληξε καὶ κατίςχυςεν δέμας,
> ἀεὶ μεθ' ἡμῶν δύςμορος πλανωμένη
> γεροντ αγωγεῖ, πολλὰ μὲν κατ' ἀγρίαν
> ὕλην ἄςιτος νηλίπους τ' ἀλωμένη,
> πολλοῖςι δ' ὄμβροις ἡλίου τε καύμαςι
> μοχθοῦςα τλήμων δεύτερ' ἡγεῖται τὰ τῆς
> οἴκοι διαίτης, εἰ πατὴρ τροφὴν ἔχοι.   (345–52)

The rhetorical structure is evident enough: ἐξ ὅτου, ἀεί, πολλὰ μέν, πολλοῖςι δ' all stress extended time and repetition, and are opposed to the home which the girl has abandoned. πλανωμένη and ἀλωμένη both end lines and clauses. Poverty and degradation is conveyed not only by ἄςιτος νηλίπους τ' but by the roughness of the elements, which a well-born maiden would escape. Creon uses a verbal structure which applies an emphatic ἀεί to both Oedipus and Antigone (746, 750), and emphasizes wandering, poverty, deprivation. Polynices brings out the length of Oedipus' suffering by a repellent personification of filth: ὁ δυςφιλὴς | γέρων γέροντι ςυγκατώικηκεν πίνος (1258–9); the whole description reactivates through language what we see on stage. Polynices connects this state with Oedipus' exile: he is ξένης ἐπὶ χθονὸς . . . ἐνθάδ' ἐκβεβλημένον (1256–7). He fails to recognize that Oedipus has now found a 'home'.

However, powerfully as the play evokes the central figure's imperfective existence, it does not expound that existence in the same lengthy and elaborate fashion as the *Trachiniae, Electra,* or *Philoctetes*; on the other hand, it devotes a great deal of its ample

---

[17] On slowness note Dunn (1992: 1). Note the depiction (whether or not of this play) in the *oecus maior* of the House of the Comedians on Delos (N, Met. 7; *LIMC* 1. 1. 820, 2). τὸν πλανήτην recalls, for example, the *strannik* (wanderer) used by Lermontov in relation to himself in the poem of exile 'Listok' ('The Little Leaf', 1841, ll. 7, 21 (*Sobr. soč.* (Moscow 1964), i. 124–5).

span to perfective events in the past and future which are connected to or contrasted with this protracted period.

Most fundamentally, the play sets the supreme event of the play, Oedipus' death, against the long time which has preceded it. The shape is already set out plainly, with the authority of an oracle, at the start of the play: Apollo ταύτην ἔλεξε παῦλαν ἐν χρόνωι μακρῶι (88, cf. βίου . . . πέρασιν . . . καὶ καταστροφήν τινα 102–3, with the rest of the sentence). One sees here the link of the perfective moment with place, in the striking phrase χώραν τερμίαν (89); one sees also the effect this moment will have in the future on Athens and Thebes.

The moment itself, the death, is heralded at the end of the play by thunder; this thunder appears for the moment to sweep away all the entanglements of sons and Thebans. It was forecast as a sign in the prologue (94–5); characteristically, this event itself seems less perfective when experienced in stage time: the terrifying sound and sight occur repeatedly. But the decisiveness of the happening is clear, and its meaning as bringing an end to Oedipus' life (1460–1, 1472–3, etc.). The speed and resolution with which Oedipus himself now guides the others, following the god, eerily marks a contrast with the movement at the beginning of the play, and with the life he is now ending (1551–2).[18]

In a speech to his daughters reported by the messenger Oedipus proclaims that 'this day' (1612) sees the end of his life, and of their labours in looking after him. As hitherto, the girls' sufferings are partly a way of talking about Oedipus' sufferings, but are partly distinct. The speech ends in a potent contrast with its beginning: Oedipus will end his life, and so the girls their toil; but they will live on, unlike him, and spend the rest of their lives mourning for him, οὗ τητώμεναι | τὸ λοιπὸν ἤδη τὸν βίον διάξετον (1618–19). The very end of the play makes clear the reality of this division, and also the further irony of Antigone's short life. Ismene in lament sets the death she wishes she could share with her father against the unendurable life she must now lead (1689–92). In a poignant

---

[18] In my view, the thunder must come before 1447; whether audible or (more likely) imagined, its sudden appearance after the penultimate line of the strophe would be unlike tragic lyric. 1456, if the thunder is imagined, would explain what precedes; the asyndeton is either 'explanatory', or produced by the brevity of the clause. With the παρ' to follow, μοι is not comfortably read as 'ethical'; if it depends on ἦλθε, it makes much clearer sense to refer the lines to the thunder.

turning round of Oedipus' speech, Antigone declares that her past life of suffering is now something she longs for (1697–9).

The death of Oedipus acquires a significance far beyond the boundaries of the perfective event. It is not so much the point that he will now become a hero, a chthonic near-divinity. We may set aside the considerable problems over the contemporary hero-cult. In the play there is little stress even on Oedipus' consciousness after death, something much more to the fore with, say, the dead Agamemnon in *Electra*. The blood of Oedipus' foes will be drunk not by Oedipus as 'a vengeful Fury', but by his cold and sleeping corpse, οὑμὸς εὕδων καὶ κεκρυμμένος νέκυς | ψυχρός . . . (621–2).[19] It is more important that the fact of his death on Attic soil has large consequences for the future. These can be represented as extending endlessly, γήρως ἄλυπα (1519), in forceful contrast to the old age of Oedipus, and of all mortals (607–8). The secret will transcend the death of the individual king (1530–1), and it will be passed on over the generations (1531–2). On the other hand, there is also a crucial moment envisaged in the future, a battle between Athens and Thebes by the site of Oedipus' grave; the presence of Oedipus' body will bring victory to Athens (411, 605, 621–2, 644–7, etc.).[20]

Oedipus makes his choice within the play to help Athens, not his own city, or his own son (1323); but the future event as well as the present is important. Oedipus will then himself, through the Athenian victory, overcome those who have harmed him, κρατήσω τῶν ἔμ' ἐκβεβληκότων (646). The reversal of power here is evident; so, in the following sequence of nervous antilabe (652–7), is the contrast with Oedipus' physical powerlessness now. One links too the earlier dialogue with Ismene, where Creon and the

---

[19] Cf. Segal (1981: 375).

[20] The historical event is discussed most recently, and helpfully, by Edmunds (1996: 95–6). On the question of the hero-cult cf. Kearns (1989: 50–2, 208–9). The best evidence in the play for Oedipus' consciousness after death is 411, where it is most natural that ὀργῆς should be referred to the time of the battle. Even 1565–7 need not be taken to imply heroic status (in the thought of the play the honour of the specific power conferred on Oedipus' body would be quite sufficient to justify αὔξοι, cf. 394). 1563–4, and 1568–78, do not greatly support an emphasis on the role of hero in 1565–7. (The text of 1565–7 themselves does not seem wholly satisfying even in the *OCT*.) Perhaps Sophocles was reluctant for aesthetic reasons to bring heroization (or deification) too openly and emphatically into his plays; this may be relevant to the *Trachiniae* too. *Phil*. 726–9, 1418–20, not part of the action of the play, would on this view be a different matter.

sons depend for their κράτος on Oedipus, and for this very reason are eager to gain κράτος over him (392, cf. 372; 400, 405, 408). This single moment in the future is thus vital to the themes and action of the play, and the larger shape in time which it foreshadows. An exceedingly impressive part of the play is the speech (607–28) in which Oedipus sets mortal mutability against the unchanging eternity of the gods, and depicts the vast and fluctuating period after his death; but at the end of it all, precisely because the gods are unchangeable and omniscient, will come his moment of power and revenge. This huge vista opens on no extrinsic piece of aetiology, but on an event which is vital to everyone in the play, and most of all to Oedipus.[21]

Highly characteristic of the play, and of Oedipus, is the unwearying scrutiny devoted to the past. Even the moment of killing Laius is explored for its motivation at that instant: would one not react with perfective action, not inquiry, to the imperfective situation of someone trying to kill one (991–6)? Oedipus' question to Creon is full of oratorical acumen.[22] Oedipus' period of wandering is not simply given a terrible perfective event which begins it, as with the sufferings of Electra and Philoctetes. Oedipus resentfully expounds, more than once, a complicated state of affairs. In his condition of mind immediately after the revelation of his deeds, he was eager for a perfective act of punishment, to be stoned (435) or to leave in exile (766); no one granted this (imperfective) desire. His feelings gradually altered with time (437–9, cf. 768–9), and he wished to remain; but there were then plans to exile him, in the midst of which his sons could have intervened but did not (440–4). 'Aspect' is important to this elaborate analysis, and is elaborately handled; the depiction of emotion weakening over time after an immediate response (433–9) reminds one of Hellenistic philosophy. The play is here typically probing, argumentative, explicit. In this respect, it is extremely different from the *Oedipus Tyrannus*.[23]

The play shows a different treatment again of imperfective

---

[21] With 607–28 one may compare and contrast Dem. 20. 161–2, which is related in its presentation of mutability but does not convey the same vastness of time.

[22] Cf. Isae. 2. 25. Edmunds (1996: 134–8) connects the self-defence with the republication of Dracon's legislation on homicide.

[23] The handling of Oedipus' past in both plays may rewardingly be contrasted with the effect of Enescu's *Œdipe*, where the whole span of Oedipus' life is accommodated into the structure of a single work.

suffering; we come to see once more the divisions in characters' perspectives on what happens. A single perfective event is placed in manifold and expressive relations to imperfective periods and perfective moments outside it. Seemingly perfective events even from the past are made to expose a greater complexity.

We have arrived at plays which are not based around an imperfective period of suffering. 'Aspect' may be thought much less relevant to the *Oedipus Tyrannus* than to the *Oedipus Coloneus*; in fact, contemplation of this matter leads one deeply into the design and nature of the play. But statements on this matter as on many other features of the work must be particularly guarded. The *OT*, despite its reputation for infernal lucidity, is in many respects less explicit and explanatory than, not only the *OC*, but Sophocles' other extant plays. It often proceeds by insidious transition rather than emphatic contrast; and the meaning and implications of the catastrophe remain in many respects unstated. The contrast with the *OC* is especially illuminating; for example, the question of Oedipus' guilt and innocence is discussed much more fully and plainly there. Part of the impact of the *OT* lies in its incommensurability and uncanniness; in consequence, criticism has to be unusually cautious in spelling out what the play suggests. This means that the things which 'aspect' enhances without being explicitly perceived are themselves further than usual from explicit perception by the spectator. But some points are clearly of importance, and may be swiftly noted.

Underlying the whole play is the notion of perfective solutions to imperfective situations. The identity of these situations shifts or glides as the play progresses. Some at least of these situations are not, as especially in *El. Phil. OC*, situations which stretch far back into the past and have created the consciousness of the central figures; rather, they are urgent crises in the present. The first imperfective situation to be solved is the plague, which the early part of the play presents with immense descriptive power. A multiplicity of misfortunes, stressed with abundant anaphora and other devices, are presented as all occurring at this time together (ὁμοῦ . . . ὁμοῦ, 4–5; 25–6; ἄλλον . . .ἄλλαι, 174, ἄλλοθεν ἄλλαι, 184; ἀνάριθμα, 168, corresponding to ἀνάριθμος, 179). Present verbs given an urgent sense of a continuous situation now. In both the Priest's speech and the parodos, the two main descriptions of the plague, the account of the present is rhetorical: it is part of a

demand for perfective help. The Priest helps Oedipus for aid (ἀλκήν
τιν' εὑρεῖν ἡμῖν, 42); the chorus, with especially forceful oppositions
of imperfective and perfective, beg the gods (εὐῶπα πέμψον ἀλκάν,
188, cf. 190–3 etc.). The Priest looks back to the perfective
deliverance which Oedipus provided from the imperfective crisis
produced by the Sphinx: ἐξέλυcαc . . . δαcμὸν ὃν παρείχομεν (35–6).
The stems λυ- and ῥυ- will be important for the play. Oedipus uses
ἐρυcαίμην (72) of the rescue he wants Apollo to show him how to
achieve; he later uses ἔκλυcιν . . . νόcηματος (306–7) of the rescue
that would be brought by punishing Laius' slayer. He uses ῥῦcαι in
threefold anaphora (312–13) to Teiresias as he begs him to rescue
the city from the plague which it is in (νόcωι cύνεcτιν, 303). That
appeal is to be conjoined with the appeals from the Priest and
chorus, though it forgoes description (302–3); like the Priest's
appeal to Oedipus, it has some affinities with prayer. In the ensuing
argument, Oedipus looks back to the situation of the Sphinx, and
how Teiresias, unlike Oedipus, failed to provide τι . . . ἐκλυτήριον
(392; contr. 397, ἔπαυcά νιν). The plague, then, is the first situation
of crisis that needs to be ended.

The quarrel with Teiresias leads the play into a different sort of
crisis, with Oedipus' construction of a conspiracy. The conspiracy is
not a crisis which is actually as grave as the plague; but that is part of
the point. Jocasta rebukes Oedipus and Creon for stirring up private
misfortunes at a time of public disaster (635–6); the chorus do not
want these woes for the land to be added to the plague (665–8). The
two sets of problems are clearly being put together; it is notable that
the penalties of exile and death (e.g. 622–3), and indeed Oedipus'
own exile (658–9, 669–70, cf. 690–6) are involved with both. The
point is partly to mark through the very disproportion between
these problems an alteration in Oedipus, as he moves from public-
spirited father of his people to, for the moment, self-concerned
tyrant; we also see the play narrowing its focus, moving inward. For
this factitious crisis, not rescue but resolution is required; on the
stage we have Jocasta and the chorus pressing for the present
situation to be sorted out: τὸ νῦν παρεcτὸc νεῖκοc εὖ θέcθαι (633;
cf. παύcαcθε 631). This animated and elaborate piece of drama, with
three actors and lyric dialogue, intensifies the idea of an imperfective
situation set against the moment of its ceasing. This cessation is
grudgingly conceded by Oedipus.

The ensuing conversation brings in a different kind of imperfectivity requiring an end: Oedipus' fear. This is another movement inward: the play had proceeded from national crisis to a personal conflict with political significance and now proceeds to the inner state of mind of two people. The entry of fear into the play is graphically marked at 726–7: οἷόν μ' ἀκούσαντ' ἀρτίως ἔχει, γύναι, | ψυχῆς πλάνημα κἀνακίνησις φρενῶν. (Contrast 67, where it is for the city that Oedipus has been πολλὰς . . . ὁδοὺς ἐλθόντα φροντίδος πλάνοις.) The description vividly conveys the imperfectivity of emotion.

The fear takes different forms and has different objects as the play twists and turns. Sometimes it appears as an emotion which has only just begun, a thing of the present; sometimes it is a continuation of emotion long experienced. For we soon learn of Oedipus' fears about his 'parents' in the past, again expressively described: ἔκνιζέ μ' ἀεὶ τοῦθ'· ὑφεῖρπε γὰρ πολύ (786). At the start of the next scene Jocasta prays to Apollo to provide rescue from Oedipus' present wild state of distress and fear, ὅπως λύσιν τιν' ἡμὶν εὐαγῆ πόρῃς (921). The form of an entreaty, prominently placed, joins this passage with the earlier appeals and prayers; the identity of the god is particular important. The Priest, at the end of the prologue, had wanted Apollo to come as saviour and finish the plague (149–50); we now see the connecting will of the grim divinity behind both situations, and at the same time perceive the movement in the concerns of the play. Jocasta's final remark that all are afraid because all look to Oedipus their helmsman (921–2) again draws in the city and again shows how the focuses of the play are changing. The generality of Jocasta's own fear is highly ironic for her.

Soon a messenger brings exultant release from long-standing fear. Oedipus has long (πάλαι, 947) feared that he might kill his supposed father Polybus; Polybus is now dead. In a striking and pathetically intimate moment, the married couple look back together in satisfied surprise on the recent situation of unresolved worry (note the imperfects): Ἰο. οὔκουν ἐγώ σοι ταῦτα προὔλεγον πάλαι; | Οι. ηὔδας· ἐγὼ δὲ τῶι φόβωι παρηγόμην (973–4). A fresh long-standing worry promptly occurs to Oedipus, the marrying of his mother; this promptness in the substitution of one anxiety with another could be seen as psychologically acute. The messenger believes he can free Oedipus from his fears: ἐξελυσάμην is the verb he uses (1003). A rich vocabulary of synonyms for fearing (1000, 1011, 1014), and vigorous repetition (1013), express the fear

Oedipus has always had: τοῦτ᾽ αὐτό, πρέcβυ, τοῦτό μ᾽ εἰcαεὶ φοβεῖ. The messenger is no saviour now, whatever he may have been when Oedipus was a baby (1030 cοῦ δ᾽ ὦ τέκνον cωτήρ γε τῶι τότ᾽ ἐν χρόνωι, cf. 1179–80). But Oedipus is excited, Jocasta appalled. Soon Oedipus will be in a state of disaster beyond rescue; he, rather than the city, will have to endure a terrible νόcημα (1293).[24]

A further area where 'aspect' is important is in the nature of Oedipus' unwitting sins. In general, this play concentrates its scrutiny of the past on specific perfective moments; it is these moments which Oedipus seeks to reconstruct and make sense of. This gives the play a very different atmosphere from say the *Philoctetes*, where, for all the stress on the single action of the Atridae and Odysseus, the imperfective past is the most important. However, it is worth reflecting further on Oedipus' two unwitting crimes. One thinks of them as neatly symmetrical: he kills his father and marries his mother. But are the actions really both perfective? Is it really the terrible thing that he married his mother, or that he is married to her, or that they have produced children? One could say that the incest itself is the terrible thing; but how is that to be regarded in time? The presentation varies: 366–7, cὺν τοῖc φιλτάτοιc | αἴcχιcθ᾽ ὁμιλοῦντ᾽; 459, γυναικὸc υἱὸc καὶ πόcιc; 791–2, ὡc μητρὶ μὲν χρείη με μειχθῆναι, γένοc δ᾽ | ἄτλητον ἀνθρώποιcι δηλώcοιμ᾽ ὁρᾶν; 1184–5, ξὺν οἷc τ᾽ | οὐ χρῆν ὁμιλῶν, οὕc τέ μ᾽ οὐκ ἔδει κτανών (note the different tenses; cf. further e.g. *OC* 945–6); 1358–9, οὐδὲ (sc. ἂν) νυμφίοc | βροτοῖc ἐκλήθην ὧν ἔφυν ἄπο; 1496–9, τὸν πατέρα πατὴρ | ὑμῶν ἔπεφνε· τὴν τεκοῦcαν ἤροcεν, | ὅθεν περ αὐτὸc ἐcπάρη, κἀκ τῶν ἴcων | ἐκτήcαθ᾽ ὑμᾶc, ὧνπερ αὐτὸc ἐξέφυ. The imperfective and present side gives a terrible irony to the portrayal of the royal marriage, dignified yet ordinary in its sorting out of problems and worries; the mixture of 'aspects' and times gives a terrible strangeness to Oedipus' meeting with the beloved daughters whom he knows to embody his crime.[25]

---

[24] cωτήρ is used at 48 of Oedipus in relation to the Sphinx, at 150 of Apollo, at 304 of Teiresias, both in relation to the plague. Cf. also Segal (1981: 152–4).

[25] The history of the tradition probably lends further significance to the begetting of children as a distinct element in the disaster. It is likely to have been absent from some versions: Pausanias' view of Hom. *Od.* 11. 274 is probably correct, or, if not, natural for earlier readers (Paus. 9. 5. 10–11, cf. e.g. Führer (1978: 1696. 61–4)); he also mentions the *Oedipodeia* (fr. 2 Davies). Accordingly, there had been meaningful addition, omission, or retention at some point before Sophocles, which is of interest for ancient feeling; and the earlier variation gives the feature further weight in

The killing of Oedipus' father is seen as a perfective act; φονεὺς εἶναι, as one sees from Antiphon, is a way of identifying a person now as the one who killed then. The play does not engage in the *Tetralogies'* ingenious explorations of what is meant by the 'murderer' (see e.g. Γ. δ. 2–8); but it is part of the unease which the play inspires that the killing of Laius was an island in the past, not preceded by evil intention, not followed by guilt. The chorus' notions of anxious guilt and luxuriating wickedness are significantly far from the mark. And yet the moment determines what Oedipus is. The climactic speech where he proclaims himself the child of Fortune is an appalling mixture of error and truth (1080–5); it displays the shadowed question which the play never overtly discusses, of the severance, and the unbreakable connection, between what Oedipus is and what he did.

The shape, and the sombreness, of the play can be more fully perceived by pondering on 'aspect'. We may emerge from the compelling obscurity of that work to touch on one more. There is not space to consider the *Ajax*; but there would be much to say here too, not least about the differing perspectives of different individuals on what occurs. We turn, however, to the *Antigone*, which offers a striking example of how 'aspect' affects the action and themes of a play.

The most important area is death. The significance of 'aspect' in the treatment of death has already emerged in our discussion of other plays. One may add the great scene where Ajax contemplates in advance the perfective moment of suicide and its consequences, dwelling drastically on the idea of a speedy decease (*Aj.* 815–16, 833–4), and bidding himself make haste (853).[26] However, in some ways death receives fuller and more central attention in the *Antigone* than in most of Sophocles' surviving plays; the exploitation of 'aspect' in this regard is correspondingly involved.

Some general points may be mentioned to begin with. Beyond the

Sophocles himself. For discussion of the tradition cf. March (1987: ch. 5); Mastronarde (1994: 20–2).

[26] Exekias' image seems similarly to contemplate the perfective moment from an imperfective time before it (belly amphora, Boulogne 558, *ABV* 145, 18). The chronological relation of the *Ajax* to the depiction perhaps by the Alkimachos Painter is more uncertain (lekythos, Basle (loan); Schefold, (1976)); for one view see March (1991–3: 32–3). How much of the speech 815–65 is interpolated is a difficult question; note Lloyd-Jones and Wilson (1997: 24–5).

perfective moment of death lie various extended periods of time. Polynices' dead body itself lingers hideously on, decaying and smelling (410, 412, cf. 1197–8). Dying is seen by Antigone as the start of unending coexistence with one's dead family: so she remarks, with dry understatement, πλείων χρόνος | ὃν δεῖ μ' ἀρέσκειν τοῖς κάτω τῶν ἐνθάδε (74–5). The world of the dead is seen by Antigone and others as having its gods, whose laws share in the eternity of the divine, unlike the momentary proclamations of Creon and the laws of men (451, 518–21, 749, al.). These imperfective elements are important to the thought and the feelings about death in the play. But the death of Antigone within the play introduces more elaborate complexities.

There is a general contrast in the play between the final scene with Antigone and the final scene with Creon. The peculiar atmosphere of the scene with Antigone is part of this contrast, which furnishes the moral structure of the play. Antigone has so far thought of dying as a simple moment, on which she has heroically decided (72, 95–7, 555; cf. 497, 546); it is premature, but it will close only an existence of woe (460–4). Indeed, at 559–60, advancing on 555 and closing her dialogue with Ismene, she elides the event altogether: cὺ μὲν ζῇc, ἡ δ' ἐμὴ ψυχὴ πάλαι | τέθνηκεν. Creon knowingly predicts a change of attitude when death is seen from closer to (580–1).[27]

Creon's own talk of death has been similarly perfective. He has not indicated much about how the breaker of his edict will die. Even when he knows it is his son's betrothed, he speaks imperviously of Hades 'stopping' that marriage (Ἅιδης ὁ παύcων τούcδε τοὺς γάμους ἐμοί, 575). In his rage with Haemon, he cruelly purposes to have Antigone slain immediately, αὐτίκα, in front of Haemon's eyes (760–1). But when this plan is thwarted, he arranges, still more cruelly but cunningly, to have Antigone immured in an underground cave, with a modicum of food; she will, he imagines, eventually die without direct action by the state (773–80).

This form of death, which resembles the apparently non-fatal punishment to be inflicted on Electra (El. 380–2, note 392), suggests the reverse of a decisive moment. The treatment in the play makes it something paradoxical and liminal. In the elegant formulation presented by Teiresias, Creon has blurred the categories of upper and lower, living and dead. Polynices is a dead person kept on earth,

---

[27] Cf. Phil. 518–21.

Antigone is a living person put in the underworld, in a 'tomb'
(1066–71); she is still alive (note 1100–1). Antigone presents
herself, with emphatic paradox and asyndeton, as belonging to οὐ
ζῶcιν, οὐ θανοῦcιν (852). The Chorus also emphasize the paradox:
she is the only person (μονὴ δή, 821) to go living into Hades (819–
21, cf. 811, etc.). Creon stresses nastily that the choice of life or
death there is her own; even he uses the paradoxical metaphor of the
tomb (885–90). The Chorus's mythological elaborations on caves
and imprisonment enhance rather than reduce the strangeness of
Antigone's fate; but the most haunting comparison is Antigone's
own with Niobe. Like her she will be enveloped by rock; but the
extension of the comparison, and the chorus's comments, suggest
Niobe's continued consciousness and grief (823–37, cf. El. 150–2).
However we interpret the comparison, a peculiar atmosphere is
made to surround Antigone's undecided, ambiguous death in life.[28]

This way of death is, then, the opposite of perfective. The actual
scene in which Antigone proceeds to the cavern is expressively
drawn out (whatever the original length of Antigone's speech 891–
928). Creon, as usual in a hurry, brings out its protraction by his
demands for speed (883–90, 931–2). The range of reference and the
changes in form and metre make the scene seem particularly ample.
It seems so all the more because the official business of the scene is a
single movement across stage, as Antigone is conducted by guards
on her final journey (807–8, 877–8, 885, 939 ἄγομαι δὴ 'γὼ κοὐκέτι
μέλλω). The slowness of the scene has particular force, since it
marks the change in Antigone's attitude. Now that death is actually
upon her, she confronts it not with cowardice, as Creon had
surmised (580–1), but with deep grief and a bitter sense of injustice.
She is now facing and contemplating the event; she is lamenting at
length before it occurs (cf. 883). The stage movement itself becomes
an embodiment of her fate. It presents a reversal or perversion of
the wedding-procession she has been denied (810–17, 891–4; 876–
8, 916–18).[29] It also suggests and perverts a funeral procession:
Antigone is still alive, and no member of her extinguished family
mourns for her (847–9, 877, 881–2; 919–20). The lingeringly

---

[28] For the significance of rock here cf. Brown (1987: 192), and also Wecklein
(1910: 69). Later authors (developing Hom. Il. 24. 617) treat the combination of
consciousness and rock more paradoxically, e.g. Call. H. 2. 22, Prop. 3.10. 8, Sen. HF
391; so too, I think, in the fragment discovered by Hollis (1997), cf. CIRB 129. 8.

[29] Cf. esp. Rehm (1994: 62–3).

imperfective scene drives home the pathos, cruelty, and strangeness of the death, and Antigone's movingly altered perceptions.

The deaths of Haemon and Eurydice are the terrible punishment which answers and contrasts with the unjust punishment of Antigone; the final part of the play (1155–1353) answers and contrasts with this scene. There is nothing lingering here. Both the narrative of the messenger and the subsequent movements on stage present a tumult of action. Creon has hurried to the vault (1102–10). Antigone has already hanged herself, a swift and as it were normal close after all that had preceded. Haemon's death takes place in a confused rush of violence. He dies abruptly with the sword, an end the chorus had even contrasted with Antigone's abnormal fate (820). His death too is seen as a perversion of marriage (1236–41, cf. 1205); but here we are shown, not Antigone's slow procession, but an instantaneous perversion of the act of physical union.[30]

The death of Eurydice gives a ghastly speed and tumult to the final scene it would not otherwise have had. The perfectivity of Haemon's and Eurydice's deaths becomes the more pointed and dreadful because Creon sees himself as the agent who has performed these killings (1319, 1340–1). Eurydice herself intensifies this notion from outside: she curses Creon τῶι παιδοκτόνωι (1305). But Creon, although he says that Hades is destroying him (1284–5) through these deaths, and although he says he is no more than nothing (1325), does not himself obtain the perfective release of death. He wishes he had been struck a fatal blow with a sword (ἀνταίαν, 1308–9); he wishes the day of death would come now (1328–32). He remains alive, with the bodies of his son and his wife, and his consciousness of what he has done.

'Aspect' has now been explored in most of Sophocles' extant plays. We have looked at it on various scales: in the overall shaping of works, in the drama of particular scenes, in the detail of individual speeches and lines. We have seen the power with which Sophocles evokes long periods of misery, the subtlety with which apparently perfective events are made more complicated, and are perceived from different angles by different people. We have observed the elaborate relations within plays between a number of imperfective situations and perfective happenings, and how these relations give the play shape and force. We have noticed all kinds of

[30] Cf. Seaford (1987: 120–1; 1994: 381).

connections and contrasts between plays; we have perhaps intensified our awareness of the individuality of each and its distinctive
world. The framework for the analysis is highly abstract; but it helps
one (in my own case at least) to articulate things one had felt more
obscurely and to notice things one had missed. That suggests the
conception may be of critical use; and may even seem enough to
justify this general style of approach.

REFERENCES

BAKKER, E. J. (1997), 'Verbal Aspect and Mimetic Description in Thucydides', in E. J. Bakker (ed.), *Grammar as Interpretation: Greek Literature in
its Linguistic Contexts*, Mnemosyne Suppl. 171 (Leiden), 1–54.

BROWN, A. L. (1987), *Sophocles: Antigone, Edited with Translation and
Notes* (Warminster).

DUMANOIR, J.-R. (1996), 'Les semailles et la peine: Héraklès et les femmes
dans les *Trachiniennes*', in A. Moreau (ed.), *Panorama du théâtre antique*
(Montpellier), 53–68.

DUNN, F. M. (1992), 'Beginning at Colonus', *YCS* 29: 1–12.

EDMUNDS, L. (1996), *Theatrical Space and Historical Space in Sophocles'
Oedipus at Colonus* (Lanham).

FANNING, B. M. (1990), *Verbal Aspect in New Testament Greek* (Oxford).

FÜHRER, R. (1978), 'ἄφαρ', in B. Snell *et al.* (eds.), *Lexikon des frühgrie-
chischen Epos* (Göttingen), i. 1695–7.

GALTON, H. (1976), *The Main Functions of the Slavic Verbal Aspect*
(Skopje).

GIORGI, A., and PIANESI, F. (1998), *Tense and Aspect: From Semantics to
Morphosyntax* (Oxford).

HAMON, PH. (1981), *Introduction à l'analyse du descriptif* (Paris).

HARDER, M. A. (1995), ' "Right" and "Wrong" in the *Electra*'s', *Hermathena* 159: 15–31.

HEIDEN, B. A. (1989), *Tragic Rhetoric: An Interpretation of Sophocles'
Trachiniae* (New York).

HOLLIS, A. S. (1997), 'A New Fragment on Niobe and the Text of
Propertius 2. 20. 8', *CQ* 47: 578–82.

KEARNS, E. (1989), *The Heroes of Attica*, BICS Supp. 57 (London).

LLOYD-JONES, H., and WILSON, N. G. (1990), *Sophoclea: Studies on the Text
of Sophocles* (Oxford).

——— (1997), *Sophocles: Second Thoughts*, Hypomnemata H. 100
(Göttingen).

MARCH, J. R. (1987), *The Creative Poet*, BICS Supp. 49 (London).

MARCH, J. R. (1991–3), 'Sophocles' *Ajax:* The Death and Burial of a Hero', *BICS* 38: 1–36.

—— (1996), 'The Chorus in Sophocles' *Electra*', in F. M. Dunn (ed.), *Sophocles' Electra in Performance*, Drama Bd. 4 (Stuttgart), 65–81.

MASTRONARDE, D. J. (1994), *Euripides:* Phoenissae, *Edited with an Introduction and Commentary* (Cambridge).

MELLET, S. (1988), *L'Imparfait de l'indicatif en latin classique. Temps, aspect, modalité* (Paris).

PAULSEN, T. (1989), *Die Rolle des Chors in den späten Sophokles-Tragödien* (Bari).

REHM, R. (1994), *Marriage to Death: The Conflation of Wedding and Funeral Rituals in Greek Tragedy* (Princeton).

REID, J. H. (1993), *Narration and Description in the French Realist Novel* (Cambridge).

SCHEFOLD, K. (1976), 'Sophokles' Aias auf einer Lekythos', *AK* 19: 71–8.

SEAFORD, R. (1987), 'The Tragic Wedding', *JHS* 107: 106–30.

—— (1994), *Reciprocity and Ritual* (Oxford).

SEGAL, C. (1981), *Tragedy and Civilization: An Interpretation of Sophocles* (Cambridge, Mass., and London).

—— (1995), *Sophocles' Tragic World: Divinity, Nature, Society* (Cambridge, Mass.).

TOBIN, Y. (1993), *Aspect in the English Verb: Process and Result in Language* (London and New York).

WECKLEIN, N. (1910), *Sophokles, Antigone*, 7th edn. (Munich).

WINNINGTON-INGRAM, R. P. (1980), *Sophocles: An Interpretation* (Cambridge).

ZIELINSKI, TH. (1896), 'Exkurse zu den Trachinierinnen', *Philologus* 9: 491–540, 577–633.

5

Sophocles and the Democratic City

JASPER GRIFFIN

At school in the early 1950s, the first Attic tragedy we read was Euripides' *Iphigenia in Tauris*: in retrospect, perhaps an eccentric choice. To help us we had a small school edition with notes in the back. The notes, broadly speaking, were concerned with questions of two kinds only. One was the reason why the verb in a given verse was in the infinitive, or the noun in the dative. That is, the note gave, in an oracular manner, a name to the case or the mood: an 'ethic' dative, a 'historic' infinitive. The other kind of note, the kind which we really disliked, gave curt and (again) oracular answers to inscrutable disputes between German scholars about the reading of the text. Discussion in class dealt with grammatical questions, not literary criticism; as for discussing the function of tragedy in the democratic city of Athens, such a thing never crossed the mind of any of us, teacher or pupil. The play was simply *there*. We set about it very much for the same reason, and in the same frame of mind, as climbers tackling Mount Everest: roped together by our shared sessions of translation in class, and with our survival kit in the form of our edition with notes in the back.

At Oxford in the late 1950s we advanced from the nineteenth to the early twentieth century. Now we met with books which did venture a fairly straightforward and unselfconscious literary criticism. Literary it was; so much so that in 1954 Victor Ehrenberg, publishing his *Sophocles and Pericles*, opened defensively by saying that it was 'a prevalent trend of our time' that 'the basis for any discussion of poetry seems to be the idea that a poet ought to be judged by poetical standards only', as against the 'chiefly trans-atlantic tendency of "sociology"':

I too live under the shadow of that towering bastion from which the literary critics dominate the intellectual and artistic countryside;

and yet after all, he daringly pleaded, it must be possible to discuss tragedy and the history of Athens.[1]

All that was in the 1950s; it seems now as remote as the 1850s. As late as 1986 a scholar could still write

The present study may also serve as a corrective to the tendency, discernible in the most recent work on Greek drama, to ignore its political aspects entirely.[2]

Since then, what a change there has been! Clio, Muse of history, has moved massively into the territory of her tragic sister Melpomene. It is now not surprising to read that

The tragedies and comedies composed for production at the Athenian dramatic festivals in the fifth and early fourth centuries BC are priceless historical documents,[3]

and that

Greek tragedies are perceived as important manifestations of political thought,[4]

and indeed that

Die attische Tragödie war eine Institution der attischen Demokratie. Das heisst: sie war eine politische Institution.[5]

So completely has the fashion changed that the question seems now to be, not whether tragedy is political, but exactly how its obviously political purpose is to be defined. Thus in the new *Cambridge Companion to Greek Tragedy* it seems almost natural that the first

[1] Ehrenberg (1954: 2). He goes so far as to say, in the spirit of that time, that to literary critics 'it will seem a kind of sacrilege to regard one of the great tragedies of the Attic theatre as anything but a masterpiece of literary genius and theatrical art . . . the essential nature of which is outside all merely historical values' (8).

[2] Podlecki (1986: 76). That was perhaps already not quite an up-to-date statement of the situation.

[3] Alan H. Sommerstein in Pelling (1997: 63).

[4] Raaflaub (1989: 49). Cf. also J. Peter Euben in Euben (1986: 29): 'Tragedy was as close as one could come to a theoretical institution. In its form, content, and context of performance, tragedy provided, by example and by precept, a critical consideration of public life.'

[5] Wolfgang Rösler in Sommerstein et al. (1993: 81).

chapter should be on 'Theatre as Process in Greek Civic Life', and that it should pronounce immediately that

The play-festivals of Dionysus . . . served further as a device for defining Athenian civic identity, which meant exploring and confirming but also questioning what it was to be a citizen of a democracy.[6]

Elsewhere we find such generalizations as these:

Tragedy might thus mirror aspects of current political thinking; in doing so it fulfilled its intended educative function by creating an awareness of the achievements of the *polis* or the problems it faced, or by reflecting the nature of politics, while presenting them in a largely nonpartisan manner.[7]

Very often we find it confidently asserted that

Tragedy . . . must be viewed as reflecting the aims and methods of the democracy. First, tragedy was funded either directly by the *polis*, which paid the honorarium to competing poets, or through the system called the liturgy . . .[8]

and, again, that

Greek tragedy is the dramatization of aetiological myth . . . shaped by the vital need to create and sustain the *polis*.[9]

Since the city paid the bills, it is obvious in this post-Thatcher world that the city must have called the tune; and a highly political tune it turns out to be. I quote as representative an influential recent book of essays on tragedy:

The patron (let us call it more generally the polis, understood as a social institution) operates towards the public with an end in view that might be roughly formulated as 'consolidating the social identity, maintaining the cohesion of the community'.[10]

It has in fact become a problem in its own right, with a growing learned literature, to wonder why Attic tragedy, although it was so political and, more specifically, so democratic, none the less continued to set its plays in the world of the old regal and

---

[6] Easterling (1997a). The first chapter is by Paul Cartledge: significantly, a historian. The passage quoted comes on p. 6.

[7] Meier (1990: 88).

[8] Croally (1994: 3).

[9] Richard Seaford in Silk (1996: 293).

[10] O. Longo in Winkler and Zeitlin (1990: 14).

aristocratic heroes of the myths.[11] That fact is perhaps not really so surprising. The ubiquitous presence of the myths and their high-born people in the tragic theatre of democratic Athens does not seem to have presented contemporaries with anything like the problem that it poses for modern scholars. That might make us pause and wonder whether they really did expect their tragic poets to be so constantly concerned with democratic ideology and democratic propaganda.

In the words of Denis Feeney, 'The current dominant model is J.-P. Vernant's "democratic moment", the intimate bond between the novel artistic and political institutions of democratic Athens'.[12] He goes on to predict, 'One feels that the consensus is about to crack.' A recent article mounts a general criticism of this approach, which shows signs of having hardened from a consensus almost into an orthodoxy,[13] and suggests a different kind of connection between tragedy and the events of fifth-century history. In this chapter I hope to question one part of it, and to give some pleasure to a scholar who has contributed so much to our understanding of Sophocles, both in the fine details of his text and in the broader patterns of his thought, by turning particularly to that poet in connection with this vexed question of politics and tragedy.

One might take as a marker for comparison a tragedy of Shakespeare, for instance *Romeo and Juliet*. That play does indeed have a message that can be called political: the feuds of foolish old men, and the privileged violence of their reckless young kinsmen, are a disaster for the whole community. At the end the Prince enunciates it:

> Capulet! Montague!
> See what a scourge is laid upon your hate,
> That heaven finds means to kill your joys with love;
> And I, for winking at your discords too,
> Have lost a brace of kinsmen. All are punished. (v. iii. 291 ff.)

So there it is: the lesson of *Romeo and Juliet*. But! we want to protest; but, of course, we know that already! We do not go to the theatre to be taught that sort of elementary political truth. And, of course, the

---

[11] I single out the subtle papers by Mark Griffith (1995) and P. E. Easterling in Pelling (1997: 21–38).

[12] Feeney (1998).

[13] Griffin (1998).

interest of the play lies not there but in the suffering and the poetry of the star-crossed lovers. To insist on a political interpretation can mean missing the real point of tragedy.

The only one of the three great Attic tragedians who actually held high elective office at Athens, serving both as *Hellenotamias* and as *strategos*, the only one not to leave democratic Attica and work for foreign dynasts, the only one not to die abroad, Sophocles is also the one who has not bequeathed to us anything which makes explicit propaganda for democracy in the manner of Aeschylus' *Eumenides* or of Euripides' *Supplices*. That cannot be from lack of patriotism. No reader of *Oedipus at Colonus* can miss the feeling of the poet both for his birth-place of Colonus and for the city of Athens. No more splendid praise of a place was ever composed than its First Stasimon:

> εὐίππου, ξένε, τᾶσδε χώ-
> ρας ἵκου τὰ κράτιστα γᾶς ἔπαυλα . . .   (*OC* 668 ff.)

But even in this play it is hard to evade the conclusion that what is central is not the politics of Athens, except in an ethical and very general sense (Athens is hospitable, generous, civilized, rich in cults, favoured by the gods[14]), but the sufferings and destiny of the aged hero and his children. Perhaps there is not one of the extant plays of this most elusive poet which does not need a good deal of careful re-description, sometimes tendentious, before it can plausibly be claimed as propaganda for democracy.

Let us begin with a play for which we are fortunate enough to possess the perfect comparative material: *Electra*.[15] The *Oresteia* of Aeschylus contains, especially in its last play, highly political elements. In the next generation both Sophocles and Euripides decided to dramatize the theme of Orestes' vengeance. When Aeschylus dealt with that story, he had in mind the numerous passages in the *Odyssey* on Agamemnon's death at the hands of Aegisthus, and on Aegisthus' death at the hands of Orestes. He seized on the aspects of the story which Homer had minimized or

[14] Cf. recently M. Whitlock Blundell, 'The Ideal of Athens in *Oedipus at Colonus*', in Sommerstein *et al.* (1993: 287–306). Richard Rutherford points out to me that the Theseus of this play is much less democratic than the Argive king in Aeschylus' *Supplices* or the Athenian king in Euripides' *Supplices* (349–51), both of whom make a point of getting the agreement of their citizens before acting. We are further from 5th-cent. Athens in the *Coloneus*.

[15] See the illuminating discussion by Bernard Knox (1983), esp. 8–10.

omitted altogether: the role of Clytemnestra in the murder of
Agamemnon; and Orestes' act of matricide, justified but still
appalling. He also decided to give a role to one of Agamemnon's
daughters, who are ignored in the *Odyssey*; and Electra is shown
mourning her father, recognizing her brother, and joining in the
great lyric *kommos* at the tomb. She then disappears. She has no role
in the killings. Aeschylus enriched this story with a striking
compound of Athenian history, recent and remote, secular and
sacred.

His successors, in their turn looking for aspects of the story which
had not been used up by a great predecessor, both turned to Electra.
Aeschylus had not exhausted her possibilities. Euripides made his
Electra play more 'political' than that of Sophocles; but he can only
do that, it seems, by making it political in a very different sense from
that of the *Oresteia*. Effects cannot simply be repeated. Euripides'
Electra is obsessed with questions of social status. Banished to the
outback from the city and the royal palace, neutralized by a marriage
which makes her *déclassée*, she broods resentfully on her social
grievances.

Sophocles saw the opportunity for something else. This is not the
place to discuss the question whether he wrote before or after
Euripides; it cannot be definitely answered, and Lloyd-Jones himself
long ago declared 'Those who confidently claim to know the date of
Sophocles' *Electra . . .* are living in a private world.'[16] What strikes us
about Sophocles' play is its unpolitical character. The real subject of
the play is the emotions of the heroine,[17] who is further illuminated
by the creation of a sister with a contrasting character. Electra's
reactions and sufferings are lovingly displayed to us over more than
a thousand lines, from her entry at line 77 all the way to her reunion
with her brother—artfully delayed until 1221 ff., although he had
already recognized her at line 80—and in her role in the two killings;
not forgetting her terrible cry to Orestes, after he has struck his
mother, παῖσον, εἰ σθένεις, διπλῆν (1432): brilliantly explained by
Lloyd-Jones and Wilson, not as 'Hit her a second time!', but as 'Hit
her twice as hard!'.[18]

Electra mourns Agamemnon not as a political figure, a rightful
king assassinated and replaced by an usurper, but as her father,

---

[16] *Ant. Class.* 33 (1964), 372.
[17] Schadewaldt (1928: 57).
[18] Lloyd-Jones and Wilson (1990: 74).

pitifully dead;[19] she laments him like Niobe, like the nightingale, the great exemplars in myth of unending grief for death within the family.[20] When she thinks of Aegisthus, it is not as the usurper of power but as her father's murderer, wearing her father's robes as he sits on his throne, and pouring libations on the spot where he slew him (264 ff.). When she asks her sister for help against Aegisthus, she begs her 'to do this for yourself, for me, and for the dearest of all men, the dead father of us both':

> ὅμως δ', ἀδελφή, σοί θ' ὑπούργησον τάδε
> ἐμοί τ' ἀρωγὰ τῷ τε φιλτάτῳ βροτῶν
> πάντων, ἐν Ἅιδου κειμένῳ κοινῷ πατρί   (461–3).

Orestes, too, seems to think of Aegisthus' offence more as 'the squandering of my father's property' than as usurpation of the kingship:

'Don't tell me how Aegisthus is squandering the wealth of the house, pouring it out and scattering it abroad':

> ὡς πατρῴαν κτῆσιν Αἴγισθος δόμων
> ἀντλεῖ, τὰ δ' ἐκχεῖ, τὰ δὲ διασπείρει μάτην   (1290–2).

As Orestes enters the palace the chorus sing, 'Crafty footed, the avenger of the dead is brought into the house, the seat of his father's wealth of old':

> παράγεται γὰρ ἐνέρων
> δολιόπους ἀρωγὸς εἴσω στέγας,
> ἀρχαιόπλουτα πατρὸς εἰς ἐδώλια,   (1391–3)

Again: vengeance for the dead, and the property of his father. The political consequences of Aegisthus' crime for the community are not what interests us. Orestes does not say, as he did in the *Choephoroe*, that one of his motives is to free Argos from the usurpers:

'My citizens, glorious men, the sackers of Troy, subjected to two

---

[19] 95 ff., 115, 132, 145 ff., 241 f., 341, 399, 525, 530, 587 f., 811, 954 ff., etc. When she thinks of killing the adulterous pair herself, she imagines people saying 'These are the sisters who have saved their father's house, who have slain their enemies when they seemed so firmly footed, at the risk of their own lives: they should be loved and honoured by all for their courage', 977–83. There is no mention of delivering the community from usurpation or tyranny, only a personal act of heroism for family motives.

[20] 145 ff., 150 f.

women'; nor does he proclaim the death of Aegisthus and Clytemnestra with the words 'Behold the two tyrants of our country' (ὁρᾶτε χώρας τὴν διπλῆν τυραννίδα[21]). What we do see is the princess Electra forced by her grief and her desire for vengeance for her father into behaviour which she knows to be unseemly,[22] but which cannot be abandoned; lamenting and keening, trembling between hope that her brother will come back and despair of his return.[23] We see her in lively and contrasted conversations with her sister and with her mother; we see her hopes revive when she hears of offerings at her father's tomb; we watch her receive the shattering news of her brother's death, in the presence of her hateful mother; we hear her form the desperate plan of avenging her father herself, alone; and we look on, through tear-filled eyes, as she laments over the urn that she believes to hold the ashes of her brother, and the ashes, too, of her hopes. By contrast with the intensity of all this, Orestes and his deadly plot are of secondary interest. The line just quoted, Electra's chilling cry to her brother, is the most vivid and memorable point in the matricide: even at that supreme moment of his story, Orestes is up-staged by his sister. As for the present or future state of the *polis* of Argos, our attention is never directed to them.

What are we to make of this? The poet has taken a myth which had been shown to be capable of intensely political treatment, and he has chosen to handle it in a completely different way. His Electra is a cousin of the deserted Ariadne of Catullus' Sixty-Fourth poem, and of Virgil's forsaken Dido, and akin to the *Heroides* of Ovid, and to the musical *scene* composed in such numbers for sopranos in the eighteenth century. All are works which allow some passionate woman to run for us through the gamut of her emotions: tenderness, anger, vengeance, pride, self-abnegation, nostalgia, hope, despair. Euripides did something not entirely different, though with a different atmosphere, in his depiction of Medea. She, too, goes through her repertoire of female emotions before our fascinated gaze.[24] In other times and other arts, we can think of Madama Butterfly, or Violetta; or of Madame Bovary, or Moll Flanders, or

---

[21] *Choeph.* 302–4; 973.

[22] *Electra* 221 f., 307–9, 616–18.

[23] 164–72, 303–5.

[24] This is part of what is going on in the great monologue of the heroine, Eur. *Medea* 1019–80; it is sad that the excellent OCT mutilates the passage by drastic excision. Where the excised verses supposed to have come from—if not (in spite of Ockham's Razor) from another play exactly like Euripides' *Medea*?

Jane Eyre; or of Giselle; or of *Fatal Attraction*. Sophocles' *Electra* is
for us a very early example. She differs from virtually all her
successors in that her emotions do not include the erotic. Sophocles,
we are tempted to say, here marks a transitional point between
archaic reticence about female sexuality and the strongly erotic
colouring which will be regular hereafter.[25]

The motives of Orestes in this play, and the emotions of Electra,
have very little to do with the ideology of the democratic city. It is
not easy to see the play as endorsing the values of the democracy, or
(a common claim in many recent writers[26]) strengthening the
cohesion of the community. It is not even the case that those
values are 'subverted' or 'called into question', a line taken by some
scholars, perhaps more sophisticated, to be a distinctive function of
tragedy.[27] Rather, they seem not to exist. Nor, to turn for a moment
to another attractive line of recent scholarship, can we say that the
end of the play marks a happy future, with the self-destruction of
the old regal family and the institution in the city of democracy.[28]
Such an analysis must surely fail with a play like *Electra*, which ends
with Orestes presumably back on his father's throne, and with the
least possible reference to the future political set-up in Argos.[29]
There is not even a patriotic mention of the traditional help given to
Orestes by Athens.

The Electra of Sophocles exhibits her emotional range, and also
its depth, not only to us in the audience, but also to her brother on
stage. The speech she makes with the urn in her arms was celebrated
in antiquity. Aulus Gellius retails a story of an actor performing it
over an urn which really held the ashes of his recently dead son, and
the rhetorical writers found it a source for illustrations of *eleos*.[30] It
is, in fact, a perfect example of what most displeased Plato about

[25] In *Trachiniae* sexual love does play a part, but the poet handles the motif with
notable delicacy. The situation of sexual rivalry between mistress and slave woman is
handled with brutal frankness, by contrast, in Euripides' *Andromache*.
[26] Thus, for instance, O. Longo, in Winkler and Zeitlin (1990: 14): the aim of the
city in sponsoring tragedy 'may be roughly formulated as "consolidating the social
identity, maintaining the cohesion of the community"'.
[27] So e.g. S. Goldhill, in Winkler and Zeitlin (1990: 124 ff.), and elsewhere. Some
shrewd points in reply are made by R. Friedrich, 'Everything to Do with Dionysus?',
in Silk (1996: 262 ff.).
[28] This is the view of tragedy taken by Richard Seaford (1994). Cf. Griffin (1998).
[29] We do not hear of any exile for Orestes, either temporary or permanent;
contrast Eur. *Electra* 1249 f., *Orestes* 1643 ff.
[30] Gellius 6.1 f.; *Rhetores Graeci*, ed. Spengel, 1. 400. 25 ff., 402. 18 f.; 3. 20. 23 f.

tragedy: the working up of emotion over something unreal. For not only is the whole action not real life but a play, a *mimesis*: even within the play Orestes is not dead, and Electra mourns and weeps as the result of a mistake. In that Platonic sense, it is a doubly representative tragedy.

Sophocles, then, was so far from feeling it incumbent on him to give his *Electra* a political point, that he turned away from the hints in that direction in the work of his fellow playwrights and applied himself instead to the development of feminine emotion and heroic pathos. That suggests that he regarded a political colouring as just one among many possibilities for a play. Some plays were strongly political. We think at once of *Eumenides*, or of the argument about the merits of democracy in Euripides' *Supplices* (399 ff.); but even that will be followed by the pure pathos of Evadne's act of suttee and her father's grief (990–1113), which can have very little relevance indeed either to endorsing or to questioning the democracy.[31] Some plays were at the opposite extreme, like the *Electra* of Sophocles, or *Alcestis*, or *Trachiniae*; and they were no less acceptable than the more political tragedies, both to archon and to audience.

Of *Trachiniae* we need say little. Here, too, it is hard to believe that the attention of audience or playwright was much focused on questions of political ideology. Heracles is a solitary superman, battling with monsters, possessing more women than any other man (459 f.); he fought with a river for his bride, and he shot a centaur to defend her. He kills an enemy by guile and is enslaved to an Asiatic queen. He starts a war and destroys a city just to get hold of a princess. In death he forces his son to marry his concubine, 'So that no other man shall take her, after she has lain beside me' (1225 f.). Even in his admirable qualities, he has little resemblance to a democrat. After death he is evidently to be succeeded not by democracy but by his son Hyllus; on whom he has just imposed an unwanted wife, in a way so sadly characteristic of monarchies, then and since. What is the play about? Evidently 'the main theme is the destructive power of beauty and love';[32] to which we may add,

---

[31] Or even its policy towards displays of mourning, as suggested by Foley, in Sommerstein *et al.* (1993: 125 f.). There is a remarkable contradiction, in that volume, between the political interpretations of the main action of the play by Foley (117–29) and by E. Krummen (207 f.); but disagreements of that sort are, as we have seen, regular in the recent literature of political interpretation.

[32] Michael Ewans in Silk (1996: 441).

once again, the trembling heart and fascinating emotions of a woman, presented in the most extreme possible contrast with the utter masculinity of the hero, his male strength and male insensitivity alike exaggerated to superhuman proportions. It is noticeable that recent writers on the political nature of Attic tragedy seldom mention *Trachiniae*.[33]

So, again, the archon who gave a chorus for this play, too, seems to have failed in his job; if, that is, his job was to ensure the presentation of politically strengthening plays, which would send the audience out of the theatre with a heightened sense of citizen solidarity. Or, perhaps, he interpreted his function differently.

Space does not permit an exhaustive survey of all seven extant Sophoclean plays. Very little can be said here about the two which do most clearly raise interesting questions of a sort that can be called political: *Antigone* and *Oedipus the King*. It is not my purpose to deny that there are tragedies in which that element was important. There were even some to which it was central; though it is far from clear that in either *Antigone* or *Oedipus* the point has anything to do with democracy. Instead I shall briefly discuss a play which falls somewhere between the strongly political interests of *Antigone* and the apolitical manner of *Electra* and *Trachiniae*, namely *Ajax*. It has been the subject of much recent discussion.

One recent interpretation of the play, explicitly 'historicizing',[34] argues that its thrust is 'toward the validation of Ajax as the best political leader' (65). This is at first sight a surprising conclusion, since after all what we see is an Ajax who has gone mad in brooding over a slight, who has tried to massacre his fellow commanders, and who kills himself, disregarding the desperate pleas of his dependants. It is reached by way of the argument that the poet 'uses all the means at his disposal to present in Ajax an abstracted image on a grand scale of an Athenian *strategos*' (69). Thus the feebleness of the chorus of Athenian sailors represents the dependence of contemporary Athenians, who would identify with them, on a series of commanders who came from the upper class: Athens still needed such leaders! All this must 'reinforce and validate a hierarchical,

---

[33] Michael Vickers (1995: 41–53) gives a detailed exposition of the play as being about the Spartan colony at Heraclea in Trachis of 427/6 BC, conveying a warning to the Athenians 'of what their fate might be if the Spartans did invade and sack Euboea, and if the Spartans did win the war'.

[34] Peter W. Rose, 'Historicizing Sophocles' *Ajax*', in Goff (1995: 59–90).

patriarchal, and paternalistic image of Athenian society' (71 f.);
while as for Odysseus, who has often been thought to come out
rather well at the end of the play, he 'adroitly fawns on the Spartan
tyrant'(sic; it is in fact not Menelaus but Agamemnon with whom
Odysseus reasons, and with whom he prevails), and he 'cannot
constitute a viable political or social alternative' to the leadership of
an Ajax (74).[35] One might think such a verdict on the Ajax of this
play hard to reconcile with his fearful dying curse on the whole
Greek army, 'go on, you swift and vengeful Furies: do not spare
them, taste the whole army':

$$\text{ἴτ, ὦ ταχεῖαι ποίνιμοί τ' Ἐρινύες,}$$
$$\text{γένεσθε, μὴ φείδεσθε πανδήμου στρατοῦ.} \quad (843 f.)$$

Is that, one asks oneself in some bewilderment, really the utterance
of an irreplaceable 'best political leader'?

Another very recent writer takes a very different view.[36] For him,
Ajax 'sees only the city, the *polis*, but since there is more than the
polis in the world ... Ajax' view of the world is necessarily distorted'.
Ajax' distorted view is 'peculiarly political' (149). This emphasis on
the *polis* may seem surprising, as the word is very rare in *Ajax*, much
rarer than in any other play of Sophocles, and is uttered by the hero
only once, in reference to the cry of lamentation which his mother
will raise in *her* city, back home, when she learns of his death (line
873). But, we read, 'the city has been implicitly present (*sic*) since
the beginning of the play' (156). In fact this Ajax seems a barely
political creature, acting on his own, with no reference to anybody
else, whether commander, subordinate, ally, or wife; much less as
fellow citizen; and the argument about his burial is not obviously
about the *polis*, as the whole thing takes place abroad, under military
discipline, in an armed camp.[37]

The *polis* seems to have made its way into the discussion

---

[35] In extreme contrast, Rainer Friedrich sees Odysseus as 'the authentic representative of the *polis*' in Silk (1996: 267). One is repeatedly struck by the arbitrariness
of these political interpretations: how—on what principle—are we to choose
between such contradictory assertions? What Odysseus says recalls the last book
of the *Iliad*: even before the *polis*, gods forbade, and men hated to see, an unburied
corpse.

[36] Michael Davies, 'Politics and Madness', in Euben (1986: 142–61).

[37] Menelaus makes the only significant reference to the city when he says that
obedience and subordination are vital to an army, as they are to a city, too: οὐ γάρ
ποτ' οὔτ' ἂν ἐν πόλει νόμοι καλῶς | φέροιντ' ἄν, ἔνθα μὴ καθεστήκῃ δέος (1073 f.).

uninvited, because of an *a priori* conviction that tragedy must be political, and political in something like our sense. The grounds on which Odysseus secures Agamemnon's reluctant agreement to the hero's burial are in fact two. One is universal human nature: Odysseus recognizes that he, too, will die and need others to bury him (1365). The other is the supremacy of the divine law (1343 f.). What opposes that law is the spiteful whim of tyrannical power; but while in *Antigone* that whim dresses itself, at least for a time, in the garb of the interest of the *polis*, in this play what the Atridae plead is not civil but military discipline. The *polis* does not seem to be the point.

It is, however, again seen as central by Christian Meier,[38] who says: 'In interpreting *Ajax* it becomes obvious that one is dealing with a highly political play' (185). For Meier, the ideas expressed by Odysseus 'are the foundation on which the polis must stand',[39] and Odysseus himself 'stands for a new phase in the evolution out of the ancient era: the phase where a polis recognizes its conditions of existence' (183). To be quite specific, in the mind of the poet there must have been anxieties about the 'gradual growth of the [Athenian] empire and the despotism that was characteristic of Athens' internal and external relations' (185); this was leading to 'encroachments' in 'certain areas which till then had been regarded as inviolable' (ibid.). The play was, in fact, 'an attempt to make people aware of the problems associated with the ethics and the intellectual infrastructure of Athens' (186).

We remember, with some perplexity, that the question of withholding or granting burial to an enemy already forms the dominant subject of the last two books of the *Iliad*; while the burial of Ajax himself was opposed in the Cyclic *Little Iliad* (F3 Davies) 'through the anger of the king' (διὰ τὴν ὀργὴν τοῦ βασιλέως). As in Sophocles' play, what opposes the divine law is, in both these epic episodes, nothing new, nothing democratic, nothing more 'political' than the

---

[38] Meier (1993: 166–87). Bernard Knox (1983) uses similar language: cf. pp. 10 and 26, [*Ajax* and *Antigone*], 'raise questions about the right of the *polis* to demand obedience in all things', etc.

[39] For Bernard Knox (1983: 13) on the other hand, it is the Atridae who are the representatives of the polis: 'The claims of the polis are advanced by unworthy spokesmen whose mean and spiteful ranting enhances the dignity of (the) heroic corpse'; cf. also ibid. 26. Once again the interpreters know that the play is political, but their political interpretations contradict each other: flatly, but also blandly. Cf. n. 44 below.

imperious will of an angry commander. Herodotus, too, is concerned with the theme of burying an enemy, the Persian Mardonius, in a context which involves no Athenian but a Spartan king.[40]

To be confident that this age-old wisdom has here a specifically Athenian application, and to see in the odious Atridae of this play a representation of the *polis* of Athens and of Athenian leaders, is a step that one must surely hesitate to take. Reluctance may be strengthened by the cliché of political display oratory which Euripides dramatizes in his *Supplices*: the Athenians selflessly took up arms to prevent the Thebans from leaving unburied the bodies of the Seven. The audience is regaled with large helpings of Athenian self-congratulation.[41] This favourite Athenian myth must surely make us wonder whether an Athenian audience would have taken the action of the Theban Creon, in *Antigone*, or the Peloponnesian Atridae, in this play—the wicked refusal of burial—as standing, in the absence of any evident clue, for Athens. More likely, surely, that they were seen as standing for the human species generally; particularly, I should guess (and guessing is what we are all doing, disguise it as we may) in a period in which there were many men in the Greek world who thought that the end justified the means, and that political calculations were supreme. Thucydides picked Corcyra as the place in which to set a discussion of them.[42]

That current of sceptical thought, rather than the democracy of Athens, looks like a target here; but the pupils of the sophists and the friends of Critias were by no means all Athenians, and the city herself was not identical even with those who were; while the Spartans who, in dooming the suppliants at Plataea, rejected every argument but their own advantage, had nothing to learn from Athens about political cynicism or political sophistry.[43] It is worth mentioning, to illustrate the subjectivity of all this, that while on Meier's view the Atridae of *Ajax* represent Athens, other scholars, no less distinguished, explain their repulsiveness by insisting that they stand for Athens' Peloponnesian enemies.[44] It is not clear on

[40] Herodotus 9. 78–9. The king rejects the temptation, not on any ground which might be called democratic, or even political, but because: 'We leave that kind of thing to barbarians, and even in them we regard it as hateful.'

[41] Cf. Loraux (1986: 67 ff.).

[42] Thucydides 3. 82–5.

[43] Thucydides 3. 68.

[44] Thus Seaford in Silk (1996: 292): 'The petty and vindictive Atreidai do not, as Goldhill claims, represent the *polis*. They are rather the ancestors of Athens'

what rational basis the reader is to choose between such contradictory assertions, which have in common only that they are
political. And it is made strikingly apparent that an approach to
Attic tragedy which promised to be hard-headed, undeceived,
rooted not in the subjectivities of literary criticism but in political
realities, is in fact at least as subjective as any 'literary' interpretation.

Two last political views of *Ajax*. In 1964 F. Robert[45] argued that
the emphasis in the play on the parentage of Eurysaces, Ajax' son by
the captive woman Tecmessa, but still his true son and heroic heir,
was meant to reflect unfavourably on Pericles' law restricting
citizenship to the children of two Attic citizens: 'La pièce prend
parti avec vigueur pour la conception aristocratique.' Such specific
suggestions are nowadays out of fashion,[46] and historicist scholars
prefer to stick to more general accounts of the relation of tragedy
and history; but the idea can no more be refuted now than it could
thirty years ago. What it suffers is perhaps worse than refutation: it
is simply not in the modern style.[47]

More modern, because more collective, is the theory advanced in
another recent book.[48] For Seaford, various points in the play 'seem
to prefigure the cult of Ajax' as a hero (129 f.).[49] Ajax, in fact, as 'the

enemies.' ὄνειδος ἥκει τόδ' ἀντ' ὀνείδους, δύσμαχα δ' ἐστὶ κρῖναι (Aesch. *Ag.* 1560 f.).
Claim and counter-claim, and it is hard to decide between them; even harder,
perhaps, to give systematic or objective reasons for one's choice.

[45] Robert (1964: 213 ff.).
[46] See the classic criticism of this approach by G. Zuntz (1955: 55 ff.): 'The most
commonly accepted instances of allusions to contemporary events are discussed
next. They prove imaginary', etc.
[47] A vigorous defence of this procedure of finding specific references to events
and persons in Attic drama, tragic and comic, is made by Michael Vickers (1997:
pp. xix ff.).
[48] Seaford (1994).
[49] See the rather different arguments of P. Burian (1972) and A. Henrichs
(1993). The absence of clear reference in the play to cult calls forth from
Henrichs some subtle arguments: in this play the poet 'explores tentatively,
almost reluctantly' hero cult (165), 'seen *in statu nascendi*'. On this view lines
1175–80 are crucial. They show that the corpse of Ajax has already supernatural
power: 'The choral voice emerges as the instigator and guarantor of ritual
performance' (170); in fact, 'The choral voice also creates the power the corpse
holds in the mind of Teukros. It holds this power only because the chorus has
effectively buried Aias in an imaginary performance that anticipates the actual
burial' (173); and the Athenian audience is to be reminded not only of the tomb
far away in the Troad but also of Aias' island of Salamis, and of cult in Athens

recipient of the cult, on the point of abandoning ruinous hostile reciprocity for the permanence of collective cult, acquires a lofty perspective' (136). As Ajax approaches death, his language takes on echoes of the mysteries (392 ff.); he achieves 'mystic insight into the changeability of all things' (397). This insight 'includes the instability of all personal relations, whether friendly or hostile. It is in principle inconsistent . . . with excessive hostility to his enemies' (ibid.). Thus we can say:

Ajax, already poised (like the mystic initiand) in the liminal space between life and death, is reconciled to his own unjust and piteous death by his insight into the cosmic principle of the perpetual transformation into each other of opposites, including, we may infer (*sic*), his own death and life in the perpetuation of his cult. The political significance of his insight is that it underlies both the communality of cult . . . and its perpetuation.   (400)

There are, surely, two difficulties with this account. One is that there is no clear allusion in the text of the play to a collective cult of Ajax, or indeed to any cult of him at all. The other is that what the text does show us is an Ajax who at his death expresses undiminished emotional attachment to his distant parents: they will mourn bitterly for his fate; and who, so far from transcending hostility, still hates the whole Achaean army and curses it to destruction by the Erinyes (835–51). Ajax dies unreconciled, still passionate in love and hate, and alone.

The extreme difficulty of getting objectively reliable conclusions from the text on such questions may be neatly illustrated. Charles Segal describes Ajax receiving 'a warrior's funeral with an entirely masculine focus'; Odysseus is excluded, and 'these funerary rites . . . say nothing of Tecmessa or female lamentation in general'.[50] In the same collection of essays P. E. Easterling replies that what we see is not the burial rite itself but only a procession towards it, and 'One might think of Tecmessa (and her attendants?) taking part in lamentations at some point after the military honours are over . . . there is no explicit (or implicit) exclusion of Tecmessa from the end of the play' (179). In another place she goes still further: Odysseus

(175 f.). Such fine-spun ingenuities surely take us far from the possible experience of an audience; not to mention the fact that what secures the burial of Aias is not the power of the dead but the reasoned pleading, the λόγος, of Odysseus, as Agamemnon tells him with great emphasis at 1370 ff.

[50] In Silk (1996: 161).

does indeed go off, but 'There is nothing to indicate that he and some unspecified number of soldiers will not do as Teucer suggests [*sc.* 1396 f.] and witness the funeral when the time comes.'[51] It is clear how subjective these fascinating speculations are,[52] with all their consequences for the interpretation of the work.[53]

What has this whirlwind tour taught us? First, a political element is one of the possible ingredients of an Attic tragedy, but only one. Second, many scholars are now determined that the *polis* shall enter in, even where the text seems to offer it no foothold: Attic tragedy is defined as a political form, and political messages are to be found in it everywhere. That goes with a conviction that the whole experience of tragedy is, in some way which is important but not easy to define exactly, collective.

Second, there is the great difficulty of determining just what the political content of a play, or of a passage in a play, should be taken to be. Alternative explanations and accounts are freely on offer, and it is hard to see a rationale for choosing between them; yet it must be a question, for instance, whether *Ajax* can both be about the establishment of a mystical hero-cult which will heal the division of society, and at the same time be a demonstration that aristocratic leaders are indispensable to the armies and fleets of the *demos*; a warning against the perils of Athenian imperialism, and at the same time an attack on Pericles' restrictive citizenship law. And can the unappetizing Atridae stand both for the Athenian democracy and for its Peloponnesian enemies?

But perhaps all this is possible. We must ask: what is the status of these proposals for the interpretation of the tragic texts? If one member of the audience, or one modern reader, claims that he finds such and such a political or ideological message, does it make sense for someone else to deny that it is 'there', or to find an opposite one? Must we acquiesce in a Protagorean state of subjectivity: if it

[51] In R. Scodel (1993: 14).

[52] For another example see Easterling (1993: 191–9), who lists seven interpretations of the 'political' passage, 919–23.

[53] This suggests the question, how was the end of the play staged, when it was first put on? A producer may show Tecmessa, and other women, following the cortège; he may send them off another way; he may add a short, or a long, file of soldiers. It often happens that we are not in a position to make a confident decision between alternatives, all of which were possible in the Attic theatre. But it is clearly unsound to settle such a point in one's mind, and then to treat one's own solution as a basis for the interpretation of the play.

feels hot to me, then it is hot to me,[54] if it seems political to me, then it is political to me; and it feels political to me in *this* sense, even if it seems to you to be political in *that*? Some of these suggested readings seem to be open, if not to refutation in the sense that a proposition in logic can be refuted, then at least (which is the appropriate degree of ἀκρίβεια for this subject matter), to being rendered by argument ἀπίθανα, implausible, hard to accept.

But, third, there is another aspect. What sort of experience was it, to sit in the theatre through a set of Attic tragedies? Were the audience on the lookout for subtly disguised or obliquely presented political meanings, or were they absorbed in the primary meaning of the words and events? Were they expecting a lesson in civics, something that would send them on their way more ideologically admonished, more collectively minded, more solid in their democratic citizenship, than they had been when they came into the theatre? Such questions cannot, in so simple a form, receive a simple answer. For one thing, audiences are not monolithic. A rustic making a rare visit to the theatre did not look for, or find, the same things in a Sophoclean trilogy as the poets Euripides and Agathon, when they sat through one. Some spectators will have seen more, some less, in these complex works.

But there are at least three points of caution which need to be borne in mind. The first is that the city did not make the experience of watching tragedies free to its citizens.[55] In the middle of the fifth century admission to the theatre cost two obols; not a trivial price, especially as in general festivals in Greece cost nothing. The city, that is, did not place so much value on indoctrinating its citizens with the ideology of democracy that it paid for them to get it for nothing. I suppose that tragedy was one of the ἀνάπαυλαι, the breaks, the refreshments, which Pericles in the Funeral Speech claimed were more numerous at Athens than anywhere else.[56] Tragedy was a pleasure (τέρψις) that you paid for, not a duty imposed on you by the state.

Second, it is worth observing that it was not only under the democracy that tragedy was loved and performed. Soon every Greek

---

[54] 80 Diels–Kranz B1.

[55] Cf. Alan H. Sommerstein in Pelling (1997: 65 ff.).

[56] Thucydides 2. 38. 1: καὶ μὴν καὶ τῶν πόνων πλείστας ἀναπαύλας τῇ γνώμῃ ἐπορισάμεθα, ἀγῶσι μέν γε καὶ θυσίαις διετησίοις νομίζοντες . . . ὧν καθ' ἡμέραν ἡ τέρψις τὸ λυπηρὸν ἐκπλήσσει.

city had its theatre for the performance of Attic tragedies. The kings and the oligarchies that dominated the cities evidently did not realize that the purpose of tragedy was political, and indeed specifically democratic. Still less, presumably, was that evident to the Roman aristocrats who in the half-Hellenized city on the Tiber patronized the translating and staging of Greek tragedies in Latin.[57] Propaganda for democracy? Hardly. Even the questioning of democracy does not seem likely as a motive.

Finally, and most importantly, we come to the question of the nature of the tragic pleasure itself. Were the spectators really looking through the surface meaning and content of the action for subtle hidden political messages? Surely the answer to this question is, broadly and for the great majority of spectators of most tragedies, No. That answer can perhaps not claim to be wholly free of the subjective, but it has at least the merit of being supported by the ancients themselves. Those who describe the state of mind of the audience in the theatre, whether they approve of it, like Gorgias, or strongly disapprove, like Plato, agree that the audience was 'deceived', emotionally swallowed up, abandoning itself to the pleasure of sympathetic emotion with the sufferings of the characters. Surrendering ourselves, ἐνδόντες ἡμᾶς αὐτούς, says Plato,[58] we follow the poet wherever he impels our emotions; by pity and terror (or 'sympathy and alarm'), says Aristotle,[59] we effect the

---

[57] It is with surprise that one reads that 'When the conquering Romans introduced the arts of captive Greece to Latium, it was not Aeschylus, Sophocles or Euripides who provided the chief source of popular dramatic inspiration (though political tragedy modelled on Euripides was not unknown in Rome), but Menander' (P. Cartledge in Easterling (1997: 35)). The tragedies of Ennius, Pacuvius, and Accius, based of course on Attic models, were still powerful a century later, in the days of Cicero, who quotes Roman tragedy constantly. On Ennius, e.g. F. Leo (1913: 187): 'Als Tragiker hat er das Theater beherrscht, und zwar in einer sein Leben überdauernden Wirkung.' On Pacuvius, ibid. 227; he was fond of using plays by Sophocles, and for Varro (Aulus Gellius 6. 14) he was the paradigm of the grand style. And so on.

[58] *Republic* 605de.

[59] This, of course, is when the play worked. Sometimes it did not work, as when the audience allowed the tension to be shattered if an actor mispronounced a word (see Dover's note on Aristophanes, *Frogs* 304); or when a passage was felt to be absurdly bombastic, ψυχρόν. As Timotheus was performing his *Artemis*, one of the audience stood up and ridiculed a vulnerable line (*Poetae Melici Graeci* frag. 778(b) Page)—though in that case it is worth remembering that the kibitzer was Cinesias, a rival composer. The line might not have been such a failure with all the audience.

purgation of such feelings. Where do we find ancient passages that speak of a cool and analytic sophistication in the spectators?

Intense emotion is one of the things which seem to come off rather short, on these political interpretations,[60] necessarily, if the audience, so far from surrendering themselves, are constantly on the watch for secondary meanings, in what might be called a post-modern manner and frame of mind. Another is religion. The plays have so much to say about the gods, and our most recent guides so little. Religion was not less important than politics to playwright and audience; above all, perhaps, to Sophocles.[61]

It has not been the intention of this paper to deny that Attic tragedy, like other forms of literature, has its roots in the healthy loam of contemporary history and the society in which, and for which, it was produced. It is true, too, that a tragedy may have at its very heart something that can properly be called political: a few extant tragedies do. What does surely emerge is that the political element in this art-form can be greatly exaggerated and misconceived; that politics is only one of the possible elements of a tragedy; and that interpretation in excessively political terms can lead to damaging mistakes. Such questions are often far from being dominant. Other aspects of the human heart may be more intense and more central, and so may other questions connected with the eternal problems of man's relation with the divine. That is part of the reason why Attic tragedy continues, long after the passing of Attic democracy, to engross modern readers and modern audiences, to command their attention, and to draw their tears.

REFERENCES

BURIAN, P. (1972), 'Supplication and Hero Cult in Sophocles' *Ajax*', *GRBS* 13: 151–6.
CROALLY, N. T. (1994), *Euripidean Polemic* (Cambridge).
EASTERLING, P. E. (1993), 'Sophocle: le texte, les personnages', *Actes du colloque international d'Aix-en-Provence: Études rassemblées par A. Machin et L. Pernée*: 191–9.
——(1997*a*) (ed.), *The Cambridge Companion to Greek Tragedy* (Cambridge).

[60] On this central point there is much to agree with in Heath (1987).
[61] See above, ch. 2.

——(1997*b*), 'Constructing the Heroic', in Pelling (1997), 21–38.

EHRENBERG, V. (1954), *Sophocles and Pericles* (Oxford).

EUBEN, J. P. (1986) (ed.), *Greek Tragedy and Political Theory* (Berkeley).

FEENEY, D. (1998), Review of Easterling (1997a), *TLS*, 29 May 1998, 11.

FOLEY, H. P. (1993), 'The Politics of Tragic Lamentation', in Sommerstein *et al.* (1993), 101–42.

GOFF, B. (1995) (ed.), *History Tragedy Theory* (Austin).

GRIFFIN, J. (1998), 'The Social Function of Attic Tragedy', *CQ* 48: 39–61.

GRIFFITH, M. (1995), 'Brilliant Dynasts: Power and Politics in the *Oresteia*', *Class. Ant.* 14: 62–129.

HEATH, M. (1987), *The Poetics of Greek Tragedy* (London).

HENRICHS, A. (1993), 'The Tomb of Aias and the Prospect of Hero Cult in Sophocles', *Class. Ant.* 12: 165–80.

KNOX, B. (1983), 'Sophocles and the *Polis*', *Entretiens Hardt* 29: *Sophocle*, 1–27.

KRUMMEN, E. (1993), 'Athens and Attica: *Polis* and Countryside in Tragedy', in Sommerstein *et al.* (1993), 191–218.

LEO, F. (1913), *Römische Literaturgeschichte* (Berlin).

LLOYD-JONES, H., and WILSON, N. G. (1990), *Sophocles* (Oxford).

LORAUX, N. (1986), *The Invention of Athens* (Eng. trans., Cambridge, Mass.).

MEIER, C. (1990), *The Greek Discovery of Politics* (Eng. trans., Cambridge, Mass.)

——(1993), *The Political Art of Greek Tragedy* (Eng. trans., Cambridge).

PELLING, C. (1997) (ed.), *Greek Tragedy and the Historian* (Oxford).

PODLECKI, A. J. 'Polis and Monarch in Early Attic Tragedy', in Euben (1986), 76–100.

RAAFLAUB, K. (1989), 'Contemporary Perceptions of Democracy in Fifth Century Athens', *Classica et Medievalia* 40: 33–70.

ROBERT, F. (1964), 'Sophocles, Périclès, Hérodote et la date d'Ajax', *Rev. de Philol.* 38: 213 ff.

SCHADEWALDT, W. (1928), *Monolog und Selbstgespräch* (Berlin).

SCODEL, R. (1993) (ed.), *Theater and Society in the Ancient World* (Ann Arbor).

SEAFORD, R. (1994), *Reciprocity and Ritual: Homer and Tragedy in the Developing City State* (Oxford).

SILK, M. S. (1996) (ed.), *Tragedy and the Tragic* (Oxford).

SOMMERSTEIN, A. H., HALLIWELL, S., HENDERSON, J., and ZIMMERMANN, B. (1993) (eds.), *Tragedy, Comedy and the Polis* (Bari).

VICKERS, M. J. (1995), 'Heracles Lacedaemonius: The Political Dimensions of Sophocles *Trachiniae* and Euripides *Heracles*', *Dialogues d'histoire ancienne* 21 no. 2.

——(1997), *Pericles on Stage* (Austin).

WHITLOCK BLUNDELL, M. (1993), 'The Ideal of Athens in *Oedipus at Colonus*', in Sommerstein *et al.* (1993), 287–306.

WINKLER, J. J., and ZEITLIN, F. (1990) (eds.), *Nothing to do with Dionysus? Athenian Tragedy in its Social Context* (Princeton).

ZUNTZ, G. (1955), *The Political Plays of Euripides* (Manchester).

6

Plain Words in Sophocles

P. E. EASTERLING

Writing a commentary on *Oedipus at Colonus* has made me think about how to do justice to the extraordinary poise and power of Sophoclean language, despite its seeming simplicity in this late play. Hence the 'plain words' of my title, but plain in the spirit of Shakespeare's Lear:

> Pray do not mock me.
> I am a very foolish fond old man
> Fourscore and upward, not an hour more or less;
> And, *to deal plainly*,
> I fear I am not in my perfect mind.
> Methinks I should know you and know this man;
> Yet I am doubtful: for I am mainly ignorant
> What place this is, and all the skill I have
> Remembers not these garments; nor do I know
> Where I did lodge last night. Do not laugh at me;
> For, as I am a man, I think this lady
> To be my child Cordelia.

> (*King Lear* IV. viii. 60–71)

What I mean by 'plain words' or 'dealing plainly' is not artless naivety or homely colloquialism; I am well aware that Sophoclean discourse—like Shakespeare's—is typically artful in the extreme, relying on a range of vocabulary that includes many abstract nouns and many synonyms, often coinages, which make possible an elaborate use of *variatio*. This subtlety of variation is evident too in syntax, in word-order, sentence-structure, and the rhetorical shaping of arguments, not to mention verse rhythm, and there is a network of references to other texts that further enriches the whole.[1] So it is an intricate plainness, *simplex munditiis*, and (to my mind) all the more appealing because of its austerity.

What I am looking for is a way of analysing the concentration and power of this language without falling back on overworked terms like ambiguity, irony, undercutting, deferral.

There are three images, or models, that I have found useful in trying to account for the depth of Sophocles' plain dealing, though all, of course, are makeshift: (1) the notion of the tension of opposites, or the holding together of contradictory forces; (2) the idea of oscillation, or shading between literal and metaphorical meaning; (3) the idea of the 'charging' of themes through concentration and the ever-varied use of repetition. Rough and sketchy as they are, they have the advantage of not being mutually exclusive, and at least they should not run the risk of being reductive.[2]

Lines 1–13 will serve as a convenient starting point:

Τέκνον τυφλοῦ γέροντος Ἀντιγόνη, τίνας
χώρους ἀφίγμεθ' ἢ τίνων ἀνδρῶν πόλιν;
τίς τὸν πλανήτην Οἰδίπουν καθ' ἡμέραν
τὴν νῦν σπανιστοῖς δέξεται δωρήμασιν,
σμικρὸν μὲν ἐξαιτοῦντα, τοῦ σμικροῦ δ' ἔτι   5
μεῖον φέροντα, καὶ τόδ' ἐξαρκοῦν ἐμοί;
στέργειν γὰρ αἱ πάθαι με χὠ χρόνος ξυνὼν
μακρὸς διδάσκει καὶ τὸ γενναῖον τρίτον.
ἀλλ', ὦ τέκνον, θάκησιν εἴ τινα βλέπεις
ἢ πρὸς βεβήλοις ἢ πρὸς ἄλσεσιν θεῶν,   10
στῆσόν με κἀξίδρυσον, ὡς πυθώμεθα
ὅπου ποτ' ἐσμέν· μανθάνειν γὰρ ἥκομεν
ξένοι πρὸς ἀστῶν, ἂν δ' ἀκούσωμεν τελεῖν.

[1] Aspects of Sophoclean language, syntax, and style are analysed by Campbell (1879: 1–107); Bruhn (1899); Earp (1944); Long (1968); Easterling (1973); Moorhouse (1982). Sophoclean criticism over the last fifty years has given great emphasis to the thematic use of language. Goheen (1951) and Knox (1957) were early pioneers; Knox (1964), Winnington-Ingram (1980), and Segal (1981) have been particularly influential. But, as Michael Silk points out in an illuminating essay (1996: 458), direct 'attempts to elucidate tragic language' have been surprisingly few and far between. For Sophocles, Jebb's commentaries remain the richest resource. A couple of pages by Mackail (1910: 150–1) adumbrate the central concerns of this paper.

[2] It would be absurd, of course, to claim that *any* approach could be comprehensive.

Child of a blind old man, Antigone, to what regions, or to what men's city
have we come? Who on this day shall receive Oedipus the wanderer with
scanty gifts? I ask for little, and I get even less, but for me that is sufficient;
for my sufferings; and the time that has long been my companion, and
thirdly my nobility teach me to be content with it. But come, my child, if
you see any seat, either near ground unconsecrated or near the precincts of
the gods, stop me and let me sit there, so that we may find out where we
are; for we have come as strangers, and must learn from the citizens and do
as they tell us.   (trans. Hugh Lloyd-Jones[3])

1. *Contradiction.* The strongest contradiction within this speech
is that between the *magnitude* of Oedipus' experience (αἱ πάθαι, (ὁ)
χρόνος ξυνὼν μακρός, and τὸ γενναῖον (7–8), with τρίτον marking
out this triad as offering three major clues to the understanding of
the whole action) and the *smallness* of what he now asks for,
receives, and accepts: σμικρὸν μὲν ἐξαιτοῦντα, τοῦ σμικροῦ δ' ἔτι
μεῖον φέροντα, καὶ τόδ' ἐξαρκοῦν ἐμοί (5–6). As the play develops we
shall find that strong emphasis is given to the question whether
Oedipus' request to Theseus and the men of Colonus is *small or
great*, and to the idea of the *little word* that can exert unexpected
power for good or evil. But even at this stage the contrast between
great and small is striking. The last word of his speech is worth
noting, too: τελεῖν, 'perform', 'fulfil', is a word of some dignity,
often used of carrying out ritual, as at 513, when Ismene offers to
perform the rite of purification, or of the action of gods, supernatural forces or time 'bringing things to pass', as in Oedipus'
famous words after his self-blinding, Ἀπόλλων τάδ' ἦν . . . ὁ κακὰ
κακὰ τελῶν ἐμὰ τάδ' ἐμὰ πάθεα (*OT* 1329–30). Not what a helpless
beggar might be expected to say of himself and his daughter, not
(that is) if he were not also Oedipus (τὸν πλανήτην Οἰδίπουν, 3). The
speaker, of course, is not any old anonymous wanderer: like
Antigone, he is a famous character of the tragic stage. The meaning
of Oedipus' identity is going to be at the centre of the play's
meditations; what, if anything, he can fulfil is going to matter.

2. *Shading from literal to metaphorical,* an extremely familiar
feature in poetry ancient and modern,[4] works particularly well in

---

[3] All passages of translation are taken from Lloyd-Jones (1994). It will be obvious
throughout how much I have learned from Sir Hugh's penetrating analysis of
Sophocles' text.

[4] On differing ancient and modern distinctions between literal and metaphorical
meaning see Padel (1992: 9–10).

drama because everything in a play is in a sense metaphorical, in that it presents past and/or fictitious events *as if* they were happening here and now before the audience's eyes. When the audience watches Oedipus, the name can with equal propriety be used both of him as a character in the story and of the actor playing the part. Movement between literal and metaphorical is thus very easy: the journey of Oedipus, symbolized by the actor's movements on the stage, can be both his journey to Colonus and his passage from life to death.[5] In this speech the clearest example of such shading is in the idea of *teaching* and *learning*: at 7–8 the subjects of διδάσκουσι are all abstract nouns—Oedipus' 'teachers' are his sufferings, the passage of time, and his nobility. At 12–13 he envisages a more literally didactic process: he has come in order to learn from the citizens and to carry out what he hears from them. Even so, this is not the formal relationship of teacher and pupil, and the lesson is evidently to be more than a factual or practical one. So far, the process of learning seems to have been characterized by suffering, by experience over time, and by reliance on some inborn quality of mind and temper which has made him capable of grasping the lesson. The lesson itself has been 'endurance' (στέργειν, 7). But now he is ready to learn from these people and act on what he learns; there is thus a strong implication that Oedipus' quest is to be one of discovery leading to action, and there may even be a clue here as to how we as audience are to learn.

3. *'Charging'*. Everything I have mentioned so far turns out to belong to the set of strands or themes that are constantly reworked and elaborated as the action develops. These first thirteen lines introduce all the play's leading ideas: personal/social relationships (child (1, 9), strangers and citizens (13)); Oedipus as wanderer and exile, blind, old, dependent on others (1–6), (although the scanty gifts (4) that he receives will later be replaced by the gift of asylum and reciprocated by a great benefit to the Athenians, the protective gift of his body (578–9, 635)); the journey of Oedipus and his daughter (ἀφίγμεθ', 2; ἥκομεν, 12); the place they have come to (1–2; ὅπου ποτ' ἐσμέν, 12), which may be a city of men (2); the seat where O. will sit (θάκησιν, 9, an unusual word marking an important feature of the setting, which will turn out to be a suppliant's seat, ἕδρα, 45);[6] the question of hallowed or unhallowed ground (10) that

---

[5] Cf. Seale (1982: 136–8); Segal (1981: 368–9).
[6] On the seat, see e.g. Easterling (1967); Burian (1974).

is, the religious meaning of the place where Oedipus establishes himself. Oedipus knows how to endure (7), he asks for little and is content with less (5–6), but has been taught by great things (7–8). He has been taught by his experiences, and yet he has come to learn (7, 12) and also to fulfil (13). Later he will be found to be a teacher, too (593-4, 1518).

With these strands of thought in mind we can turn to Oedipus' famous speech on time and change (607–28), a passage of great solemnity but one also of seeming directness and simplicity, which might make a good test case for the application of these three models:

> ὦ φίλτατ' Αἰγέως παῖ, μόνοις οὐ γίγνεται
> θεοῖσι γῆρας οὐδὲ κατθανεῖν ποτε,
> τὰ δ' ἄλλα συγχεῖ πάνθ' ὁ παγκρατὴς χρόνος.
> φθίνει μὲν ἰσχὺς γῆς, φθίνει δὲ σώματος,   610
> θνῄσκει δὲ πίστις, βλαστάνει δ' ἀπιστία,
> καὶ πνεῦμα ταὐτὸν οὔποτ' οὔτ' ἐν ἀνδράσιν
> φίλοις βέβηκεν οὔτε πρὸς πόλιν πόλει.
> τοῖς μὲν γὰρ ἤδη, τοῖς δ' ἐν ὑστέρωι χρόνωι
> τὰ τερπνὰ πικρὰ γίγνεται καὖθις φίλα.   615
> καὶ ταῖσι Θήβαις εἰ τανῦν εὐημερεῖ
> καλῶς τὰ πρὸς σέ, μυρίας ὁ μυρίος
> χρόνος τεκνοῦται νύκτας ἡμέρας τ' ἰών,
> ἐν αἷς τὰ νῦν ξύμφωνα δεξιώματα
> δόρει διασκεδῶσιν ἐκ σμικροῦ λόγου·   620
> ἵν' οὑμὸς εὕδων καὶ κεκρυμμένος νέκυς
> ψυχρός ποτ' αὐτῶν θερμὸν αἷμα πίεται,
> εἰ Ζεὺς ἔτι Ζεὺς χὠ Διὸς Φοῖβος σαφής.
> ἀλλ' οὐ γὰρ αὐδᾶν ἡδὺ τἀκίνητ' ἔπη,
> ἔα μ' ἐν οἷσιν ἠρξάμην, τὸ σὸν μόνον   625
> πίστον φυλάσσων· κοὔποτ' Οἰδίπουν ἐρεῖς
> ἀχρεῖον οἰκητῆρα δέξασθαι τόπων
> τῶν ἐνθάδ', εἴπερ μὴ θεοὶ ψεύδουσί με.

Dearest son of Aegeus, for the gods alone there is no old age and no death ever, but all other things are submerged by all-powerful time! The strength of the country perishes, so does the strength of the body, loyalty dies and disloyalty comes into being, and the same spirit never remains between friends or between cities, since for some people now and for others in the future happy relations turn bitter, and again friendship is restored. And if now all is sunny weather between Thebes and you, time as it passes brings forth countless nights and days in which they shall shatter with the spear the present harmonious pledges for a petty reason. Then shall my dead body, sleeping and buried, cold as it is, drink their warm blood, if Zeus is still Zeus and his son Phoebus speaks the truth! But since there is no pleasure in speaking words that should not be touched on, leave me in the course I have begun, but only keep your word, and you shall never say that Oedipus whom you received into these regions was a useless inmate, if the gods do not deceive me! (trans. Hugh Lloyd-Jones)

This is marked as one of the play's 'big speeches' by the formality of address[7] (ὦ φίλτατ' Αἰγέως παῖ) and its dramatic placing: it leads up to the moment when Theseus, the proto-democratic king, makes the right response to Oedipus' supplication—despite the unprepossessing appearance of the suppliant and his gift—and takes seriously his offer of a secret source of protection for the city. Theseus' acceptance of Oedipus as an Athenian 'dweller in the city' 637)[8] and promise to protect him, followed by the Chorus' song in praise of Colonus and Attica, make a solemn climax in the action so far.

How is Oedipus' speech presented in this significant place? It is identified as a lesson, in language already familiar from the opening of the play: at 575 Theseus has urged Oedipus to teach him so that he may learn (at 593–4 there has been some rather pointed play with these ideas of teaching and learning; the theme will be recalled at 1154–5, 1518–39, and 1643–4). Oedipus is explaining the Athenians' need for protection from friends (the Thebans) who may one day become enemies, and he bases his argument on truths about time and change in the natural world and (even more) in political life (especially 611–15). But if it is a lesson it is not an easy one: it also raises serious questions to which Oedipus can give only a

---

[7] 'Dearest son of Aegeus' is both intimate and formal: 'dearest' is echoed in Oedipus' words of farewell to Theseus at 1552 (φίλτατε ξένων, cf. ὦ φίλον κάρα at 1631), but the address of a character as a child of his or her father is always a marker of the importance of the dramatic moment, as at *Ajax* 134 and 331 or *Ant.* 211. (Not surprisingly, there are many instances in *Philoctetes*, a play which explicitly examines the nature of a son's inheritance from his father.) Two solemn moments later in *OC* are marked by the formula 'child (τέκνον) of Aegeus': at 1154, when Oedipus asks Theseus to 'teach' him (about the arrival of an unknown suppliant—the cue for the Polyneices scene), and at 1518, when he announces that he will 'teach' Theseus the future of his city. Creon, too, uses the expression (940) at the beginning of what he misguidedly hopes will be a dignified speech of self-defence.

[8] See Burian (1974: 416–17) and Easterling (1996: 34–6) on the interpretation of this passage.

conditional answer. The problem, as at *Ajax* 646–92,[9] can be simply put: if *everything* changes, how can you be sure that anything matters?

1. *Contradiction.* There is a powerful concentration of contradictions in this speech. On the one hand, all nature and all human activity, indeed the whole of human history, are subject to radical change, and even the strongest social bonds can be loosened: faith (πίστις) dies, faithlessness (ἀπιστία) flourishes (611), both between individuals and between communities. The process can be reversed, too: 'happy relations turn bitter, and again friendship is restored' (615). On the other hand, the promise that Oedipus is making to Athens depends on Theseus keeping his word (τὸ σὸν μόνον | πιστὸν φυλάσσων, 625–6). You can believe, and indeed must try to believe, the speech seems to say, in the power of human commitment in the matter of friendship and supplication, just as you can and should believe in the possibility that the gods have a benign purpose, but you can't *know*: the best you can do (and the best Oedipus ultimately can do, for all his prophetic conviction) is to wish and to pray. Four times in the play he prays for Athens, the last time in his solemn parting words at 1552–5; when he first hears that he has reached the grove of the Eumenides he twice prays to them for fulfilment of Apollo's oracle (86, 101–5).

This speech includes an extremely strong prediction of the posthumous power that Oedipus will one day exert on behalf of the Athenians against their present allies the Thebans. Its strength is intensified by the link between these aetiological references and promises made elsewhere in the play, which seem to foreshadow what the contemporary audience would recognize as hero cult.[10] The inner contradiction of the expression—Oedipus' *sleeping* and *cold* corpse will *drink* the *hot* blood of the fallen Thebans (621–2)— is another intensifying factor, but this confident assurance is immediately followed by a conditional clause, 'If Zeus (is) still

---

[9] It is hard not to detect an element of Sophoclean self-quotation in the wording of *OC* 607–23, particularly of *Aj.* 646–9 and 669–83. Cf. Seaford (1994: 136–7, 395–9) on the similarities between the two passages.

[10] The language here seems designed to evoke the familiar practice of making liquid offerings at the tombs of those whose bodies were thought to have talismanic power. For other references in the play to the coming power of Oedipus to help or harm after his death cf. 92–3, 287–8, 389–402, 457–60, 576–82, 787–8, 1489–90, 1508–9, 1518–55, 1760–5. For recent discussion see Edmunds (1981 and 1996), Henrichs (1983, 1993, and 1994); Burkert (1985); Kearns (1989); Krummen (1993).

Zeus and Zeus's son Phoebus (is) sure' (σαφής, 623).[11] And again, the claim (627–8) that Theseus will never have occasion to say that Oedipus has been a useless 'resident' (οἰκητῆρα)[12] is at once followed by the conditional 'if the gods are not deceiving me'.[13] How can one know, except through humanly limited processes and experiences, the correct way to interpret the enigmatic words of the gods?[14]

So there is a strong sense of precariousness here: Oedipus, and his secret, matter if—and only if—Theseus and his successors can maintain faith, and if the gods are understood well enough by the sufferer who has spent his life trying to learn their lessons. When he came to the grove, after all, he had to make a leap of faith in order to identify it as *the* place destined for his passing.

The same effect of precariousness is created by τἀκίνητ' ἔπη at 624. The secret (the precise location of Oedipus' passing) must stay a secret, 'words not to be stirred',[15] and yet the keeping of it will depend not only on Theseus holding to his side of the agreement (τὸ σὸν μόνον | πιστὸν φυλάσσων) but, after his death, on the loyalty of

[11] For this use of σαφής (meaning 'unerring', 'reliable') in connection with oracles cf. 791–3, quoted in n. 19 below.

[12] For the cultic resonance of οἰκητῆρα see Edmunds (1981: 223 and n. 8); Henrichs (1976: 278).

[13] As Lloyd-Jones and Wilson (1990) point out ad loc., K's ψεύδουσι is more likely to be the original reading than ψεύσουσι in the rest of the MSS; and the sense 'are not deceiving me' is more appropriate than 'will deceive', given that Oedipus received the oracle long ago. The implication is almost 'have not all along been deceiving me'.

[14] There are some further instances in *OC* of εἰ-clauses used in the context of the divine purpose: at 664–5, Theseus encourages Oedipus to be confident, 'if it was Phoebus who sent you' (Φοῖβος εἰ προὔπεμψέ σε); at 1380–2 Oedipus declares to Polyneices, 'Therefore these curses overcome our supplication and your thrones, if Justice sits of old beside the throne of Zeus according to the ancient laws' (εἴπερ ἐστὶν . . . ξύνεδρος, where περ strengthens the confident tone); at 1480–1, in response to the claps of thunder, the Chorus pray to the *daimon*: 'Kindly, O god, kindly be your coming, if you are bringing something wrapped in darkness to the earth our mother!', where the εἰ-clause implies anxious foreboding rather than assurance. In all these cases the conditional phrasing deepens the impression that the divine will is not transparent; the phrasing at 623, with no verbs expressed, makes it even more elusive.

[15] For possible links with the language of mysteries cf. Seaford (1994: 397–8). Silence and secrecy are both important ideas in *OC*: cf. 128–33 for silence in the cult of the Semnai Theai and 1050–3 for the 'golden key' on the tongues of the initiates in the mysteries at Eleusis.

his successors from generation to generation, and we have heard at
610 ff. in language suggestive of the ineluctable processes of nature
(death, growth, birth, the weather) that all human activities are
subject to change and only the gods are exempt, enjoying eternal
existence and (by implication) eternal knowledge. If the safety of
Athens is to depend on words passed faithfully and secretly from
one human generation to the next, there is no possibility of its not
being vulnerable.

 2. *'Shading'*. Much that is relevant under this heading is equally
apposite under the next, since by this stage in the action many
words have acquired a charge of complex associations. But it is
worth looking at the verbs that carry the weight of the argument:
time submerges, destroys ($\sigma\upsilon\gamma\chi\epsilon\hat{\imath}$, 609), the strength of the land and
of the body perishes ($\phi\theta\acute{\imath}\nu\epsilon\iota$, 610), faith dies ($\theta\nu\acute{\eta}\sigma\kappa\epsilon\iota$), faithlessness
comes into being, shoots forth ($\beta\lambda\alpha\sigma\tau\acute{\alpha}\nu\epsilon\iota$, 611) and the same spirit
does not persist for ever between friends, whether individuals or
cities (612–13). 'Spirit' perhaps sounds too inward and abstract as a
translation of $\pi\nu\epsilon\hat{\upsilon}\mu\alpha$, while 'wind' might at first sight seem almost
too metaphorical: the image of the inconstancy of the weather, with
winds repeatedly changing direction, seems to have been a familiar
one in Greek for human intercourse, as in our cliché 'see which way
the wind is blowing'. Yet in this context, preceded by verbs
suggestive of growth and death and followed by the stronger
weather image of $\epsilon\mathring{\upsilon}\eta\mu\epsilon\rho\epsilon\hat{\imath}$ (616) of the good relations between
Athens and Thebes, the phrase $\pi\nu\epsilon\hat{\upsilon}\mu\alpha\ldots\beta\acute{\epsilon}\beta\eta\kappa\epsilon\nu$ must contribute
to the sense of a pattern of forces that shape the natural world and
human society within it.[16] The most powerful of these forces, time,
the destroyer at 609, is also the generator of new life: it gives birth to
a countless succession of nights and days (618) in which the most
unexpected events can happen;[17] in this case the day will come when
'they' will 'scatter with the spear' the present harmonious pledges,
'they' being the Thebans, currently in alliance with Athens. Spears
are normally used to cause the scattering of troops, but here their
victims are the solemn words of a treaty ($\xi\acute{\upsilon}\mu\phi\omega\nu\alpha\ \delta\epsilon\xi\iota\acute{\omega}\mu\alpha\tau\alpha$,

---

[16] In any case, as Ruth Padel has pointed out, we should be alert to the Greeks'
more integrated perception of the world: 'Air is both wind—breath in the world—
and breath within a human being. It is part of the patterned system within and
without' (1992: 51).

[17] Solon's famous calculation for Croesus of the days in a typical human life-span
(Herodotus 1. 32) makes a similar point: $\pi\hat{\alpha}\nu\ \mathring{\epsilon}\sigma\tau\iota\ \mathring{\alpha}\nu\theta\rho\omega\pi\sigma\varsigma\ \sigma\upsilon\mu\phi\sigma\rho\acute{\eta}$.

619). The absence of an expressed subject for διασκεδῶσιν contributes to the sense of violent irruption after the stately sequence of
nouns with present indicative verbs, and the violence will be
perpetrated 'on some minor pretext' (ἐκ σμικροῦ λόγου, 620),
suggesting the force, randomness, and triviality of conflict. The
idea of the cold corpse drinking hot blood continues the sense of
distortion; but when Oedipus reaches the gods they have no verbs at
all: εἰ Ζεὺς ἔτι Ζεὺς χὠ Διὸς Φοῖβος σαφής (623).

3. 'Charging'. If the delicate oscillation between literal and
metaphorical is hard to capture without simplification (or indeed
over-elaboration), it is even more of a challenge to chart all the ways
in which the words of this speech gain power from cumulative
associations with earlier passages in the play, or give weight to newly
developing themes. The resonances are no less strong because the
words themselves are so plain: thus the emphasis on friends and
enemies (607; especially 612–13) relates to one of the leading
questions of the play: who are the φίλοι of Oedipus? Old age and
death (608, 610, 611) are the context for thinking about what
happens to him in the course of the action. Time, which destroys
and brings to birth (609, 618) was identified by Oedipus at 7–8 as
his teacher, and reciprocal teaching and learning characterize his
dealings with Theseus and the Athenians. Land and body (610) are
easily linked with the play's insistent stress on place (cf. 627) and on
the body of Oedipus and its potential meaning (cf. 621); relations
between cities are the immediate topic, both of this speech, in
response to Theseus' question at 606, and of its sequel, in his
promise to incorporate Oedipus into the city of Athens (ἔμπολιν
κατοικιῶ, 637), and the matter of faith and faithlessness in the
dealings between cities (611) will become the focus of close
attention in the scenes between Oedipus, Theseus, and the representatives of the Thebans. The 'little word'[18] of 620, the trivial pretext
that will spark hostilities between Thebes and Athens, recalls 443,
Oedipus' allegation that the two brothers Eteocles and Polyneices
forced him into exile 'for the sake of a little word', that is, by
refusing to revoke the sentence of exile imposed on him. But if
something one says (or refrains from saying) can do harm, a little
word can also be creative and transformative, as at 1615–16 when

---

[18] On the 'little word' cf. Mackail (n. 1 above); Kirkwood (1958: 245); Segal
(1981: 398–9).

(in the Messenger's report) Oedipus tells his daughters that just a single word (in this case φιλεῖν) relieves all the pain of caring for him. And the phrase σμικρὸς λόγος can also mean 'a short speech' as it does at 569–70, when Oedipus responds to Theseus' generous welcome by saying that the king's nobility, briefly expressed, has saved his suppliant the distress of making a long speech of self-identification. Theseus and Oedipus 'talk the same language', and only brief exchanges are needed between them, so secure is their understanding of one another.

At 623 Zeus and Phoebus are cited as the guarantors of Oedipus' predictions: Zeus, whose mysterious will, and Apollo, whose translation of that will into oracular messages, have shaped his life of suffering and learning. 'If Zeus (is) still Zeus and Phoebus (is) sure': σαφής recalls the whole story of Oedipus' relations with oracles and his struggle to interpret them.[19] Like Apollo's enigmatic oracles, Oedipus himself is a potential source of illumination: at 74 in answer to the man of Colonus who has asked 'And what help can be given by a man who cannot see?' Oedipus has claimed 'Everything I say will have sight' (πάνθ' ὁρῶντα λέξομεν). But for most of the action there is fear and anxiety on his part (e.g. at 652–6, 822–3, 1486–7), and the threat from the Thebans is soon shown to be real enough.

Even so, his words carry conviction. The Chorus tells Theseus that Oedipus has been making promises like these from the first and seems set to fulfil them (ὡς τελῶν ἐφαίνετο, 630). Theseus, too, is impressed, though he gives a range of reasons for accepting him: in addition to Oedipus' goodwill (εὐμένεια, 631) he singles out his status as ally and the religious obligation he imposes as suppliant.

The implication of these responses is that Oedipus' speech has indeed exerted power; and the play seems to invite audiences and readers to endorse the faith of Theseus and the old men in Oedipus' 'seeing' words. The power, I suggest, comes from the profundity of his teaching: his didactic speech makes clear that from the mortal point of view all structures entail mutability and therefore vulner-ability, but at the same time it demonstrates the intense need for something or someone to trust.[20] Oedipus as human sufferer,

---

[19] Cf. esp. 791–3 (Oedipus to Creon): ἆρ' οὐκ ἄμεινον ἢ σὺ τὰν Θήβαις φρονῶ; | πολλῶι γ', ὅσωιπερ κἀκ σαφεστέρων κλύω, | Φοίβου τε καὐτοῦ Ζηνός, ὃς κείνου πατήρ.

[20] At 1518–19, in his final speech on stage, Oedipus begins his solemn account of the secret on which the safety of Athens will depend with words which strongly recall

teacher and learner, blind yet a seer, suppliant and saviour, outsider
and indweller, can begin to fulfil the role of interpreter of the divine
will. But what he can offer is (at best) a tentative reading of the
meaning of his fate, and (as the play goes on to show) he can curse
as well as bless: the little word can destroy as well as transform.

The end of the play, full of the 'wonder' of what has happened to
Oedipus (1586, 1665), indeed offers something for the audience to
trust, and to pray for, but in more literal terms it proves nothing. It
leaves gaps in the 'evidence' for Oedipus' coming role as protector
of Athens: the divine voice is reported, not heard; Theseus has seen
the mystery, but his response is enigmatic (he is seen covering his
eyes, and saluting both earth and heaven, 1654–5). The play ends in
the daughters' desire for lamentation, which is forbidden, and in
hopes of resolving conflict between their brothers, which we know
will not be fulfilled. The Chorus may sing of 'confirmation' ($\kappa\hat{\nu}\rho\sigma$,
1779) but the audience is left with unresolved[21] plain words.

REFERENCES

BRUHN, E. (1899, repr. 1963), Sophokles erkl. von Schneidewin/Nauck,
   Anhang (Berlin).
BURIAN, P. (1974), 'Suppliant and Saviour: Oedipus at Colonus', Phoenix:
   408–29.
BURKERT, W. (1985), 'Opferritual bei Sophokles. Pragmatik–Symbolik–
   Theater', AU 28. 2: 5–20.
CAMPBELL, L. (1879), Sophocles, i, 2nd edn. (Cambridge).
EARP, F. R. (1944), The Style of Sophocles (Cambridge).
EASTERLING, P. E. (1967), 'Oedipus and Polynices', PCPhS 13: 1–13.
——(1973), 'Repetition in Sophocles', Hermes, 101: 14–34.
——(1996), 'Weeping, Witnessing and the Tragic Audience: Response to
   Segal', in Silk (1996), 173–81.
——(1979), 'Constructing the Heroic', in Pelling (1997), 21–37.
EDMUNDS, L. (1981), 'The Cults and the Legend of Oedipus', HSCP 85:
   221–38.
——(1996), Theatrical Space and Historical Place in Sophocles' 'Oedipus at
   Colonus' (Lanham, Md.).

this speech: ἐγὼ διδάξω, τέκνον Αἰγέως, ἅ σοι | γήρως ἄλυπα τῇδε κείσεται πόλει.
Oedipus' further stress on 'teaching', and his claim that his words will be 'without
the pains of old age' address the same need for permanently reliable guidance.

[21] For different readings of the end of the play see e.g. Winnington-Ingram (1980:
275); Seaford (1994: 134–5); Easterling (1996: 174–7).

GOHEEN, R. F. (1951), *The Imagery of Sophocles' Antigone* (Princeton).

HENRICHS, A. (1976), 'Despoina Kybele', *HSCP* 80: 253–86.

—— (1983), 'The "Sobriety" of Oedipus Misunderstood', *HSCP* 87: 87–100.

—— (1993), 'The Tomb of Aias and the Prospect of Hero Cult in Sophokles', *Cl. Ant.* 12: 165–80.

—— (1994), 'Anonymity and Polarity: Unknown Gods and Nameless Altars at the Areopagos', *ICS* 19: 27–58.

KEARNS, E. (1989), *The Heroes of Attica* (*BICS* Supplement 57; London).

KNOX, B. M. W. (1957, repr. 1998), *Oedipus at Thebes* (New Haven and London).

—— (1964), *The Heroic Temper* (Berkeley, Los Angeles, and London).

KIRKWOOD, G. M. (1958), *A Study of Sophoclean Drama* (Ithaca, NY).

KRUMMEN, E. (1993), 'Athens and Attica: *Polis* and Countryside in Tragedy', in Sommerstein *et al.* (1993), 191–217.

LLOYD-JONES, Sir H. (1994), Sophocles, *Antigone, The Women of Trachis, Philoctetes, Oedipus at Colonus*, Loeb Classical Library (Cambridge, Mass.).

LLOYD-JONES, Sir H., and WILSON, N. (1990), *Sophoclea* (Oxford).

LONG, A. A. (1968), *Language and Thought in Sophocles* (London).

MACKAIL, J. W. (1910), *Lectures on Greek Poetry* (London).

MOORHOUSE, A. C. (1982), *The Syntax of Sophocles* (Leiden).

PADEL, R. (1992), *In and Out of the Mind* (Princeton).

PELLING, C. (ed.) (1997), *Greek Tragedy and the Historian* (Oxford).

SEAFORD, R. (1994), *Reciprocity and Ritual* (Oxford).

SEALE, D. (1982), *Vision and Stagecraft in Sophocles* (London).

SEGAL, C. (1981), *Tragedy and Civilization: An Interpretation of Sophocles* (Cambridge, Mass.).

SILK, M. S. (1996) (ed.), *Tragedy and the Tragic* (Oxford).

—— (1996), 'Tragic Language', in Silk (1996: 458–96).

SOMMERSTEIN, A. H. *et al.* (1993) (eds.), *Tragedy, Comedy and the Polis* (Bari).

WINNINGTON-INGRAM, R. P. (1980), *Sophocles: An Interpretation* (Cambridge).

7

Sophocles' *Antigone* and Herodotus Book Three

STEPHANIE WEST

When we were blessed with a new Oxford Classical Text of Sophocles in 1990, many readers surely looked first to see whether the editors had voted for or against the authenticity of the passage (*Ant.* 904–20) where Antigone defends her commitment to Polynices with reasoning more at home in another kind of story, where a wife, being given the opportunity to save one of the three men closest to her, husband, son, or brother, opts for the last, thus so disconcerting the ruler who has given her this dreadful choice that she gains more than was originally offered. Goethe robustly expressed his objections to the passage;[1] but our editors were unmoved by his hope that a competent scholar would show these lines to be interpolated.[2] While few passages in Sophocles can have

I am greatly indebted to Maria Brosius, Martin Ostwald, and Chris Pelling for learned and constructive criticism of an earlier version of this chapter, which has also benefited greatly from the editor's comments and from those of other participants in the *Sophoclea*.

[1] 'So kommt in der Antigone eine Stelle vor, die mir immer als ein Flecken erscheint, und worum ich vieles geben möchte, wenn ein tüchtiger Philologe uns bewiese, sie wäre eingeschoben und unächt. Nachdem nämlich die Heldin im Laufe des Stückes die herrlichsten Gründe für ihre Handlung ausgesprochen und den Edelmuth der reinsten Seele entwickelt hat, bringt sie zuletzt, als sie zum Tode geht, ein Motiv vor, das ganz schlecht ist und fast ans Komische streift' (J. P. Eckermann, *Gespräche mit Goethe*, 28 March 1827). A. L. Jacob (1821) had already attempted the demonstration desiderated. Less often quoted is the criticism of Jean Jacques Barthélemy, *Voyage du jeune Anacharse* (1788), iv. 65 f.: 'Est-il de la dignité de la tragédie ... qu'Antigone nous assure qu'elle sacrifieroit un époux, un fils à son frère, parce qu'elle pourroit avoir un autre fils et un autre époux; mais qu'ayant perdu son père et sa mère, elle ne sauroit remplacer le frère dont elle est privée?'

[2] See further Lloyd-Jones (1971: 117), Lloyd-Jones and Wilson (1997: 81).

been so much debated,[3] virtually everyone is agreed that there is a
direct relationship between these lines and the argument which
Herodotus ascribes to the wife of the Persian grandee Intaphernes
(3. 119), condemned to death (unjustly) as the leader of a
conspiracy against Darius, in which the king assumed the complicity
of other family members. The assumption of Clement of Alexandria
(*Strom.* 6. 19. 3) that Herodotus was indebted to Sophocles has not
found many adherents;[4] an overwhelming majority of scholars,
whether or not they hold the passage to be authentic, see in
Antigone's speech a borrowing from Herodotus. But other indica-
tions of the influence on this play of Herodotus' narrative of the
reigns of Cambyses and Darius have not received much attention.

I must first forestall a chronological objection. The date of the
Antigone's production is uncertain, but it is generally thought to be
early.[5] Most scholars, indeed, are more reluctant than our honorand
to sacrifice the tradition mentioned in the ancient hypothesis
associating the play with the revolt of Samos (441–439); to its
success, we are told, it was thought that Sophocles owed his election
as *strategos* in Samos (a slightly odd phrase).[6] Herodotus cannot
have completed his work before the outbreak of the Peloponnesian
War, since he refers to the killing of the Spartan envoys (7. 137. 1–
3), dated by Thucydides to late summer 430 (2. 67. 1–4).[7] Of course
'publication' was a less datable event before the invention of

---

[3] See further below, n. 87.

[4] But see Erbse (1992: 70 f.). I have not come across any proponent of a further
theoretical possibility, a common source.

[5] Cf. Lloyd-Jones (1994: 8 f.): 'With great caution one may say that *The Women of
Trachis* and *Antigone* seem to show a less advanced technique than the other plays,
and may be comparatively early.'

[6] φασὶ δὲ τὸν Σοφοκλέα ἠξιῶσθαι τῆς ἐν Σάμωι στρατηγίας εὐδοκιμήσαντα ἐν τῆι
διδασκαλίαι τῆς Ἀντιγόνης (Arph. Byz. *Hypoth.* (*TrGF* 4. 45 T 25)); cf. *Vita* 9,
στρατηγὸν εἵλοντο . . . ἐν τῶι πρὸς Ἀναίους πολέμωι. It is obviously tempting to guess
that the source of this detail was the *Epidemiai* of Ion of Chios (*FGrHist* 392 F 4–23).
Command in the aftermath of the Samian rebellion may be meant; as general 'in
Samos' Sophocles would have been involved in the campaign against the rebel
oligarchs based on the mainland at Anaea. See further Lewis (1988), who argues
persuasively for 438 as the date of production. For the sceptic's case see Reinhardt
(1947: 241 = Eng. trans. 1979: 240).

[7] He may of course have continued work for some years longer. Fornara (1981)
has made a strong case for supposing that Herodotus' literary activity extended
throughout the Archidamian War (against the objections raised to Fornara (1971)
by Cobet (1977)).

printing, and there was no reason why Herodotus should not have presented the earlier parts of his work as lectures (or even let them circulate in written form) before he had finished the later. Indeed his insistence on the historicity of the Constitutional Debate (3. 80. 1; 6. 43. 3) is most naturally construed as a response to audience reaction, implying that the section of his history which particularly concerns us had been tried out on the public before he composed his final version.

That some part, at least, of his work was favourably received by the Athenian public in the mid-440s is indicated by the entry in Eusebius (*Chron.* Ol. 83. 4) for 445/4, where it is recorded that Herodotus was honoured by the Athenian *boule* after reading his books to them.[8] There is no obvious reason to reject the substance of this testimony, though we should be cautious about combining it with the information given by Plutarch (*De Herod. mal.* 26, 862 B), citing the Athenian historian Diyllus (*c.*357/6–297/6), that on the motion of Anytus Herodotus received from Athens a gift of ten talents (*FGrHist* 73 F 3);[9] as remuneration for a visiting lecturer the sum is disproportionately generous (notwithstanding some observations highly complimentary to Athens (1. 60. 3; 7. 139)),[10] and if this information is to be trusted, some further service to this city should be inferred.

We have what is generally taken to be evidence of friendship between Sophocles and the historian in the opening of an epigram

---

[8] Ἡρόδοτος ἱστορικὸς ἐτιμήθη παρὰ τῆς Ἀθηναίων βουλῆς ἐπαναγνοὺς αὐτοῖς τὰς βίβλους.—well discussed by Ostwald (1991). We do not of course know the source of Eusebius' date; is it to be connected with the foundation of Thurii? The story that the young Thucydides was reduced to tears at one of Herodotus' readings (*Vita Marcellini* 54) cannot be regarded as reliable evidence.

[9] ὅτι μέντοι δέκα τάλαντα δωρεὰν ἔλαβεν (sc. Ἡρόδοτος) ἐξ Ἀθηνῶν, Ἀνύτου (Turnebus: ἀντὶ τοῦ codd.) τὸ ψήφισμα γράψαντος, ἀνὴρ Ἀθηναῖος οὐ τῶν παρημελημένων ἐν ἱστορίαι, Δίυλλος εἴρηκεν. As Jacoby (1913: 229) observes, the name Anytus is not so uncommon that there is any call to identify this man (*PA/APF* 1321; Ἄνυτος (1) Fraser and Matthews) with the Anytus who prosecuted Socrates (*PA/APF* 1324; (4) Fraser and Matthews). Diyllus' father Phanodemus is very likely to be identified with the Atthidographer. 'außer dem Faktum der Zahlung ist nichts sicher . . . es bleibt also auch fraglich, in welchem Zusammenhang die Angabe stand (Lob der Geschichtsschreibung in einem Prooimion? . . .). die Urkunde, die er nicht im Wortlaut gab, mag der Sohn des Atthidographen selbst gefunden haben' (Jacoby ad loc.).

[10] A similar gift to Pindar amounted to merely 10,000 drachmae (= $1\frac{2}{3}$ talents) (Isocr. 15. 166).

quoted by Plutarch (*An seni* 3, *Mor.* 785 B), ὠιδὴν Ἡροδότωι τεῦξεν
Σοφοκλῆς ἐτέων ὢν πέντ' ἐπὶ πεντήκοντα,[11] evidently a dedication
intended to accompany the song. Jacoby was sceptical about the
identification of the addressee with the historian;[12] but though it
would be rash to use these lines as a basis for much further
argument, the identification must be judged highly probable. That
these two writers were in some ways of a rather similar cast of mind
is indisputable. But personal relationships are rather peripheral to
my argument. What is clear is that Herodotus' work had made a
notably favourable impression at Athens in the 440s, and though,
even if Herodotus repeated his lectures to many different groups,
only a small proportion of Sophocles' audience can have heard him,
the content of his lectures may well for a time have been the talk of
the town. Though we should not look for subtle effects of intertextuality, it is not unreasonable to suppose that Sophocles expected
some members of his audience to be reminded of Herodotus'
account of Persian affairs under Cambyses and Darius.

We may start with Creon's vehement rejection of Teiresias'
warning (1037–44):

> κερδαίνετ' ἐμπολᾶτε τἀπὸ Σάρδεων
> ἤλεκτρον, εἰ βούλεσθε, καὶ τὸν Ἰνδικὸν
> χρυσόν· τάφωι δ' ἐκεῖνον οὐχὶ κρύψετε,
> οὐδ' εἰ θέλουσ' οἱ Ζηνὸς αἰετοὶ βορὰν
> φέρειν νιν ἁρπάζοντες ἐς Διὸς θρόνους,
> οὐδ' ὡς μίασμα τοῦτο μὴ τρέσας ἐγὼ
> θάπτειν παρήσω κεῖνον· εὖ γὰρ οἶδ' ὅτι
> θεοὺς μιαίνειν οὔτις ἀνθρώπων σθένει.

Creon resorts to a familiar gambit for discounting unwelcome
counsel from a seer;[13] his indiscriminate accusations of corruption[14]

---

[11] Fr. eleg. 5 West, Page *Epigrammata Graeca* 466–7; Sophocles was born in the
490s, most probably 496 or 495.

[12] Jacoby (1913: 233 f.). With his usual fair-mindedness he notes that the name
Herodotus is rare at Athens; the *Lexicon of Greek Personal Names* ii gives no datable
examples from Attica before the Hellenistic period. It was correspondingly much
favoured in Ionia and the islands: 'Es wäre garnicht unmöglich, daß die Ode an
einen schönen ionischen Knaben ging . . . Wer gern phantasiert, könnte daraufhin
den von Sophokles bewunderten Knaben in Chios, von dem Ion (Athen.
xiii.503F ff.) so niedlich erzählt, H. nennen.'

[13] Cf. *Od.* 2. 185 ff., S. *OT* 387 ff.

[14] A constant preoccupation in the earlier part of the play (cf. 221 f., 293–303,

display anachronistically wide horizons, coterminous to west and east with Darius' view of his empire.[15] For the heroic world the utmost east is normally represented by Colchis and the Phasis[16] or by the Ethiopians.[17] By the land of the Indoi we should understand not the subcontinent as a whole but the northwestern region, not easily demarcated from Scythia, now belonging mainly to Pakistan, which came to the knowledge of the Greeks as a result of the extension of the Persian Empire to the Indus valley;[18] even as a legendary country it apparently attracted little interest before Alexander's campaigns. Apart from a questionable reference (quite possibly an intrusive gloss) in Aeschylus (*Suppl.* 284), as Pelasgus perplexedly attempts to place Danaus' exotic-looking daughters,[19] this is the only mention of India in extant tragedy. The country does not figure in Io's wanderings (A. *Pr.* 786 ff.) or in Dionysus' itinerary (E. *Ba.* 13 ff.); more remarkably, Indians find no place in Aeschylus' catalogue of Persian forces (*Pers.* 12 ff., 302 ff.).[20] This is not just a matter of tragic convention; there is no reference to India in extant Pindar and Aristophanes. Even more significantly, Indians are absent from the wide-ranging ethnography of Hippocrates, *Airs, Waters, and Places.*[21] Thus, while Lydian wealth was a

311–14, 325 f.), but illogical now that Antigone has made it clear that she acted on her own and had no accomplices. On Athenian attitudes to bribery see Harvey (1985).

[15] Cf. DPh (Apadana foundation text; Kent 1953: 136–7): 'Saith Darius the King: this is the kingdom which I hold, from the Scythians who are beyond Sogdiana, thence unto Ethiopia; from Sind, thence unto Sardis which Ahuramazda the greatest of the gods bestowed upon me.'

[16] Cf. E. *Hipp.* 3 (with Barrett's n.).

[17] Cf. *Od.* 1. 22–4; on Ethiopians in tragedy see Hall (1989: 140 ff.).

[18] See further Karttunen (1989), esp. 32–59, 65–79. The study of the Indo-Achaemenid provinces is still a relatively neglected area, and classical sources, in particular Herodotus, remain immensely important; see further Vogelsang (1990).

[19] Ἰνδῶν τ᾽ ἀκούω νομάδας ἱπποβάμοσιν | εἶναι καμήλοις ἀστραβιζούσας χθόνα: Ἰνδῶν Hartung: Ἰνδούς M: Ἰνδάς anon., τοίας Tucker, τοίους Musgrave; the word must be considered in relation to the complex of problems presented by 284 f.

[20] 'The tour of the imperial lands in the parodos (33–58) reveals an accurate assessment of the extent of the dominions. Only three and a half lines are however devoted to the whole of the eastern empire (52–5), which probably indicates that Aeschylus knew little about it except the name Babylon itself' (Hall (1989: 93)). This rather short measure should probably be taken to reflect what Aeschylus might suppose to be meaningful to his audience rather than the limitations of his own geographical knowledge.

[21] See further Karttunen (1989: 86–8).

commonplace, Indian gold in the mid-fifth century was strikingly untraditional.[22]

The innovation has attracted little attention, and scholars have been wary of postulating the direct influence of Herodotus' account of the Indian contribution to the Persian exchequer (3. 94. 2).[23] Yet there were not many channels by which information about India might reach Athens, and Herodotus' report is certainly impressive, forming the climax to his survey (89–94) of the administrative and financial organization established by Darius: Ἰνδῶν δὲ πλῆθός τε πολλῶι πλεῖστόν ἐστι πάντων τῶν ἡμεῖς ἴδμεν ἀνθρώπων καὶ φόρον ἀπαγίνεον πρὸς πάντας τοὺς ἄλλους ἑξήκοντα καὶ τριηκόσια τάλαντα ψήγματος. The figure 360 is clearly stereotypical.[24] India, the twentieth satrapy, is El Dorado, and gold is central to Herodotus' description of this (very vaguely demarcated) region, some rather random remarks about Indian manners and customs[25] being organized round a description of the collection of the gold from the lairs of ant-like creatures somewhat larger than foxes.[26]

The association between India and gold, then, would seem natural

---

[22] Easterling (1985: 6) refers very briefly to this passage to illustrate the way in which tragedy veils references to coinage: 'There is an ultimate Homeric model—Achilles' rejection of all the wealth of Egypt (*Il.* ix. 381 ff.)—and the choice of electrum and gold gives Creon's words an appropriately heroic feeling, but the reference to Sardis must owe something to the theme of Lydian luxury made familiar by the lyric poets.' But the region itself, under the name Maeonia, was already associated with luxury in Homer (cf. esp. *Il.* 4. 141).

[23] Cf. Riemann (1967: 4 n. 4): 'Die Nennung von Ἰνδικὸν χρυσόν (*Ant.* 1038) scheint nur zu allgemein, um als Anspielung auf H.3. 94 aufgefasst werden zu können'; similarly Cobet (1977: 25).

[24] On Herodotus' use of typical numbers, see further Fehling (1989: 216–39).

[25] We get an impression of a primitive region; unusually, Herodotus has nothing to say about religious practice. His belief (104. 2) that dawn here is the hottest time of day (a natural corollary of a flat earth) undermines our confidence in his Indian information in general. On the deficiencies of his account see Dihle (1990: 59 f.).

[26] The identification of these animals as marmots (first suggested, so far as I know, by C. Ritter in 1833) has long been popular. Herodotus does not claim to have seen the creatures (unlike the skeletons of flying snakes, 2. 75) and some linguistic confusion may reasonably be postulated. A strong case has recently been made for interpreting Herodotus' account in the light of the traditional mining practices of Dardistan, where the energetic burrowing of marmots in the gold-bearing soil was regularly exploited; see further Peissel (1984). Unfortunately, Peissel's work was apparently not known to Karttunen (1989), but there is much of value in the latter's discussion (171–8) of the gold-digging 'ants' and their north-eastern counterparts, the gold-guarding griffins (3. 116. 1; 4. 13. 1; 27).

and obvious to anyone who had paid attention to Herodotus' account of Darius' reorganization of the Empire.[27] But we have already been made aware of this eastward extension of Persian hegemony when Indians are introduced as representatives of the far east to confront Greeks in Darius' famous study of funerary practice (3. 38. 3–4): Darius, at the heart of his empire, summons some of his Ionian subjects, and asks them how much they would take to eat their deceased fathers. (The form of the question, ἐπὶ κόσωι χρήματι, nicely fits Darius' reputation for undue concentration on Treasury questions (cf. 89. 3; 1. 187).) No price is high enough. He then puts a similar question to Indians for whom, we are told, such funerary cannibalism was regular practice, asking them what sum would induce them to undertake cremation, a suggestion which they reject with uninhibited expressions of horror.[28]

Both groups take for granted a duty to dispose of their dead kin in accordance with custom; the obligation to protect the corpse from casual dissolution is not questioned. Herodotus here explores ideas which must have occurred to many Greeks who associated with foreigners, whether they went abroad as traders or mercenaries or had dealings with foreign visitors (or, for that matter, talked to their own slaves). Funerary ritual lies outside the realm of rational gesture,[29] but so long as we do not have to face an alternative to familiar custom, conformity to traditional practice goes unquestioned. Contact with equally well-established foreign customs, or problems about performing familiar rituals in an alien environment (where, for example, it is hard to excavate graves or shortage of fuel precludes cremation) must stimulate discussion about what is truly

[27] It is easy to overlook his failure to tell us how this region was added to the Persian Empire. What little he has to say on this topic amounts to a footnote to his digression on the relationship between the continents in his narrative of Darius' Scythian campaign (4. 44).

[28] We note that Darius needs an interpreter to communicate with the Indians but not, it seems, with Greeks; the detail reinforces our sense of the alienness of this eastern group, a remote people of whom next to nothing is known.

[29] It might be thought appropriate to refer here to the evidence for Neanderthal burials, above all the well-known 'flower burial' from Shanidar Cave (in the Zagros Mountains of north-eastern Iraq), on which see Solecki (1972), esp. 154–92. But this interpretation of the data can be questioned: see further Sherratt (1997: 282 n. 28), who argues that what have been interpreted as Neanderthal burials may simply be 'sleeping hollows', filled with insulating vegetation, whose occupants died there. I am indebted to Dr Sherratt for warning me against uncritical acceptance of a most appealing hypothesis.

essential, required by religion or by common humanity, and what is
optional. This episode particularly well illustrates Edith Hall's view
of the importance of comparative ethnography as a catalyst for the
development of the philosophers' distinction between nature and
nomos.[30]

Indians and Greeks must have met in the great cities of the
Persian Empire, and were no doubt brought together in the army,
but we shall seek in vain for other direct evidence from the classical
period for any exchange of ideas.[31] Some scepticism as to the
historicity of Darius' seminar may be in order. Herodotus, in
common with most ethnographers and travellers, was generally
interested in funerary customs,[32] and it is his way to enliven abstract
analysis by presenting it as a confrontation between representatives
of different views (as, most famously—we might even say, pro-
grammatically—in Solon's interview with Croesus (1. 29–33).[33] The
Persian king, lord of all men from the rising to the setting of the
sun,[34] is pre-eminently suitable as the organizer of such an enquiry
because of the vast extent and ethnic diversity of his dominions.[35]
He summons subjects from its westward and eastward limits and
confronts whose who practise the familiar rite of cremation with a
group[36] for whom the utterly alien (and indeed mythical) custom of
funerary cannibalism is hallowed by tradition.[37] This is not asso-

[30] Hall (1989: 185).

[31] Cf. Karttunen (1989: 48–50).

[32] Persian 1. 140. 1; Babylonian 1. 198; Egyptian 2. 85–90; Ethiopian 3. 4;
Scythian 4. 71–3; Libyan 4. 190; Thracian 5. 8; Spartan royal 6. 58.

[33] So too with the conversation of Hecataeus with the Theban priests (2. 143; see
further West 1991: 145–54) and Demaratus' discussion with Xerxes contrasting
Greek and Persian attitudes (7. 101–4; 209). For further anecdotes concerning
representatives of different cultures see Fehling (1989: 193 f.). Should we see in this
mannerism the influence of tragedy?

[34] Aeschin. 3. 132. For a fine discussion of this phrase, which 'never lost the mark
of its origin in Oriental grandiloquence' see Fraenkel (1957: 451) (I owe this
reference to Jasper Griffin).

[35] Similarly the fabulously wealthy king of Lydia may direct a comparative
investigation into the reliability of oracles (1. 46–9). These enquiries, like Psamme-
tichus' experiment to establish the original language (2. 2), suggest intellectual pipe-
dreams inspired by sophistic discussion.

[36] It is interesting that the Kallatiai are specified here (cf. 97. 2, Hecat. *FGrHist*
1 F 298), whereas in Herodotus' ethnographic section the practice is associated with
the Padiaioi (99), who, however, are specifically said to kill their aged relatives as
well as eat them.

[37] See further Karttunen (1989: 197–202). There is very little satisfactory evidence

ciated with India by any other source, though Herodotus also ascribes the custom to the savage Massagetae (1. 216)[38] and to the Issedones (4. 26); but these peoples were not at Darius' command. In Darius himself we see an unprejudiced chairman, to whom both practices are equally alien.

Persian funerary custom consisted in secondary interment after exposure of the corpse to birds of prey. This practice was once very widespread; in our own islands it is clearly evidenced from a neolithic tomb at Isbister on the Orcadian island of South Ronaldsay, and it still continues in Tibet and among the Parsees.[39] The procedure is, and so far as our evidence goes, normally was, as ceremonious and well regulated as other forms of funerary ritual, special sites being set aside for the exposure of the corpse and frequented by raptors. However, what Herodotus has to say about Persian practice suggests that he thought it was rather casual (1. 140. 1): it is said that the corpse of a male Persian is not interred πρὶν ἂν ὑπ' ὄρνιθος ἢ κυνὸς ἑλκυσθῆι. The last few words express what to Greek ideas represents the ultimate horror. More relevant to the present purpose, since we are focusing on Book 3, are his recollections (3. 12) of the battlefields of Pelusium (525) and Papremis (459) where, he would have us believe, the skeletons of Egyptians and Persians alike had simply been left undisturbed for decades:

τῶν γὰρ ὀστέων κεχυμένων χωρὶς ἑκατέρων τῶν ἐν τῆι μάχηι ταύτηι πεσόντων (χωρὶς μὲν γὰρ τῶν Περσέων ἔκειτο τὰ ὀστέα, ὡς ἐχωρίσθη κατ' ἀρχάς, ἑτέρωθι δὲ τῶν Αἰγυπτίων), αἱ μὲν τῶν Περσέων κεφαλαί εἰσι ἀσθενέες οὕτω ὥστε, εἰ θέλοις ψήφωι μούνηι βαλεῖν, διατετρανέεις, αἱ δὲ τῶν Αἰγυπτίων οὕτω δή τι ἰσχυραί, μόγις ἂν λίθωι παίσας διαρρήξειας . . . εἶδον δὲ καὶ ἄλλα ὁμοῖα τούτοισι ἐν Παπρήμι τῶν ἅμα Ἀχαιμένεϊ τῶι Δαρείου διαφθαρέντων ὑπὸ Ἰνάρω τοῦ Λίβυος.

for cannibalism as customary and socially approved anywhere (survival cannibalism under stress conditions is another matter); the practice is regularly associated with others, either in the past or at a distance. See further Arens (1979).

[38] Cf. *Dissoi Logoi* 2. 14: Μασσαγέται δὲ τὼς γονέας κατακόψαντες κατέσθοντι, καὶ τάφος κάλλιστος δοκεῖ ἦμεν ἐν τοῖς τέκνοις τεθάφθαι· ἐν δὲ τᾶι Ἑλλάδι αἴ τις ταῦτα ποιήσαι, ἐξελαθεὶς κακῶς κα ἀποθάνοι ὡς αἰσχρὰ καὶ δεινὰ ποιέων.

[39] On the Isbister tomb see further Hedges (1984: 133–42); the extraordinary vulture shrine of Çatal Hüyük in Central Anatolia (c.6150 BC) shows the great antiquity of the practice; see further Mellaart (1967: 166–8, pls. 45, 48, 49). Classical authors associate it particularly with Central Asia (cf. e.g. Cic. *Tusc.* 1. 108, Strab. 517, 714); for contemporary Tibetan practice see e.g. Seth (1983: ch. 14); Buckley and Strauss (1986: 58 f.); for illustrations N. Tomašević (1981: pls. 98-100).

Since Egypt was under Persian rule it was reasonable to infer that such neglect was perfectly acceptable to the authorities, deeply abhorrent as it must be to Egyptian feeling. The alert reader may view this chapter with some scepticism, but its manifold improbabilities[40] do not affect its relevance to my argument. Darius ought to have found edification in the intensity of feeling displayed by the representatives of Greek and Indian funerary custom. The defiance of normal Greek ideas expressed in Creon's welcome to the eagles, with its outrageous suggestion that they might bring carrion to the throne of Zeus, is thus associated with a callousness towards the disposal of the dead which Herodotus regards as characteristically Persian.[41]

Darius' funerary investigation forms a rather artificially contrived coda to the first section of Herodotus' narrative of Cambyses' activity in Egypt; it is appended to a catalogue of his offences against Egyptian religion (an indictment not confirmed by Egyptian evidence), irrefutable evidence in Herodotus' view that Cambyses was mad (38. 1–2): πανταχῆι ὦν μοι δῆλά ἐστι ὅτι ἐμάνη μεγάλως ὁ Καμβύσης· οὐ γὰρ ἂν ἱροῖσί τε καὶ νομαίοισι ἐπεχείρησε καταγελᾶν. This chapter, reiterating νόμος and its cognates,[42] well illustrates the centrality of this concept in Herodotus' anthropology;[43] he sees

[40] See further Asheri ad loc., Fehling (1989: 28–30).

[41] Creon's welcome to the eagles (1040 f.) embodies an interesting irony if we are aware that where excarnation is effected by birds of prey their alacrity in disposing of a corpse is a good omen, even apparently being regarded as a sign of the merits of the deceased; but 5th-cent. Athenians can hardly have known this. On this point the reports of medieval western travellers (well discussed by Greenblatt (1991: 44 f.)) can be confirmed by more recent observation: see e.g. Wu (1930: 210): 'After three days . . . if the body has been completely devoured by wild beasts the friends of the dead man rejoice, knowing him to have been pure of heart. If the corpse is found still unconsumed there is great distress, and the lamas are called upon to make intercession for one so stained by sin that even the wild beasts reject his flesh. The priests call upon the beasts and birds of the desert to do their work quickly, crying out that the dead man is less sinful than they think him. Eventually the flesh is consumed and all are at peace.'

[42] νόμος 5 ×, νομίζω 3 ×, νόμαιον 1 ×.

[43] Cf. Burkert (1990: 4): 'Er verfügt über einen Begriff, der das jeweils Fremde an seinem Ort in seinem Zusammenhang erfassbar macht und Andersartigem als gleichwertig an die Seite stellt: Nomos.'; 22–4. (However, we notice a more judgemental attitude at 1. 199. 1, in his account of Babylonian sacred prostitution.) On the connotations of nomos in the 4th cent. see Ostwald (1969: 20–54); he draws attention (35) to Herodotus' extensive use of νόμος/-οι for the social practices current among a given group, which frequently amount to a characteristic

clearly that any attempt to disturb the norms regarded as valid and binding by a given society must be expected to meet with strenuous resistance, and that those who bear rule over others should hesitate to impose their own ideas in place of what is customary. In this we have what might be regarded as an uncontroversial administrative commonplace. But Herodotus is not thinking merely in terms of human relationships; when his narrative returns to Cambyses, we see that divine forces have been provoked, as he himself comes to realize, by his sacrilegious folly (64. 3–5).

The centrality of νόμος for the *Antigone* is unarguable.[44] Creon himself acknowledges, even before catastrophe has struck, (1113 f.):

> δέδοικα γὰρ μὴ τοὺς καθεστῶτας νόμους
> ἄριστον ἦι σώιζοντα τὸν βίον τελεῖν.

His punishment comes through the natural reactions of his son and wife, though Tiresias leaves us in no doubt that divine forces are at work. Cambyses and Creon are alike made to realize their folly in violating religious custom, and each must face the knowledge that he is responsible for his lack of a successor.[45] The resemblance between these two arrogant rulers brought low is surely more than an interesting coincidence. It has been suggested before that Sophocles' presentation of Creon is indebted to Herodotus' Cambyses,[46] who is made to embody much of the potential for evil inherent in one-man rule, and has thus played a leading role in the creation of the stereotype of the Oriental autocrat, the royal megalomaniac whose whims affect the well-being of vast subject populations.

It is worth looking in some detail at Herodotus' portrayal of

differentiating it from other groups, and notes a contrast with the rarity of this use of the word in Hippocrates, *Airs, Waters, and Places*.

[44] See further Ostwald (1980: 148–61).

[45] Hdt. 3. 66.2, cf. 32. 4; 34. 5; the report of Eurydice's death (*Ant.* 1305) reminds us that Creon has already sacrificed his elder son to secure Thebes' safety (cf. 993, 1058, 1191, 1250).

[46] Cf. Schmid and Stählin (1934: 356 n. 5) on Creon: 'Der Typus des gebrochenen ὑβριστής erinnert an den Xerxes des Aischylos und ist von Herodotus in seinem Kambyses wieder aufgenommen.' See further Podlecki (1966), who concludes, 'Creon is a character whom Herodotus would certainly have recognized, and perhaps even helped to create.' Much the same point is made by those who comment on the affinity between Creon and the tyrant as adumbrated by Otanes in the Constitutional Debate (3. 80), e.g. Funke (1966: 38 n. 46).

Cambyses.[47] He tells us nothing about this king before his departure
for Egypt in 525 and makes little of his achievement in adding Egypt
to the Persian Empire, though the conquest of this vast, strange
country must have presented many serious problems to an invader.
His account of Cambyses is thus a catalogue of failure and crime.
But at least up to the capitulation of Memphis he presents him
acting in accordance with legitimate and reasonable motives.[48]
However, a serious deterioration is observable when Cambyses
moves to Sais (the capital of the last dynasty), where he subjects
to an outrageous and prolonged assault the mummy of the recently
deceased philhellenic pharaoh Amasis;[49] the contravention of both
Egyptian and Persian custom is emphasized (16. 1–4). Amasis had
died some months before the battle of Pelusium; Cambyses'
violation of his corpse cannot be palliated by reference to the
exhilaration of a victor fresh from the battlefield triumphing over
an opponent who might have treated him similarly. Cambyses
rejoices in pursuing a vendetta beyond the grave; there were to be
further insults to the dead (37. 1).

Even more offensive to Egyptian sentiment was of course his
mockery and wounding of the Apis bull (27–9).[50] To this outrage

[47] On Herodotus' presentation of Cambyses see further Hofmann and Vorbichler
(1980), Brown (1982), Munson (1991). On Cambyses in Egypt see Ray (1988; 254–
61, 275). It is customary to note that Cambyses' reduction of Egyptian temple
revenues must have created a prejudice against him in the priestly circles to whom
Herodotus would have us believe that he owed his information. But he must have
learnt much about Egypt during his time in Samos (see below, pp. 131 f.), and his
Samian sources (anti-Persian, anti-tyrant aristocrats) would have presented a
tradition hostile to Cambyses; misconception may have contributed to Greek
demonization of this king. Athenian support for Egyptian nationalism would have
predisposed Athenians to take a black view of the conqueror responsible for the loss
of Egypt's independence. Darius had no interest in seeking to rehabilitate Cambyses,
and Persian informants would hardly have helped to counteract Greek and Egyptian
hostility.

[48] His test of Psammenitus' endurance (14 f.) leaves an unfavourable impression,
but hardly more so than the experimental spirit in which Herodotus describes Cyrus
consigning Croesus to the funeral pyre (1. 86. 3).

[49] Amasis qualifies for Herodotus' only use of the adjectve φιλέλλην (2. 178. 1);
Graeco-Egyptian relations were unusually close during his reign and he was clearly
popular with the Greeks (cf. 172–4). 'Amasis is a striking departure from Herodotus'
usual conception of royal character, and his shrewd, vulgar, easy-going disposition is
a natural protection against the besetting sin of ὕβρις' (Lattimore (1939: 32)).

[50] As has been clear since Mariette's excavation of the Serapeum, Cambyses'
sacrilegious assault must be a malicious fabrication; see Asheri ad loc. It may well

the Egyptians ascribed Cambyses' madness (30. 1): Καμβύσης δέ, ὡς λέγουσι Αἰγύπτιοι, αὐτίκα διὰ τοῦτο τὸ ἀδίκημα ἐμάνη, ἐὼν οὐδὲ πρότερον φρενήρης. But Herodotus had already described him as ἐμμανής . . . καὶ οὐ φρενήρης (25. 2) and ὑπομαργότερος (29. 1), connecting his insanity with epilepsy (33); he reminds us repeatedly that Cambyses was mad (34. 1; 35. 1, 4; 37. 1; 38. 1). The diagnosis has no exculpatory force, but conveys the difficulty of coming to terms with a disregard of normally accepted standards apparently beyond understanding.

Cambyses' madness is variously displayed in his dealings with his kin and his courtiers. Having arranged for the murder of his brother Smerdis by Prexaspes, his most trusted subordinate (30), he causes the death of his pregnant sister/wife, who had provoked his wrath by a rather Aesopian attempt at advice (31–2). In explaining the background to this incestuous union, Herodotus stresses that it was then contrary to Persian custom (31. 2): οὐδαμῶς γὰρ ἐώθεσαν πρότερον τῆισι ἀδελφεῆισι συνοικέειν Πέρσαι. Cambyses, having fallen in love with his sister, displayed a disconcerting regard for legality; the royal judges, being consulted, were unable to produce any law positively commanding the king to marry his sister, but drew Cambyses' attention to a law permitting the king to do as he pleased (31. 2–5). We observe the pressure of fear on those who should guide and counsel the king, as the Persian judges supply *ad hominem* legislation. The horror with which the Greeks regarded the acceptability of incestuous marriages in Persian society is reflected in the notion that the practice originated with the passion of a mad king; Cambyses' insanity had enduring consequences for his people.[51]

In what follows we see Cambyses' appallingly frivolous attitude towards human life combined with a dangerous failure to value his

have been invented as a crime fitting the punishment seen in Cambyses' inglorious death; see further n. 57. No Egyptian source confirms the Greek tradition of Cambyses' offences against Egyptian religion, and we should treat with caution the testimony of the Jewish community of Elephantine, writing in 408 to the Persian governor of Judaea, that, while their temple suffered no harm, the Persian invaders overthrew all the temples of the gods of Egypt (see Cowley 1923: no. 13, 13 f.). Similarly Xerxes' alleged offences against Babylonian religion appear to be the creation of Hellenic prejudice; see further Kuhrt (1988: 133–5).

[51] For arguments against the historicity of Cambyses' incestuous marriages see Brosius (1996: 45–7). For a survey of Greek and Roman animadversions see Chadwick (1979: 146 ff.).

subordinates' loyalty. Prexaspes, who had been trusted to dispose of the heir apparent, sees his son shot down, as Cambyses seeks to prove his sanity by an insane act; we may be reminded of Astyages' brutal killing of the son of his most trusted subordinate, Harpagus (1. 119), but Harpagus was undoubtedly guilty of a serious breach of orders. Twelve noble Persians are buried alive on a trivial charge, ἐπ᾽ οὐδεμιῆι αἰτίηι ἀξιοχρέωι (35). We look for someone to take a stand (the royal judges, as we have seen, are not prepared to offer any resistance), and Herodotus casts the aged Croesus for this kamikaze role (36. 1–2).[52] Cambyses does not take this warning well, and having failed to kill Croesus on the spot,[53] orders his execution. His servants, however, are used to his regretting ill-considered death-sentences, and decide to conceal Croesus for the moment, in the hope of a reward if the king changes his mind (36. 5). They are not motivated by goodwill or compassion or respect for disinterested courage, but simply by considerations of personal profit; as often in Herodotus, we observe how autocracy corrupts its servants.[54] But their scheme is counter-productive; when, shortly afterwards, Cambyses, as they had hoped, regrets his decision and learns with delight of Croesus' survival,[55] they are killed for disobeying orders.[56]

[52] Delphic tradition may be credited with the idea that Croesus did not perish at the fall of Sardis, but hardly with the invention of his second career as a pensioner at the Persian court, which looks like a demythologization of his translation to the land of the happy Hyperboreans as related by Bacchylides (3. 57 ff.); his transformation from blinded tyrant to wise counsellor suits Herodotus' narrative purposes so well that we should suspect that it originated with him. See further Lattimore (1939), Burkert (1985), Fehling (1989: 207), Erbse (1992: 22 n. 20).

[53] The only case in Herodotus of an assault on an adviser.

[54] Cf. Harpagus' devious behaviour (1. 108 f.). The Persian abhorrence of falsehood (1. 138. 1, cf. 136. 2) should be taken with a grain of salt (cf. Darius on 'necessary lies', 3. 72. 4).

[55] Aly (1921: 21, 87) may have been over-optimistic in claiming this episode as evidence that the *Story of Ahiqar* was already known to the Greeks; there are significant differences between Croesus' case and Ahiqar's, and the motif of the counsellor unjustly condemned to death, concealed, and finally reinstated long flourished where autocrats were familiar (cf. Thompson (1955–8: K. 2101, P. 111); Aarne and Thompson (1961: 922A)). For an early 19th-cent. case from Egypt see Curzon (1849: 64 f.). I wonder whether Sophocles had this passage of Herodotus in mind at *El.* 62–4 (where many have seen an allusion to Herodotus' account of Zalmoxis (4. 95); these possibilities are not of course mutually exclusive); I hope to discuss this motif at greater length elsewhere.

[56] Cf. 8. 118. 4; the same principle is involved in Astyages' punishment of Harpagus (1. 118–19).

Having returned briefly to the theme of Cambyses' violations of Egyptian religious custom (37), he concludes this section of narrative with Darius' funerary seminar, before turning to events in Samos and their background (39–60). We are thus left in suspense for some time before we learn how Cambyses died (64–6). His fatal accident is clearly to be understood as retribution for his assault on the Apis bull (64. 3): τρωματισθεὶς . . . κατὰ τοῦτο τῆι αὐτὸς πρότερον τὸν τῶν Αἰγυπτίων θεὸν Ἄπιν ἔπληξε.[57] Now at last he comes to his senses (64. 5): ἐσωφρόνησε. Herodotus does not suggest that this is simply an Egyptian view of Cambyses' end; he sees here evidence that the king had provoked divine wrath, not merely offended the religious sensitivities of one among the many nations comprising the Persian Empire. To Greeks (and no doubt to other foreigners) Egyptian religion, and above all, the prominence afforded to zoolatry, appeared perplexingly alien, if not downright repugnant,[58] and the mockery of the Apis cult which Herodotus puts in Cambyses' mouth (29. 2) surely expresses ideas which had occurred to many Greeks in the age of the sophists. But Egyptian religious custom deserved particular respect by reason of its extraordinary antiquity;[59] odd as it might seem, it had certainly stood the test of time. Cambyses' fate offers a grim warning to intolerant rationalists that, while men's conceptions of the divine are all more or less equally inadequate,[60] God is not mocked.

In Cyrus Herodotus showed us an attractive picture of monarchy, when the king is a father to his people (cf. 89. 3).[61] In Cambyses we see the antithesis, an autocrat who is χαλεπός . . . καὶ ὀλίγωρος, whose ὕβρις provides most of the material for Otanes' argument in favour of democracy (3. 80), which is almost entirely an indictment

[57] Little light is thrown on Cambyses' end by Darius' enigmatic statement 'Cambyses died his own (natural) death' (DB I 11, as translated by Schmitt (1991: 51)), though certainly this is consistent with Herodotus' account of death by blood-poisoning from an accidentally inflicted wound (64. 3–5; 66. 1–2), and the way in which the *akinakes* was worn would have made this type of injury very easy; of course, the malefactor's death from a self-inflicted accident is a familiar folktale motif. See further Walser (1983), Friedrich (1973: esp. 116–20).

[58] See further Smelik and Hemelrijk (1984).

[59] Which Herodotus immensely exaggerates (2. 142 f.).

[60] Cf. Herodotus' explanation for an apparent deficiency in his account of Egyptian religion (2. 3. 2): τὰ μέν νυν θεῖα τῶν ἀπηγημάτων οἷα ἤκουον, οὐκ εἰμὶ πρόθυμος ἐξηγέεσθαι, ἔξω ἢ τὰ οὐνόματα αὐτῶν μοῦνον, νομίζων πάντας ἀνθρώπους ἴσον περὶ αὐτῶν ἐπίστασθαι.

[61] Surely we are meant to recognize a Homeric reminiscence: cf. *Od.* 2. 46 f., 5. 6 f.

of monarchy.[62] Greek ideas about the megalomania of the Kings of Kings may at times have been fostered by a failure to distinguish institutional from individual characteristics.[63] But Cambyses' ὕβρις as Herodotus presents it as a more personal quality, manifested in a terrifying combination of malice, paranoid policies, and a sadistic sense of humour, and supported by an unassailable conviction that neither Persian nor Egyptian norms need count for anything. His career starkly illustrates the worst features of monarchy where Amurath to Amurath succeeds. The dreadful consequences of the exercise of supreme authority by a psychopath demonstrate the lack of any legitimate means of controlling the ruler under an autocratic system. The Sultan's will (or whim) is paramount.

Such is the style which we see Creon adopt in the *Antigone*. First impressions are always important; we should bear in mind that the costume of a king on the tragic stage resembled noble Persian dress.[64] Creon gives the Chorus no chance to greet him; he does not wait for a spontaneous expression of respect and confidence.[65] With his brusque ἄνδρες (162) we should contrast the forms of address by Antigone (ὦ γᾶς πατρίας πολῖται, 806; ὦ πόλεως πολυκτήμονες ἄνδρες, 843–4; Θήβης οἱ κοιρανίδαι, 940) and Tiresias (Θήβης ἄνακτες, 988). The autocratic tone of his opening speech (162–210) is unmistakable. Just before his entry the Chorus had prayed that strife might be forgotten as the city united in victory celebrations (150–4), but the register of Creon's speech is that of war; it is important for his authority that a commander-in-chief should still be deemed necessary.[66] Eteocles' state funeral, potentially an occasion for uniting the city in patriotic thanksgiving, receives signific-

---

[62] It is interesting to compare the objections to monarchy voiced in vain by the prophet Samuel in response to popular demand for a king (1 Sam. 8: 11–20). In view of Herodotus' insistence that Greek scepticism about the historicity of the Constitutional Debate is unjustified (80. 1; 6. 43. 3), it is worth considering the possibility that Herodotus knew of (but could not himself read) a dialogue in some Near Eastern language (most likely Aramaic) comparing various forms of government within a Persian frame-story; Job sufficiently demonstrates that the use of the dialogue form was not a Greek monopoly.

[63] See further Sancisi-Weerdenburg (1993: 151).

[64] See further Alföldi (1955); for Creon thus attired see Steiner (1984: pls. 1, 2). On 'metaphorical orientalism' in tragic costume for figures without oriental connections, denoting transgressive behaviour, see Sourvinou-Inwood (1997; 281–7).

[65] Cf. Müller's note on 162–74.

[66] As Antigone's use of στρατηγός (8) in her opening speech indicates.

antly fewer lines (194–7) than the ban on any funerary ritual (including lament) for Polynices (198–206):

τὸν δ' αὖ ξύναιμον τοῦδε, Πολυνείκη λέγω,
ὃς γῆν πατρώιαν καὶ θεοὺς τοὺς ἐγγενεῖς
φυγὰς κατελθὼν ἠθέλησε μὲν πυρὶ
πρῆσαι κατ' ἄκρας, ἠθέλησε δ' αἵματος
κοινοῦ πάσασθαι, τοὺς δὲ δουλώσας ἄγειν,
τοῦτον πόλει τῆιδ' ἐκκεκήρυκται τάφωι
μήτε κτερίζειν μήτε κωκῦσαί τινα,
ἐᾶν δ' ἄθαπτον καὶ πρὸς οἰωνῶν δέμας
καὶ πρὸς κυνῶν ἐδεστὸν αἰκισθέν τ' ἰδεῖν.

Creon makes no pretence of consulting the elders, but takes for granted their acceptance of the edict which he has already issued. His first official act as ruler of Thebes seems an unpromising start to tackling the problems of a state recovering from the horrors of fratricidal war; it would have been reassuring to hear of provision for the wounded and for the orphans, widows, and elderly parents of the men slain while defending their city.

Self-promotion is the keynote of his speech;[67] its reiterated first-person pronouns are picked up by the emphatic position of σοί in the Chorus' reply (211–14):

σοὶ ταῦτ' ἀρέσκει, παῖ Μενοικέως, ποεῖν
τὸν τῆιδε δύσνουν καὶ τὸν εὐμενῆ πόλει·
νόμωι δὲ χρῆσθαι παντί, τοῦτ' ἔνεστί σοι
καὶ τῶν θανόντων χὠπόσοι ζῶμεν πέρι.

We sense a reluctant acceptance of some curtailment of political discussion during the present emergency. The following sticho-mythia reveals a polite lack of enthusiasm on the elders' part; the readiness with which they shortly suggest that the covering of

[67] In its egocentricity and self-advertisement, its confidence of divine support and its relish for the physical humiliation of a defeated enemy Creon's speech has much in common with the *Res Gestae* of Near Eastern rulers (as has the Aeschylean Agamemnon's opening speech (*Ag.* 810–54)). Many Greeks must have been familiar with texts like that of the Bisitun inscription; Darius wanted that *apologia* for his rule to be widely read (DB IV 70), and it is more likely than not that there was a Greek version. In any case, many Greeks must have had a working knowledge of Aramaic, the language of commerce and diplomacy. Darius' letter to Gadatas (Meiggs and Lewis 1988: no. 12), if indeed it is authentic, shows how quite a short text could convey an impression of Persian absolutism.

Polynices' corpse is prompted by the gods implies positive dis-
approbation of Creon's edict. (278 f.):

> ἄναξ, ἐμοί τοι μή τι καὶ θεήλατον
> τοὔργον τόδ' ἡ ξύννοια βουλεύει πάλαι.

Creon's furious reaction to this attempt to warn him, culminating in
his fearsome threats to the watchman, discourages them from
further attempts at guidance until Tiresias' intervention has brought
Creon's folly home to him. The scholion on 872 well characterizes
their attitude for much of the play: οἱ τοῦ χοροῦ τὸ μὲν ἔργον τῆς
παιδὸς ἐπαινοῦσιν, οὐ μὴν δὲ θαρσοῦσιν καὶ τὴν γνώμην τοῦ βασιλέως
διελέγχειν ὡς μοχθηράν.[68] As we saw at Cambyses' court, autocracy
stifles the free expression of opinion, and those who by reason of
their proven loyalty and experience should be the ruler's trusted
advisers may be tempted to appear to approve when they should
protest.

Creon betrays an attitude unlikely to appeal to a democratically
minded audience in the imagery with which he speaks of restive
elements among the citizens (289–92):

> ἀλλὰ ταῦτα καὶ πάλαι πόλεως
> ἄνδρες μόλις φέροντες ἐρρόθουν ἐμοὶ
> κρυφῆι, κάρα σείοντες, οὐδ' ὑπὸ ζυγῶι
> λόφον δικαίως εἶχον, ὡς στέργειν ἐμέ.[69]

It becomes increasingly clear that not only has he lost sight of the
distinction between citizens and slaves (οὐ γὰρ ἐκπέλει / φρονεῖν μέγ'
ὅστις δοῦλός ἐστι τῶν πέλας, 478 f.)[70] but he is more concerned with
his personal authority than with the interests of the state. The first
suggestion that he should no longer take the city's support for
granted comes from Antigone (504–5):

---

[68] See further Petersmann (1982).

[69] Cf. Funke (1966: 35): 'Wie man ὡς στέργειν ἐμέ 292 auch grammatisch
auffasst, jedenfalls stellt Kreon selbst, in dem er die πόλεως ἄνδρες in seine Schranken
zurückweist, eine Diskrepanz zwischen seinem Willen und dem Urteil der Stadt über
diesen fest.'

[70] We may be reminded of the Persian application even to nobles of a term
rendered in Greek by δοῦλος (e.g. Xen. Anab. 1. 9. 29; 2. 5. 38 (of the king's own
brother), Hdt. 7. 39. 1), a usage which seemed to the Greeks (who were not alert to
the connotations of ba(n)daka) to epitomize the absolutist character of Persian rule:
see further Missiou (1993).

τούτοις τοῦτο πᾶσιν ἁνδάνειν
λέγοιμ' ἄν, εἰ μὴ γλῶσσαν ἐγκλήιοι φόβος.

Haemon, to whom it falls to play the part of the counsellor whose advice goes unheeded, confirms Antigone's diagnosis (690 ff., 733), provoking from Creon a response which reveals the hollowness of his earlier display of high principles (175–90):[71] πόλις γὰρ ἡμῖν ἁμὲ χρὴ τάσσειν ἐρεῖ; (734), ἄλλωι γὰρ ἢ 'μοὶ χρή με τῆσδ' ἄρχειν χθονός; (736), οὐ τοῦ κρατοῦντος ἡ πόλις νομίζεται; (738).[72] 'Für den Gewaltmenschen Kreon ist . . . der Staat das Eigentum des Königs, ebenso wie dies für die Grosskönige der Fall war.'[73] The more clearly Creon is displayed as an autocrat, the more our thoughts should turn to Persia, for fifth-century Greeks the paradigm of despotism. His conviction, manifested in his repeated accusations of corruption, that Antigone's action reflects a conspiracy to dethrone him, despite her insistence on the claims of *pietas*, well exemplifies one aspect of Otanes' typical monarch (80. 4): φθονέει γὰρ τοῖσι ἀρίστοισι περιεοῦσι καὶ ζώουσι . . . διαβολὰς δὲ ἄριστος ἐνδέκεσθαι. The characteristic is clearly illustrated by Darius' reaction to Intaphernes' hot-headed response to what he wrongly supposed to be unjustified interference with his well-earned privileges (118–19); Darius at first suspects a conspiracy by the six grandees who had joined him in disposing of Smerdis, and when this suspicion proves groundless, infers a plot involving Intaphernes' sons and τοὺς οἰκηίους πάντας. When Antigone adverts to the lack of any restraint on tyranny (506–7), ἀλλ' ἡ τυραννὶς πολλά τ' ἄλλ' εὐδαιμονεῖ κἄξεστιν αὐτῆι δρᾶν λέγειν θ' ἃ βούλεται, we may compare the authorization which the royal judges supplied to Cambyses (31. 5): τῶι βασιλεύοντι Περσέων ἐξεῖναι ποιέειν τὸ ἂν βούληται; compare Otanes' criticism (80. 3) κῶς δ' ἂν εἴη χρῆμα κατηρτημένον μουναρχίη, τῆι ἔξεστι ἀνευθύνωι ποιέειν τὰ βούλεται; Cambyses condemned men to death with little or no consideration, and might indeed regret his decision (14. 11–15. 1; 36);[74] Ismene

---

[71] Cited with approval by Demosthenes (19. 247). (I find rather surprising the view of Knox (1968: 749) that 'The story that Sophocles owed his election as strategos to the success of the "Antigone", whether true or not, makes little sense except in the light of the lasting impression made by Creon's speech.')

[72] Creon's attitude corresponds to the Danaids' view of monarchy (A. *Suppl.* 370–5) marked out as unhellenic by Pelasgus' reaction (esp. 397 ff.).

[73] Alföldi (1955: 31).

[74] Not that Cambyses was the only Persian king over-hasty with capital sentences,

escapes a death-sentence only because of a choral reminder (770 f.).[75] In Creon's decision to change the prescribed penalty to perpetual immurement (773 ff.)[76] we should surely see an admission that he lacks the general support required for public stoning.[77] The sentence is treated as tantamount to burial alive (804–22, 847–52, 885–96, 1069),[78] for Herodotus a characteristically Persian practice (7. 114. 2 Περσικὸν δὲ τὸ ζώοντας κατορύσσειν, cf. 3. 35. 5).

This cruel and unusual punishment of course leaves scope for a change of heart on Creon's part. To the play's first audience it might have suggested a hope of rescue (as apparently in Euripides' *Antigone*[79]), a reasonable expectation for anyone familiar with stories of the grateful dead.[80] Sophocles did not invent Antigone,[81] but if we reject the end of the *Septem* the story of her protest cannot be traced back earlier,[82] and the plot almost certainly contains an

despite the principle singled out by Herodotus for commendation (1. 137. 1): τὸ μὴ μιῆς αἰτίης εἵνεκα μήτε αὐτὸν τὸν βασιλέα μηδένα φονεύειν, μήτε μηδένα τῶν ἄλλων Περσέων μηδένα τῶν ἑωυτοῦ οἰκετέων ἐπὶ μιῆι αἰτίηι ἀνήκεστον πάθος ἔρδειν ἀλλὰ λογισάμενος ἢν εὑρίσκηι πλέω τε καὶ μέζω τὰ ἀδικήματα ἐόντα τῶν ὑπουργημάτων, οὕτω τῶι θυμῶι χρᾶται; cf. 7. 194. 1–2.

[75] 'So leichtfertig geht Kreon mit dem Leben seiner Untertanen um, dass eine Unschuldige vernichtet worden wäre, wenn nicht ein Dritter ihn auf sein gleichgültig und fast unbewusst hingeworfenes Urteil aufmerksam gemacht hätte' (Funke 1966: 45).

[76] On the imprisonment of women in tragedy see Seaford (1990).

[77] Cf. Müller ad loc.: 'Steinigung bedeutet kollektive Verdammung und setzt der Idee nach voraus, dass das einheitliche sittliche Gefühl aller verletzt ist'; see also Fraenkel on A. *Ag.* 1616, Fehling (1974: 59–79). Creon also of course avoids a further problem about the disposal of Antigone's corpse.

[78] It is probably futile to try to establish precisely Sophocles' conception of Antigone's tomb; but if, as many have thought, he envisaged something like the 'Treasury of Atreus', the puzzling phrase ἁρμὸν χώματος λιθοσπαδῆ (1216) would very neatly fit the relieving triangle above the entrance.

[79] In which Antigone's story included marriage to Haemon and the birth of a child, Maeon; for a convenient summary see Webster (1967: 181–4). (*P. Oxy.* 3317 includes two lines ascribed to this play by Stobaeus, but seems not to add significantly to our knowledge, and the identification has in any case been questioned; see further Taplin (1988: 37 f.).)

[80] See Pease on Cic. *De div.* 1. 56; Aarne and Thompson (1961: 171–5, nos. 505–8); Thompson (1955–8: E. 341).

[81] Pherecydes (*FGrHist* 3 F 95) mentioned Antigone and Ismene as Oedipus' children by Euryganeia, whom he married after Jocasta's death.

[82] I assume that there is no need to rehearse the arguments against the authenticity of the final scene of the *Septem* (1004–78); the controversy is reviewed

unusually high proportion of free invention[83] even if Sophocles had some precedent for it. It should not surprise us if he found inspiration in Herodotus' narrative.

We return now to the passage where there is virtually no dispute about the debt to Herodotus; the question is whether it was incurred by Sophocles or another. There is little doubt that Antigone's strange reasoning at 904 ff. derives from the argument which Herodotus puts in the mouth of Intaphernes' wife (3. 119) who, being offered a reprieve for one of her male kin, so surprises Darius by the explanation with which she supports her choice of her brother that he grants her the life of her eldest son as well. We have here an adaptation of a widely attested type of story; though Herodotus offers the oldest extant version of this migratory motif,[84] it does not quite fit a situation where the condemned are not on an equal footing, Intaphernes being the only one against whom there are any grounds for suspicion, and it would be quite irrational for Darius to spare the man he regards as the ringleader of a conspiracy. As this type of story is usually told, the wife's unexpected answer brings a reprieve for all three men;[85] success, after all, is usually the result won by intelligence and a cool head in such tales, but we ought to understand that the woman concerned is taking a calculated risk rather than frankly expressing her priorities.[86]

at some length by Zimmermann (1993: 98–112)—without, however, any reference to the discussion in Hutchinson (1985).

[83] See further Petersmann (1978), Zimmermann (1993: 59–137), esp. 115–37. Gantz (1993: 521) well says that 'The intensely confrontational nature of the whole situation might seem to argue that it was created for drama.'

[84] I deliberately avoid the term 'folktale', which is too imprecise to be helpful.

[85] See further Aarne and Thompson (1961: no. 985); Thompson (1955–8: P. 253.3); *Enzyklopädie des Märchens* (Berlin and New York, 1979), ii. 861–4 ('Bruder eher als Gattin oder Sohn gerettet' (U. Masing): a very popular theme in Ireland), Bremmer (1997: 97–9).

[86] I do not want to suggest that a preference for brother over husband or son is in itself incredible: contrast Edith Durham's experience in Albania early in this century (Durham (1909; 90): 'Here, as in Montenegro, women tell you frankly that, of course, a woman loves her brother better than her husband. She can have another husband and another child, but a brother can never be replaced. Her brother is of her own blood—her own tribe'; the wording might suggest the influence of Antigone's speech, but the point is illustrated by a tale of a woman who slew her husband and two sons in vengeance for her brother. ('The book literally reeks of blood', alleged a reviewer who judged that the author devoted too much attention to vendettas.)

The difficulties presented by Antigone's adoption of this reasoning are too well known to need rehearsing;[87] μακρά μοι νεῖσθαι κατ' ἀμαξιτόν. If the passage had not been cited as genuine by Aristotle, its authenticity would surely now find few to defend it (though once successful interpolation on this scale is admitted the implications for the text of the play in general are disturbing). Goethe's objection[88] can of course be partly met: throughout the play Antigone's arguments may be best regarded as rationalizations of a conviction taken for granted as a fundamental moral principle normally treated as beyond question; we need not be disturbed by some inconsistency with the grounds for her action previously offered. But her reasoning here is simply irrelevant to her situation, while her oddly legalistic calculation hardly suggests the emotional turmoil which, natural enough in her circumstances, would make consideration of the relevance of her words seem misplaced. Paradoxically, these inconcinnities argue in favour of authenticity. An actor who wanted to increase the impact of this speech would hardly have chosen to elaborate this unemotional ordering of priorities irrelevant to Antigone's actual situation. It is surely much more likely that the passage was composed when Intaphernes' ingenious wife's ratiocination was still a novelty which appealed to the poet.[89] The strikingly similar phraseology is put to a very different purpose. Intaphernes' wife makes a real choice among living kin; Antigone's selection is quite hypothetical. In her case there is a certain irony in the common-sense observation that, both her parents being dead, she could never have another brother; we are reminded that she and her siblings were the products of an incestuous union, Herodotean material has been reworked to serve a very different purpose,[90] and the effects of intertextuality contribute powerfully to a passage my discussion of which, if it is to remain within reasonable limits, can

---

[87] It is almost impossible to keep up with publication on this passage. From the last decade I may single out Sourvinou-Inwood (1987–8), Zimmermann (1993: 128 n. 40); Rösler (1993), Riemer (1991: 12, 44–8); Neuberg (1990), Müller (1996).

[88] See above, n. 1.

[89] So Nussbaum (1986: 64), Bees (1993: 239).

[90] Similarly with the other conspicuous Sophoclean debt to Herodotus, IC 337–41, the material is used to very different effect; what in Herodotus (2. 35) is presented as an ethnographical curiosity in Sophocles takes on connotations of oriental decadence and perversion. (This point is well made by C. W. Müller (1996: 210), though he regards both passages as additions by the younger Sophocles (the poet's grandson).)

hardly avoid the charge of superficiality. This conspicuous borrowing from Herodotus needs to be viewed in relation to the less obvious (because better integrated) evidence of pervasive Herodotean influence on this play.

Herodotus' dovetailing of Persian history with Samian (and within that, Corinthian) leads to a remarkable accumulation of monarchs whose pride precedes an exemplary fall. Polycrates and Periander confirm the image of autocracy memorably displayed in Cambyses, and partially paralleled in what Herodotus records about the other Persian kings. The juxtaposition with Persian events might be thought to lend an exaggerated importance to Samian affairs, but certainly it is fundamental to the narrative structure of this book. Persian and Samian strands are closely integrated,[91] and skilful cross-cutting increases the narrative tension. Was this already his manner of presentation in the 440s?

Certainly his Samian material should have held a powerful appeal for an Athenian audience. Trouble between Athens and Samos was clearly brewing for some time before the outbreak of the revolt,[92] and Persian interest in the island's affairs could not be ignored. If the ten talents' honorarium reported by Diyllus is excessive as a lecturing fee, we might consider the possibility that the Boule recognized Herodotus' value as a source of Samian intelligence over and above what he recorded for us to read; he had, after all, spent some time there when he was in exile as a young man,[93] and whatever doubts we may entertain about his travels in general, his Samian material was clearly got at first hand. If we bear in mind the importance of Persian gold in fifth-century Greek politics in general[94] and in particular the support which Pissuthnes, the

[91] The linkage via Otanes, the conqueror of Samos (3. 141–9), is particularly noteworthy. The differences between Herodotus' narrative of the circumstances surrounding Darius' accession (3. 68–72) and the version given in the Bisitun inscription centre on Otanes (of whom Phaedymie is merely an extension). See further Brosius (1996: 52–64).

[92] See Shipley (1987: 113–22).

[93] *Suda* s.v.: μετέστη δ' ἐν Σάμωι διὰ Λύγδαμιν τὸν ἀπὸ Ἀρτεμισίας τρίτον τύραννον γενόμενον Ἁλικαρνασσοῦ. See further Mitchell (1975: 75–91); Shipley (1987: 69–109). Herodotus was clearly aware that some might judge his treatment of Samian affairs disproportionately lengthy (3. 60. 1, 4). Note, too, an interesting ambiguity at 3. 139. 1: μετὰ δὲ ταῦτα Σάμον βασιλεὺς Δαρεῖος αἱρέει, πολίων πασέων πρώτην Ἑλληνίδων καὶ βαρβάρων. I strongly suspect that much of his information about Cambyses in Egypt derived from Samian sources.

[94] See further Lewis (1989).

satrap of Sardis, could offer to disaffected Samians,[95] Creon's anachronistically wide horizons (1037–9) assume a remarkable contemporary relevance.[96] Indeed, many in Sophocles' audience must have seen an aptness not immediately apparent to us in the opening words of his speech (1033 f.), πάντες ὥστε τοξόται σκοποῦ τοξεύετ' ἀνδρὸς τοῦδε. The imagery is common enough to pass without comment. But it gains a heightened significance if we are aware that Persian darics, produced specifically for circulation in Asia Minor, to pay currency-oriented mercenaries, acquired the nickname 'archers' from the mural-crowned archer represented on their obverse.[97] Here, with the monarch as the image of the Empire, we have the iconography of the autocracy to which Creon's style of government appears to aspire.

REFERENCES

AARNE, A., and THOMPSON, S. (1961), *The Types of the Folktale* (Helsinki).

ALFÖLDI, A. (1955), 'Gewaltherrscher und Theaterkönig', in K. Weitzmann (ed.), *Late Classical and Mediaeval Studies in Honor of Albert Mathias Friend, Jr.* (Princeton), 15–55.

ALY, W. (1921), *Volksmärchen, Sage und Novelle bei Herodot und seinen Zeitgenossen* (Göttingen; repr. 1969).

ARENS, W. (1979), *The Man-Eating Myth* (New York).

ASHERI, D. (1990), *Erodoto, Le Storie: Libro III, La Persia* (Rome).

BADIAN, E. (1993), *From Plataea to Potidaea: Studies in the History and Historiography of the Pentecontaetia* (Baltimore and London).

BARRETT, W. S. (1964), *Euripides: Hippolytos* (Oxford).

BARTHÉLEMY, J. J. (1788), *Voyage du jeune Anacharse en Grèce dans le milieu du 4ᵉ siècle avant J.C.* (Paris).

BEES, R. (1993), *Zur Datierung des Prometheus Desmotes* (Stuttgart).

BREMMER, J. (1997), 'Why did Medea Kill her Brother Apsyrtus?', in James J. Clauss and Sarah Iles Johnston (eds.), *Medea: Essays on Medea in Myth, Literature, Philosophy and Art* (Princeton), 83–100.

BROSIUS, M. (1996), *Women in Ancient Persia 559–331 BC* (Oxford).

BROWN, T. S. (1982), 'Herodotus' Portrait of Cambyses', *Historia* 31: 387–403.

---

[95] Thuc. 1. 115. 4 f. On Pissuthnes' activity see Badian (1993: 33 f., 38 f.).

[96] Cf. Lewis (1988: 41 n. 22).

[97] Plut. *Ages.* 15, *Art.* 20. On the extent to which Achaemenid coinage was familiar in 5th-cent. Athens see Miller (1997), 73 f.

BUCKLEY, M., and STRAUSS, R. (1986), *Tibet: A Travel Survival Kit* (Victoria and Berkeley).

BURKERT, W. (1985), 'Das Ende des Kroisos: Vorstufen einer Herodoteischen Geschichtserzählung', in C. Schäublin (ed.), *Catalepton: Festschrift f. Bernhard Wyss* (Basel), 4–15.

—— (1990), 'Herodot als Historiker fremder Religionen', in Nenci (1990): 1–32.

CHADWICK, H. (1979), 'The Relativity of Moral Codes: Rome and Persia in Late Antiquity', in W. R. Schoedel and R. L. Wilken (eds.), *Early Christian Literature and the Classical Intellectual Tradition: In Honorem Robert M. Grant* (Paris), 135–64.

COBET, J. (1977), 'Wann wurde Herodots Darstellung der Perserkriege publiziert?', *Hermes* 105: 2–27.

COWLEY, A. E. (1923), *Aramaic Papyri of the Fifth Century B.C.* (Oxford).

CURZON, R. (1849), *Visits to Monasteries in the Levant* (London).

DIHLE, A. (1990), 'Arabien und Indien', in Nenci (1990): 41–61.

DURHAM, E. (1909), *High Albania* (London).

EASTERLING. P. E. (1985), 'Anachronism in Greek tragedy', *JHS* 105: 1–10.

Enzyklopädie des Marchens (1975–), ed. K. Ranke (Berlin and New York).

ERBSE, H. (1992), *Studien zum Verständnis Herodots* (Berlin and New York).

FEHLING, D. (1974), *Ethologische Überlegungen auf dem Gebiet der Altertumskunde* (Munich).

—— (1989), *Herodotus and his 'Sources': Citation, Invention and Narrative Art* (Leeds).

FORNARA, C. W. (1971), 'Evidence for the Date of Herodotus' Publication', *JHS* 91: 25–34.

—— (1981), 'Herodotus' Knowledge of the Archidamian War', *Hermes* 109: 149–56.

FRAENKEL, E. (1950), *Aeschylus: Agamemnon* (Oxford).

—— (1975⁷), *Horace* (Oxford).

FRASER, P. M., and MATTHEWS, E. (1987–), *A Lexicon of Greek Personal Names*: ii, *Attica*, ed. M. J. Osborne and S. G. Byrne, 1994 (Oxford).

FRIEDRICH, W.-H. (1973), 'Der Tod des Tyrannen. Die poetische Gerechtigkeit der alten Geschichtsschreiber u. Herodot', *AuA* 18: 97–129 (= *Dauer im Wechsel: Aufsätze*, ed. C. J. Classen and U. Schindel (Göttingen, 1977), 336–75).

FUNKE, H. (1966), 'Κρέων ἄπολις', *AuA* 12: 29–50.

GANTZ, T. (1993), *Early Greek Myth: A Guide to Literary and Artistic Sources* (Baltimore and London).

GREENBLATT, S. (1991), *Marvellous Possessions: The Wonder of the New World* (Oxford).

HALL, E. (1989), *Inventing the Barbarian* (Oxford).

HARVEY, F. D. (1985), 'Some Aspects of Bribery in Greek Politics', in P. Cartledge and F. D. Harvey (eds.), *Crux: Essays Presented to G. E. M. de Ste Croix* (London), 76–117.

HEDGES, J. W. (1984), *Tomb of the Eagles* (London).

HOFMANN, L., and VORBICHLER, A. (1980), 'Das Kambysesbild bei Herodot', *AOF* 27: 86–105.

HUTCHINSON, G. O. (1985), *Aeschylus: Septem contra Thebas* (Oxford).

JACOB, A. L. (1821), *Sophocleae Quaestiones* (Warsaw).

JACOBY, F. (1913), 'Herodotos', *RE Supplement* 2: 205–520.

KARTTUNEN, K. (1989), *India in Early Greek Literature* (Helsinki).

KENT, R. G. (1953), *Old Persian: Grammar, Texts, Lexicon* (New Haven).

KNOX, B. M. W. (1968), review of Müller (1967), *Gnomon* 40: 747–60.

KUHRT, A. (1988), 'Babylonia from Cyrus to Xerxes', *CAH*² iv. 3a. 112–35.

LATTIMORE, R. (1939), 'The Wise Adviser in Herodotus', *CPh* 34: 24–35.

LEWIS, D. M. (1989), 'Persian Gold in Greek International Relations', *REA* 91: 227–35 (= *Selected Papers in Greek and Near Eastern History*, ed. P. J. Rhodes (Cambridge, 1997), 369–79).

LEWIS, R. G. (1988), 'An Alternative Date for Sophocles' Antigone', *GRBS* 29: 38–50.

LLOYD-JONES, H. (1971), *The Justice of Zeus* (Berkeley and Los Angeles).

—— (1994), *Sophocles* i: *Ajax, Electra, Oedipus Tyrannus* (Cambridge, Mass. and London).

—— and WILSON, N. G. (1997), *Sophocles: Second Thoughts* (*Hypomnemata* 100, Göttingen).

MEIGGS, R., and LEWIS, D. M. (1988), *A Selection of Greek Historical Inscriptions to the end of the Fifth Century B.C.* (Oxford).

MELLAART, J. (1967), *Çatal Hüyük* (London).

MILLER, M. C. (1997), *Athens and Persia in the Fifth Century BC: A Study in Cultural Receptivity* (Cambridge).

MISSIOU, A. (1993), '*ΔΟΥΛΟΣ ΤΟΥ ΒΑΣΙΛΕΩΣ*: The Politics of Translation', *CQ* 43: 377–91.

MITCHELL, B. M. (1975), 'Herodotus and Samos', *JHS* 95: 75–91.

MÜLLER, C. W. (1996), 'Die thebanische Trilogie des Sophokles und ihre Aufführung im Jahre 401. Zur Frühgeschichte der antiken Sophoklesrezeption u. der Überlieferung des Textes', *RhM* 139: 193–224.

MÜLLER, G. (1967), *Sophokles, Antigone* (Heidelberg).

MUNSON, R. V. (1991), 'The Madness of Cambyses (Hdt. 3. 16–38)', *Arethusa* 24: 43–65.

NENCI, G. (1990) (ed.), *Hérodote et les peuples non grecs* (*Entretiens Hardt* XXXV, Vandoeuvres-Geneva).

NEUBERG, M. (1990), 'Like a Woman: Antigone's Inconsistency', *CQ* 40: 54–76.

NUSSBAUM, M. (1986), *The Fragility of Goodness: Luck and Ethics in Greek Tragedy and Philosophy* (Cambridge).

OSTWALD, M. (1969), *Nomos and the Beginnings of Athenian Democracy* (Oxford).

—— (1980), *From Popular Sovereignty to the Sovereignty of Law* (Berkeley, Los Angeles, and London).

—— (1991), 'Herodotus and Athens', *ICS* 16: 137–48.

PEASE, A. S. (1920–3), *M. Tulli Ciceronis de divinatione libri duo* (Urbana).

PEISSEL, M. (1984), *The Ants' Gold: The Discovery of the Greek El Dorado in the Himalayas* (London).

PETERSMANN, H. (1978), 'Mythos u. Gestaltung in Sophokles' Antigone', *WSt* 12: 67–96.

—— (1982), 'Die Haltung des Chores in der Sophokleischen Antigone', *WSt* 16: 56–70.

PODLECKI, A. J. (1966), 'Creon and Herodotus', *TAPA* 97: 359–71.

RAY, J. D. (1988), 'Egypt 525–404 BC', *CAH* [2] iv. 3g. 254–86.

REINHARDT, K. (1947), *Sophokles*, 3rd edn. (Frankfurt am Main; trans. F. D. and H. Harvey, Oxford, 1979).

RIEMANN, K.-A. (1967), *Das herodoteische Geschichtswerk in der Antike* (Munich).

RIEMER, P. (1991), *Sophocles, Antigone—Götterwille u. menschliche Freiheit*, *AAWM* 12.

RÖSLER, W. (1993), 'Die Frage der Echtheit von Sophokles, *Antigone* 904–30 und die politische Funktion der attischen Tragödie', in A. H. Sommerstein, S. Halliwell, J. Henderson, and B. Zimmermann (eds.), *Tragedy, Comedy and the Polis* (Bari): 81–99.

SANCISI-WEERDENBURG, H. (1993), 'Political Concepts in Old-Persian Royal Inscriptions', in K. Raaflaub (ed.), *Anfänge politischen Denkens in der Antike: Die nahöstlichen Kulturen u. die Griechen* (Munich), 145–63.

SCHMID, W., and STÄHLIN, O. (1934), *Geschichte der griechischen Literatur*, i:2 (Munich).

SCHMITT, R. (1991), *The Bisitun Inscriptions of Darius the Great: Old Persian Text* (London).

SEAFORD, R. (1990), 'The Imprisonment of Women in Greek Tragedy', *JHS* 110: 76–90.

SETH, V. (1983), *From Heaven Lake* (London).

SHERRATT, A. S. (1997), 'Climatic Cycles and Behavioural Revolutions: The Emergence of Modern Humans and the Beginning of Farming', *Antiquity* 71: 271–87.

SHIPLEY, G. (1987), *A History of Samos, 800–188 B.C.* (Oxford).

SMELIK, K. A. D., and HEMELRIJK, E. A. (1984), ' "Who Knows not what Monsters Demented Egypt Worships?" Opinions on Egyptian Animal

Worship in Antiquity as Part of the Ancient Conception of Egypt',
ANRW II xvii. 4 (Berlin), 1852–2000.

SOLECKI, R. S. (1972), *Shanidar: The Humanity of Neanderthal Man*
(London).

SOURVINOU-INWOOD, C. (1987–8), 'Sophocles, Antigone 904–20: A Reading', *AION: sezione filologico-letteraria* 9–10: 19-35.

——(1997), 'Medea at a Shifting Distance: Images and Euripidean
Tragedy', in James J. Clauss and Sarah Iles Johnston (eds.), *Medea:
Essays on Medea in Myth, Literature, Philosophy and Art* (Princeton),
253–96.

STEINER, G. (1984), *Antigones* (Oxford).

TAPLIN, O. (1998), 'Narrative Variation in Vase-Painting and Tragedy: The
Example of Dirke', *Antike Kunst* 41: 33–9.

THOMPSON, S. (1955–8), *Motif-Index of Folk Literature* (Copenhagen).

TOMAŠEVIĆ, N. (1981), *Tibet* (London).

VOGELSANG, W. (1990), 'The Achaemenids and India', in H. Sancisi-
Weerdenburg and A. Kuhrt (eds.), *Achaemenid History* iv: *Centre and
Periphery: Proceedings of the Groningen 1986 Achaemenid History Work-
shop* (Leiden), 93–110.

WALSER, G. (1983), 'Der Tod des Kambyses', in H. Heinen, K. Stroheker,
and G. Walser (eds.), *Althistorische Studien Hermann Bengtson zum 70.
Geburtstag dargebracht* (Wiesbaden), 8–23.

WEBSTER, T. B. L. (1967), *The Tragedies of Euripides* (London).

WEST, S. (1991), 'Herodotus' Portrait of Hecataeus', *JHS* 111: 144–60.

WU, A. K. (1930), *Turkistan Tumult* (London).

ZIMMERMANN, C. (1993), *Der Antigone-Mythos in der antiken Literatur und
Kunst* (*Classica Monacensia* 5, Tübingen).

8

Sophocles' *Philoctetes*:
A Problem Play?

MALCOLM HEATH

> This play has a highly developed conceptual and intellectual
> dimension: here if anywhere in Greek tragedy we have a
> 'problem play'.

Thus Oliver Taplin.[1] I concur, and propose in this paper to examine
some of the problems which the *Philoctetes* poses. This may seem a
paradoxical aim, in view of the footnote attached to Taplin's statement: 'I am not persuaded that I should give up this sort of
interpretation by M. Heath's *The Poetics of Greek Tragedy* . . .'. But
although, on rereading that book a decade after publication, I can see
how readily it lends itself to misconstruction, it was in fact no part of
my aim in writing the book to persuade its readers that they should
give up that sort of interpretation. I wish therefore to begin by
clarifying some aspects of the view of Greek tragedy for which I was
then arguing. This will bring to light one important respect in which
that view is inadequate; acknowledging the defect will in turn lead us to
the larger questions that I have in mind in the present chapter. Readers
impatient of such prolegomena should feel free to proceed directly to
§II, where the discussion of the *Philoctetes* itself commences.

I. INTRODUCTION

Despite Taplin's footnote, *The Poetics of Greek Tragedy* (henceforth:
PGT)[2] does not maintain that the conceptual and intellectual

---

[1] Taplin (1987: 69, with n. 2). Cf. Blundell (1989: 184); '*Philoctetes* is the most
ethically complex of all Sophocles' plays.'

[See p. 138 for n. 2]

dimension of tragedy is necessarily underdeveloped, or that tragedies must be problem-free. Indeed, if the book's central contention is
correct, and tragedy aimed primarily at achieving an intense
emotional effect,[3] then we should surely expect tragedy to be
problem-prone. To achieve its powerful impact on the audience's
emotions tragedy typically deals with extreme situations, as Aristotle
was aware (*Poet.* 53ᵃ21 f.: ὅσοις . . . συμβέβηκεν ἢ παθεῖν δεινὰ ἢ
ποιῆσαι). Such abnormal situations may well prove recalcitrant to
the ethical norms and habits of judgement which are developed in
us through the experiences of everyday life. The highly emotive
situations in which tragedy specializes are therefore likely to be
morally problematic as well.

But there is an important distinction between the inherent
complexity of the situations with which tragedy deals and the
complexity of tragedy's dealings with those situations. It is possible
that tragedies sometimes deal with material that is inherently
complex and morally problematic in a way which circumvents or
conceals the problems. This is an eventuality which a critical
discourse as intellectually sophisticated and as problem-oriented
as our own may find it easy to mistake. In exploring the inherent
complexity of the situation, we may take it for granted that
reflections occasioned *by* the play are embedded *in* the play. But
that is not a valid inference. The intellectual complexity of our
engagement with a tragedy is not of itself evidence that the tragedy's
engagement with its material is equally complex.

In *PGT*, *Antigone* was read as unproblematic in this sense. There

---

[2] Heath (1987*a*), part of a doctoral thesis supervised by Hugh Lloyd-Jones, whose
scholarship remains a stimulus and inspiration.

[3] Taplin's note continues (1987: 69 n. 2): 'Though there is much of interest in
the book, it seems to me to have two basic flaws on the topic of "intellectualisation". One is the confusion of intellectual content with a "moral" or "message".
The other is the insistence that either the emotional or the intellectual dimension
must be primary and the other secondary.' *PGT* argues that one set of aims was *in
fact* primary, but it nowhere asserts or implies that one or other dimension *must* be
primary (i.e. that this conclusion is predetermined in principle, independently of
internal and external evidence for the tragedians' actual practice). As for the
intellectual content of tragedy, see e.g. *PGT* 38: 'It is certainly *possible* for a play
to be the vehicle at once of ideas and of emotions—indeed, in some sense it must be
so'; 71: 'To deplore the intellectualisation of tragedy is naturally not to deny that
there is an intellectual element in our response to tragedy. To deny that would be
absurd . . . Tragedy has intellectual (moral, theological, metaphysical) *content*, and
this content must be understood.'

are indeed profound moral complexities latent in the situation which Sophocles has dramatized, but in *PGT* I argued (73–7) that the way in which Sophocles has elected to present that material tends to pre-empt those complexities and to weight the audience's responses to the issues (or, more precisely, to the characters engaged with those issues). This interpretation would not, of course, be universally accepted, but I still find it broadly speaking persuasive. However, to take this view of *Antigone* is obviously not to claim that tragedy always treats inherently complex material in this way, or that tragedy never seeks to pose problems. Euripides' *Hecuba* could be cited as a tragedy designed to leave the audience with an unresolved set of conflicting responses. The unresolved moral complexity at the end of this play is one of the factors which create an effect that *PGT* describes as 'complex and disturbing' (83).[4]

The argument of *PGT* was not, therefore, that because it was primarily emotive in intent tragedy must be problem-free, nor that the simplification of moral problems in any one tragedy implies that all Greek tragedy works in the same way. Rather, the simplification of complex moral problems in so great a tragedy as *Antigone* is evidence that Sophocles' primary concern was not with the exploration of the situation's moral and intellectual complexities as such, but with its emotional impact; conversely, intellectual simplicity is not appropriate grounds for adverse judgement on a tragedy (at any rate, from the perspective of what tragedy aimed to achieve).[5] Greek tragedians sometimes evade the moral complexities of the material they have chosen to dramatize, and sometimes exploit them. Engagement with complexity in Greek tragedy is a variable; but a constant underlying that variation (*PGT* maintained) is the aim of providing an intense and satisfying pattern of emotional stimulus.

There is therefore no conflict in principle between the primacy of emotion for which *PGT* argued and the discernment of intellectual complexity in tragedy or the existence of 'problem plays'. But another dimension of tragedy needs to be considered which (it

---

[4] Cf. Heath (1987*b*), esp. 65 f.; on this view the play poses more of a problem than it does for the many interpreters who find Hecuba's revenge unproblematically bad. A good discussion in Mossman (1995: 164–203).

[5] The starting-point for *PGT*'s critique of intellectualization (37) was the adverse judgement of Aeschylus' *Persians* which Winnington-Ingram based on its lack of intellectual depth.

might be thought) is likely to have exercised a counterbalancing pressure towards the dissolution or resolution of problems: its didactic function. Here, too, *PGT* stands in need of clarification. Some have understood it as denying that tragedy was didactic. But its attempt to summarize and evaluate the evidence for a didactic strand in ancient thinking about tragedy, although it makes a number of cautionary observations, concludes not with a rejection of the didactic view of tragedy, but with its 'qualified approval' (*PGT* 47). Unfortunately, this point was not made with sufficient clarity or emphasis. An index of the extent to which *PGT* laid itself open to misunderstanding in this respect can be found in Croally's comment:[6]

Heath offers no evidence as to why tragedians should be blind to the cultural conditions in which they lived and worked. As regular members of the audience themselves, there seems no reason to doubt that they were aware that tragedy was expected to be paideutic.

True: *PGT* offers no such evidence. But the omission should occasion no surprise in an argument which concludes (and for the very reason Croally states) that tragedians were *not* blind to these conditions and *did* accommodate their work to the audience's didactic expectations.[7]

Croally and the author of *PGT* agree, therefore, in holding that tragedy had a recognized didactic function. They also agree in finding the ancient understanding of that didactic function disappointing and uninteresting.[8] Here we should part company with

[6] Croally (1994: 35).

[7] *PGT* 46: 'It might still be argued that a Greek tragedian would probably have shared in the common assumption that his work would have moral and educative effects on its audience, and would certainly have been aware of the didactic applications that the audience would be inclined to make outside the theatre; that he would therefore probably have recognised a responsibility to ensure that his work had a good effect and provided edifying material for didactic application; and that didactic intentions therefore cannot be excluded as rigorously as the foregoing argument implies. This seems to me correct . . .'. As well as overlooking this further step in an ongoing analysis, Croally gives a thoroughly muddled report of the discussion which precedes it.

[8] *PGT* 47: 'when a Greek spoke of the poet as teacher he meant something that is, from our point of view, rather disappointing: that one could find in the poets moral exemplars, cautionary tales and formulations in gnomic utterance of moral, and indeed technical, wisdom.' Cf. Croally (1994: 37): 'the claim that tragedy taught by providing simple moral lessons, and by acting as a storehouse for pithy maxims, would indeed describe a disappointing and reductive form of teaching.'

them both. One of the major flaws of *PGT* is that, having acknowledged tragedy's didactic dimension, it fails to do anything constructive with it. It notes (correctly) that tragedy's didacticism, as it was conceived in antiquity, is far removed from the kind of intellectualization of tragedy that is practised in much modern criticism; but it did not attempt to develop a positive account of it, or try to find a perspective from which tragic didacticism in something like its ancient form might become fruitful or interesting. As is often the case with polemical writing, its perspective was too narrowly determined by the position against which it was reacting, but whose assumptions it still unwittingly shared. *PGT*, in other words, was insufficiently radical.[9]

Croally adopts a different strategy in dealing with this issue. Having established a didactic dimension to tragedy by reference to the evidence for the ancient views of the matter, and having found the didactic dimension in its ancient form 'disappointing', he simply substitutes a different and more congenial concept of tragic didacticism, for which no ancient evidence is provided: 'What we have now is a three-word description of tragic didacticism: tragedy questions ideology' (43). Anticipating the objection that 'ideology prefers to affirm rather than question itself' (45), Croally appeals to Socrates' judgement in the *Apology* (38a5 f.) that a life lived without self-examination is wasted.[10] The argument here

[9] To this extent I have some sympathy with the criticism made by Feeney (1995: 306). But the larger context of Feeney's remarks fails to engage with the project of *PGT* and its extended footnote, *Unity in Greek Poetics* (Heath 1989). I certainly maintain that attention to ancient criticism is methodologically important, and that it casts more light on the structure of ancient literary aesthetics than is generally recognized. But it is simply false to say that I have 'claimed . . . that ancient literary criticism is in effect the only apparatus which the modern scholar may use' (301). Indeed, the reference to 'Heath's claim that ancient testimony is our sole legitimate interpretative key' (303, soon becoming 'Heath's law') is refuted by the very quotation (from *PGT* 3) used to illustrate it. For that quotation speaks of a 'presumption of general reliability': presumptions are by their very nature defeasible; general reliability is consistent with particular fallibility; and both defeasibility and fallibility logically entail the existence of legitimate kinds of evidence which may be judged to counterbalance the testimony of ancient criticism. That 'we are all (including Malcolm Heath) doing modern literary criticism all the time' (307) has never been in doubt, and is not the issue. My concern is with the extent to which our modern literary criticism is willing to learn from ancient literary criticism— which must of course be treated (as any teacher must be) critically.

[10] Blundell (1989: 273) likewise invokes Socrates in connection with the

slides from inferring the 'possibility that this his expressed value was shared by other Athenian citizens' (some others? most others? all others? It makes a difference) to the conclusion: 'It may be, then, that self-examination was a constituent of Athenian ideology' (46). This conclusion falls short of what is needed: 'it may be' does not mean that it was. Moreover, the reference to Socrates is double-edged, not just because of the ultimately fatal outcome of Socrates' habit of questioning, but because Socrates himself denies that the Athenians in general engage in the critical life to which he aspires;[11] the tragic poets are included in this judgement (*Ap.* 22a9). Plato certainly did not regard tragedy as a vehicle for reflection and ideological self-criticism. Part of his objection to tragedy was that it tended to confirm and reinforce the debased values of the society it addressed.

Yet Croally's formula does express an instinct which I (as a modern reader) also share. 'Questioning', with the complexity that we expect will go with it, interests us; we suspect (perhaps) that a didacticism which inclines to affirm, rather than to question, ideology must tend to be simplistic, evasive, and fundamentally uninteresting. With these concerns in mind, therefore, let us turn to *Philoctetes*.

II. NEOPTOLEMUS' PRINCIPLES

At the start of the play Neoptolemus is unreservedly hostile to the use of deception (88, 91): he would prefer to fail by direct means than to succeed by what he regards as shameful means (94f.). The echo of Achilles in *Iliad* 9. 312f. has been recognized since antiquity (sch. *Phil.* 94), and is particularly pointed in the context of references to Neoptolemus' inherited nature (79f.) and to his father (88f.). But we should not forget the occasion of Achilles' remark. He is speaking to envoys who claim to be his friends, but who are (he suspects) more concerned with another's advantage than with his;[12] and he is preparing those friends for a response to their request that he knows will be unwelcome. He is saying, in effect, 'I understand that what I am going to say will be painful, but

'dialectical' view of tragedy which she adopts in preference to the 'naive view of the didactic function of tragedy' found in ancient sources (12f.).

[11] Cf. Griffin (1998: 49f.).
[12] Cf. Pratt (1993: 58).

among friends it is best to be completely frank'; and there is a hint of suspicion that they have been less than completely frank with him. Elsewhere he takes a positive attitude to ambush (*Il.* 1. 226–8),[13] and he is complicit in the deception of the Trojans when Patroclus puts on his armour (cf. 16. 40–2). So it would be rash to conclude that Homer's Achilles disapproved of deceit without qualification.[14]

Unqualified disapproval would indeed be strange. Consider a real example. In the spring of 396 Agesilaus took command of the Greek forces operating against Persia in Asia Minor. When he arrived a temporary armistice was in force, to which he scrupulously adhered, even though the Persian satrap Tissaphernes did not. But when war broke out, Agesilaus acted vigorously. He made elaborate preparations for an invasion of Caria, and then (when the Persians had deployed to meet this threat) he launched his attack in a completely different direction. He was even more devious in his next campaign. He announced that he was going to attack Sardis, and did so; the Persians, falsely assuming that this was another bluff, were again wrong-footed. Xenophon records these events in the *Hellenica* (3. 4) and his encomium of Agesilaus, where he provides a moralizing commentary (1. 10–17; cf. *Mem.* 4. 2. 13–18). He points out that by adhering to the terms of the truce in the face of Tissaphernes' provocations Agesilaus won the trust of potential allies, who realized that he was someone who kept his word; but, Xenophon adds, when war was declared and it became religiously and morally legitimate (ὅσιόν τε καὶ δίκαιον) to deceive, he showed that Tissaphernes was a mere novice at deception. In Xenophon's view, skill in deception is a proper, and indeed a necessary, part of a general's expertise.[15]

[13] The ambush is a supreme test of courage: *Il.* 13. 277; *Od.* 11. 504–37 (on Neoptolemus). Edwards (1985: 18–35) argues that the *Odyssey* 'develops the positive view of the λόχος evident in Idomeneus' speech [sc. *Il.* 13. 277], or on the shield of Achilles' (34), but that in the *Iliad* 'it is viewed as a stratagem of cowardice and treachery' (27). The passages he cites to counterbalance Idomeneus and the shield are (i) Diomedes' response to Paris (11. 369–95); but taunts by the target of an ambush do not provide an objective evaluation; and (ii) the ambushes of Tydeus (4. 376–400) and Bellerophon (6. 155–95): both involve treachery (in one case, against an envoy) as well as deception, and so do not allow inferences to be drawn about ambush as a military tactic in general. See now van Wees (1996: 37, with 72 n. 94).

[14] This is not to deny that the generalization of Achilles' remark was possible in the 5th and 4th cent.; Pl. *Hipp.* 365ab.

[See p. 144 for n. 15]

Neoptolemus' attitude is therefore an extreme one. If we are meant to acquiesce in it,[16] then we should surely have to recognize this as an instance in which Sophocles has evaded an underlying complexity in his material; for on this hypothesis he is trying to induce his audience to accept a moral position that in other contexts they would recognize as over-simplified. Alternatively, if we do not acquiesce in Neoptolemus' attitude, we may conclude that it is naïve and immature. He is, after all, a young man, and it was a common-place that young men, because they lack experience and judgement, can be expected to act in foolhardy ways. This is a point stressed by the servant of Euripides' Hippolytus (*Hipp.* 114, 188 f.), a young man comparably extreme and foolish in his attitude to sex. Neoptolemus' youth is repeatedly emphasized in the course of the play, for example in the way other characters persistently address him as παῖ or τέκνον (201, 236, etc.). Odysseus makes this very point in 96 f.: 'I was just the same when I was young.' Neoptolemus' exaggerated aversion to guile might therefore be read as a mark of his moral immaturity.

It may not matter much which reading we prefer. Once Neoptolemus has adopted that position, it is clearly wrong for him to go along with a plan that involves deceit. The readiness with which he abandons his ethical position and complies with Odysseus' proposal is undeniable evidence of moral immaturity, or of moral weakness. This in turn prepares the way for the instability of purpose displayed in what follows. He gives up the deception (895–917), but not the bow which the deception has placed in his hands (925 f.); at this stage he has no intention of allowing Philoctetes to stay behind (so he must envisage the use of force to compel compliance). Philoctetes' appeal sways him (965–74); but when he is on the point of giving way Odysseus reappears, and he tamely capitulates again. But then he changes his mind again, again. It is only now, when he has definitively rejected Odysseus' plan, that he at last shows an ability to abide by a decision in difficult circumstances. The process of achieving a stable moral judgement is thus prolonged and erratic. The play dramatizes Neoptolemus' growth in moral maturity and in

[15] On the ethics of deception see Pratt (1993: 55–94), outlining some principles. On ambush and trickery in war: Pritchett (1974: 177–89); Wheeler (1988); Whitehead (1988) stresses the ambivalence of Greek attitudes.

[16] A similarly hostile view of deception may have been taken in other tragedies (cf. Soph. fr. 79, 352): but what were the contexts?

the ability to stick to his moral judgements. Or does it? The end of
the play, with its allusion to the death of Priam, reminds us that his
expressed willingness to comply with Heracles' instructions will not
survive the stress of the sack of Troy (cf. sch. *Phil.* 1441).[17]

III. IN DEFENCE OF ODYSSEUS

Xenophon's judgement on deception applies to the deception of an
enemy in war. But Philoctetes is not at war with the Greeks. How far
does this alter the moral situation? Several points can be made. First,
although the Greeks are not at war with Philoctetes, they are at war,
and the outcome of the war depends on the success of the mission
to Philoctetes. Odysseus uses the term σωθῆναι (109); he is trying to
save the army from disaster. Second, the legitimate use of deception
is not restricted to enemies in a state of war, as the *Odyssey* shows.
The suitors are not at war with Odysseus; they are his personal
enemies.[18] Third, although Philoctetes is not at war with the Greeks,
he is in a state of enmity with them. This is one of the few things on
which Odysseus and Philoctetes agree. Philoctetes is very insistent
that he is the ἐχθρός of the Atreids and Odysseus, and indeed (in
1216) of the Greeks in general; in 1302 f. he refers to Odysseus as
πολέμιος as well as ἐχθρός. Neoptolemus, too, shares the assumption
that Philoctetes is an enemy and (therefore) a legitimate target for
hostile action: when he says he is unwilling to use deception, he at
once goes on to say that he would be quite happy to use force
against him—'He won't put up much of a fight: after all, he's only
got one leg!' (A loose paraphrase of 90–3.) We must not sentimen-
talize Neoptolemus. He is a warrior, violence is his way of life, and
violently appropriating someone else's livelihood for one's own use
is a part of that; he is perfectly happy to prey on those weaker than

[17] Taplin (1987: 76): 'The ending is smudged' (an example of the device of
foreshadowing briefly touched on in *PGT* 104). The innovative choice of Neoptolemus as Odysseus' companion may perhaps alert the audience to this prospect from
the outset; and it might be argued that his reputation, precisely because it leaves
open the possibility of brutal and immoral behaviour, makes him an ideal candidate
for this dramatic role.

[18] Admittedly, if the suitors discover who he is they will do their best to kill him,
so the distinction may seem beside the point. But Odysseus is bent on killing them
irrespective of their reaction; he is out for personal vengeance, and his policy
towards them is dictated by that aim.

himself, so long as he does it by forthright brutality. So Odysseus, Neoptolemus, and Philoctetes himself all concur in the view that Philoctetes is an enemy of the Greeks. This implies that Philoctetes is a legitimate target for hostile action.

In this light, Odysseus' moral position might look quite strong. He is a member of the Greek army, and bound to them as comrades. Their desperate need for the one thing that can break the deadlock at Troy places on him a genuine obligation; it cannot simply be shirked. How is the need to be met? The analysis Odysseus offers at the beginning of the play proves to be correct: Philoctetes cannot be persuaded;[19] the bow makes force impractical; so he has to be tricked. There is no other way in which Odysseus can bring to his friends the help they need. Since Philoctetes is an enemy, the use of hostile action against him, whether force or deception, raises no moral problem.

That conclusion overlooks one important complication. Philoctetes is an enemy because the Greeks betrayed and abandoned him. He was part of the army, and as such a *philos*; but the Greeks violated the obligations this entailed, and it is their betrayal that has made him an enemy. There is a moral problem, therefore, and Odysseus' handling of the point in the opening lines is decidedly evasive and unsatisfactory. But even if he openly conceded that Philoctetes had been wronged, that would not annul the obligations Odysseus is under now to his allies. Would the fact that one ally was betrayed ten years ago justify betraying other allies now?

There are (then) things to be said in Odysseus' favour, and some of them are said in the play: the chorus pleads his obligations to the army in his defence (1143–5). But most of them are not said in the play, and they are not said by Odysseus. Odysseus himself never engages in an *agon* (1047 f. is almost ostentatious in declining the opportunity). The opening dialogue with the young and naive Neoptolemus is the only sustained attempt which Odysseus makes in the play to persuade anyone of anything.[20] It may not be very surprising that he does not bother to argue with Philoctetes; but when Neoptolemus tries to give the bow back, why not reason with

---

[19] Neoptolemus fails, even when he has given Philoctetes good reason to trust him by returning the bow; so it is hard to imagine that persuasion would have succeeded at any earlier stage.

[20] 997 f. is an isolated gesture of persuasion in a series of peremptory commands and threats.

him? Is it not strange that a man who has already expounded the supremacy of the spoken word so readily resorts to threats of force (1241–3, 1250–8)?

Moreover, in his one attempt at persuasion, so far from putting an attractive gloss on his approach, Odysseus needlessly advertises its amorality. When he makes his comments on Neoptolemus' immaturity in 96–9, he refers to the supremacy not (as I did just now) of the spoken word, but of the tongue (γλῶσσα), a word which in the late fifth century often carries hostile implications (Philoctetes uses it in this hostile sense at 408, 440). This is not the only instance of Odysseus undermining his case by his choice of words: he did not have to say κλοπεύς (77), τεχνᾶσθαι κακά (80), or ἀναιδές (83). It should be noted that Neoptolemus reacts adversely to the idea of τέχνη κακή (88): so this choice of words does not function only to communicate Odysseus' character to the audience; it conveys a moral message between the characters themselves. Thus the point is put in its least attractive guise, a fact which might be thought surprising in someone who is meant to be a master of persuasive speech.[21] This is not to deny that Odysseus' approach might be read as in some respects skilfully adapted to Neoptolemus' character and aspirations; and the fact that Neoptolemus succumbs to so blatant an appeal certainly reinforces the impression of his moral fragility. But in making Odysseus load the moral case against himself in this way Sophocles has concealed an element of complexity in the underlying situation; and he is arguably willing to put the consistency of Odysseus' characterization as a master of persuasive speech at risk in order to achieve this concealment.[22]

IV. NEOPTOLEMUS' DILEMMA

It if were not for the compromise of his principles over deception, Neoptolemus' moral position would appear to be even stronger

---

[21] For a different view see e.g. Buxton (1982: 125): 'That Odysseus' persuasion is subtle is not surprising, for he is a past master of the art.' Cf. Gibert (1995: 67): 'Odysseus skilfully overcomes Neoptolemus' reluctance to deceive Philoctetes in two stages: first he confuses him as to the meaning of moral terms . . . and then he clinches the case with an appeal to profit . . .'.

[22] Gibert (1995: 38 f.) points that that non-focal characters (such as villains often are) tend to lack 'the ethical complexity we find in the case of many focal characters' (for the terminology see *PGT* 95–8).

than that of Odysseus. In joining the Greeks at Troy he has accepted
them as *philoi* (cf. 66 f.), and thereby accepted obligations of loyalty
towards them. Moreover, friendship and enmity are contagious.
When I enter into friendship, I enter into a network of relations
which ramifies far beyond the immediate point of contact. If I am
obliged to assist my friend, that implies an obligation to assist him
in his attempts to satisfy the dual imperative to help friends and
harm enemies. So my friend's friend is my friend; my friend's enemy
is my enemy. Conversely, my enemy's friend is my enemy, because
he is obliged to help my enemy's attacks on me; and my enemy's
enemy is my friend, because we share a common interest in harming
the same person. Thus (to return to *Iliad* 9) towards the end of the
embassy Achilles warns Phoenix not to plead Agamemnon's case:
for in so doing, he will make himself *ekhthros* to Achilles: 'It is good
for you to join me in harming whoever harms me' (9. 613–15). It is
in this spirit that Neoptolemus explains how the Atreids, whom he
had regarded as friends (cf. 361), have wronged him; consequently
anyone who hates them is now his friend (389 f., 585 f.; cf. sch. *Phil.*
59). This is, of course, part of the deception; but for the deception to
work the motivation, although false in point of fact, must be
regarded as in principle both credible and creditable.

Two consequences follow. First, Neoptolemus, in being a *philos* to
the Greek army, has acquired the relationship to Philoctetes of being
an enemy; hence the assumption, as we have already noticed, that
Philoctetes is a legitimate target of violence. Second, Philoctetes will
reciprocate this attitude: if Neoptolemus were to approach him
openly as an ally of the Greeks, Philoctetes would automatically be
inclined to treat him with suspicion and hostility. This can be seen
in the way Philoctetes reacts to Neoptolemus' attempts to persuade
him to go to Troy even after the bow has been returned: he is
confused, angry, and resentful at what he sees as Neoptolemus'
friendly attitude towards people who should be his enemies (1376 f.,
1384 f.). Hence Odysseus is quite right to say that Neoptolemus can
best win Philoctetes' confidence by a pretence of shared enmity
towards the Greek leaders (54–69).

Since Neoptolemus had never been Philoctetes' friend, the past
betrayal does not complicate his moral position as it does Odysseus'.
But the moral complications which are initially lacking are brought
into being by the execution of Odysseus' plan itself. The way in
which the deception exploits the conventions of friendship and

enmity makes Neoptolemus' moral position progressively more difficult to sustain.

The question of friendship arises in Philoctetes' first speech: speak, if in fact you have come as *philoi* (229). Neoptolemus gives no direct answer to the implied question, but the whole deception is designed to answer it indirectly. By presenting himself as someone wronged by the Greek leadership, and therefore as their enemy, Neoptolemus in effect establishes himself as Philoctetes' friend. At the end of his account of the fictitious quarrel (389 f.) he expresses the idea that my enemy's enemy is my friend, as an encouragement to Philoctetes to draw the appropriate conclusion. He does so, saying (403) that Neoptolemus has a σύμβολον, in their respective grievances against the Greek leaders they have the two matching halves of a token which establish that they are indeed *philoi* to each other. Neoptolemus, for his part, claims to be Philoctetes' *philos* in 585 f., and again in 671–3 (where the implications of the claim in terms of mutual assistance are spelled out). The fact that friendship has ostensibly been established explains the strength of Philoctetes' reaction when Neoptolemus tells him the truth: he interprets these events as betrayal by someone who appeared to be his friend—and indeed, someone who (given their shared enmities) ought to be his friend.

It is all a pretence, of course: Neoptolemus was in reality acting as Philoctetes' enemy all along. But in sustaining this pretence of friendship Neoptolemus encounters and incurs genuine obligations towards Philoctetes. Most concrete is the fact that Philoctetes makes a formal supplication (468–70), which Neoptolemus accepts.[23] But the ritual of supplication simply formalizes something that was recognized in any case, that helplessness should be pitied rather than exploited. All human life and prosperity is precarious, and the human being who withholds pity is forgetting or denying the limits of mortal existence: Philoctetes stresses this point at the end of his appeal (501–6).[24] Thus there are limits to how far enmity can be pursued without incurring disapproval. And Neoptolemus does feel pity (965 f.); it is this which prevents him from proceeding as planned. Significantly, the crisis-point comes at the very moment when Philoctetes' dependency is physically

---

[23] Belfiore (1994) examines *xenia* and supplication as elements in the relationship established between Neoptolemus and Philoctetes.

[24] Or 501–3, if the deletion of the last three lines is accepted.

enacted, when he leans on Neoptolemus before their abortive exit (895).

So Odysseus' plan involves a manipulation of the institution of friendship, which is at the basis of Greek society and ethics; it requires Neoptolemus to violate Philoctetes' status as suppliant; and it oversteps the limits of legitimate enmity in its ruthless exploitation of helplessness. So although Neoptolemus' first objection, that the plan involves deceit, may be naive and simplistic, and although a case can be made out in defence of Odysseus' position, in the last analysis the execution of the plan forces Neoptolemus to confront a far more substantial set of moral problems. It is this accumulation of concrete moral difficulties, rather than a simple distaste for deception, that makes it ultimately impossible for him to go through with the plan.

And yet . . . The problems that beset the plan do not make Neoptolemus' obligations to the Greeks disappear; Neoptolemus is now caught in a dilemma. To satisfy the obligations which he has incurred towards Philoctetes he must abandon the plan; but to abandon the plan is a breach of loyalty towards the Greeks. As Odysseus points out (1250, 1258), and as Neoptolemus acknowledges (1404), choosing to side with Philoctetes will automatically make him an enemy to the rest of the army. The one possible way out of the dilemma is to persuade Philoctetes to come to Troy, which he cannot even begin to do with any hope of success until he has re-established his claim to being Philoctetes' *philos* by returning the bow. But in doing that, he guarantees that if Philoctetes will not be persuaded, he cannot be forced—in other words, he guarantees the failure of the Greek expedition. Thus the only chance that Neoptolemus has of being able to satisfy both sets of obligations commits him to siding with Philoctetes if Philoctetes is unpersuadable: as, in the circumstances, he is likely to be.

But Philoctetes too is in a dilemma. He is compelled to acknowledge Neoptolemus as a friend when the bow is returned, and that puts him under obligations towards Neoptolemus that are irreconcilable with his long-standing enmity towards the Greek leadership. This dilemma is only, and perhaps only partially, resolved by the fact that the bow gives him a way to defend Neoptolemus when he incurs the consequences of his abandonment of his allies.

V. A PROBLEM PLAY

Clearly, then, *Philoctetes* is a problem play, in the sense that it dramatizes a profoundly problematic situation—one in which the characters are made to confront difficult, and perhaps insoluble, moral dilemmas. Sophocles has, I suggest, simplified at least one aspect of the moral situation, by making Odysseus undercut his own position. But the complexity of the problems which face Neoptolemus and Philoctetes is allowed to emerge, and must be allowed to emerge. Without some awareness of the ethical complexities of the situation the audience will be unable to appreciate and respond appropriately to the painful contradictions in which the characters find themselves entangled. The emotional impact of the situation is inextricably bound up with its ethical complexity.

At this point we may feel tempted to take a further step, highly attractive to modern sensibilities: to infer from the dramatization of moral problems a problematization of the underlying moral or ideological codes. Croally's description of tragic didacticism is apposite: 'tragedy questions ideology'. But is the inference justified? We must return now, in the light of our discussion of the play, to the concerns raised at the end of the introduction. I shall discuss two interpretations of the *Philoctetes* which, in very different ways, take this further step; and I shall argue that it need not be taken.

VI. GOLDHILL: IDEOLOGICAL TRANSGRESSION

In an influential paper on the civic Dionysia, Simon Goldhill has described and sought to interpret the ceremonies performed in the theatre before the beginning of the tragic competition, arguing that there is a 'tension' (115) between these ceremonies and the tragic texts.[25] 'The tragic texts' (he suggests) 'seem to question, examine, and often subvert the language of the city's order' (114), which the ceremonies assert. *Philoctetes* is one of the plays chosen to illustrate this claim; the role of the youthful Neoptolemus in particular makes it possible to examine the interaction of the text with one of the

---

[25] Goldhill (1990). For an ambiguity in Goldhill's argument (are the ceremonies in tension with a *reading* of the tragic texts or with the *texts*?) and its implications see Heath (1997: 243 f.).

'preplay ceremonies', the parade of war-orphans, educated and equipped at the city's expense.[26]

In Goldhill's reading the 'preplay ceremonies' all serve to stress 'the power of the *polis*' and 'the duties of the individual to the *polis*' (114). By contrast, *Philoctetes* is seen as dramatizing 'a conflict between moral and social values and a commitment to the collective need of the Trojan expedition' (122). It is in this conflict that the tension between the tragic text and 'the preplay ceremonies' emerges (122 f.):

Neoptolemos' *uncertainty* and awareness of a conflict in his system of beliefs contrast strikingly with the opening ritual's assuredness. In the ephebic oath, the young Athenian promised to stand by his colleague wherever in the line he was stationed; Neoptolemos shows that it is not always clear what this might involve.

So the text of *Philoctetes*, 'seems to question . . . and set at risk the direct assertion of ideology that the preplay ceremonies seem to proclaim' (123).

Goldhill's reading of the 'preplay ceremonies' is, I would argue, too one-sided in its emphasis on the collective. Consider, for example, the proclamation and crowning of civic benefactors. This ceremony does not simply assert the duties owed by every citizen to the *polis*, but singles out individuals who have been outstanding in their services to the community and reciprocates by bestowing an outstanding honour on them. The element of reciprocation on the part of the community is present in the parade of orphans, as well: the *polis* has accepted an obligation towards the dependants of those who have died in its service, and the ceremony demonstrates that this obligation has been discharged.[27]

As for the play, Neoptolemus' commitment to the Trojan expedition is a voluntary one. The fact that he is not under oath or constraint is highlighted as a key point in Odysseus' plan (72 f.);

[26] Goldhill also discusses *Ajax*, another play relevant to this theme. For a discussion which pays particular attention to Goldhill's interpretation of *Ajax* see Friedrich (1996), esp. 263–8.

[27] Note that in Aeschines' account (3. 154) the proclamation acknowledges the fathers' sacrifice (τούσδε τοὺς νεανίσκους, ὧν οἱ πατέρες ἐτελεύτησαν ἐν τῷ πολέμῳ ἄνδρες ἀγαθοὶ γενόμενοι), affirms that the *polis* has discharged its responsibility of care towards them (μέχρι μὲν ἥβης ὁ δῆμος ἔτρεφε), and sends the young men to see to their own (not the collective's!) affairs (ἀφίησιν ἀγαθῇ τύχῃ τρέπεσθαι ἐπὶ τὰ ἑαυτῶν).

this sets him apart from an Athenian who had sworn the ephebic oath. Everyone in the play accepts that, if he had been treated as insultingly as he describes in his deception, Neoptolemus would have grounds for leaving the army.[28] So his obligations to the collective enterprise are circumscribed in a way that an Athenian citizen's never were; he has a degree of autonomy that an Athenian did not; the loyalty he owes towards the other Greeks is not the same as that of an Athenian towards the *polis*; and the dilemma he faces cannot be straightforwardly assimilated to the situation of an Athenian citizen. But these differences, though important, do not wholly undermine the parallel. The uncontested limits of Neoptolemus' obligations to the collective enterprise have not, in fact, been reached; but he has still been placed in a position in which fulfilling those obligations is morally impossible.

There is, however, still a question to be posed of Goldhill's interpretation: what assumptions have to be operative for the play to 'question' and 'set at risk' the ideology expressed in the 'preplay ceremonies'? Clearly, it has to be assured that the ideology expressed in those ceremonies implicitly denies that the obligations it imposes on individual citizens might be uncertain or unclear, and implicitly excludes any possibility of conflict between an individual's obligations. For an ideology that admits the possibility of uncertainty, unclarity, and conflict in a citizen's obligations is not threatened or 'set at risk' by a play that exhibits them. But the assumption that Athenian civic ideology denied or excluded these possibilities seems to me gratuitous, and indeed false. To go no further afield, the acceptance by the *polis* of responsibility for the care of war-orphans acknowledges a potential conflict between the citizen's obligations towards the community (whose interests are served by his readiness to die in battle) and his obligations towards his family (whose interests are threatened by his readiness to die in battle). In undertaking the care of the orphans, the community goes some way towards resolving this conflict of obligations; the element of reciprocity which we have already identified shows that the

---

[28] Odysseus regards his abandonment of the plan as a betrayal, but that is because he knows that the supposed insult is a fiction and is unable to see that Neoptolemus has any other valid grievance; the plan itself presupposes that the insult would have been good grounds for leaving the army. Philoctetes, as we have seen above, always remains under the impression that Neoptolemus does have good reason to break with the Greeks.

community refrains from asserting its own claims on the individual as absolute over against his other obligations.

If it is accepted that a citizen may be called upon to make difficult judgements between conflicting obligations, then the dramatization of Neoptolemus' entanglement in such a conflict is a dramatization of a possibility already embedded in civic ideology. As such, it scarcely warrants epithets such as 'paradoxical', 'questioning', 'transgressive', 'subversive', and 'unsettling'. At any rate, it would only unsettle the most naïve and simplistic. To be sure, people can be naive and simplistic—young men, especially (as Neoptolemus is arguably naive and simplistic in his attitude to deception). Perhaps, then, it could be said that it is salutary for those who have taken the ephebic oath to be reminded that observing it properly may be difficult. But that is far from being a 'subversion' of the civic ideology;[29] it would be more reasonable to see it as part of their induction into that ideology. In other words, if Athenian civic ideology admits the possibility of uncertainty, unclarity, and conflict in a citizen's obligations, then the dramatization of such problems might be thought not to subvert so much as to illustrate and illuminate that ideology.

One of the obligations which Neoptolemus has to weigh up (or at least cites to justify himself at one point: 925 f.)[30] is obedience to his commanders. This was something specifically included in the ephebic oath; and 'subversion' here would be particularly futile, since the principle that obedience is owed to lawful authority is essential to social and especially military cohesion, and hence to the existence of the *polis*—one of the things which Goldhill accepts is *not* questioned in tragedy.[31] So we might ask whether a more

---

[29] Friedrich (1996: 282 n. 70): 'the dramatization of conflicts inherent in the ethical life and the civic discourse of the *polis* cannot automatically be equated with subversion and the celebration of transgression.'

[30] As noted above, Neoptolemus' military service is voluntary, not obligatory; hence in the opening scene he is not a subordinate who can be ordered, but a colleague who must be persuaded to co-operate. As Blundell (1989: 185 n. 5) observes, Odysseus uses language which implies Neoptolemus' subordination (15, 53), while Neoptolemus represents himself as a colleague (93); we should not let Odysseus' attempt to manipulate the relationship go unchallenged. Odysseus' insinuation of subordinate position can be compared to his attempt in the opening lines to acquit himself with regard to the abandonment of Philoctetes on the grounds that he was acting under orders (6); when at 925 Neoptolemus appeals to the duty of obedience he too seems to be engaged in tendentious self-exculpation.

[31] Goldhill (1990: 120): 'Obedience towards "the authorities" . . . is a standard

constructive reading of Neoptolemus' dilemma is possible. Athenian citizens were not, as Neoptolemus was, free to choose whether or not they will serve; but they did (collectively) choose the people they would have to serve under. They chose their leaders, either positively by election or (in the case of sortitive offices) negatively through the *dokimasia* designed to screen out unsuitable office-holders. If the principle of obedience to authority is accepted, it is important that people like Odysseus and the Atreids do not occupy positions of authority.[32] A play that portrays the consequences of bad men exercising power offers a salutary reminder of the obligations involved in the exercise of democratic rights. This, again, might be thought to illuminate and reinforce democratic ideology, rather than to subvert or question it.[33]

VII. BLUNDELL: MORAL CRITIQUE

My second example comes from Mary Whitlock Blundell's important and instructive study, *Helping Friends and Harming Enemies*.[34] According to Blundell (261):

Sophocles handles the ethical issues that centre round the talio and Help Friends/Harm Enemies in such a way as to provoke critical questioning of conventional moral assumptions.

requirement, of course, for the maintenance of the bonds of a democratic as well as a more hierarchical society'; 114: 'I do not think that the *polis* is seriously questioned as the necessary basis of civilization.'

[32] In this connection one could cite 385–8, if authentic. For the deletion see Lloyd-Jones and Wilson (1990: 187). But the shift in the focus of Neoptolemus' anger from Odysseus (383f.) to the Atreids (389f.) is then disconcertingly abrupt; and οἱ ἀκοσμοῦντες may mean 'behaving badly' (e.g. Hyp. fr. 14; Pl. *Symp.* 188b5, *Laws* 764b6; Aristot. *Ath. Pol.* 3. 6) rather than specifically 'resisting authority'. These lines are also discussed by Blundell (1987: 325 f.); she goes on to argue (with sch. *Phil.* 99) for a connection with contemporary Athenian politicians.

[33] The first of the four preplay ceremonies is the pouring of libations by the generals, described by Goldhill as 'the ten most powerful military and political leaders . . . the most influential and important representatives of the state' (101); hence this ceremony's inclusion in the claim that 'all' the preplay ceremonies stress 'the power of the *polis*, the duties of the individual to the *polis*' (114). But it is important to bear in mind that the generals were not the citizens' masters, but their appointees and agents; and an essential element in democratic ideology was the *accountability* of the generals.

[34] Blundell (1989).

Thus, for example, in *Philoctetes* the impasse reached by the human characters is evidence of 'the danger of incoherence in Help Friends/ Harm Enemies' (224). The argument for this conclusion has two stages. First Blundell exhibits the possibility of conflicting loyalties and 'a permanent risk of internal inconsistency' (263) between the two sides of the Help Friends/Harm Enemies principle. But the fact that Help Friends/Harm Enemies can generate conflicts of loyalties and obligations is not in itself enough to call it into question. Blundell is aware of this, commenting that 'the potential for inconsistency is present in any moral code' (264). She therefore proceeds to a second phase, in which these potential conflicts are taken as 'symptoms of a more fundamental problem' (265). This is the fact that Help Friends/Harm Enemies is agent-relative, not agent-neutral (265). Consequently, it is not strictly a *moral* code in Blundell's sense: for 'any moral code faces the challenge of convincing us that we should at least sometimes step outside this perspective and adopt criteria for moral judgement that are independent of personal interest' (265).[35]

The critique of Help Friends/Harm Enemies developed from this position urges, first, that agent-relative principles 'provide little incentive to curtail the impulses of passion in the interests of the desires or needs of others' (266). But that is clearly untrue: Help Friends/Harm Enemies positively enjoins the curtailment of one's own impulses in the interests of another's desires or needs, if the other is a friend. Second, it is argued that 'different personal perspectives are bound to clash . . . the result is insoluble conflict' (266). There is an obvious retort: if conflict is an ineradicable part of human existence, the idea that a moral code can be evaluated by whether it eliminates the possibility of insoluble conflicts is unrealistic. So the critique of the Help Friends/Harm Enemies code that Blundell claims to elicit from Sophocles' plays requires an assumption about the place of conflict in human existence which is not, so far as I can see, a given in the plays themselves, and which is certainly contestable. Blundell has therefore failed to show that Sophoclean tragedy has revisionary implications for someone who is not already and independently committed to a set of moral beliefs

[35] 265 n. 8 adds 'This follows from the nature of morality as I have been using the term (above, p. 3, n. 8)': but p. 3 n. 8 claims to use the term 'in the broadest sense', and does not advertise the latent restriction that excludes Help Friends/Harm Enemies as a moral code in advance.

that entail the inadequacy of Help Friends/Harm Enemies.[36] To someone who takes a different view about conflict, Sophocles might seem instead to be dramatizing a potential for tragedy that is of necessity inherent in the basic structures of human society.

Moreover, what we see in a play is never the action of a moral code in the abstract. We see the actions of individuals trying to implement the code as they understand it in particular circumstances—circumstances which (to recur to a point touched on in §I) in tragedy are likely to be extreme and to resist the application of our habitual standards of moral judgement. In this play, what makes the conflict insoluble is not the Help Friends/Harm Enemies principle *per se* but Philoctetes' understanding of the principle and of the circumstances in which it is being applied,[37] and his consequent intransigence in applying it. So even if we were to concede that the insoluble conflict provokes critical questioning, why should it be the general principle of Help Friends/Harm Enemies that is called into question rather than Philoctetes' attitude?

If we were to question Philoctetes' attitude, it would not of course follow that we had to condemn him personally for taking that attitude. In the circumstances in which he finds himself, his intransigence is understandable: he has been treated in a way that has left him embittered, savage (cf. 226, 132) and isolated from human society. But that point itself invites a further reflection. The intractable savagery that makes the conflict insoluble is a result of a previous violation of the Help Friends/Harm Enemies principle. If you betray a friend, treating him in a way that leaves him in a state

---

[36] Blundell (1989: 272): 'In the process of exploring the tragic consequences of traditional ethics, an implicit critique of such values emerges.' But 'emerges' is misleading; the critique is the *product* of an exploration conducted by Blundell herself on the basis of certain specific assumptions.

[37] Blundell (1989: 218 f.) sees him as attaching greater weight to Harm Enemies than to Help Friends. But in a sense the choice for him is between Helping Enemies (by going to Troy) or Harming Enemies (by not going to Troy); Neoptolemus' involvement in the triangle potentially changes the choice—except that Philoctetes (who still believes that Neoptolemus has been treated outrageously by the Greeks) cannot see any good reason why Neoptolemus should want to go to Troy. Neoptolemus' insistence on going to Troy is therefore bound to raise suspicions about his good faith (1384); and for Neoptolemus to correct the misperception by explaining this part of the deception would only confirm that he is the friend of Philoctetes' enemies, making it even harder to establish himself as a friend of Philoctetes.

of profoundly embittered alienation, this may well create a situation with which Help Friends/Harm Enemies finds it difficult to cope. So what conclusion are we to draw: that there is something wrong with Help Friends/Harm Enemies? Or that Help Friends/Harm Enemies should be upheld, not violated? On the latter view, the play might lead us to reflections like these: do not betray your friends; do not cynically manipulate the conventions of friendship; be careful who your friends are. These reflections tend to reaffirm the principle Help Friends/Harm Enemies, rather than questioning it.[38]

VIII. CONCLUSION

It must be stressed that I am not *asserting* the interpretations that have just been sketched out in response to Blundell and Goldhill. They are offered *exempli gratia*, to illustrate my contention that the presence of problems, conflicts, and complexity in a play does not of itself compel us to read the play as questioning, subversive, critical of the underlying ideology or morality; other readings are available. Which conclusions we reach will depend on the assumptions and expectations which we bring with us when we read. Change the assumptions about the *kind* of meaning to be looked for in serious drama, and we may end up with ideologically affirmative readings instead of ideologically subversive ones.

The evidence suggests that ancient audiences of tragedy expected something closer to an affirmation of ideology than to ideological critique. If that is right, then contemporary appropriations of *Philoctetes*, problem-play though it is, are likely to have been situated more in the general direction that I have been pointing towards than in the direction of Goldhill's or Blundell's readings. And, on the principle (which I share with Croally) that Sophocles, as a regular member of the ancient audience, would have been alert to 'the cultural conditions in which he lived and worked', such appropriations are more likely to have been—I will not say *intended* by Sophocles (since I am still not persuaded that Greek tragedians set out to teach specific moral lessons): but they are more likely to have been *envisaged* by the poet with approval and pride.

[38] The fact that, at the end of the play, Philoctetes' isolation is overcome by a friend whose loyalty to him is beyond question, and who reassures him of his future status, could be seen as pointing in the same direction.

That is not, of course, to say that *we* cannot draw other (and ideology-questioning) implications from the text ourselves; nor does it mean that we should not do so.[39] My point is that, if we choose to do so, we should not unthinkingly project our choice onto 'the text', or onto the fifth century. To do that runs the risk of serious confusions. If, for example, we read tragedy as characteristically subversive, we might look for an explanation for the apparent paradox of such texts playing a central role in an ideologically significant civic festival.[40] But the paradox may be merely apparent: perhaps the reason why texts which *can be* read as subversive were accorded the role they were is that, at the time, they *were not* read in that way. If that is so, then it would be fruitless to seek to resolve the paradox in terms of ancient patterns of ideological or theological thought; for on this hypothesis, the subversiveness of the tragic texts is an artefact of modern practices of reading and lay outside the range of interpretations standardly accessible in the fifth century. The attempt to reconstruct ancient responses to tragedy, therefore, while it cannot tell us everything that we might want to know about the plays, may tell us something that, as classicists, we need to know.

REFERENCES

BELFIORE, E. (1994), '*Xenia* in Sophocles' *Philoctetes*', *CJ* 89: 113–29.
BLUNDELL, M. W. (1987), 'The Moral Character of Odysseus in *Philoctetes*', *GRBS* 28: 307–29.

[39] See the final paragraph of Heath (1989: 155), an assertion of interpretative pluralism to which I am (despite one reviewer's scepticism) fully committed. It is precisely because I set no *a priori* limit to the diversity of interpretation that I have always been strenuous in asserting what kind of interpretative project it is that my own work is pursuing.

[40] Goldhill (1990: 114) comments: 'after such preplay ceremonies, the performance of tragedy and comedy that follow could scarcely seem—at first sight—a more surprising institution.' I would be more cautious: collocation does not of itself amount to an interpretatively significant contextualization, and we cannot know *a priori* the extent to which tragedy's audiences made an interpretative connection between the plays and the civic ceremonies that began the festival (for the principle cf. Heath (1997: 238, 242 f.); for more concrete doubts about the specific relevance of the ceremonies to tragedy see Griffin (1998: 47, with 43 f.))). But from the point of view of ancient understanding of tragic didacticism there might indeed be grounds for surprise.

BLUNDELL, M. W. (1989), *Helping Friends and Harming Enemies* (Cambridge).

BUXTON, R. (1982), *Persuasion in Greek Tragedy* (Cambridge).

CROALLY, N. T. (1994), *Euripidean Polemic* (Cambridge).

EDWARDS, A. T. (1985), *Achilles in the Odyssey* (Beiträge zur klassischen Philologie 171; Meisenheim).

FEENEY, D. (1995), 'Criticism Ancient and Modern', in D. Innes, H. Hine, and C. Pelling (eds.), *Ethics and Rhetoric: Classical Essays for Donald Russell* (Oxford), 301–12.

FRIEDRICH, R. (1996), 'Everything to do with Dionysus? Ritualism, the Dionysiac, and the Tragic', in M. S. Silk (ed.), *Tragedy and the Tragic* (Oxford), 257–83.

GIBERT, J. (1995), *Changes of Mind in Greek Tragedy* (*Hypomnemata* 108; Göttingen).

GOLDHILL, S. (1990), 'The Great Dionysia and Civic Ideology', in J. Winkler and F. Zeitlin (eds.), *Nothing to Do With Dionysus?* (Princeton), 97–129.

GRIFFIN, J. (1998), 'The Social Function of Attic Tragedy', *CQ* 48: 39–61.

HEATH, M. (1987*a*), *Poetics of Greek Tragedy* (London).

——(1987*b*), '"Iure principem locum tenet": Euripides' *Hecuba*', *BICS* 34: 40–68.

——(1989), *Unity in Greek Poetics* (Oxford).

——(1997), 'Aristophanes and the Discourse of Politics', in G. Dobrov (ed.), *The City as Comedy* (Chapel Hill), 230–49.

LLOYD-JONES, H., and WILSON, N. G. (1990), *Sophoclea* (Oxford).

MOSSMAN, J. (1995), *Wild Justice* (Oxford).

PRATT, L. H. (1993), *Lying and Poetry from Homer to Pindar* (Ann Arbor).

PRITCHETT, W. K. (1974), *The Greek State at War*, ii (Berkeley).

TAPLIN, O. (1987), 'The Mapping of Sophocles' *Philoctetes*', *BICS* 34: 69–77.

VAN WEES, H. (1996), 'Heroes, Knights and Nutters: Warrior Mentality in Homer', in A. B. Lloyd (ed.), *Battle in Antiquity* (London), 1–86.

WHEELER, E. L. (1988), *Stratagem and the Vocabulary of Military Trickery* (*Mnemosyne* Suppl. 108; Leiden).

WHITEHEAD, D. (1988), 'κλοπὴ πολέμου: "Theft" in Ancient Greek Warfare', *C&M* 39: 45–53.

9

Three Places of the *Trachiniae*

ROBERT L. FOWLER

My purpose in this brief discussion is to suggest that in three places of the *Trachiniae* hitherto unnoticed or unexploited parallels may improve our understanding of the play.

I

At lines 153 ff., Deianeira tells the chorus that a novel kind of suffering has attended her husband's latest absence:

> Πάθη μὲν οὖν δὴ πόλλ' ἔγωγ' ἐκλαυσάμην·
> ἐν δ', οἷον οὔπω πρόσθεν, αὐτίκ' ἐξερῶ.
> Ὁδὸν γὰρ ἦμος τὴν τελευταίαν ἄναξ
> ὡρμᾶτ' ἀπ' οἴκων Ἡρακλῆς, τότ' ἐν δόμοις
> λείπει παλαιὰν δέλτον ἐγγεγραμμένην
> ξυνθήμαθ', ἀμοὶ πρόσθεν οὐκ ἔτλη ποτέ,
> πολλοὺς ἀγῶνας ἐξιών, οὕτω φράσαι,
> ἀλλ' ὥς τι δράσων εἷρπε κοὐ θανούμενος.
> Νῦν δ' ὡς ἔτ' οὐκ ὢν εἶπε μὲν λέχους ὅ τι
> χρείη μ' ἑλέσθαι κτῆσιν, εἶπε δ' ἣν τέκνοις
> μοῖραν πατρῴας γῆς διαιρετὸν νέμοι,
> χρόνον προτάξας ὡς τρίμηνος ἡνίκα
> χώρας ἀπείη κἀνιαύσιος βεβώς,
> τότ' ἢ θανεῖν χρείη σφε τῷδε τῷ χρόνῳ,
> ἢ τοῦθ' ὑπεκδραμόντα τοῦ χρόνου τέλος
> τὸ λοιπὸν ἤδη ζῆν ἀλυπήτῳ βίῳ.

Knowledge of this fate, she goes on to say, was imparted to Heracles by the oracle of Zeus at Dodona; and as the allotted time has now passed, she is feeling justifiably fearful.

Oliver Taplin has well commented that the *Trachiniae* is a

nostos-play like Aeschylus' *Agamemon* and *Persae* and Euripides' *Heracles Furens*.[1] Commentators have picked up this hint and usefully explored the similarities and contrasts between these plays. I should like to suggest that an equally fruitful comparison can be made with the archetypal *nostos*, that of Odysseus; indeed, the audience might think of this one sooner, not only because of the familiarity of the text, but because it reproduces more faithfully the archetypal folktale of the departing husband who leaves instructions against his failure to return.[2] The story pattern includes the fixing of a time after which the wife is to act. Heracles states a time, or at least reports it as it was given to him, in the passage quoted; Odysseus, we learn in book 18 (257 ff.), told Penelope to take action when Telemachus had grown his beard. The instructions in both cases pertain to domestic and marital arrangements; Deianeira is to repossess her dowry, Penelope is to remarry. Time being the essence of the traditional story, much is made of it in both the *Odyssey* and the *Trachiniae*. Those left behind are on the edge of despair as the date draws near, facing the possibility that the hero might not return after all. The arrival of the stated time precipitates the crisis in both cases; each heroine takes steps which provoke it. The story pattern requires, of course, that the hero return in the nick of time. Odysseus does so in disguise, with triumphant results. Heracles' return is also postponed to the very last minute, and is initially reported in triumphant language.

But here the differences begin. After the jubilant hyporchema celebrating the hero's return Lichas enters with the captive women. It is instantly clearly that something is going to go wrong, not only because such celebrations in tragedy always turn out to be premature, but because Deianeira has already made her marriage, and its possible termination, the central issue. In the *Odyssey* the threat to Penelope's marriage comes from her husband's presumptive death after twenty years of absence, which has brought the suitors to her door; in the *Trachiniae* the threat to Deianeira's marriage ironically comes from the husband himself after his return. The *Odyssey* ends with the serene reunion of husband and wife; in the *Trachiniae*, after all the anticipation, the reunion never happens, for the wife is dead before the husband

---

[1] Taplin (1977: 124 f.); cf. Hall (1997: 107).
[2] Hölscher (1988: 50 ff., 250 ff., and *passim*).

arrives.[3] The husband dies not long afterwards, through the wife's agency.

Nor is this the end of the ironies. In the *Odyssey*, the time limit had been set by Odysseus on his own authority and quite reasonably as the time at which Telemachus reached manhood; in the *Trachiniae* the time limit had been set by an oracle This introduces the element of fate, so essential to Sophoclean tragedy. It also increases the irony of Deianeira's procedure. She would have proceeded against Iole in any case, one feels; but once the audience knows about the oracle, it knows also that her actions ironically ensure the oracle's fulfilment, for the worse. It seems the time-limit has not expired just yet; but Deianeira's actions ensure that it does, in such a way as to preclude all but one possible outcome of the prophecy. Heracles was to have either death or repose; now these two alternatives turn out to be one. The ironic self-infliction of a preordained end is strongly reminiscent of the *Oedipus Tyrannus*, and encourages one to identify this pattern of events in the *Trachiniae* as the heart of the Sophoclean design.[4]

A further indication that Sophocles was thinking of the *Odyssey* as a pattern lies in his innovations to the myth.[5] It is very likely he who made Deianeira an innocent and thus tragic perpetrator of the death of her husband; in earlier versions Deianeira the 'man-slayer' was probably exacting straightforward revenge.[6] Certainly Sophocles has laid all his dramatic stress on her innocence. In her virtue she becomes Penelope-like. Furthermore, he is very likely the first to specify the date of Deianeira's marriage; at any rate, he makes a great deal of it: it was long ago, and Deianeira has been suffering patiently for many years, waiting for the restoration of domestic happiness, like Penelope. One can justifiably compare Deianeira's abandonment to Penelope's, for, as she says in the prologue,

---

[3] As several critics have noted, e.g. Silk (1985: 3), Easterling (1981: 57 f.).

[4] Cf. Ewans (1996: 440 ff.). March (1987: 63 f.) argues that Nessus' connection with the death of Heracles is a Sophoclean innovation like those discussed immediately below; he too is part of fate's design (see §2).

[5] March (1987: 49 ff.); Davies (1991: pp. xxx f.).

[6] Dietrich von Bothmer points out the name is not the exclusive property of the wife of Herakles (another early Deianeira, mother of Lykaon, in Pherecydes *FGrHist* 3 F 156; others of uncertain date in Diod. Sic. 4. 16. 3, Hyg. *Fab.* 31); perhaps this circumstance may allow its generic meaning to come more to the fore. A non-mythological example is suggestive; one of the comic poets' nicknames for Aspasia, along with Hero and Omphale, was Deianeira (adesp. 704 Kassel–Austin).

Heracles has really never been at home during the long years in which Hyllus has grown to manhood. The number of years in question is thus approximately the same. The final irony is that in the end her actions conform to those of the other waiting wife of the *Odyssey*, Clytaemnestra.[7]

Sophocles did not have to make this a *nostos*-drama. If one were to speculate on his reasons for doing so, one might suggest that, in contemplating the death of Greek religion's greatest hero, he thought that the best way of intimating its dimensions would be to see it through the eyes of others—a device he uses to stupendous effect in the *Ajax*. An obvious choice for these others would be the members of his family, and especially the woman whom tradition made his killer. Sophocles would have been quick to realize the dramatic possibilities of the contrast between the secluded world of the heroine and the active outside world of the hero, which he exploits to the full in the play.

Ultimately more interesting, however, is the unpredictable transformation the contrast undergoes, from one of ordinary and extraordinary mortals, to one of mortals and gods. The domestic atmosphere is stressed by many details in the first part of the play, so that when the rough lord of the house finally does return, the shock is violent. We inevitably see the ensuing events through the eyes of the family, because of the way the play is constructed. But as the action progresses, and particularly from the moment when Heracles himself recognizes the role of fate, the stress changes; Deianeira is mentioned no more, and the death-throes of the greatest of heroes occupy all our attention. But Deianeira has been the focalizer of audience perceptions for 970 lines, and the familial point of view is sustained by Hyllus in the exodus; we therefore continued to see the hero from this domestic and distanced point of view, but the focus of our contemplation is now assuming new dimensions. Heracles is in the process of becoming either hero or god (or, more likely, both). The sense of distance from him that Deianeira felt as his wife, in which the audience shared, is now the sense of distance that we feel from him in this moment of transformation. We can no more aspire to his status than we can comprehend his agony. We can only watch in bewilderment and awe. Both of these are primal religious emotions, in response to divine mystery. The world to which

[7] As Jasper Griffin (to whom I am grateful for useful criticism) notes. On Deianeira and Clytaemnestra see, among other discussions, March (1987: 69–70).

Heracles belongs is as incommensurate with ours as it was with Deianeira's. We must be able to generalize from her case, in fact, or the tragedy will not work; the play cannot merely be the story of a domestic mishap. There has to be a sense of contact with a different dimension of reality. In the end the play is not about Deianeira at all, but about the death of Heracles, and the events which led to it.[8] The startling originality of the setting, which brings together—like water and electricity—god and man, death and salvation, the domestic and the cosmic, the fated and the contingent, is the outcome of long contemplation of the great hero's life by one of the world's great religious thinkers.

II

The second passage is the decisive moment when the dying Heracles hears the name of Nessus (1141). As has often been remarked, the name marks a change in his bearing and in the direction of the play. The meaning of the oracles is now all too clear. Heracles resigns himself to his fate and prepares for death. His numerous instructions to Hyllus about the funeral begin immediately.

As many critics have noted, oracles and knowledge too lately acquired play a comparable role in *OT*; but the moment in Sophocles most comparable to Heracles' moment of realization, when he hears the name of Nessus, is Oedipus' in *OC*, at the very beginning of the play, when he hears the name of the Eumenides. In his case too the meaning of an oracle is instantly clarified, and everything else flows from that. Actually, there are two comparable moments in *OC*. After the main action of the play involving Theseus, Creon, and the children of Oedipus, the moment of realization is repeated like a kind of echo. This time the omen is thunder (1466); Oedipus recognizes its portent instantly, as no one else does. It is just as the oracle foretold, he says. His translation to the other world ensues immediately; he issues sharp instructions to those around him, like Heracles.

---

[8] So Lloyd-Jones (1982: 230). Cf. Easterling (1982: 1); Davies (1991: p. xix); March (1987: 71). That Heracles is 'zugleich Mensch und mehr als Mensch' (Nesselrath) is at once the source of his attraction as a tragic figure, and of the difficulty he poses the dramatist who would write about him; see Nesselrath (1997), and compare Silk (1985).

Both heroes, before the moment of revelation, were passive and helpless victims. With their new knowledge they take imperious control of their situations. They proceed with the absolute conviction which springs from divinely vouchsafed knowledge. Both know more than they are willing to tell; Oedipus is explicit about this, saying he can reveal everything only to Theseus, while it is implicit in Heracles' concessions that Hyllus need not light the pyre himself,[9] and perhaps also in his insistence that Hyllus marry Iole.[10] Furthermore, the final goal of the dramatic movement in both plays is the death of the hero. In *OC*, of course, a quite different atmosphere prevails, as Oedipus has been told that his death will be his vindication, and the movement towards it occupies the whole of the play; in *Trachiniae*, nothing in Heracles' own words justifies the belief that he has any such idea as Oedipus', and the movement towards his death, as a visible part of the drama, occupies the exodus only. But of course the actual death of Oedipus occupies only the exodus of *OC*, following upon his recognition of the second omen, and (conversely) the goal of *Trachiniae* is just as obvious from an early stage to any alert member of the audience. The subject of the play, indeed, is the death of Heracles as ordained by the will of Zeus, of which Deianeira is the instrument. Heracles' father is mentioned a disproportionate number of times merely in order to underscore this larger perspective, and the several references to Mt. Oeta throughout the play have the same purpose.[11] As in other Sophoclean plays, the larger perspective, often in the form of a family curse, is impossible to ignore for all that it remains understated.[12] It is brought very much to the foreground by Heracles' moment of realization and the conviction with which he proceeds from that point; his conviction mirrors the certainty of fate, and his attitude to events is inevitably shared by the audience. A sense of significance beyond the immediate framework of the action is engendered by this movement, and underscored by subtle but unmistakable allusions. The great power of *OC* springs from its situation on the border between myth and cult, between stage and

---

[9] Lloyd-Jones (1983: 128); the honour was reserved for Philoctetes or Poeas.

[10] See further §3.

[11] Holt (1989: 75). Note the powerful build-up to the mention of Oeta in line 1191: twelve lines of stichomythia to underscore the point that Hyllus MUST do what Heracles says, then, 'Do you know Mt. Oeta, which belongs to highest Zeus?'

[12] Lloyd-Jones (1983: ch. 5); cf. West, Ch. 3 above.

real life; the movement is from one to the other.[13] The same movement gives the *Trachiniae* its real power; without it, all the fuss about the pyre is simply pointless.[14] As in *OC* we are seeing the cult *in statu nascendi*; the same is true of the *Ajax*, as Albert Henrichs has remarked.[15] The differences between these three plays are clear, but so are the similarities. In the case of *OC* and *Trachiniae*, the endings are imbued with elemental religious power. Oedipus and Heracles are beings in touch with forces far above the audience; their deaths leave us with a feeling of mystery and incomprehension, of which one can only say, there is nothing here which is not Zeus.

III

The third passage comes from the instructions of Heracles to Hyllus (1193 ff.).

> Ἐνταῦθά νυν χρὴ τοὐμὸν ἐξάραντά σε
> σῶμ' αὐτόχειρα καὶ ξὺν οἷς χρῄζεις φίλων,
> πολλὴν μὲν ὕλην τῆς βαθυρρίζου δρυὸς
> κείραντα, πολλὸν δ' ἄρσεν' ἐκτεμόνθ' ὁμοῦ
> ἄγριον ἔλαιον, σῶμα τοὐμὸν ἐμβαλεῖν,
> καὶ πευκίνης λαβόντα λαμπάδος σέλας
> πρῆσαι. Γόου δὲ μηδὲν εἰσίτω δάκρυ,
> ἀλλ' ἀστένακτος κἀδάκρυτος, εἴπερ εἶ
> τοῦδ' ἀνδρός, ἔρξον· εἰ δὲ μή, μενῶ σ' ἐγὼ
> καὶ νέρθεν ὢν ἀραῖος εἰσαεὶ βαρύς.

There are many ritual prescriptions Sophocles might have made his character pronounce; why these two about the pyre and lamentation? The only other instruction in the scene pertains to Iole. The

---

[13] The point remains valid whether the cult actually existed or not; the play assumes that it does. On the question of the cult's existence see Kearns (1989: 50), with App. 2.

[14] Easterling (1981: 57, 65) quoting Linforth (1952: 255–67). As both pyre and apotheosis are well attested in Sophocles' day, it is unreasonable to insist on keeping them separate because we have no text explicitly connecting them before *Trach.*; March (1987: 74) is right to speak of an 'excess of caution' in those who do. The only alternative, that Heracles went to Hades after cremation, cannot have been entertained by many people, if anyone. On Eur. *Hcld.* 910–14 see Holt (1989: 72 f.).

[15] Henrichs (1993). On the endings of the *OC* and *Ajax* see also Easterling (1996: 174ff.), and, for another view, Griffin, Ch. 5 above, pp. 87 f.

significance of the pyre and Iole are agreed by everyone; the former refers to the cult on Oeta, and the latter to the descendants in historical times of Hyllus and Iole. These instructions point beyond and outside of the play; the instruction about lamentation ought to as well. Heracles lays the utmost stress on the point; he ensures obedience with the ferocious threat of a curse from beyond the grave. This is no rhetorical exaggeration; it is a curse of the most grievous kind. Thus it is not enough to say that Heracles is merely afraid lest Hyllus show feminine weakness at the funeral. There must be some more compelling reason why it is vital to get things right.

Another great death scene may shed some light: the end of Plato's *Phaedo*. When at last Socrates drinks the hemlock, his companions are unable to hold back their tears any longer. Socrates chides his friends: 'Come come, gentlemen,' he says, 'this is the reason why I have sent the women away. And besides,' he adds, 'I have heard that one ought to die ἐν εὐφημίᾳ' (1173). Socrates' comment about unmanliness nicely parallels Heracles' explicit reason. Perhaps the comment about εὐφημία supplies the unspoken reason. From Socrates' casual manner we may infer that silence, though desirable, was a requirement not always enforced, presumably because unenforceable in the face of overpowering grief; if religion absolutely required it, one would expect Socrates to show a little more pious indignation and a little less avuncular remonstration. It is clear from the manner of Socrates' remark, however, and more particularly from Plato's incorporation of it into his dialogue at its most crucial juncture, that the desirability of silence was generally known and understood; for Plato's purpose, whatever it was, would have been frustrated if this requirement were a private invention.

That it was not is confirmed by the existence of the verb ἀνευφημέω. It occurs three times in classical Greek. Once is in the *Trachiniae* itself, when the messenger reports the response of the people to Heracles' throwing Lichas off the cliff (783 f.):

> ἅπας δ' ἀνηυφήμησεν οἰμωγῇ λεώς,
> τοῦ μὲν νοσοῦντος, τοῦ δὲ διαπεπραγμένου.

The second instance is in Euripides' *Orestes*, when Hermione asks what the cries in the house signify. Electra deceitfully replies (1326) that events deserving lamentation have befallen them (ἄξι' ἡμῖν τυγχάνει στεναγμάτων); the last word suggests mourning for death, so that Hermione instinctively responds, εὔφημος ἴσθι. Upon learning the truth, she remarks,

> ἐπ' ἀξίοισί τἄρ' ἀνευφημεῖ δόμος,

echoing Electra's ἄξια, and her own εὔφημος ἴσθι. Here, for once, lamentation is justified; Electra responds, περὶ τοῦ γὰρ ἄλλου μᾶλλον ἂν φθέγξαιτό τις; The third passage is in the *Phaedo* again, when Socrates' friends enter to find Xanthippe and the children with him (60a):

> εἰσιόντες οὖν κατελαμβάνομεν τὸν μὲν Σωκράτη ἄρτι λελυμένον, τὴν δὲ Ξανθίππην—γιγνώσκεις γὰρ—ἔχουσάν τε τὸ παιδίον αὐτοῦ καὶ παρακαθη-μένην. ὡς οὖν εἶδεν ἡμᾶς ἡ Ξανθίππη, ἀνηυφήμησέ τε καὶ τοιαῦτ' ἄττα εἶπεν, οἷα δὴ εἰώθασιν αἱ γυναῖκες, ὅτι "Ὦ Σώκρατες, ὕστατον δή σε προσεροῦσι νῦν οἱ ἐπιτήδειοι καὶ σὺ τούτους."

Socrates feels obliged to send his family away. As at the end of the dialogue, it is the lack of εὐφημία that he cannot abide. That is what the verb must denote: failure, through lack of control,[16] to observe εὐφημία. The ἀν- is the negative prefix, not the preposition ἀνά.[17] Burnet in his commentary on the *Phaedo* declared that the word ought to mean 'raise a cry of εὐφημεῖτε', and commentators have followed him; but ἀναβοᾶν, if that is what Burnet had in mind, is not at all analogous (it does not mean 'raise a cry of βοᾶτε'). It is true that LSJ offers no examples of verbs in ἀνευ- from Greek of the period, but there are some examples from later Greek and there is nothing against the possibility in principle. The normal opposite of εὐφημέω is δυσφημέω, so the point of this coinage lies in its stress: the sin is not one of commission (δυσφημέω, uttering words of ill omen), but omission (failure to keep silent). The circumstances, then, in which one would use this word must be precisely those which require silence. In all three instances of its use, death is in prospect. We infer that the approach of death was a time when silence was appropriate.

Why? Margaret Alexiou has an intriguing suggestion which may be along the right lines.[18] The idea in Plato, she comments, seems to be the same as it still is in Greek belief, that premature lamentation

---

[16] οἷα δὴ εἰώθασιν αἱ γυναῖκες is one illustration among many that in the view of Greek men women lacked self-control.

[17] Cf. Wilamowitz on Eur. *HF* 1188 and M. L. West on *Or.* 1337.

[18] Alexiou (1974: 4 f.).

will interfere with the proper progress of the soul to its appointed destination. The moment when the soul struggles to separate itself from the body is perilous, and words of ill omen could only make it more so.[19] The notion of the struggle of the soul at the point of death is attested by the verb ψυχορραγεῖν[20] and by the folktale of wrestling with Thanatos in the *Alcestis*. One may object that the modern Christian ideas of the soul's destiny can hardly be read back into the ancient Greek belief, and that, if they are present in Plato, it merely goes to show that he has invested the ordinary practice with a new meaning in the light of his philosophy which, after all, has notable similarities to Christianity. But conventional Greek belief did hold that death involved a journey to a new abode, and the practice which Plato is, on this view, reinterpreting, must at the very least have supposed that words of bad omen would interfere dangerously with the operations of the divine, which is never closer than at death. The analogy of sacrifice is pertinent; εὐφημία gives way to ὀλολυγή, as εὐφημία in the presence of death gives way to lamentation, only when it is safe, only when events have unmistakably taken their decisive turn. Disaster will ensue if the sacred proceedings are compromised. Presumably, then, untimely lamentation would make the whole process more difficult for the dying person than it needed to be. The stress on silence concentrated attention on the sanctity of the moment—in Sophocles' play, on the sanctity of *this* particular moment.

On a perfectly ordinary level, one can understand the reason for the prescription. Even when death is a certainty, to underscore the fact by mourning at the deathbed can seem unbearably inappropriate.[21] This is part of Socrates' feeling with Xanthippe. But the *Trachiniae* and the *Phaedo* are not ordinary contexts. One is the death of the greatest hero of mythology, the other is the death of the greatest hero of philosophy. We are entitled, even required, to press the references. Socrates has spent the whole dialogue arguing

[19] Cf. Danforth (1982), 39: 'no crying or lamenting is permitted in the presence of the dying person, since that . . . is believed to hinder the soul's departure from the body.'

[20] Eur. *Alc.* 20, 143, *HF* 324.

[21] Premature lamentation actually presages death; Alexiou (1974: 4 f.) cites *Iliad* 6. 500, where the women mourn Hector ἔτι ζωόν. She might have cited Thetis' lament for Achilles (*Iliad* 18. 51 ff.), which explicitly forecasts his death. Cf. Seaford (1994: 166 f.). *Trachiniae* 783 f., quoted above, may be read in the same way; the lamentation comes too soon and only shows that Heracles will die.

that death is a transition, the preparation for which is the philosopher's purpose in life; that moment is at hand. Here, if anywhere, εὐφημία is to be commended, to ensure that nothing interferes with this transition. The *Trachiniae*, too, implicitly presents the death of Heracles as a transition. The only explicit reason Heracles gives for his prohibition is his contempt for unmanly weeping, and perhaps no argument will persuade readers who want everything spelled out for them that any other reason needs to be supplied.[22] Others will agree that these words, like his others, say more than even he knows.

At the very least we may say that, without lamentation, there is no funeral.[23] Heracles' prohibition, strictly speaking, applies to the moments leading up to his death; as Hyllus rightly understands (1207), Heracles will not yet be dead when placed upon the pyre. That in itself is worth noticing: one would normally hope to have a proper corpse to cremate. Heracles cannot die during the play (how could he, without contradicting prevailing belief?), and this startling peculiarity about the funeral arrangements must make one wonder what *really* happens on the pyre. The moment of death is left completely vague, and the injunction against lamentation must continue in force. The funeral is cancelled.

A final parallel confirms the reading. In the exodus of Euripides' *Iphigeneia at Aulis*, which, though bedevilled by problems of authenticity, is based on a Euripidean design, Iphigeneia, convinced of the rightness of her sacrifice, emphatically forbids mourning (1433 f., 1466). She will have no tomb, she says (just like Heracles); her memorial will be the altar of Artemis. Furthermore, she calls upon the chorus to sing a paean of celebration—the verb is ἐπευφημήσατε (1467)—and enjoins ritual εὐφημία on the Argive host (1564). Diggle in his *OCT* judges that these lines (except the last) are probably by Euripides. Her utterly mysterious disappearance is reported in the messenger's speech which, though judged spurious by editors, must have had a counterpart in the original version. Iphigeneia has no real funeral because her death is an easy transition to semi-divine status. She is fully conscious of this; in

---

[22] The messenger says of Theseus in the *OC* that he ὡς ἀνὴρ γενναῖος οὐκ οἴκτου μέτα | κατῄνεσεν τάδ' ὅρκιος δράσειν ξένῳ (1636 f.); Heracles' own weeping in *Trach.* causes him deep shame (1071 ff.; cf. Eur. *HF* 1354 f.). On manly resistance to grief cf. Dover (1974: 167).

[23] Holt (1989: 76).

Sophocles' play, it is the audience that knows it. Heracles' death too is not really a death.[24]

In the exodus, one's attention is naturally fixed on what is mentioned: the instructions about the pyre and so on. What is not mentioned can be equally significant. Heracles omits from his instructions the most obvious thing of all: what should be done with the bones after the cremation.[25] The disposition of the remains is the focal point with Patroclus and Achilles, with Elpenor, with Ajax, and with countless others. In the *Phaedo* (115c), Crito asks Socrates how he would like to be buried; Socrates like Heracles had omitted to mention it. Socrates replies that if Crito wishes to bury him he will have to catch him first; he himself will be elsewhere, and all that will remain behind is a lifeless corpse. Heracles' failure to give instructions on this point is quite striking when one thinks of it, and the reason is, of course, that there will be no grave of Heracles in the real world. Sophocles' tactful omission of the topic is another indication that his inner eye was on the coming transformation.

It seems beyond doubt that Sophocles hints at the broader, real-world significance of the stage events. That being so, it is useless to

[24] This passage in *IA* provides a bridge to the topos of the funeral oration that a glorious death should not be lamented, because the dead have won immortal fame; see Thuc. 2. 44. 1, Lys. 2. 77–81, Xen. *Ages.* 10. 3, Pl. *Menex.* 247–8, [Dem.] 60. 32, Hyper. *Epit.* 41–2; Charondas *apud* Stob. 4. 2. 24 (iv. 153 Hense); Kassel (1958: 40 ff.); Loraux (1986: 44). Simonides' poem for the dead of Thermopylae (*PMG* 531), as Loraux notes, provides close parallels for this topos (πρὸ γόων δὲ μνᾶστις, ὁ δ' οἶκτος ἔπαινος); he says also, like Iphigeneia, that their tomb will be an altar. Lloyd-Jones at the conference noted *OC* 1751 ff., where Theseus says it would be νέμεσις to mourn Oedipus for whom death is a χάρις (cf. 1777); Martin West quoted Ennius' epitaph *nemo me lacrumis decoret nec funera fletu | faxit. cur? volito vivos per ora virum.* Note that in the *OC* the children wept copiously even before Oedipus died (1646)—a nice confirmation of what was said above, that the prohibition was neither enforceable nor universally enforced, and of the supposition that when an author chooses to make something of it, there is a good reason. Incidentally, Seaford's defence of the text ξύν' ἀπόκειται in 1752 (1994: 135 n. 141)—he understands it to mean that it is νέμεσις to mourn one whose death is a common blessing to the city, i.e. a hero worshipped in cult—sits ill with the widespread practice of ritual lamentation in such cults (documented by Seaford 139 nn. 151–2); Theseus' comment (with ξυνά) sounds like a general rule (not just one for this cult, as Seaford n. 152). It reads much better as a version of the epitaphian topos that the dead, having attained peace, need no mourning. Charondas loc. cit. says that excessive grief constitutes ἀχαριστία towards the chthonian spirits; χάρις being a reciprocal affair, the passage provides something of a parallel to the *OC*. Lloyd-Jones and Wilson (1997: 137) defend the conjecture νύξ.

[25] Holt (1989: 32).

speculate on how or whether this interferes with the realism of stage representation. Both elements are simply there: the stage Heracles thinking that this is his mortal end, side by side with a Heracles whom the audience can hardly forget as a potent god in their own lives. One could if one wished excogitate various ways of reconciling these conflicting tendencies, and arbitrarily choose one that satisfies. One could, for instance, imagine a scenario in which the oracles impressed upon Heracles the extreme importance of getting to Oeta and building the pyre, and of marrying Iole to Hyllus; he passes on these commands to his son, thus encouraging the audience to remember the real-life reasons for them, even though he himself is unaware of them. But such ingenuity would be wasted, and would come close to the documentary fallacy. For most viewers the play is over before such problems even begin to obtrude themselves. In the course of watching this scene the first audience would, I believe, have thought of Heracles' coming immortality, whether as hero, god, or both; if they happened to think also, as I think they would not, that it is odd for Heracles to hint at such things, it would be easy enough to suppose that he knows not whereof he speaks; Sophocles' words are carefully chosen to be consistent with that supposition. We who come after him know the true significance.

An argument advanced from time to time is that any hint of Heracles' coming immortality ruins the tragic effect.[26] The difficulty with this argument is that it presumes to tell Sophocles what the 'tragic effect' should be. Unmitigated disaster may be connoted by the English word 'tragic', but it is not necessarily what dramatists at the Dionysia thought they had to represent. On purely dramatic grounds the argument is weaker than it seems, for even if a spectator catches these hints is it impossible to remain unmoved by Heracles' screams, and say, with a shrug of the shoulders, 'This is all only temporary: glory awaits him in heaven above.' No more does Christ's ultimate ascension mitigate the suffering of the crucifixion or the tragedy of Good Friday. But it is probably altogether wrong to think of death and transfiguration as alternative readings of the scene. Rather, knowledge of the coming transformation is exactly what puts the death in perspective. It raises disturbing questions and emotions in the audience as they watch Heracles' agony, questions that strike to the heart of Greek religion as Sophocles

---

[26] So, insistently, Stinton (1990: 479, 482, 489).

understood it.[27] Is this the price to be paid for heroization? *Does* Heracles die in utter ignorance and undiluted pain? Is Zeus as cruel as Hyllus thinks (1264 ff.)? Can others follow this path? How could they, if ignorance is our lot (1270), and any course of action might be frustrated by the gods? But if this fate is peculiar to Heracles the god-man, can it teach us anything at all? Is not the hero's eventual exaltation violently incongruous with the bathetic cause of his death? Many questions without answers: one can only shake one's head and say, there is nothing here which is not Zeus. Now *that* is a truly tragic effect. Without Zeus, and Oeta, and the oracles, and the coming exaltation, this is only a sad and ironic story about a housewife who accidentally killed her great warrior husband; it is not a story fit for the Dionysia, as Sophocles conceived it. The sense of a larger dimension is precisely what makes the ending both mysterious and powerful. The *Trachiniae*—dare we call it a passion play?—ends in a maelstrom of conflicting religious emotions; and Greek tragedy is about nothing if not religion, as our honorand has so often taught us.

REFERENCES

ALEXIOU, M. (1974), *The Ritual Lament in Greek Tradition* (Cambridge).

DANFORTH, L. M. (1982), *The Death Rituals of Rural Greece* (Princeton).

DAVIES, M. (1991), *Sophocles:* Trachiniae (Oxford).

DOVER, K. J. (1974), *Greek Popular Morality in the Time of Plato and Aristotle* (Basil Blackwell).

EASTERLING, P. E. (1981), 'The End of the Trachiniae', *BICS* 6: 56–74.

—— (1982), *Sophocles: Trachiniae* (Cambridge).

—— (1996), 'Weeping, Witnessing, and the Tragic Audience: Response to Segal', in Silk (1996), 173–81.

—— (1997) (ed.), *The Cambridge Companion to Greek Tragedy* (Cambridge).

EWANS, M. (1996), 'Patterns of Tragedy in Sophokles and Shakespeare', in Silk (1996), 438–57.

FRIIS JOHANSEN, H. (1986), 'Heracles in Sophocles' *Trachiniae*', *C&M* 37: 47–61.

HALL, E. (1997), 'The Sociology of Athenian Tragedy', in Easterling (1997), 93–126.

---

[27] Friis Johansen (1986: 61) reads the ending in a similar way; cf. also Easterling (1981: 68; 1996: 174 ff.).

HENRICHS, A. (1993), 'The Tomb of Aias and the Prospect of Hero Cult in Sophokles', *ClAnt* 12: 165–80.

HÖLSCHER, U. (1988), *Die Odyssee: Epos zwischen Märchen und Roman* (Munich).

HOLT, P. (1989), 'The End of the *Trachiniae* and the Fate of Heracles', *JHS* 109: 69–80.

KASSEL, R. (1958), *Untersuchungen zur griechischen und römischen Konsolationsliteratur (Zetemata* 18).

KEARNS, E. (1989), *The Heroes of Attica (BICS* Suppl. 57).

LINFORTH, I. M. (1952), 'The Pyre on Mount Oeta in Sophocles' *Trachiniae*', University of California Publications in Classical Philology 14. 7: 255–67.

LLOYD-JONES, H. (1982), *Blood for the Ghosts* (London).

——(1983), *The Justice of Zeus*, 2nd edn. (Berkeley and Los Angeles).

——and WILSON, N. (1997), *Sophocles: Second Thoughts (Hypomnemata* 100).

LORAUX, N. (1986), *The Invention of Athens* (Cambridge, Mass.).

MARCH, J. (1987), *The Creative Poet (BICS* Suppl. 49).

NESSELRATH, H.-G. (1997), 'Herakles als tragischer Held in und seit der Antike', in H. Flashar (ed.), *Tragödie. Idee und Transformation (Colloquium Rauricum* 5), 307–31.

SEAFORD, R. (1994), *Reciprocity and Ritual* (Oxford).

SILK, M. S. (1985), 'Heracles and Greek Tragedy', *G&R* 32: 1–22.

——(1996) (ed.), *Tragedy and the Tragic* (Oxford).

STINTON, T. C. W. (1986), 'The Scope and Limits of Allusion in Greek Tragedy', in M. J. Cropp, E. Fantham, and S. E. Scully (eds.), *Greek Tragedy and its Legacy: Essays Presented to D. J. Conacher* (Calgary), 67–102 = Stinton (1990), 454–92.

——(1990), *Collected Papers on Greek Tragedy* (Oxford).

TAPLIN, O. (1977), *The Stagecraft of Aeschylus* (Oxford).

10

Comic Patterns in Sophocles' *Ichneutae*

NETTA ZAGAGI

Sophocles' *Ichneutae* is one of a group of satyr-plays which are only loosely connected with tragedy in their themes and in their poetic atmosphere. One can safely assume that it does not constitute a direct parody of any individual tragedy—but that, after all, is one of the salient characteristics of the satyric *genre*. Moreover, the theme of this play itself, albeit mythological, is in its very nature and essence non-tragic. Its plot consists mainly of the story of the search for Apollo's lost cattle, ending successfully with the exposure of the thief, the baby Hermes; but at the same time we also have the discovery of Hermes' wonderful invention, the lyre, which is to become the main musical instrument used by Apollo himself. The fragmentary nature of our evidence makes it difficult to guess to what extent, if at all, this pretty but rather marginal myth, a brief episode in the biography of the two Olympian brothers, had ever attracted the attention of the major tragedians; but it is clear that, as far as its subject-matter goes, it has nothing to offer which would be even faintly reminiscent of the intensity of the tragic *genre*.

Things look different when we consider the opposite dramatic *genre*, comedy. Amusing adventure stories with a happy ending; successful searches for lost or merely wished-for objects; acts of theft, inventions, miraculous creatures and happenings—all these are among the staple themes not only of the satyr-play, but also of Old and Middle Comedy—and, with the exception of the magic and miraculous elements, of New Comedy as well—subject, of course, to

I am deeply grateful to my colleague Professor John Glucker and to Mr P. McC. Brown for their generous help in the various stages of the preparation of this chapter. Thanks are also due to the editor for his useful criticism.

generic differences in the execution.[1] Yet the striking affinity in theme between *Ichneutae* and the comic tradition has not been sufficiently noticed by scholars. The majority of scholars have concentrated on comparing this satyric text with tragedy,[2] or with the Homeric Hymn to Hermes, clearly one of Sophocles' main sources of inspiration for this play,[3] while the comic parallels, in the few cases where scholars have noticed them at all, are treated as side issues.[4] My starting-point in the present study is the assumption that the key to understanding Sophocles' dramatic art in *Ichneutae* consists above all in recognizing the comic qualities of the characters and events depicted in this play; for, important as the analogies to tragedy may be, they can hardly enable us to throw light on the working methods of Sophocles the author of a satyr-play, as distinct from Sophocles the author of solemn dramas. The approach that has prevailed in recent scholarship is just the opposite of that delineated here. It appears to me that too much effort has been expended on fruitless attempts to reconcile the art of Sophocles in his tragedies with his achievement in that light and somewhat licentious reflection of tragedy, the satyr-play, as we have it in the remains of *Ichneutae*. Such attempts have, of necessity, led scholars into underrating the achievement of Sophocles in the satyric medium. A comparison with comedy, the aims and methods of which are in many ways the same as those of the satyr-play, and which is as accustomed to parody and burlesque of tragedy and myth as is the satyr-play, may assist us in

[1] On the thematic and structural affinity between comedy and satyr-play, see e.g. Guggisberg 1947: 36 ff.; Sutton 1980: 136 f., 144 f., 162 f., 169, 172 f.; id. 1985: 102; Seaford 1984: 18 ff.; Seidensticker 1979: 247 ff. = Seidensticker 1989: 350 ff. I have not been able to consult L. T. Murphy, 'Quae ratio intercedat inter fabulas satyricas et comoediam antiquam' (Diss. Harvard, 1935).

[2] Sutton 1980: 167: 'The sailors' frantic search for the missing Ajax seems parodied by the satyrs' search in *Ichneutae*'; id. 1985:97: 'The description in *Ichneutae* of Apollo searching for his missing cattle and their thief distinctly recalls that of Odysseus searching for the killer of the Achaean herd; the divided chorus of searching satyrs (*Ichn.* 85 ff.) seems to parody the divided chorus of searching sailors (*Aj.* 866 ff.), and both plays conclude with a scene of reconciliation'; Pöhlmann 1989: 48; below, nn. 30, 31. See in general, Maltese 1982: 12–17.

[3] On the question of the relation between the Homeric Hymn to Hermes and Sophocles' *Ichneutae* see in general Maltese 1982: 17–20.

[4] See below, nn. 23, 40, 41, 44, 50; Guarini (1925: 313–29) and Ussher (1974: 130–8) are concerned almost exclusively with Sophocles' exploitation of comic terms and expressions.

placing Sophocles' achievement in *Ichneutae* in a more realistic perspective.

I should make it clear, at this point, that it is not my intention to deal with problems of chronology, or to attempt to establish a direct influence of this or that extant comedy on *Ichneutae*, or of *Ichneutae* on other plays. The ancient theatre was a *living* industry, with techniques and motifs being borrowed, stolen, and exchanged among authors/producers, without necessarily depending on the few written plays and fragments which have reached us through a *literary* tradition. In particular, the Greek comic tradition was characterized by a fruitful synthesis between formal conservatism and intellectual daring. Motifs which were first introduced in the earliest stages of its development continued to leave their mark on comedy, even in its latest transmutations, in differing shapes and proportions; and, although our fragmentary evidence does not allow us to form a complete picture of the various stages of the development of comedy, it is none the less clear that in the world of comic poetry—as in ancient poetry in general—*convention* never lost its force: on the contrary, in many ways it served both the audience and the author himself as the main (if not the only) criterion for identifying and assessing variation and originality. It is not only possible but actually vital to discuss the relationship between *Ichneutae* and comedy in general terms, to ensure a fruitful discussion of the interrelations between the two *genres*.

Our concern here—as already shown by the title of this study—is with comic *patterns*, which exercise an influence not so much on the character and development of the plot of the play as a whole, as on the formation of the characters and of their experiences in individual situations and scenes. Silenus' entrance-speech provides us with the first of these patterns:

> ἐπεὶ θ]εοῦ φώνημα τὼς ἐπέκλυον
> βοῶ]ντος ὀρθίοισι σὺν κηρύγμασι,
> σ]πουδῇ τάδ᾽ ἦ πάρεστι πρεσβύτῃ [τελῶν,
> σ]οί, Φοῖβ᾽ Ἄπολλον, προφιλὴς εὐε[ργέτης
> θέλων γενέσθαι τῷδ᾽ ἐπεσσύθην δρ[ό]μω[ι,
> ἤν πως τὸ χρῆμα τοῦτό σοι κυνηγέσω.   (45–50)[5]

---

[5] I quote the Loeb edition of H. Lloyd-Jones (1996) since it is the latest edition so far, and it incorporates materials and suggestions which are later than Radt's *TGF* iv. 274–308. For the purpose of my arguments, the full apparatus of Radt's edition is not usually required. The plays of Aristophanes are cited from the Budé edition of

Silenus' appearance on the stage comes in direct response to Apollo's public appeal to all the residents of Cyllene (see below) to assist him in discovering his lost cattle, in exchange for a fitting remuneration. But important as the motivation for Silenus' appearance may be, what the spectator is expected to notice, while the father of the satyrs is directing his steps towards the god, is that *it is an old man who is here about to offer his help*. This emphasis on the advanced age of the protagonist who is entering the stage has a considerable number of parallels in comedy. We shall supply a few of the more typical examples:

> οἴ—
> μοι τάλας τῶν ἐτῶν τῶν ἐμῶν·
> οὐκ ἂν ἐπ' ἐμῆς γε νεότητος, ὅτ' ἐ—
> γὼ φερων ἀνθράκων φορτίον
> ἠκολούθουν Φαύλλῳ τρέχων, ὧδε φαύλως ἂν ὁ
> σπονδοφόρος οὗτος ὑπ' ἐμοῦ τότε διωκόμενος
> ἐξέφυγεν οὐδ' ἂν ἐλαφρῶς ἂν ἀπεπλίξατο.
>
> νῦν δ' ἐπειδὴ στερρὸν ἤδη τοὐμὸν ἀντικνήμιον
> καὶ παλαιῷ Λακτρατείδῃ τὸ σκέλος βαρύνεται,
> οἴχεται.

(Aristoph. *Ach.* 208 ff.)

> χώρει, πρόβαιν' ἐρρωμένως. Ὦ Κωμία, βραδύνεις.
> μὰ τὸν Δι' οὐ μέντοι πρὸ τοῦ γ', ἀλλ' ἦσθ' ἱμὰς κύνειος·
> νυνὶ δὲ κρείττων ἐστὶ σοῦ Χαρμίδης βαδίζειν.
> ὦ Στρυμόδωρε Κονθυλεῦ, βέλτιστε συνδικαστῶν,
> Εὐεργίδης ἆρ' ἐστί που ἐνταυθὶ Χάβης ⟨θ'⟩ ὁ Φλυεύς;
> πάρεσθ', ὃ δὴ λοιπόν γ' ἔτ' ἐστίν, ἀπαπαπαῖ παπαιάξ,
> ἥβης ἐκείνης, ἡνίκ' ἐν Βυζαντίῳ ξυνῆμεν
> φρουροῦντ' ἐγώ τε καὶ σύ· . . .
> ἀλλ' ἐγκονῶμεν, ὦνδρες, ὡς ἔσται Λάχητι νυνί·
> . . .
> . . . ἀλλὰ
> σπεύδωμεν, ὦνδρες ἥλικες, πρὶν ἡμέραν γενέσθαι.

(Aristoph. *Vesp.* 230 ff.)

Coulon and Van Daele 1923–30. References of the form '[author] fr. [ ] K.-A. are to Kassel's and Austin's *PCG*. References to Austin's *Comicorum Graecorum Fragmenta in Papyris Reperta* (1973) are indicated by *CGFP*. References to Menander follow the OCT, and its numeration, of Sandbach (1990). The plays of Plautus are cited from the OCT of Lindsay (1910), those of Terence from the OCT of Kauer and Lindsay (1965).

οὔκουν ὁρᾷς ὁρμωμένους ἡμᾶς πάλαι προθύμως,
ὡς εἰκός ἐστιν ἀσθενεῖς γέροντας ἄνδρας ἤδη;
σὺ δ' ἀξιοῖς ἴσως με θεῖν, πρὶν ταῦτα καὶ φράσαι μοι
ὅτου χάριν μ' ὁ δεσπότης ὁ σὸς κέκληκε δεῦρο.[6]

(Aristoph. Plut. 257 ff.)

Ut aetas mea est atque ut hoc usu' facto est
gradum proferam, progrediri properabo.
sed id quam mihi facile sit hau sum falsus.
nam pernicitas deserit: consitus sum
senectute, onustum gero corpu', vires
reliquere: ut aetas mala est! mers mala ergost.

(Plaut. Men. 753 ff.; Menaechmus I's father-in-law)

It is obvious that we are faced here with a comic convention, of which Silenus' speech can be regarded as representative. What seems to set the Sophoclean treatment of this convention at variance with the traditional comic pattern is the dissimilarity between action and speech in the protagonist's demeanour. While in the other examples just quoted there is, most probably, a full accord between the description of the slow progress of the old men—whether delivered by themselves or by some other character present on the stage—and what actually takes place before the audience, in *Ichneutae* old Silenus' excessive emphasis on the speed of his arrival—τῷδ' ἐπεσσύθην δρ[ό]μῳ[ι, to use his own words[7]—is, as far as we can judge, an exaggeration due to sheer boastfulness.[8] We shall soon return to this characteristic of Silenus.

The bargaining scene between Apollo and Silenus, coming after the latter's dubious self-presentation as 'a nimble old man', presents us with another comic pattern, which is entirely different from our first one. Silenus, the god's self-styled προσφιλὴς εὐε[ργέτης (48), is

---

[6] Cf. Plaut. *Poen.* 522–6: liberos homines per urbem modico magi' par est gradu | ire, servoli esse duco festinantem currere. | praesertim in re populi placida atque interfectis hostibus | non decet tumultuari. sed si properabas magis, | pridie nos te advocatos huc duxisse oportuit. 545–6: si quid tu placide otioseque agere vis, | operam damus; | si properas, cursores meliust te advocatos ducere. 568–9: bene vale igitur. te advocatos meliust celeris ducere; | tardi sumu' nos.

[7] Cf. 92: ἔοικεν ἤδη κ[ἀμὲ πρὸς τοὔργον δραμεῖν.

[8] For boastfulness as a character trait of Silenus in *Ichn.* see further 153–60 (on which see recent discussion by Lloyd-Jones 1994: 139 f.); Siegmann 1941: 67–9; Guggisberg 1947: 54 f. Cf. Eur. *Cycl.* 1–9; Aesch. *Dict.* 47a Radt. For satyric boasting in general see Soph. fr. 1130 Radt. (= *P. Oxy.* VIII 1083 on which see Maas 1912: 1426–9 = *Kleine Schriften* 50–3); Seaford 1984: nn. ad 1, 596, 635–55.

willing to do Apollo the favour of attempting to find his lost cattle—
but not without Apollo's express undertaking, here and now, that he
will give him the promised reward.⁹ This conditional undertaking
causes Apollo to make a counter-condition, and, at the end of what
appears like a commercial negotiation, reminiscent in its mutual
verbal repetitions of the formal structure of verbal contracts like the
Roman *stipulatio*, the god finds himself bound by a *double* promise:
both his original promise of financial remuneration, and a promise
to rescue Silenus and his sons from slavery:

τ[ὸ] γὰρ γέ[ρα]ς μοι κείμενον χρ[υ]σο[σ]τεφέ[ς
μά[λι]στ᾽ ἐμ[αῖς κόμ]αισ[ι π]ροσθέσθ[αι χρεώ]ν.
παῖδας δ᾽ ἐμ[οὺ]ς ὅσσοισι [. . .]. . . ε[.]β. [. .].[
π[έμποιμ᾽ ἄ]ν, εἴπερ ἐκτελεῖς ἅπερ λέγεις.
⟨ΑΠ.⟩
σάφ᾽ ἴσθι, δ]ώσω· μοῦνον ἐμπ[έδου τ]άδε.
⟨ΣΙ.⟩
τὰς βοῦς ἀπάξω σ]οι· σὺ δ᾽ ἐμπέδου [δόσι]ν.
⟨ΑΠ.⟩
ἕξει σφ᾽ ὅ γ᾽ εὑ]ρών, ὅστις ἔσθ᾽· ἐτ[οῖμ]α δ[έ.
[*fragments of four lines*]
⟨ΣΙ.⟩
τί τοῦτο; πῶ[ς *about 16 letters*] εις.
⟨ΑΠ.⟩
ἐλεύθερος σὺ [πᾶν τε γένος ἔσται τέκν]ων. (51–63)

Although Apollo's 'legal standing' *vis-à-vis* Silenus and the satyrs
is not all that clear in our play, and the satyrs are traditionally
regarded as the servants and companions of *Dionysus*,¹⁰ it can hardly

⁹ A recurrent feature of Silenus' characterization in satyric drama was his
noticeable tendency towards business negotiation with other characters to his own
profit: Guggisberg 1947: 54 f.; Sutton 1980: 139.

¹⁰ The identity of the master to whom the satyrs are supposed to be enslaved in
Ichneutae has been the subject of much dispute. Three deities have been mentioned
as suitable candidates for the job: Dionysus, their traditional master in surviving
satyr drama, Apollo himself, and Pan, whose cult is closely associated with Arcadia
(for a critical evaluation of the main theories put forward in this matter, see
Siegmann 1941: 46–54; also Maltese (1982: 21 f.)). Although the fragmentary state
of our evidence makes certainty impossible on the point, I am inclined to surmise
that in our play, just as in e.g. Euripides' *Cyclops* and Aeschylus' *Isthmiastae*, the
lawful master of the satyrs is no other than Dionysus. Cf. Lloyd-Jones 1996: 142 '. . .
Apollo is promising emancipation from their regular servitude to his brother
Dionysus. It is true that they usually enjoy being slaves to Dionysus, but it may
well have been imagined that they would prefer not to be slaves at all.' However,

be denied that in this scene, as well as in later parts of this play, the underlying assumption is that Apollo has both the right and the power to release them from their bondage. Since in everyday life this is the exclusive right of the legal owner of a slave, one may be justified in regarding this scene as something of an intentional inversion of the master–slave relation, in addition to the more obvious inversion of the god–man relation which is one of the fundamental patterns of Greek comic perception. New Comedy—especially in Plautus' Latin adaptations—is full of such inversions of the master–slave relationship;[11] but Old Comedy, too, largely based as it is on depicting the social world-order upside-down, hardly neglected the wealth of comic possibilities which this well-known technique of inversion can derive from the area of master–slave relations. A prime example of such an inversion—also presented in a mythological attire—can be seen in the vicissitudes in the relations between Dionysus and his slave Xanthias on their way to Hades in Aristophanes' *Frogs*.[12]

given the conventional nature of the satyrs' position as slaves in satyr drama (see below), one should be wary of attaching too much importance to the question of the identity of their master in our play. Note Wilamowitz's balanced approach to this question 'Ich ahne nicht, wer der Herr sein konnte, vermutlich ist er am Ende bei der Freilassung der Satyrn gennant worden; aber die Zuschauer haben offenbar eine Aufklärung gar nicht nötig gehabt. Sklaven sind die Satyrn im "Kyklops", wo das besonders motiviert wird; man vermutet, dass es ein konventionelles Motiv des Satyrspiels war, um die Tiere überall einführen zu können' (1912: 454 = *Kleine Schriften I*: 354 = Seidensticker 1989: 94). The captivity, servitude, and liberation of the satyrs is one of the most common themes of satyric drama: see e.g. Guggisberg 1947: 60 ff.; Sutton 1980: 137 ff., 147 ff.; id. (1985: 98 f.; Seaford 1984: 33 ff.; Seidensticker 1979: 244 f. = 1989: 346 ff.; Lasserre 1973: 289 ff. = 'Das Satyrspiel' in Seidensticker 1989: 271 ff.

[11] See esp. the conclusion of the plays *Epidicus* and *Pseudolus*; Plautus' play *Asinaria* is largely based on the device of role-reversal in master–slave relations: see esp. 650 ff.; also *Bacch.* 702–3, 726–60; *Capt.* Act II; *Cas.* Act III. vi; *Mil.* 610–11, 805–6, 812, 1009, 1129; *Most.* 406; *Poen.* 145–6; cf. 447–8; *Rud.* 1265–80. On the role and place of this particular feature of master–slave relationship in Plautine comedy see in general, Segal (1987: ch. 4), 'From Slavery to Freedom'. For Plautus' farcical representation of slaves and master–slave relationships, see Fraenkel 1922: 194 f., 231 ff.; Spranger 1984.

[12] Wehrli (1936: 35 n. 1, 51). See also Aristoph. *Plut.* 20–5, 45 ff. The dramatic device of role-reversal of the purely farcical kind found in the comedies of Aristophanes and Plautus has no parallel in surviving Menander: see Zagagi (1994: 38–40, 45). A milder form of role-reversal in the relations between master and slave may be found in Men. *Asp.* 299 ff. (Austin 1970: n. ad loc. [Arnott's]);

Yet, even more than the pattern of an inversion in the master–
slave relation, the mere promise to release someone from bondage in
exchange for special services rendered is sufficient to indicate a
striking affinity between the poetic world of *Ichneutae* and that of
comedy. It is true that this motif is not to be found in the remains of
Old Comedy; but in view of its widespread use in later comedy,[13]
and considering the increasing significance of slaves in comedy (and
also in Euripidean tragedy) in the fifth century,[14] it is reasonable to
assume that the silence of our sources here is merely an accident of
the transmission. It is worth noting, in this context, that as in many
of the plots of New Comedy, so also in *Ichneutae*, the dramatic
importance of this typical element is not limited merely to the
bargaining scene, but makes its mark, to a greater or lesser extent,
also on later stages of the plot.[15] On the other hand, in *both* cases,
the bargaining scene between slave and master is given some special
emphasis, since it is perceived as a comic focus of interest in its own
right.

It is worth pointing out how well Sophocles had already prepared
us for the commercial nature of the negotiations between Silenus
and Apollo in the god's own opening speech which precedes this
transaction. Apollo's formal language both at the beginning and at
the conclusion of the speech; the request for help, which is couched

Peric. 267 ff. (Handley and Hurst 1990: 158 (Zagagi's note)). See also Ter. *Heaut.*
350–2.

[13] Plaut. *Epid.* 726 ff. (Epidicus); *Men.* 1023 ff., 1055 ff., 1146 ff. (Messenio); *Rud.*
927 ff., 1394 ff., 1410 ff. (Gripus); 1216–20 (Trachalio); Ter. *Ad.* 960 ff. (Syrus and
his wife); *And.* 35 ff. It seems reasonable to assume, using the analogy of the above
examples, that Habrotonon in Menander's *Epitrepontes* (see 538–41, 557–60) and
Strobilus in Plautus' *Aulularia* (see 823 ff.) gained their freedom in the end. The
same could be argued for Daos, the intriguing slave in Menander's *Aspis*, who,
initially believing his young master Cleostratos to be dead in battle, claims to have
lost any hope of manumission (ll. 11–12; see Webster 1974: 40 f.), but with his
master's safe homecoming may have ended up as a free man in return for his
exceptionally good services to him. In the following cases the stock reference to
manumission, in so far as it is treated as a plot-constituent, takes the form of a
promise, not to be fulfilled in the course of the play: Men. *Peric.* 982–3 (Doris);
Plaut. *Asin.* 650 ff. (Libanus, Leonida); *Mil.* 1193–5 (Palaestrio); *Poen.* 420, 428–30
(Milphio). Austin, *CGFP* fr. 253. 16–17 (= fr. 1006 K–A) and possibly also Austin,
CGFP fr. 259. 7 ff. (= fr. 1013 K–A) further demonstrate, however fragmentarily,
New Comedy's stock treatment of the theme of liberation from slavery.

[14] See Aristoph. *Ra.* 947 ff.

[15] *Ichn.* 159–65, 457; see esp. Plaut. *Asin.* 650 ff.; *Men.* 1023 ff., 1055 ff.; *Rud.*
1410 ff.

in general terms; the special mention of a remuneration for the finder—all these reflect (as has been well observed by Maltese[16]) the stylistic and structural mechanisms of official public proclamations aimed at the detection of lost property, and in particular of runaway slaves. The gap between Apollo's divine nature and his need to employ formal patterns of action derived from the ways of life of contemporary Athenian society, places both speech and speaker within the well-known territory of divine parodies, one of the salient characteristics of Old Comedy. Indeed, a closer analysis of Apollo's speech would make it clear that his image loses progressively more of its divine quality as his public proclamation gains in length and detail. Take, for example, the emphasis on Apollo's ignorance concerning the circumstances of the disappearance of his cattle (13 ff.)—an emphasis accompanied by a touch of dramatic irony typical of Sophocles: θεῶ]ν ὡς τέχνῃ[σιν (15); or take his evident embarrassment in face of that event having occurred at all (15–17); or his emotional report of his own wide-ranging and utterly confused search, conducted in a mental state bordering on madness (18–38; see 18–21: ἐκπλαγεὶς ὄκνῳ | σκοπ]ῶ ματεύω . . . ἐμμανὴς κυνηγετῶ). The very Apollo who had begun his speech with a formal appeal for help addressed both to gods and men (7–8), and has repeated his appeal, in the same manner, after first reporting on the disappearance of his cattle (19–20), abandons, towards the end of his speech, his divine *milieu*. From the initial general appeal directed equally to gods and men he has now descended to the concrete appeal to the local peasant population of Cyllene, including the satyrs (39 ff.).[17] Indeed, if we accept the supplement δῶρα in line 8 (as nearly all editors do), what was presented originally, in the opening part of the speech, as a mere generous remuneration, which has the appearance of a personal act of kindness on the god's part

---

[16] Maltese (1982: 67 f.). Apollo's speech has commonly been interpreted as a *Hilferuf* analogous to the one found in Aeschylus' satyr play *Dictyoulcoi* (fr. 46a. 17 ff. Radt) and Sophocles' *Ajax* (879 ff.): e.g. Pfeiffer 1938: 3 ff. = Seidensticker 1989: 58 ff.; Siegmann 1941: 28 ff.; Steffen 1965: 38 ff.; but see Maltese 1979: 117ff.; id. 1982: 15, 66–9; n. ad 1–44.

[17] 'This treatment of Apollo suggests the way in which Pindar conducts implicit polemic against stories that Apollo had to depend on informers to find out things: in *Pythian* 9, the identity of Cyrene; in *Pythian* 3, the truth about Coronis. In the second case we know that Hesiod made a raven bring the news to Apollo; in the first it is natural to make a similar inference. Pindar is uncomfortable with these stories about the oracular god' (Jasper Griffin).

towards the finder, has been transformed in the final lines of the speech into a fully fledged commercial undertaking:

τὰ ἔλ]ωρα τοῦ Παιῶνος ὅστις ἄ[ν λάβῃ,
τῷδ' α]ὐτόχρημα **μισθός** ἐσθ' ὁ κε[ίμενος   (43–4)

Such a starkly realistic presentation, by Apollo himself, of the promised remuneration, stands in sharp contrast to the first, and subjective (one should emphasize this), attitude of Silenus to the same issue. Silenus, in his boastfulness, transfers the act of remuneration, which has just been depicted by Apollo in plain commercial terms, from the cold and calculating world of commercial give-and-take into the glorious heroic world of the Homeric princes, presenting the promised reward metaphorically as *a prize for a victory in an agonistic contest*—that is, as an act of public recognition of his personal prowess:

τ[ὸ] γὰρ γέ[ρα]ς μοι κείμενον χρ[υ]σο[σ]τεφὲ[ς
μά[λι]στ' ἐμ[αῖς κόμ]αισ[ι π]ροσθέσθ[αι χρεώ]ν.   (51–2)

This piece of bragging by Silenus deserves our attention. It is true that we have here a trait which is characteristic of the father of the satyrs and his offspring.[18] But if we concentrate on our scene, a scene in which the status of the protagonist, the satyr, *as a bonded slave* is perceived as an important dramatic factor and as a basic ingredient of the plot about to unfold before our eyes, it would then appear hardly permissible for us to ignore the analogy between the slave-character before us here and the well-known plotting and boastful slaves of New Comedy, headed by Pseudolus, Tranio, and Chrysalus in Plautus' *Pseudolus*, *Mostellaria*, and *Bacchides* respectively. Like Silenus, these slaves also find themselves in situations where they offer their masters unusual services. Like him, they dress up their modest undertaking in the inflated jargon of classical heroism.[19]

---

[18] See above, n. 8.

[19] For military boastfulness as exemplified by Plautine slaves see e.g. *Bacch.* 640 ff., 925 ff. (see Zagagi 1980: 61–3); *Epid.* 675–8; *Mil.* 266–7, 334, 814–15, 1159; *Most.* 775 ff.; *Pseud.* 383–92, 424–6, 572, 574–91, 761–6, 1025–36, 1051. A useful collection of examples from Roman comedy is found in Lorenz 1886: 47 f.; id. 1876: 33–5. See also Ter. *Phorm.* 229 f., 346 f. On Plautus' comic application of military metaphors to servile personages, see Fraenkel 1922:184–6, 231–40; Segal 1987: 128 ff. The fragments of Greek New Comedy have no real parallel for this literary device, but see Men. *Peric.* 278–9; Page 1942: fr. 62. 43; fr. 67. 4. The discovery of Menander's *Aspis* with its intrigue conducted by a masterful slave has not changed

The comic type of the braggart slave, bursting with self-importance, finds its most sophisticated expression in *Ichneutae* in Silenus'
speech immediately following the *parodos* of the chorus of satyrs:

> θεὸς Τύχη καὶ δαῖμον ἰθυντήριε,
> τυχεῖν με πράγους οὗ δράμημ' ἐπείγεται,
> λείαν ἄγραν σύλησιν ἐκκυνηγέσαι
> Φοίβου κλοπαίας βοῦς ἀπεστερημένου.
> τῶν εἴ τις ὀπτήρ ἐστιν ἢ κατήκοος
> ἐμοί τ' ἂν εἴη προσφιλὴς φράσας τάδε
> Φο]ί[βῳ τ'] ἄνακτι παντελὴς εὐεργέτης.
> [*fragments of five lines, two by Silenus, three by the
> Chorus*]
> ⟨ΣΙ.⟩
> φησίν τις, ἢ [οὐδείς φησιν εἰδέναι τάδε;
> ἔοικεν ἤδη κ[ἀμὲ πρὸς τοὔργον δραμεῖν.   (79–92)

Silenus' prayer for success in his undertaking; the military
expressions he weaves into his description of that undertaking
(λείαν . . . σύλησιν, 81); the improvisational manner of his action
(in fact, the spectator is left in complete ignorance as to Silenus'
plans until the moment when, in a sharp reversal, he finds the time
to distribute his instructions among the satyrs: 93)—all these are
well-known and well-tested patterns of the comic tradition.[20] Even
his appeal, in 83 f., and especially at 91—rightly interpreted by
Hunt,[21] Robert,[22] and Süss[23] as addressed to the audience—is in the
nature of an acting-gesture typical of Old Comedy plays.[24] What is

the picture: 'Daos is not the arch-intriguer, glorying in the spider's web he has spun,
but rather one ordinary human being, with an individual's complex fusion of
human characteristics, in a play that concentrates on the interlocking experiences of
contrasted individuals' (Arnott 1970: 14).

[20] For the militaristic element, see above, n. 19; on the question of improvisation
in Graeco-Roman New Comedy see e.g. Slater 1985; Stärk 1989 (criticized by Zagagi
1990: 202–3); Lefèvre *et al.* 1991; Zagagi 1994: 27 ff.; eadem 1995: 71 ff.; Benz *et al.*
1995; Lefèvre 1995.

[21] Hunt 1912: [*ed pr.*] 33 (ad Col. IV 5).

[22] Robert 1912: 541 f.

[23] Süss 1935: 183 ff.; id. 1938: 134 f. See below, n. 40.

[24] Cf. Guggisberg 1947: 41 (criticized by Bain 1975: 24 f.). The nature of Silenus'
appeal and its addressee have been much disputed: see Maltese (1982: 73 with
bibliography). Although we have no evidence in fifth-century satyric drama for
breaking off the dramatic illusion (see, however, Timocles, *Icarioi Satyroi*, fr. 19. 6–7
K–A with n. ad 6; cf. Page 1942: fr. 51b 11–12 with note, p. 241), the affinity

unique to Silenus' pattern of behaviour in the speech just cited is his
marked imitation of the behaviour of Apollo himself in his
proclamation at the opening of our play. Silenus, who, once
Apollo has left, has found himself master both of the stage and
the situation, expresses his feeling of self-importance by adopting
the pose of Apollo: hence the inflated language of his opening
words, which—as observed rightly by Maltese[25]—reflects with great
precision the opening phrases of official documents. Hence also the
general appeal for help, a gesture which at this stage in the action of
the play appears to be superfluous. Silenus goes even further than
this and stresses the apparent community of interests between him
and the god, by means of the following antithesis:

$$τῶν εἴ τις ὀπτήρ ἐστιν ἢ κατήκοος$$
$$ἐμοί τ' ἂν εἴη προσφιλὴς φράσας τάδε$$
$$Φο]ί[βῳ τ'] ἄνακτι παντελὴς εὐεργέτης. \quad (83\text{–}5)$$

That Silenus' earlier description of himself as προσφιλὴς εὐε[ργέτης
(48) of Apollo is here serving—by means of separating its two
components—to create this antithesis increases the ironical effect of
the present situation.

But unlike the plotting slaves of comedy, who place themselves at
the centre of the dramatic activity initiated by themselves, Silenus
recedes to the background as soon as he has distributed his orders to
his sons (92 f.), and henceforward it is the satyrs who shoulder the
main burden of tracking down the lost cattle (100 f.). In the very act
of unfolding the hunting scene, Sophocles skilfully turns his
spectator's attention from the hunter (κυνηγέσω, 50; ἐκκυνηγέσαι,
81) to his assistants: the chorus of satyrs, who are functioning in this
particular situation as a pack of hounds. The impressive visual
effect, achieved both by means of sound and movement, of the great
number of participants in the hunting expedition, has restricted
Silenus' modest place in the action of the play to the preliminary

between the latter genre and comedy, combined with the fragmentary state of our
evidence, especially in the case of satyric drama, should put us on our guard against
any attempt to exclude the phenomenon in question from *Ichneutae*. From both the
dramatic and the comic point of view, the attribution to Silenus of a meta-theatrical
gesture involving an appeal to the *audience* in 83 f. can easily be defended against the
two, more traditional, lines of approach: the one involving an address to the chorus
(Steffen 1960: 69; Maltese 1982: 73 ff.), the other involving an address to the local
inhabitants of Cyllene (Leo 1913: 249, n. 1; Vollgraff 1914: 83; Bain 1975: 24).

[25] Maltese 1982: n. ad 79.

stages of the pursuit. As we shall soon see, this shift of emphasis is used as a preparation for the virtual removal of Silenus from the field of action in the penultimate stages of that pursuit—a surprising plot-movement, which is not without its parallels in the comic tradition.

To appreciate the comic pattern behind this act of pursuit conducted by the satyrs in their act of canine mimicry, one should make it clear from the outset that, to the best of our knowledge, what we have here are not members of the chorus masked as dogs, but a chorus of satyrs *imitating* dogs while keeping their identity as satyrs throughout the play.[26] Indeed, the improvisational and temporary appearance of the chorus as a pack of hounds, contributing as it does to its ambivalent image at a point of crucial interest in the action of the play, is one of the most impressive features of *Ichneutae*. The first appearance of the members of the chorus occurs after the negotiations between Apollo and Silenus have been concluded (76 ff.). From later parts of the play, it is clear that they are aware of the 'conditions of the contract'—financial reward and release from slavery in exchange for discovering the lost cattle (162 ff., 206 ff.). If we were to assume that the members of the chorus were equipped with canine apparel, we would find it difficult to explain—even within the grotesque world of satyr drama—the relevance of that transaction to their canine nature.[27] Add also that Silenus himself, their biological father, shows no sign of any canine qualities, either in his character or in his behaviour. What is more, if what we have in the pursuit scene is more than a mere mimetic imitation of the behaviour of dogs, how could one justify Silenus' sharp censure of his sons' cowardly reaction to the sound emanating from the depths of Cyllene's cave (124 ff.), when their behaviour at this point would be exactly what one might expect of dogs in such circumstances? It must be clear that the canine behaviour of the satyrs has one purpose and one alone: to enliven the scene of pursuit by means which are as dramatic, realistic, and economical as

[26] There is no real basis for Walton's theory (1935: 167 ff. (following Wilamowitz 1912: 453 n. 1, 454–5, 457 = *Kleine Schriften* I: 353 n. 1, 354–5, 357 = Seidensticker 1989: 93 n. 1, 94, 96)) that in this play the satyrs were made up like *dogs*: see Ussher 1974: 133 f.; Maltese 1982: 25.

[27] There is indeed a marked difference between Sophocles' exploitation here of a satyric chorus of a canine behaviour, as it were, and the device of animal choruses in comedy. In the latter case, the animal apparel of the chorus clearly represents its essential nature.

possible.[28] Once this aim has been achieved, the task of the canine pantomime is at an end, and the satyrs return to their natural and original dimension. This may be the place to point out that the depictions of satyrs on vases give us no evidence for their appearance as *dogs*.

It is, indeed the perfect mimetic character of the pursuit-scene, performed by the chorus of satyrs through their canine mimicry, which deserves attention. Admittedly, scenes of pursuit vividly presented on the stage are not uncommon in tragedy.[29] The same is true of using canine imagery in descriptions of someone in hot pursuit in the specific context of search scenes. The most famous example, of course, is the persistent pursuit of Orestes by the Erinyes in Aeschylus' *Eumenides*, 244 ff.[30] One could also point out some choreographic similarities between the chorus of *Ichneutae* and that of *Ajax*.[31] Nevertheless, when we concentrate on the mimetic dimension of the stage production, we must acknowledge the fundamental difference between the satyric scene of search and its tragic counterparts. In tragedy, the act of search is embedded in a set

[28] Some of the terms representing the apparently canine behaviour of the satyrs can easily be explained as metaphorical: note the conventional sense and usage (in satyr-play as well as in comedy) of θῆρες (221 cf. 147 κάκιστα θηρῶν); θηρία (153 ὦ κάκιστα θηρίων) as derogatory epithets: Guarini 1925: 325; Maltese 1982: 25 (from Maltese's list of references to θῆρες in *Ichneutae* the participial form θηρῶν in l. 252 should be omitted (ibid. n. 151). Tudeer 1916: 38 n. ad 147 (= 153 Lloyd-Jones): *Sophocles hic θηρίον vocabulo eodem modo ac postea Aristophanes contumeliose usus est. Mirum non est poetam hoc vocabulum adhibuisse, cum Silenum iratum satyros ignavos increpantem spectatoribus ante oculos posuerit.* See below, nn. 57, 75.

[29] See esp. Aesch. *Eum.* 244 ff.; Soph. *Aj.* 866 ff.; Eur. *Rhes.* 674 ff.; Pöhlmann 1989: 41 ff.

[30] Lilja 1976: 56 f.; Taplin 1977: 379–81. Cf. Soph. *Aj.* 5–8 where Athena's description of Odysseus as the hunter tracking out game most naturally develops into a comparison to a Laconian hound, 7 f. Lilja 1976: 61. For a comparative study of the two Sophoclean scenes, see Kamerbeek 1953: 20. Kamerbeek's claim, however, that 'the contrast between the two scenes—the concrete, literal diction of the Ichn., the semi-metaphorical diction here—is determined by the difference between satyr-play and tragedy' (ibid.) appears to ignore the essential difference in dramatic quality between the two scenes in question: for while in the *Ajax* scene we are dealing for the most part with a depicted action of an off-stage hero, in *Ichneutae* we are confronted with a 'live' performance of a similar action by the *dramatis personae* involved throughout.

[31] Sutton (1985: 97) has even gone as far as suggesting that 'the divided chorus of searching satyrs (*Ichn.* 85 ff.) seems to parody the divided chorus of searching sailors (*Aj.* 866 ff.)'. On tragic search scenes supposedly involving divided choruses see Taplin (1977: 380 f.).

of religious and ethical ideas which govern the plot, and it is therefore scarcely ever given a detailed mimetic treatment in any of its stages. As a rule, it tends to be expressed symbolically rather than have its various components physically presented in a detailed and realistic manner.[32] In *Ichneutae*, on the other hand, the same act, unfettered by any profound ideological considerations, has consciously been turned into a *mimetic event par excellence*, which constitutes, in itself, the whole of the dramatic experience. To exemplify the fundamental difference in their approach to the presentation of scenes of search between satyr-play and tragedy, we could do worse than compare our scene from *Ichneutae* with the pursuit of Orestes by the Erinyes in Aeschylus' *Eumenides* 244 ff.— a scene which also makes use of canine imagery in order to make the idea of pursuit more concrete. In the latter scene, as Taplin rightly remarks, 'the visual and choreographic picture of the Erinyes hunting by following a trail of blood evokes the entire framework of murder and revenge' which is at the basis of the whole *Oresteia* trilogy.[33] Yet it is important to observe the paucity of proper stage actions reported when we reach the act of pursuit itself. The chorus of Erinyes, which may have entered the orchestra σποράδην,[34] embarks on the chase of Orestes, following the blood-track and the scent of blood (244–7; 253). In the midst of it, the chorus reports on its previous efforts to track him down (248–51). There follows a brief visual description of the area in which it believes that Orestes is crouching to conceal himself, and the quarry is soon uncovered (252; 254–8). The rest of the *stasimon* is devoted to ethical–religious reflections on the duty of avenging blood—an idea which runs through the whole trilogy. Now compare this with the impressive accumulation of mimetic stage-acts occurring in the opening section of the scene of pursuit in *Ichneutae* (93–123)

> ἄγ' εἶα δὴ πᾶς . . .
> ῥινηλατῶν ὀσμ[αῖσι
> αὔρας ἐάν πῃ πρ[
> διπλοῦς ὀκλάζω[

---

[32] The only possible exception may be Eur. *Rhes.* 674 ff.—which, quite significantly, has its counterpart in Aristoph. *Ach.* 281 ff. Arist. *Eq.* 247 ff., too, is not so different in content and style. See below, pp. 194 f.

[33] Taplin 1977: 381.

[34] Ibid. 379 ff.

ὕποσμος ἐν χρῷ [
οὕτως ἔρευναν καὶ π[
ἅπαντα χρηστὰ κα[ὶ about 11 letters τε]λεῖν.
⟨HMIX⟩
θεὸς θεὸς θεὸς θεὸς ἔα [ἔα·
ἔχειν ἔοιγμεν· ἴσχε· μὴ . .ρ[. . .].τει.
⟨HMIX⟩
ταῦτ᾽ ἔστ᾽ ἐκεῖνα· τῶν βοῶν τὰ βήματα.
⟨HMIX⟩
σίγα· θεός τις τὴν ἀποι[κία]ν ἄγει.
⟨HMIX⟩
τί δρῶμεν, ὦ τᾶν; ἢ τὸ δέον [ἄρ᾽] ἤνομεν;
τί; τοῖσι ταύτῃ πῶς δοκεῖ; ⟨HMIX⟩ δοκεῖ πάνυ·
σαφῶ[ς γ]ὰρ αὔθ᾽ ἕκαστα σημαίνει τάδε.
⟨HMIX⟩
ἰδοῦ ἰδοῦ·
καὶ τοὐπίσημον αὐτὸ τῶν ὁπλῶν πάλιν.
⟨HMIX⟩
ἄθρει μάλα·
αὔτ᾽ ἐστὶ τοῦτο μέτρον ἐκμε[μαγ]μ[έ]νο[ν].
⟨HMIX⟩
χώρει δρόμῳ καὶ τα[about 11 letters] .ν ἔχου
. . .]ογμ[. . . .].[about 14 letters]μενος
ῥοίβδημ᾽ ἐάν τι τῶν [βοῶν ἐ]π᾽ οὖς [μόλῃ.
⟨HMIX⟩
οὐκ εἰσακούω πω [τορῶ]ς τοῦ φθέγματος.
ἀλλ᾽ αὐτὰ μὴν ἴχ[νη τε] χὠ στίβος τάδε
κείνων ἐναργῆ τῶν βοῶν· μαθεῖν πάρα.
⟨HMIX⟩
ἔα μάλα·
παλινστραφῆ τοι ναὶ μὰ Δία τὰ βήματα.
εἰς τοὔμπαλιν δέδορκεν· αὐτὰ δ᾽ εἴσιδε.
τί ἐστὶ τουτί; τίς ὁ τρόπος τοῦ τάγματ[ος;
εἰς τοὐπίσω τὰ πρόσθεν ἤλλακται, τὰ δ᾽ αὖ
ἐναντί᾽ ἀλλήλοισι συμπ[επλεγ]μένα·
δεινὸς κυκησμὸς εἶχ[ε τὸν βοη]λάτην.

The scene of pursuit in *Ichneutae* has no ideological dimension, and no ethical–religious reflection is attached to its action. Even Silenus' lengthy tirade against the shameful cowardice of the chorus at 145–68 is guided merely by utilitarian considerations. It concerns the *practical functioning* of his sons, turned huntsmen for the occasion, who for some reason or other have abandoned their pursuit prematurely.

A comparison with the divided chorus of sailors, desperately searching for Ajax in Sophocles' eponymous tragedy (866 ff.), would be no less instructive: a thorough scrutiny of the *stasimon* would reveal that, rather than a real search, what we are given here is an admission, by both groups of searchers, of their failure to find their vanished leader. One half of the chorus emphasizes the misery it feels because of the failure of all its efforts so far (866–9; 887). The other half makes a noisy entrance, which raises our expectations (870–1)—but only in order to present us with a similar report of their complete failure (872 ff.). The two halves of the chorus then unite in expressing the wish that some other factor—a fisherman, a goddess, or one of the streams of the Bosporus—will join in the search and help them find Ajax (879 ff.). The discovery of Ajax' body, following on the last line of this *stasimon*, puts an end to the state of uncertainty to which the chorus has been subjected, and at the same time to the whole action of the search. The pursuit-scene in *Ajax*, in all essentials a static scene, stands in sharp contrast to its mimetic and action-packed counterpart in *Ichneutae*, produced by the same dramatist. The difference in the dramatist's approach to the two scenes has been dictated by the difference between satyr-play and tragedy.

Our next example, from Euripides' *Rhesus* (674 ff.), presents us with a similar situation. The realistic and vivacious entry of the chorus of Trojan guards—closely reminiscent of the violent entry of the chorus of old men in Aristophanes' *Acharnians* (281 ff.)—raises the highest expectations in the spectator, who now looks forward to the most energetic action on the part of the chorus in tracking down Odysseus, Rhesus' presumed murderer:

> ἔα ἔα·
> βάλε βάλε βάλε βάλε.
> θένε θένε. τίς ἀνήρ;
> λεύσσετε· τοῦτον αὐδῶ.
> κλῶπες οἵτινες κατ' ὄρφνην τόνδε κινοῦσι στρατόν.
>
> δεῦρο δεῦρο πᾶς.
> τούσδ' ἔχω, τούσδ' ἔμαρψα.
> τίς ὁ λόχος; πόθεν ἔβας; ποδαπὸς εἶ;
>
> (674–81, Zanetto's Bibl. Teub. (1993))

Odysseus is, indeed, found; but he succeeds in slipping out of the chorus's hands before his identity has been established. The investigation stops. The chorus dismisses the idea of clamouring for help (690 f.). There follows an impetuous argument concerning the identity of the murderer, with Odysseus emerging as the preferred candidate (692 ff.). The chorus's main fear is that Hector may vent his anger on it for having failed in its undertaking (722 ff.); yet the very possibility of a further search is not even considered.

Ichneutae's uncompromising concentration on the mimetic aspect in its scene of search, so different as it is from what we have in similar scenes in tragedy, puts it in a different category as far as the tragic treatment of such a type of action is concerned: indeed, it provides us with the key to uncovering the comic pattern which underlies it. We have already mentioned the tumultuous clamour of the chorus of old men in Aristophanes' *Acharnians*, at the beginning of the confrontation scene between it and Dicaeopolis (οὗτος αὐτός ἐστιν, οὗτος· | βάλλε, βάλλε, βάλλε, βάλλε, | παῖε παῖε τὸν μιαρόν. | οὐ βαλεῖς, οὐ βαλεῖς; 280–3). Here are the chorus's words on entering the orchestra (204–36):

τῇδε πᾶς ἕπου, δίωκε καὶ τὸν ἄνδρα πυνθάνου
τῶν ὁδοιπόρων ἁπάντων· τῇ πόλει γὰρ ἄξιον
ξυλλαβεῖν τὸν ἄνδρα τοῦτον. ἀλλά μοι μηνύσατε,
εἴ τις οἶδ᾽ ὅποι τέτραπται γῆς ὁ τὰς σπονδὰς φέρων.
ἐκπέφευγ᾽, οἴχεται φροῦδος. οἴ—
μοι τάλας τῶν ἐτῶν τῶν ἐμῶν·
οὐκ ἂν ἐπ᾽ ἐμῆς γε νεότητος, ὅτ᾽ ἐ—
γὼ φέρων ἀνθράκων φορτίον
ἠκολούθουν Φαΰλλῳ τρέχων, ὧδε φαύλως ἂν ὁ
σπονδοφόρος οὗτος ὑπ᾽ ἐμοῦ τότε διωκόμενος
ἐξέφυγεν οὐδ᾽ ἂν ἐλαφρῶς ἂν ἀπεπλίξατο.

νῦν δ᾽ ἐπειδὴ στερρὸν ἤδη τοὐμὸν ἀντικνήμιον
καὶ παλαιῷ Λακρατείδῃ τὸ σκέλος βαρύνεται,
οἴχεται. διωκτέος δέ· μὴ γὰρ ἐγχάνοι ποτὲ
μηδέ περ γέροντας ὄντας ἐκφυγὼν Ἀχαρνέας,
ὅστις, ὦ Ζεῦ πάτερ καὶ θεοί,
τοῖσιν ἐχθροῖσιν ἐσπείσατο,
οἷσι παρ᾽ ἐμοῦ πόλεμος ἐχθοδοπὸς
αὔξεται τῶν ἐμῶν χωρίων·
κοὐκ ἀνήσω πρὶν ἂν σχοῖνος αὐτοῖσιν ἀντεμπαγῶ
ὀξύς, ὀδυνηρός, ⟨ἐπίω θ᾽ ἅμ᾽⟩ ἐπίκωπος, ἵνα
μήποτε πατῶσιν ἔτι τὰς ἐμὰς ἀμπέλους.

ἀλλὰ δεῖ ζητεῖν τὸν ἄνδρα καὶ βλέπειν Βαλλήναδε
καὶ διώκειν γῆν πρὸ γῆς, ἕως ἂν εὑρεθῇ ποτέ·
ὡς ἐγὼ βάλλων ἐκεῖνον οὐκ ἂν ἐμπλήμην λίθοις.

Beside the conventional phrases expressing a chase (τῇδε πᾶς ἕπου, δίωκε . . . πυνθάνου, 204; διωκτέος, 221; ἀλλὰ δεῖ ζητεῖν . . . καὶ βλέπειν . . . καὶ διώκειν, 234–5), one should point out the appeal to everyone present, in a way that seems potentially to include the audience, too, seeking its help in uncovering the hiding-place of Dicaeopolis (206 ff.; cf. *Ichn.* 83 f.),[35] and also the copious allusions to the advanced age of the members of the chorus, as a running commentary on their heavy movements and their slow progress towards the orchestra (209–22).[36] It is of course in their opening words that any chorus must establish itself as being what it is. As in *Agamemnon* and *Wasps*, where the agedness and feebleness of the chorus is heavily stressed in the *parodos*, here, too, as the chorus first appears in the play, the spectator's attention is drawn to the mimetic functioning of its members, old men who are forced to perform a physical task which is beyond their bodily strength (note especially 219–20: νῦν δ' ἐπειδὴ στερρὸν ἤδη τοὐμὸν ἀντικνήμιον | καὶ παλαιῷ Λακρατείδῃ τὸ σκέλος βαρύνεται).

Even more colourful in its mimetic expressions is the women's chorus searching for 'spies'—men who have infiltrated their assembly together with Euripides' old kinsman, who has already been caught—in Aristophanes' *Thesmophoriazusae* (655 ff.). The search is conducted with beacons. To provide themselves more freedom of movement the women tuck up their long undergarments, wearing them, as it were, in man-like fashion, and, having shed their outer garments, they apparently embark on a thorough survey of the area of the Pnyx, the tents and the passages, first with quiet and furtive steps, and then running around in a circle:

ἡμᾶς τοίνυν μετὰ τοῦτ' ἤδη τὰς λαμπάδας ἁψαμένας χρὴ
ξυζωσαμένας εὖ κἀνδρείως τῶν θ' ἱματίων ἀποδύσας
ζητεῖν, εἴ που κἄλλος τις ἀνὴρ ἐσελήλυθε, καὶ περιθρέξαι
τὴν πύκνα πᾶσαν καὶ τὰς σκηνὰς καὶ τὰς διόδους διαθρῆσαι.

εἶα δὴ πρώτιστα μὲν χρὴ κοῦφον ἐξορμᾶν πόδα
καὶ διασκοπεῖν σιωπῇ πανταχῇ. μόνον δὲ χρὴ

---

[35] See above, nn. 21–4.
[36] Cf. *Ichn.* 47–9 (Silenus' first entrance); above, pp. 179 f.

μὴ βραδύνειν, ὡς ὁ καιρός ἐστι μὴ μέλλειν ἔτι.
ἀλλὰ τὴν πρώτην τρέχειν χρῆν ὡς τάχιστ᾽ ἤδη κύκλῳ.   (655–62)

The mimetic action reaches its climax in a series of short and rhythmical instructions for the chase:

εἶά νυν ἴχνευε καὶ μά—
τευε ταχὺ πάντ᾽, εἴ τις ἐν τό—
ποις ἑδραῖος
ἄλλος αὖ λέληθεν ὤν.
πανταχῇ δὲ ῥῖψον ὄμμα,
καὶ τὰ τῆδε καὶ τὰ δεῦρο
πάντ᾽ ἀνασκόπει καλῶς.   (663–7)[37]

Before declaring that it has completed its thorough search (687), the chorus finds time for a long and solemn disquisition on the moral and social implications of the behaviour of the unknown offender (668–86). We have already encountered a similar combination of mimetic action and reflections on the character of the culprit in Aeschylus' *Eumenides*. Yet while in *Eumenides* these reflections are largely directed at a culprit *who has been caught*—Orestes—here in *Thesmophoriazusae* we must assume that they are being expressed *simultaneously with the mimetic act of the chase*,[38] which comes to an end with the chorus' declaration at 687.[39]

Although we have no evidence for postulating a direct line of influence leading from *Ichneutae* to Plautine comedy,[40] it is difficult to ignore the striking analogy between the Sophoclean search scene

[37] Compare the entrance of the chorus of women dressed like men on its return from the assembly in *Eccl.* 478 ff.

[38] Line 687 confirms that the series of activities begun at 655, and carried out according to the collective instructions of the chorus, has come to its natural end with the end of the chorus song itself. Note the striking verbal similarities between 667 (πάντ᾽ ἀνασκόπει καλῶς) and 687 (ἀλλ᾽ ἔοιχ᾽ ἡμῖν ἅπαντά πως διεσκέφθαι καλῶς), the starting-point and the end of these reflections.

[39] Compared with the scenes of search in Aristophanes which we have just discussed, the similar scene at the opening of his *Birds* is rather deficient in mimetic elements of the sort we are dealing with. The attention of the searchers is centred on the—apparently defective—functioning of the two birds they have brought along with them to serve as their guides. In attempting to establish an analogy between comedy and satyr-play in their dramatic manipulation of the search-motif, it may be useful to point out the striking analogy between Aristoph. *Thesm.* 1210 ff. and Eur. *Cycl.* 675 ff.

[40] This was postulated by Süss 1935: 182 ff.; cf. id. 1938: 134 f. Süss' view is criticized by Wehrli 1936: 119 f.; see below, n. 50.

and its later Latin counterpart in *Cistellaria* 671 ff.[41] The maid Halisca has lost the casket containing the identifying objects of her mistress Selenium during the tumult which occurred when Alcesimarchus kidnapped his beloved Selenium (iii. i). Now she is desperately searching for the casket and, *while slowly uncovering the footprints of the suspected thief, she reconstructs his movements one by one*:

> mei homines, mei spectatores, facite indicium, si quis vidit,
> quis eam apstulerit quisve sustulerit et utrum hac an illac iter
>   institerit . . .   (678–9)
>
> nunc vestigia hic si qua sunt noscitabo.
> nam si nemo hac praeteriit, postquam intro abivi,
> cistella hic iaceret. quid hic? perii, opinor,
> actum est, ilicet me infelicem et scelestam!
> nulla est, neque ego sum usquam. perdita perdidit me.
> sed pergam ut coepi tamen, quaeritabo . . .   (682–7)
>
> Halisca, hoc age, ad terram aspice et despice,
> oculis investiges, astute augura . . .   (693–4)
>
> sed is hac iit, hac socci video
> vestigium in pulvere, persequar hac.
> in hoc iam loco cum altero constitit. hic
> meis turba oculis modo se obiecit:
> neque prorsum iit hac: hic stetit, hinc il-
> -lo exiit. hic concilium fuit.
> ad duos attinet, liquidumst. attat!
>   singulum vestigium video.
> sed is hac abiit. contemplabo. hinc huc iit, hinc nusquam abiit.
> actam rem ago. quod periit, periit: meum corium ⟨cum⟩ cistella . . .
>   (697–703)

This is a lively and complex mimetic scene, clearly reminiscent of the actions, in *Ichneutae*, of the satyrs/hounds following in the steps of Apollo's lost cattle (cf. *Ichn.* 100–23 quoted earlier).

Another important mimetic feature of the act of pursuit carried out by the satyrs/hounds in *Ichneutae*—following the *scent* of the lost cattle (93 ff.)—has its most vivid and detailed parallel in Plautus' *Curculio*, in the *canticum* of the drunken old woman Leaena, desperately searching for the source of the scent of the

---

[41] Süss 1935: 182 f.; Zimmermann 1995: 199 f.

wine she is pining for, near the home of the pimp Cappadox, her master:

> flos veteris vini meis naribus obiectust,
> eiius amor cupidam me huc prolicit per tenebras.
>> ubi ubi est, prope me est. euax, habeo!
>>> salve, anime mi, Liberi lepos.
>>>> ut veteri' vetu' tui cupida sum!
>> nam omnium unguentum odor prae tuo nautea est,
>>> tu mihi stacta, tu cinnamum, tu rosa,
>>>> tu crocinum et casia es, tu telinum,
>> nam ubi tu profusu's, ibi ego me pervelim sepultam.
> sed quom adhuc naso odos opsecutust meo,
> da vicissim meo gutturi gaudium.
> nil ago tecum: ubi est ipsus? ipsum expeto
> tangere, invergere in me liquores tuos,
>> sine, ductim. sed hac abiit, hac persequar.   (96–109)

The old woman's sharp sense of smell makes the slave Palinurus, who is watching her actions from the side of the stage, compare her to a *bitch*:

> canem esse hanc quidem magi' par fuit: sagax nasum habet.   (110b)[42]

In the two Plautine examples quoted above, what we have is an act of search performed through a *canticum*: the actor/singer, we assume, accompanies his song with an appropriate mimetic dance.[43] In *Cistellaria*, the audience is called upon to participate in what is happening on the stage, through a direct appeal by the protagonist. This is an old Greek comic technique which we have already encountered in *Ichneutae* as well. This technique reaches its most successful mimetic expression in Plautus' *Aulularia*—there, too, in a *canticum*. Euclio, shocked and helpless after the disappearance of his favourite gold-laden *aula* from the temple of Apollo, where he had concealed it, appeals in desperation to the audience, asking their help in uncovering the thief. Soon enough, his request turns into blaming some members of the audience itself for the theft!

---

[42] Cf. Aesch. *Ag.* 1093 f. See also Palaestrio's self-presentation in Plaut. *Mil.* 268–9: *si ita non reperio ibo odorans quasi canis venaticus | usque donec persecutus volpem ero vestigiis.*

[43] Zimmermann 1995: 199 f.

> . . . opsecro ego vos, mi auxilio,
> oro, optestor, sitis et hominem demonstretis, quis eam apstulerit.
> quid ais tu? tibi credere certum est, nam esse bonum ex voltu
>   cognosco.
> quid est? quid ridetis? novi omnis, scio fures esse hic compluris,
> qui vestitu et creta occultant sese atque sedent quasi sint frugi.
>   hem, nemo habet horum? occidisti. dic igitur, quis habet? nescis?
>
> $(715–20)^{44}$

Let us now return to *Ichneutae*, and to Silenus' censure of the behaviour of his sons the satyrs, delivered while the act of search is being carried out (124 ff.). The satyrs, frightened by the unknown (as yet) sound of the lyre coming out of the recesses of Cyllene's cave, where Hermes, who has stolen Apollo's cattle, is hiding, immediately crouch on the ground and cease their search. Silenus, who has not yet heard the sound of the lyre, is naturally annoyed by this unexpected delay. What should interest us is his first reaction:

> τίν' αὖ τέχνην σὺ τήν[δ' ἆρ' ἐξηῦρες, τίν' αὖ,
> πρόσπαιον, ὧδε κεκλιμ[ένος] κυνηγετεῖν
> πρὸς γῇ; τίς ὑμῶν ὁ τρόπος; οὐχὶ μανθάνω.
> ἐχῖνος ὥς τις ἐν λόχμῃ κεῖσαι πεσών,
> ἤ τις πίθηκος κύβδ' ἀποθυμαίνεις τινί.
> τί ταῦτα; ποῦ γῆς ἐμάθετ'; ἐν ποίῳ τόπῳ;
> σημήνατ'· οὐ γὰρ ἴδρις εἰμὶ τοῦ τρόπου. $(124–30)^{45}$

This is a familiar comic technique: a running commentary, by one character on the stage, on the mimetic activities of another—in our case, the chorus of satyrs. This technique is particularly frequent in comedy, especially in situations where the behaviour of a character or characters which the spectators can see on the stage is regarded by another character as strange, absurd, eccentric or in need of an explanation—as is the case in our particular scene.[46] Such is also the reaction of Strepsiades in Aristophanes' *Clouds* (184 ff.) on observing Socrates' pupils crouching over their

---

[44] Süss 1938: 134 f. (following Kraus 1934: 72 f.). See also Plaut. *Rud.* 465–70 (Zimmermann 1995: 200 n. 24). Note that the search scene in Ter. *Eun.* 293 ff. is entirely lacking in all the mimetic ingredients characteristic of the Plautine scenes cited here.

[45] On this passage and the following see recent discussion by Lloyd-Jones (1994: 136–9).

[46] For tragic exploitation of this technique see Aesch. *Ag.* 1050 ff.

geological objects in a position largely reminiscent of that of the
satyrs in our scene of *Ichneutae*:[47]

> ὦ Ἡράκλεις, ταυτὶ ποδαπὰ τὰ θηρία;   (184)
>
> ἀτὰρ τί ποτ᾽ εἰς τὴν γῆν βλέπουσιν οὑτοιί;   (187)
>
> τί γὰρ οἶδε δρῶσιν οἱ σφόδρ᾽ ἐγκεκυφότες;   (191)
>
> τί δῆθ᾽ ὁ πρωκτὸς εἰς τὸν οὐρανὸν βλέπει;   (193)

In *Peace* (309 ff.), Trygaeus is annoyed with the noisy and
exuberant behaviour of the chorus of peasants, endangering, in
his opinion, the chances of rescuing the goddess of peace from the
cave of Ares, the god of war. As one should expect, the main object
of his censure is the chorus' dance—that is, the mimetic presentation of the joy of victory—the infelicitous timing of which, before
the rescue operation has even begun, has turned it into something
incongruous and unbefitting present circumstances (322–34):

> Τρ. τί τὸ κακόν; τί πάσχετ᾽, ὦνδρες; μηδαμῶς, πρὸς τῶν θεῶν,
> πρᾶγμα κάλλιστον διαφθείρητε διὰ τὰ σχήματα.
> Χο. ἀλλ᾽ ἔγωγ᾽ οὐ σχηματίζειν βούλομ᾽, ἀλλ᾽ ὑφ᾽ ἡδονῆς
> οὐκ ἐμοῦ κινοῦντος αὐτὼ τὼ σκέλει χορεύετον.
> Τρ. μή τι καὶ νυνί γ᾽ ἔτ᾽, ἀλλὰ παῦε παῦ᾽ ὀρχούμενος.
> Χο. ἢν ἰδού, καὶ δὴ πέπαυμαι. Τρ. φῄς γε, παύει δ᾽ οὐδέπω.
> Χο. ἓν μὲν οὖν τουτί μ᾽ ἔασον ἑλκύσαι, καὶ μηκέτι.
> Τρ. τοῦτό νυν, καὶ μηκέτ᾽ ἄλλο μηδὲν ὀρχήσησθέ τι.
> Χο. οὐκ ἂν ὀρχησαίμεθ᾽, εἴπερ ὠφελήσαιμέν τί σε.
> Τρ. ἀλλ᾽, ὁρᾶτ᾽, οὔπω πέπαυσθε. Χο. τουτογὶ νὴ τὸν Δία
> τὸ σκέλος ῥίψαντες ἤδη λήγομεν τὸ δεξιόν.
> Τρ. ἐπιδίδωμι τοῦτό γ᾽ ὑμῖν, ὥστε μὴ λυπεῖν ἔτι.
> Χο. ἀλλὰ καὶ τἀριστερόν τοί μ᾽ ἔστ᾽ ἀναγκαίως ἔχον.

Later in the same play, we find Trygaeus, as well as Hermes,
passing criticism on the defective functioning of some members of
the chorus, representatives of various Greek city-states, during the
act of rescue itself (460 ff.).

The eccentric and apparently unhinged behaviour of Trygaeus
himself, even before he has made his entry riding on the dung-beetle
at the opening of the play, becomes a constant object of puzzlement
and censure among his slaves. Just as Silenus is suddenly faced with

---

[47] Maltese 1982: n. ad 127. However this was staged, it is generally accepted that
the disciples were visible to the audience. See e.g. Dover 1968: pp. lxxiv–lxxvi; cf. id.
1972: 25, 107 f.; Dearden 1976: 65–7; 152.

the 'innovative method of investigation' practised by his sons the satyrs, so do Trygaeus' slaves find themselves confronted with their master's inexplicable τρόπος, or behaviour pattern:

> ὁ δεσπότης μου μαίνεται καινὸν τρόπον,
> οὐχ ὅνπερ ὑμεῖς, ἀλλ' ἕτερον καινὸν πάνυ.
> δι' ἡμέρας γὰρ εἰς τὸν οὐρανὸν βλέπων
> ὡδὶ κεχηνὼς λοιδορεῖται τῷ Διὶ
> καί φησιν· "ὦ Ζεῦ, τί ποτε βουλεύει ποιεῖν;
> κατάθου τὸ κόρημα· μὴ 'κκόρει τὴν Ἑλλάδα."
> ἔα ἔα·
> σιγήσαθ', ὡς φωνῆς ἀκούειν μοι δοκῶ.
> Τρ. ὦ Ζεῦ, τί δρασείεις ποθ' ἡμῶν τὸν λεών;
> λήσεις σεαυτὸν τὰς πόλεις ἐκκοκκίσας.
> Οι. Β. τοῦτ' ἔστι τουτὶ τὸ κακὸν αὔθ' οὑγὼ 'λεγον·
> τὸ γὰρ παράδειγμα τῶν μανιῶν ἀκούετε· [etc.]   (54–65)

The external details of his master's behaviour as reported by the slave find their expression on the stage, first through a verbal description behind the scenes (60–3), and then by the spectacle of the master riding on the back of the dung-beetle, accompanied all the while by the descriptive and critical remarks of his slaves (79 ff.).[48]

In Greek New Comedy, the allusions to the eccentric or excessive behaviour of a character are usually made in the absence of that character from the stage, and are in the nature of a prospective comment, aimed more at alerting the spectator to the approaching arrival on the stage of the character depicted than as a comment on comic action.[49] The Plautine versions on the other hand, show a

[48] Compare also *Vesp.* 1474 ff. (the censure by Xanthias and Bdelycleon of Philocleon's licentious dance; Zimmermann 1995: 196 n. 13); also Metagenes, *Thouriopersae*, fr. 7 K–A (with n. ad loc.): τίς τρόπος ἵππων· ὡς δ' ὀρχοῦνται τὸν βαρβαρικὸν τρόπον οὗτοι. A mocking attitude by one figure on the stage towards the eccentric *external* appearance of another—an important feature of the comic technique we have just considered, but without a parallel in the remains of *Ichneutae*—is typical of Aristophanes' dramatic technique: see e.g. *Av.* 93 ff. (with regard to Epops); 859 ff. (with regard to the crow); *Thesm.* 134ff. (with regard to Agathon); *Ra.* 38 ff. (with regard to Heracles).

[49] See e.g. Men. *Dysc.* 81 ff. (Cnemon); *Epitr.* 878 ff. (Charisius); *Mis.* 176 ff. (Demeas). In contrast, see *Dysc.* 147 ff.; 179–80 (Sostratus' reactions on seeing Cnemon approach); *Sam.* 360 ff. (the cook's reaction on seeing and hearing the infuriated Demeas involves a running commentary on the eccentric activities of a character both on stage and off it). The uncertainty as to the presence or absence on the stage of the hiding maiden in Men. *Theoph.* 16 ff. has made it impossible to draw

marked preference for the immediate and direct type of comment, which is also characteristic of our scene of *Ichneutae*,[50] as well as of such scenes in Aristophanic comedy. Zimmermann[51] has identified as a characteristic feature of Plautine comedy a situation in which the mimetic dance movements of one actor are depicted and interpreted by another. In the *cantica*, it is usually the actor himself who comments on his own movements, usually in the context of a symposium or a *komos*.[52] The most outstanding example of such comments made on pantomimic acts while they are being performed is, of course, the imitation of the process of thinking by Palaestrio and the running commentary made on it by Periplectomenus, *Miles* 195–230.[53] To quote but the most significant of these comments:

> illuc sis vide,
> quem ad modum astitit, severo fronte curans, cogitans.
> pectus digitus pultat, cor credo evocaturust foras;
> ecce avortit: nixus laevo in femine habet laevam manum,
> dextera digitis rationem computat, feriens femur
> dexterum. ita vehementer icit: quod agat aegre suppetit.
> concrepuit digitis: laborat; crebro commutat status.
> eccere autem capite nutat: non placet quod repperit . . .   (200–7)
>
> ecce autem aedificat: columnam mento suffigit suo.
> apage, non placet profecto mihi illaec aedificatio . . .   (209–10)
>
> eugae! euscheme hercle astitit et dulice et comoedice;
> numquam hodie quiescet priu' quam id quod petit perfecerit.
> habet opinor. age si quid agis, vigila, ne somno stude,

firm conclusions as to the nature of the running commentary on her strange behaviour. See e.g. Körte 1935: 431–8; Handley 1969: 93; Gomme-Sandbach 1973: 400 f. For tragic exploitation of this technique see Soph. *Aj.* 66 ff.; 331 ff. The eccentricity of Medea's character and excessive reaction to the impending marriage of Jason and Creon's daughter are brought to the audience's attention quite extensively shortly before Medea's own entrance to the stage in Euripides' play *Medea* (214 ff.).

[50] Süss (1935: 184) has pointed out the analogy between the *Ichneutae*-passage under consideration and Plaut. *Cist.* 728 ff.

[51] Zimmermann 1995: 193 ff.

[52] Ibid. 198 ff. The very existence of such comments is explained by Zimmermann (200 ff.) as deriving from the dramatist's need to interpret to his audience a feature of comedy which has not yet become naturalized in Roman cultural life—the language of pantomime. See also Petrone 1995: 171ff.; Hofmann 1995: 205 ff.

[53] On this scene, see Zimmermann 1995: 193–6; Petrone 1995: 177 f.; Hofmann 1995: 217.

nisi quidem hic agitare mavis varius virgis vigilias.
tibi ego dico. †anheriatus vestis† heus te adloqui, Palaestrio.
vigila inquam, expergiscere inquam, lucet hoc inquam . . .   (213–18)

Unlike Silenus and Strepsiades, here Periplectomenus is aware, right from the start, of the significance of the movements of the stage-figure he is watching (195–9). His comment should be regarded as serving an essentially comic purpose, unless we assume that the audience still found it difficult to understand the protagonist's body-language.[54] Nevertheless, we should pay attention to the critical undertones which penetrate Periplectomenus' description (210; 215 ff.) when, contrary to his expectations (see 214), Palaestrio does not turn from reflection to action but, wrapped in his thoughts, freezes motionlessly in his place.[55] At this point, where we have an unexpected delay in the progress of the action, as well as eccentric behaviour by the performing figure on the stage—at least as it is regarded by the figure commenting on his performance—here, perhaps, one could detect a connecting-link between the older techniques of Sophocles and the later techniques of Plautus.[56]

Silenus' censure of his sons for their cowardice (145 ff.)[57] provokes the demand, on their part, that he should lead them in this critical stage of the chase, while the source of their fright, the unfamiliar sound of the lyre, has not yet been identified (169 ff.). Fortified by memories of his past prowess, Silenus responds to this challenge with his characteristic haughtiness (172 ff.); but when he hears the sound of the lyre, he hastens to abandon the battle with no unnecessary pangs of conscience and despite the vociferous protest of his sons (205 ff.). Silenus thus forfeits his chance of obtaining the financial reward and of gaining his craved liberty—both of which have formerly constituted the main two incentives in his impressive

---

[54] See above, n. 52.

[55] Fraenkel (1968: 231–4) proposed a redistribution of the parts of 195–234: PA was to be inserted before *age* in line 215 and removed from before *audio* in line 218; PE was to be removed from *viden* in line 219 and inserted before *magnam* in line 228. But see Jocelyn 1997: 211–17.

[56] Compare also Charmides' censorious attitude to the apparently suspect behaviour of the sycophant sent by Callicles: *Trin.* 851 ff.

[57] The string of curses directed by Silenus towards his sons (146 ff.) represents a stylistic feature which, though not peculiar to comedy, was adopted by the comedians as one of the manners of expression most typical of a comic character: see Headlam and Knox 1922: n. ad vi. 16 (p. 287); Maltese 1982: n. ad 150 f.

rhetorical appeal to his sons to persist in their search for Apollo's cattle. The satyrs, on the other hand, find that their curiosity has got the better of their fear, and they become adamant in their determination to track down the source of the strange sound (210 ff.). They knock on the roof of Cyllene's cave, and in a last effort, they bring the process of the search to its end.

Such a dramatic pattern, in which we witness a reversal in the roles of hero and coward between Silenus and the chorus (cf. Eur. *Cycl.* 608–62), has its parallels in Aeschylus' *Choephori* in the contrasting reactions of Orestes and the chorus before and after the murder of Clytemnestra.[58] Yet I believe that we should also pay attention to the parallel uses of this pattern in comedy, later as these are in date than the Sophoclean version. The alternating feelings of fear and courage expressed by Dionysus and Xanthias in Aristophanes' *Frogs* (460 ff.) as they stand in front of the gates of Hades, represent this pattern at its best. The unsuccessful attempts by Getas and Sicon to borrow a pot from the misanthrope Knemon in the third act of Menander's *Dyscolus* (456 ff.) are clearly representative of the familiar phenomenon of haughtiness followed by fear. The same happens in the first act of the same play. Chaereas the bragging parasite, usually proud of his adeptness, as a matchmaker, in suiting himself to all seasons and situations (57 ff.), hastens to remove himself from the scene of action on hearing the alarming report by Pyrrhias of the violent personality and boorish behaviour of Cnemon, who will eventually become the father-in-law of one of his occasional patrons, Sostratus (125 ff.). Sostratus himself, who has managed to keep his cool on hearing the report, also finds it hard to face Cnemon, and even harder to disclose to him the real reason for his visit to his neighbourhood (145 ff.).[59]

To return to *Ichneutae*. Silenus abandons the stage probably after 212. As far as one can judge on the basis of our fragmentary evidence, he returns only at 458, towards the end of the play. On the external level, his departure from the stage is dictated by the

---

[58] As recognized by Siegmann 1941: 69 n. 25. The role and function of these reactions in the dramatic framework of *Choephori* have been rightly emphasized by Snell 1928: 129 f. see esp. 130: 'So bleibt das Schwanken und Zaudern die einheitliche Stimmung des Dramas—abwechselnd sind der Chor oder Orest die Träger dieser Stimmung, —und trozdem wird die Handlung zu ihrem Ziele geführt. Der Widerstreit dieser vorwärtstreibenden und hemmenden Kräfte gibt den Choephoren das Gepräge. Und dieser Widerstreit ist das Wesen des Orest.'

[59] Zagagi 1994: 85, 96 ff., 156 ff.

need for an actor who would play the part of Cyllene, or, at a later stage, that of Hermes. His long absence is explained, within the action of the play, by his cowardice, as revealed in the final stages of the search scene.[60] Be that as it may, it is only after the mystery of the disappearance of Apollo's cattle has been solved, and the secret of the strange sound emanating from Cyllene's cave has been deciphered, that Sophocles makes his hero return to the scene of action.[61]

Menander's *Samia* presents us with a similar case of a character abandoning the scene in fear in the very midst of a crucial dramatic development which has come about largely through his own interference. He is to return to it only after it has reached its successful culmination. Parmenon the slave is one of the initiators of the deceitful presentation of Moschion and Plangon's illegitimate baby as the fruit of the regular relations between Demeas and his mistress Chrysis (Act I). In the third act, Parmenon is questioned by Demeas, under threat of torture, as to the baby's ancestry (295 ff.). He manages to slip out of Demeas' hands before his part in the deception has been discovered, and finds a place of hiding out of Demeas' sight. Parmenon reappears in the fifth act, reproaching himself for his cowardice (641 ff.). Like Silenus in *Ichneutae*, the sudden escape of Parmenon and the prolonged postponement of his return have removed him from the centre of events and turned him into a minor character, absent from the culminating event of the play—the discovery of the baby's true identity—and thus naturally of no consequence to the practical result of this discovery, the forthcoming marriage of Moschion and Plangon.

If we ignore the element of fear, we may include in the same category the case of Parmeno the slave in Terence's *Eunuch*, an adaptation of a play with the same name by Menander. Parmeno here is an active partner in the planning and execution of an act of deception, whose purpose is to enable his young master Chaerea to spend some time on his own, disguised as a eunuch, in the house of the *hetaera* Thais, with a young girl he has fallen in love with (362 ff.). After some lapse of time, he returns to the scene of action out of mere curiosity as to Chaerea's success in advancing his plans (923 ff.). Like the Parmenon of Menander's *Samia*, this Parmeno is also unaware of the crucial dramatic developments which have

---

[60] Siegmann 1941: 71 f.; Maltese 1982: 85 f.
[61] Siegmann 1941: 72.

occurred during his long absence: the rape perpetrated by Chaerea on the girl, and his plans to marry her when her Athenian descent has been discovered. These developments, which are a direct result of the act of deception, provide a way out of the intricacies of the plot.

The fragmentary nature of our text makes it impossible for us to make more than plausible conjectures concerning the movements of Silenus after he withdraws from the stage. Siegmann[62] believes that in *Ichneutae* Silenus, true to his character, timed his return to the stage to coincide with the apportioning of the reward among the satyrs, in an attempt to win his own portion; but that he had to depart disgraced and empty-handed, owing to the staunch opposition of Apollo as well as the satyrs. If Siegmann's hypothesis is to be adopted, then we have here a variant of one of the basic features of the endings of comic plays—the scurrilous scene of 'settling of accounts' with the character taken, rightly or wrongly, to be 'the villain of the piece'. The general Lamachus in Aristophanes' *Acharnians* (1174 ff.); Euripides in his *Thesmophoriazusae* (1128 ff.); Smicrines the father of Pamphile in Menander's *Epitrepontes* (1078 ff.); Cnemon in his *Dyscolus* (885 ff.); Pyrgopolynices in Plautus' *Miles Gloriosus* (1394ff.); Lysidamus in his *Casina* (963 ff.); Demaenetus in his *Asinaria* (851 ff.); Thraso in Terence's *Eunuchus* (1049 ff.)—all these are links in the chain of characters which comedy has singled out for 'poetic justice', meted out in its own comic manner towards the end of the play.[63] Not a few of those about to be the victims of such 'comic justice' appear on the scene expecting to be given some prize, only to discover that this has been a mere delusion.[64] It is possible that Silenus' fate also fitted this category.

We return to the point in the action where the satyrs renew their search for Apollo's lost cattle, first under the official leadership of

[62] Siegmann 1941: 71.

[63] For further examples see Holzberg's excellent discussion of Old and New Comedy play-endings in his book 1974: 121 ff. It is tempting to accept Lloyd-Jones' proposition (1971: 189) 19 that the end of *Aspis* included the mockery of Smicrines by Daos and the cook after the manner of Cnemon's treatment by Getas and Sicon in Act v of *Dyscolos*.

[64] Mostly Plautine examples: Pyrgopolynices (*Miles Gloriosus*); Lysidamus (*Casina*); Lycus (*Poenulus*); Stratophanes (*Truculentus*); Cappadox (*Curculio*). Strepsiades' fate at the end of Aristophanes' *Clouds* may also be interpreted as falling within the same category.

Silenus, and then (176 ff.) without him. The whole scene takes place in front of Cyllene's cave, out of which the mysterious sound had emanated. Their assault on the cave is made in an effort to open its door(?) and discover the identity of its occupant. The atmosphere of hunting which characterizes this scene is created by an abundance of mimetic and suggestive devices.[65] Sophocles imparts movement and life to the whole scene in a number of ways. First, we seem to have the *sicinnis* dance, characterized by strong gestures of propulsion in different directions and accompanied by loud shouting.[66] At the same time, some member of the chorus—probably the leader of the chorus (Silenus?)—issues orders, words of encouragement, praise or restraint, and addresses the 'hounds' each by his name. As Maltese rightly observes, 'quanto al procedimento di apostrofare ὀνομαστί i singoli coreuti, esso ha riscontro soltanto nella commedia'.[67]

The choreographic constituents of this scene have no parallel in comedy, but things look different when we consider the pattern of action which underlies the scene. Indeed, this is the pattern of action at the basis of the scenes of siege laid to the house of the beloved or the pimp in New Comedy.[68] In such scenes, the imagery of hunt and hounds have given way to descriptions of 'campaigns'; but in all its other aspects—the preparation for a collective assault on a specific place of habitation on the stage; concentration on its occupant; the individual character of the protagonists, and the emphasis on the strategic nature of the action—in all these, the theatrical experience is exactly the same. A good example of all these features can be found in the scene of the siege of Thais' house in Terence's *Eunuchus*:

> THR. Hancin ego ut contumeliam tam insignem in me accipiam,
>   Gnatho?

[65] Maltese 1982: n. ad 176–202. See ibid. on the correspondence of the Sophoclean scene with Xenophon's *Cynegeticus*.

[66] Maltese 1982: 82; Séchan 1930: 200–6, 214 nn. 105–6, 108–9; Seaford 1984: n. ad 37.

[67] Maltese 1982: 82 with references. For a detailed discussion of the satyrs–hounds' individual names in question, see Maltese 1982: 82–5.

[68] See Men. *Peric.* 467 ff.; Ter. *Eun.* 771 ff. *Ad.* Act II presents us with the aftermath of a successful 'military' operation. The analogy between Aristoph. *Lys.* 845 ff. (Cinesias–Myrrhine confrontation) and the siege situation under consideration has been pointed out by Wehrli 1936: 23. On the motif we are discussing see further Wehrli 1936: 31 n. 1, 103 f., 110; Zagagi 1994: 30 f., 33 ff., 58 f., 1653 f., 174 n. 73.

mori me satiust. Simalio, Donax, Syrisce, sequimini.
primum aedis expugnabo. GN. recte. THR. virginem eripiam.
  GN. probe.
THR. male ulcabo ipsam. GN. pulchre. THR. in medium huc agmen
  cum vecti, Donax;
tu, Simalio, in sinistrum cornum; tu, Syrisce, in dexterum.
cedo alios: ubi centuriost Sanga et manipulus furum? SA. eccum adest.
THR. quid ignave? peniculon pugnare, qui istum huc portes, cogitas?
SA. egon? imperatoris virtutem noveram et vim militum;
sine sanguine hoc non posse fieri: qui abstergerem volnera?
THR. ubi alii? GN. qui malum 'alii'? solu' Sannio servat domi.
THR. tu hosce instrue; ego hic ero post principia: inde omnibus signum
  dabo.
GN. illuc est sapere: ut hosce instruxit, ipsu' sibi cavit loco.
THR. idem hoc iam Pyrru' factitavit. (771–83).[69]

The final noisy assault by the satyrs on Cyllene's cave (217 ff.),
and the nymph's angry reaction to it (221 ff.; 251 ff.), call for a
comparison with another feature of comic convention: the scene of
knocking on the stage-door.

It is true that such scenes are not unheard-of in tragedy,[70] but the
striking frequency of such knocking-scenes in Attic comedy[71] as well
as in its Latin adaptations[72] seems to confirm the impression that
the main place for such scenes, as a typically conventional feature of

---

[69] See also the knights' 'military' attack on Cleon–Paphlagon in Aristophanes'
Knights (242 ff.).

[70] See esp. Aesch. *Cho.* 653–69; Eur. *IT* 1284-308; *Hyps.* fr. I. 1. 4–5. Door-
knocking presumably takes place also in Eur. *Hel.* 430–52 and *Phoe.* 1067–9. For
tragic door scenes involving *shouting* as their main feature, see Soph. *Aj.* 69–93, 784–
8; *Phil.* 1261–6; fr. 491 Radt (= Eur. fr. 623N), 775 Radt; Eur. *Phoe.* 296–300, 1067–
9, 1264–7; *Bacch.* 170–80; *IA* 314–17, 801–20, 1532–5; *Heracl.* 642–7; *Hec.* 171–9
and the above quoted examples, *passim*.

[71] Aristoph. *Ra.* 35 ff. (quoted below, p. 28), 460 ff.; *Ach.* 393 ff., 1071–2; *Eq.*
725 ff.; *Nub.* 132 ff. (quoted below, p. 1144–6; *Av.* 53 ff., 92–4; *Eccl.* 960 ff. (see
below, n. 76); *Plut.* 1097 ff. (see below, n. 76). Door-knocking presumably takes
place also in *Ach.* 1174 ff.; *Nub.* 866 ff.; *Lys.* 1216 ff.; *Pax* 179 ff. In *Vesp.* 152 ff.,
1482 ff., the traditional pattern of the knocking-scene has been reversed. Motif-
reversal may also be recognized in *Thesm.* 65 ff. On door-knocking scenes in Tragedy
and Old Comedy see the forthcoming article by P. G. McC. Brown. My thanks are
due to Peter Brown for generously allowing me to consult an earlier version of this
article in the course of preparation of the present study.

[72] A useful discussion of the relevant material from Menander, Plautus, and
Terence is found in Brown 1995: 71–89.

the play, was in comedy. (At least in the case of Euripides, one cannot rule out the possibility of comic influences on his use of the features of such scenes.)

In our scene it is not the conventional stage-door, but the roof and the opening of the cave, which are the objects of the dramatic action.[73] The noisy and violent behaviour of the satyrs, which includes thumping the roof of the cave and kicking against it (clearly to be taken as a substitute for the conventional knocking[74]), as well as Cyllene's angry reaction as she emerges[75] conform exactly to the tendency so typical in comedy to present the scene in front of the door in an especially violent fashion—whether this is done in the form of 'stage-reality', by means of pretended action by the protagonists, or through the subjective perceptions of those inside the house.[76]

Compare, for example:

> ἀμαθής γε νὴ Δί' ὅστις οὑτωσὶ σφόδρα
> ἀπεριμερίμνως τὴν θύραν λελάκτικας . . .
>
> (Aristoph. *Nub.* 135)

> τίς τὴν θύραν ἐπάταξεν; ὡς κενταυρικῶς
> ἐνήλαθ' ὅστις.
>
> (Aristoph. *Ra.* 38)

> . . . quisnam a me pepulit tam graviter fores?
>
> (Ter. *Ad.* 788)

---

[73] In the case of our satyr-play, the stage-door is not mentioned, nor do we have any of the conventional expressions for the knocking on it (κόπτω, κρούω, ἀράσσω, πατάσσω)—but this phenomenon is not without its parallels. See Brown 1995: 75–7, 82–3, and several examples in his forthcoming article.

[74] Maltese 1982: 23.

[75] See esp. ἀλλ' ἐγὼ τάχα | φ[έρ]ων **κτύπον πέδορτον ἐξαναγκάσω** | **πηδήμασιν κραιπνοῖσι καὶ λακτίσμασιν** | ὥστ' εἰσακοῦσαι, κεἰ λίαν κωφός τις ἦ. (Cyll.) Θῆρες, τί τόνδε χλοερὸν ὑλῶδη πάγον | ἔνθηρον ὡρμήθητε σὺν πολλῇ βοῇ . . . (221–2) . . . ποῖ στροφαὶ νέαι | μανιῶν στρέφουσι; (229–30) . . . καὶ ταῦτ' ἀφεῖσα [**σὺν ποδῶν λακτ[ίσμασιν** (237) . . . ἀκούσασ' ὧδε παραπεπαισμέν[ων] (240) . . . ταῦτ' ἔστ' ἐκείνων νῦν [τρόπων πεπαίτερα, | καὶ τοῖσδε θηρῶν ἐκπύ[θοιο πλείον' ἂν | ἀλκασμάτων δ[ειλῆ]ς τε πειρατηρίων | νύμφης (251–4). For θῆρες (Cyllene's opening curse, 221) as a term of abuse, see above, n. 28. Cf. Men. *Dysc.* 481; *Peric.* 366.

[76] We find this tendency even in situations where the alleged violent knocking may have not taken place at all: see e.g. Aristoph. *Eccl.* 976 ff.; *Plut.* 1097 ff.; Plaut. *Asin.* 381 ff.

tibi Juppiter
dique omnes irati certo sunt qui sic frangas fores . . .
. . . paene ecfregisti, fatue, foribus cardines.

(Plaut. *Amph.* 1021–7)

. . . quid istuc? quae istaec est pulsatio?
quae te ⟨male⟩ mala crux agitat, qui ad istunc modum
alieno viris tuas extentes ostio?
fores paene ecfregisti.

(Plaut. *Bacch.* 583–6)

quis est qui nostris tam proterve foribus facit iniuriam?

(Plaut. *Rud.* 414)

quid hoc? occlusam ianuam video. ibo et pultabo fores.
aperite atque adproperate, fores facite ut pateant, removete moram;
nimis haec res sine cura geritur. vide quam dudum hic asto et pulto.
somnon operam datis? experiar fores an cubiti an pedes plus valeant.

(Plaut. *Stich.* 308–11)

quisnam, opsecro, has frangit fores? ubist?
tun haec faci'? tun mihi huc hosti' venis?
. . . ean gratia fores ecfringis?

(ibid. 326–7)

quis illic est qui tam proterve nostras aedis arietat?[77]

(Plaut. *Truc.* 256)

Masqueray and Séchan maintain that the *sicinnis* dance was not
necessarily accompanied by singing, and suggest as an example that
there was such a dance in *Ichneutae* between 220 and 221 (= 214–15
Masqueray)—that is, after the chorus-leader's proclamation and
before Cyllene's appearance.[78] If we accept their hypothesis, what we

[77] Note that in Men. *Dysc.* 466 ff. Cnemon's complaint is devoid of any
suggestion of violent behaviour on the part of Getas and Sicon. But see *Dysc.*
911–22. P. Köln 203 fr. C col. I, possibly of Menandrian origin, may be interpreted
as containing a rather violent door knocking scene of the type we would normally
expect to find in Aristophanes: see Maresch 1985: 20 n. ad l. 12.

[78] Masqueray 1942: 243; Séchan 1930: 214 nn. 105, 106. See also Steffan 1960:
77: 'dubitari non potest, quin secutae sint vagae satyrorum saltationes corporumque
lascivorum motus tumultuosi'; and 10: 'Satyri autem lascivis saltationibus Cyllenam
nympham ex antro prodire cogunt.' Seaford 1984: 104 (n. ad 37). Walker (1919:
185) postulates that the *sicinnis* took place at the final stages of the play, (421–8)
according to his numeration, and was expressive of the satyrs' satisfaction at having

have here is a version of the knocking-scene which is unique to Sophocles among all the numerous scenes of this sort preserved in ancient drama. What is expressed in other knocking-scenes through ordinary and predictable body gestures is presented by Sophocles in the form of a well-timed conclusive phase of a choreographic movement, perhaps even beginning at 176—that is, from the point where the satyrs led by Silenus renew their chase after Apollo's lost cattle. Sophocles' version, in its stylized form, thus stands in a vivid and impressive contrast to the usual stage action in such knocking-scenes. What should be noted above all is Sophocles' adeptness in subordinating the convention of the satyr-dance to the requirements of the satyric drama—requirements which are apparently quite different from those of both tragedy and comedy.

It would be an exaggeration to maintain that the guessing-game in the course of which Cyllene reveals to the satyrs the form, origin, and construction of the new musical instrument invented by the baby Hermes (284 ff.) reflects a uniquely comic technique. The use of γρῖφος and αἴνιγμα is an integral part of the social and cultural life of ancient Greece, and they leave their mark on virtually all areas of Greek literature and thought.[79] Yet even a cursory glance at the detailed discussion of riddles in the tenth book of Athenaeus (448b–59b) would show that comedy played a role which is central both in its importance and in its scope to the development of the literary and dramatic exploitation of this technique.[80] 'How the comic poets make mention of them [i.e. riddles]' (448c) is the central theme proposed for the discussion at the opening of Aemilianus' survey in *Deipnosophistae* X. His survey is full of examples from Middle Comedy,[81] to which we can add the direct evidence we encounter

won the double prize promised to them by Apollo. Whatever the truth of the matter may be, it must be stressed that Walker's attempt to substantiate this hypothesis is purely subjective and has no basis in the text of the play: 'As up to this point the σίκιννις, the typical dance of satyric drama, seems quite clearly, owing, doubtless, to the comparative sedateness imposed by the nature of the first portion of the play, to have found no place, and as the σίκιννις can scarcely be kept very long out of a satyric play, I conjecture that that is quite likely to be the dance here' (ibid.).

[79] See in general Ohlert (1898: 596 ff.; 1912).

[80] A fact which should not surprise us if we remember Clearchus' definition: γρῖφος πρόβλημά ἐστι παιστικόν (Ath. x. 448c).

[81] Alexis, fr. 242 K–A; Anaxandrides, fr. 6 K–A; Antiphanes, fr. 51 K–A, fr. 55 K–A, fr. 75 K–A, fr. 122 K–A, fr. 192 K–A, fr. 194 K–A; Diphilus, fr. 49 K–A; Eubulus, fr. 106 K–A; Timocles, fr. 13 K–A Old Comedy: Plato, fr. 3 K–A.

in the plays of Aristophanes[82] and Plautus.[83] As in *Ichneutae*, so in all our comic examples, what stands out is the whimsical character of the γρῖφος, in situations where simple and even trivial information is slowly supplied to the protagonists by forcing them to participate in the roundabout and taxing process of *facere coniecturam* (to use Plautus' expression), which also throws an ironic light on their personal proclivities and intellectual prowess. Here again, then, the technique employed by Sophocles in expanding and constructing his dramatic situation is mainly a feature of comedy. Even the subtle, dominant, and sexually suggestive[84] personality of

[82] *Nub.*, 319 ff.; *Ra.* 52–67.

[83] *Men.* 143 ff., 164 ff. (Menaechmus I–Peniculus; *Merc.* 888 ff. (Eutychus–Charinus); *Pers.* 215–50 (Sophoclidisca–Paegnium), 630–50 (Saturio's daughter–Dordalus); *Trin.* 883–92, 905-23 (Sycophanta–Charmides).

[84] Note Cyllene's comments, ll. 251–5, 366–8. (*a*) I take ἀλκασμάτων δ[ειλῆ]ς τε πειρατηρίων νύμφης (253–4) to contain an accusation, coquettishly expressed, of an attempted seduction. For ἄλκασμα as *ostentatio virium*, see Tudeer 1916: 12. (*b*) Although we have no parallel for πειρατήριον in the sense of 'an attempt on a woman's honour', the association of the verb πειρᾶν and its cognates with seduction and attempted sexual assault is quite common: see e.g. πειρᾶν: Aristoph. *Eq.* 517 with *scholia ad loc.*, *Plut.* 150, 1067; *Lys.* I. 12; Xen. *Cyr.* 5. 2. 28; πειρᾶσθαι: Pind. *Pyth.* II. 34; πειράζω: Apoll. Rhod. 3. 10; πειρα: Plut. *Thes.* 26, *Cim.* 1; πείρασις: Thuc. 6. 56. (*c*) Hunt's suggestion 1912: 79 (ad col. x. 13 [*ed. pr.*]) that ὀρθοψάλακτον in line 255 corresponds in sense to ὀρθιοψάλακτον 'shrill-sounding' met with general acceptance among Sophoclean scholars: see e.g. Tudeer 1916: 53; Page 1942: ll. 201–2: 'I do not like loud quarrels started in argument.' Cf. Lloyd-Jones 1996: ll. 254–5; Maltese 1982: n. ad 255. It must be stressed, however, that we are dealing here with a ἅπαξ εἰρημένον (the fragmentary compound at the beginning of l. 329 ⟨x⟩οψάλακτος has been variously supplemented (see Radt ad loc.), and, needless to say, provides no real parallel to the one under consideration). The literal sense of the word has nothing to do with sound (in marked contrast to ὄρθιος and its compounds, ὀρθός is nowhere used in the sense of 'high-pitched', 'loud' whether to characterize a voice, a melody or otherwise; ὀρθοτονέω, ὀρθοτόνησις, ὀρθότονος are used exclusively to define a pronunciation with the unmodified *accent*). Rather, its most obvious meaning would be 'erect as a result of being touched lightly'. The reference would be to the phallic situation of the satyrs here claimed by Cyllene to be responsible for the satyrs' aggressive attempt to gain entrance to her cave. Cyllene's present, sexually suggestive, characterization of the satyrs' former aggressiveness as ἔρις ὀρθοψάλακτος may be compared with her attitude toward them in l. 368: see subsequent remark (*d*) Cyllene's comment in ll. 254–5 may be paraphrased thus: 'I do not like a sexually stimulated type of quarrel—involving a *membrum virile*, aroused in response to manual handling—to be stirred up in argument.' Pearson: 1917 n. ad *Ichn.* 249: '. . . it might be suggested that the force of ὀρθός is the same as in fr. 1077. Then the whole compound would mean "violently roused".' (See, however, his reservation ad loc.) (*d*) τὸ λεῖον φαλακρὸν in line 368 has rightly been

the feminine key-figure in this guessing-game in *Ichneutae*, reminiscent in many ways of the conventional image of *demi-monde* women in Middle and New Comedy,[85] helps to place this game between Cyllene and the satyrs (despite the use of *stichomythia*) firmly within the area common to comedy and satyr-play.[86]

The riddle of the tortoise and the lyre made of it is in itself a widespread motif in ancient literature.[87] From Pacuvius' Latin imitation of Euripides' lost *Antiope* (fr. IV, *TRF*[3] Ribbeck), it emerges that Cyllene's riddle in *Ichneutae* did have a tragic parallel in classical Greek literature—the riddle presented by Amphion, the first of the citharodes, to the chorus in that lost play of Euripides. It is generally assumed that Euripides imitated here a practice of his older rival Sophocles.[88] In view of the wide popularity of this motif and our lack of reliable information for the date of *Ichneutae*, it seems that one should leave open this question of the relation between these two dramatists in this particular technical detail. It is, in any case, of no great importance.

recognized by Lloyd-Jones 1994: 142 (following Lobel's suggestion) as referring to the satyrs' *membrum virile*. While such an interpretation would reconcile itself most readily with the use of πίτνημι 'to spread out' in our present line (cf. Lloyd-Jones' translation of line 368 (1996): παῦου τὸ λεῖον φαλακρὸν ἡδονῇ πιτνάς—'Cease to expand your smooth phallus with delight'), this is far from being the case with the traditional identification of the bodily organ here depicted as φαλακρὸν with the satyrs' head. The following translations would serve to demonstrate the peculiarity of language and thought involved in adopting the 'head concept': 'cease courting pleasure with your bald pate.' (Hunt 1912: 84 (Col. xiv. 17 [*ed. pr.*])); 'Cesse d'épanouir de plaisir ton front chauve et lisse.' (Masqueray 1942); 'It's time that bald skull stopped fluttering with ecstasy.' (Page 1942); 'smettila di divertirti a ciondolare quella pelata liscia.' (Maltese 1982); see also Tudeer 1916: 73: *caput capillis nudum*. Pearson's suggestion 1917: n. ad *Ichn.* 359 that πίτνημι is used here in the figurative sense of *to flutter* or *excite* has no real basis in literary evidence and contributes little, if anything, to a better understanding of the Sophoclean line.

[85] See in general Ferguson 1911: 77 f.; Hauschild 1933; Webster 1970: 63 f.; Henry: 1985; Brown 1990: 241–66.

[86] The nymph Cyllene does not figure in the Homeric Hymn to Hermes; rather, it is Maia, Hermes' own mother, who is credited with the full responsibility of taking care of her divine offspring. It is not at all unlikely that this departure from the Homeric Hymn is an essentially Sophoclean invention, pointing out even more clearly to the dramatist's comic inspiration.

[87] See Borthwick 1970: 373–87.

[88] Following Wilamowitz's suggestion 1912: 460 f.; cf. Hunt 1912: 34 [*ed. pr.*]. On the question of the relation between Sophocles' *Ichneutae* and Euripides' *Antiope*, see in general Maltese 1982: 12 f.

One could add numerous examples to the ones I have cited; but it seems to me that even what has been said so far is sufficient to point out a relation between *Ichneutae* and ancient comic tradition which is of the essence of this play. Sophocles knew well how to use such a connection for his dramatic needs. Further comparative study of other parts of satyr-plays which have reached us may well substantiate the suggestion that there is no clear boundary, in the use of motifs, in the characterization of protagonists and situations, and in dramatic manners of expression, between the two dramatic *genres* aiming at τὸ γελοῖον, comedy and satyr-play. One can learn how ingrained the thematic coincidence between comic and satyric drama may have been from the fact that works by authors of Old and Middle Comedy could appear under the title *satyroi*, as if they had been 'normative' satyr-plays.[89] The poetical atmosphere of *Ichneutae*, satyric and comic at the same time, is an excellent example of the fruitful consequences of such a symbiosis.

REFERENCES

ARNOTT, W. G. (1970), 'Young Lovers and Confidence Tricksters: The Rebirth of Menander', *Leeds University Review* 13: 1–18.

AUSTIN, C. (1970), *Menandri Aspis et Samia* II, Subsidia Interpretationis (*Kleine Texte für Vorlesungen und Übungen* 188b; Berlin).

—— (1973) (ed.), *Comicorum Graecorum Fragmenta in Papyris Reperta* (*CGFP*) (Berlin and New York).

BAIN, D. (1975), 'Audience Address in Greek Tragedy', *CQ* NS 25: 13–25.

BENZ, L., STÄRK, E., and VOGT-SPIRA, G. (1995) (eds.), *Plautus und die Tradition des Stegreifspiels. Festgabe für Eckard Lefèvre zum 60. Geburtstag* (*ScriptOralia* 75; Reihe A: Altertumswiss. Reihe 19; Tübingen).

---

[89] Comedies entitled *Satyroi* were written by Cratinus (K–A, *PCG* iv. 232); Callias (K–A, *PCG* iv. 49); Ecphantides (K–A, *PCG* v. 127); Eupolis, fr. 479 (*Silenoi/Satyroi*; K–A ad loc.); Phrynichus (K–A, *PCG*, vii. 414–16); Ophelion (K–A, *PCG* vii. 97); Timocles (*Icarioi Satyroi*; K–A, *PCG* vii. 767–70); *Demosatyroi* (K–A, *PCG* vii. 757–8). See also *P. Oxy.* 1801 = Austin, *CGFP* fr. 343. 17; in Hermippus' play *Moirae*, fr. 47. 1 K–A, Pericles is referred to as 'king of satyrs'; *P. Oxy. 663* (= Austin, *CGFP* fr. 70; cf. K–A, *PCG* iv. 140), col. ii. 42 provides a clear evidence that satyric figures (a chorus?) were included among the characters of Cratinus' *Dionysalexandros*. It is interesting to note that the author of the *hypothesis* to Euripides' *Alcestis* finds it indeed difficult to decide whether to describe it as a δρᾶμα κωμικώτερον or a δρᾶμα σατυρικώτερον.

BORTHWICK, E. K. (1970), 'The Riddle of the Tortoise and the Lyre', *Music and Letters* 51: 373–87.

BROWN, P. G. McC. (1990), 'Plots and Prostitutes in Greek New Comedy', *PLLS* 6: 241–66.

—— (1995), 'Aeschinus at the Door: Terence *Adelphoe* 632–43 and the Traditions of Greco-Roman Comedy', *PLLS* 8: 71–89.

COULON, V., and VAN DAELE, H. (1923–30) (eds.), *Aristophanes* (Budé, Paris; corrected reprints of individual volumes, Paris, 1963–).

DEARDEN, C. W. (1976), *The Stage of Aristophanes* (London).

DOVER, K. J. (1968) (ed.), *Aristophanes: Clouds* (Oxford).

—— (1972), *Aristophanic Comedy* (Berkeley and Los Angeles).

FERGUSON, W. S. (1911), *Hellenistic Athens: An Historical Essay* (London).

FRAENKEL, E. (1922), *Plautinisches im Plautus* (Berlin).

—— (1968), 'Zur römischen Komödie, 1: Plautus *Miles* 214–232', *MH* 25: 231–4.

GOMME, A. W., and SANDBACH, F. H. (1973), *Menander: A Commentary* (Oxford).

GUARINI, G. (1925), 'La lingua degli "Ichneutai" di Sofocle', *Aegyptus* 6: 313–29.

GUGGISBERG, P. (1947), *Das Satyrspiel* (Diss. Zürich).

HANDLEY, E. W. (1969), 'Notes on the *Theophoroumene* of Menander', *BICS* 16: 88–101.

—— and HURST, A. (1990) (eds.), *Relire Ménandre* (*Recherches et Rencontres* 2; Genève).

HAUSCHILD, H. (1933), *Die Gestalt der Hetäre in der griechischen Komödie* (Diss. Leipzig).

HEADLAM, W., and KNOX, A. D. (1922) (eds.), *Herodas, The Mimes and Fragments* (Cambridge).

HENRY, M. M. (1985), *Menander's Courtesans and the Greek Comic Tradition* (*Studien zur klassischen Philologie* 20; Frankfurt am Main, Bern, and New York).

HOFMANN, W. (1995), 'Die Körpersprache der Schauspieler als Mittel des Komischen bei Plautus', in Benz *et al.* (1995), 205–18.

HOLZBERG, N. (1974), *Menander: Untersuchungen zur dramatischen Technik* (Nuremberg).

HUNT, A. S. (1912), '*The Oxyrhynchus papyri* IX, n. 1174. Sophocles, *Ichneutae*', 30–86 [*ed. pr.*].

JOCELYN, H. D. (1997), 'Plautus, *Mil.* 195–234: the Distribution of the Parts', in B. Czapla, T. Lehmann, and S. Liell (eds.), *Vir Bonus Dicendi Peritus, Festschrift für Alfons Weische zum 65. Geburtstag* (Wiesbaden), 211–17.

KAMERBEEK, J. C. (1953), *The Plays of Sophocles, Commentaries*, Part I: *The Ajax* (Leiden).

KASSEL, R., and AUSTIN, C. (1983–) (eds.), *Poetae Comici Graeci* (*PCG*) (Berlin and New York).

KAUER, R., and LINDSAY, W. M. (1965) (eds.), *P. Terenti Afri Comoediae* (2nd edn.; Oxford).

KÖRTE, A. (1935), 'Zu Menanders Θεοφορουμένη', *Hermes* 70: 431–8.

KRAUS, W. (1934), '*Ad spectatores* in der römischen Komödie', *WS* 52: 66–83.

LASSERRE, F. (1973), 'Le Drame satyrique', *RFIC* 101: 273–301 = 'Das Satyrspiel' in Seidensticker (1989), 252–86.

LEFÈVRE, E. (1995), *Plautus und Philemon* (*ScriptOralia* 73, *Reihe A: Altertumswiss. Reihe* 17; Tübingen).

—— STARK, E., and VOGT-SPIRA, G. (1991), *Plautus Barbarus: Sechs Kapitel zur Originalität des Plautus* (*ScriptOralia* 25; *Reihe A: Altertumswiss. Reihe* 8; Tübingen).

LEO, F. (1913), *Geschichte der römischen Literatur*, i (Berlin).

LILJA, S. (1976), *Dogs in Ancient Greek Poetry* (*Commentationes Humanarum Litterarum* 56; Helsinki-Helsingfors).

LINDSAY, W. M. (1910) (ed.), *T. Macci Plauti Comoediae* (2nd edn.; Oxford).

LLOYD-JONES, H. (1971), 'Menander's *Aspis*', *GRBS* 12: 175–95 = *The Academic Papers of Sir Hugh Lloyd-Jones*, ii: *Greek Comedy, Hellenistic Literature, Greek Religion, and Miscellanea* (Oxford, 1990), 7–25.

—— (1994), 'Notes on Fragments of Sophocles', *SIFC* 87: 129–48.

—— (1996) (ed.), *Sophocles*, iii: *Fragments* (Loeb Classical Library; Cambridge, Mass., and London).

LORENZ, AUG. O. FR. (1876) (ed.), *Ausgewählte Komödien des T. Maccus Plautus, 4 Bd.: Pseudolus* (Berlin).

—— (1886) (ed.), *Ausgewählte Komödien des T. Maccus Plautus, 3 Bd.: Miles Gloriosus* (2nd edn.; Berlin).

MAAS, P. (1912), 'Zu dem Satyrspiel Oxyrh.-Pap. VIII 1083', *BPhW* 32: 1426–9 = *Kleine Schriften*, 50–3.

MALTESE, E. V. (1979), 'A proposito degli Ichneutae di Sofocle', *Maia* 31: 117–26.

—— (1982) (ed.), *Sofocle: Ichneutae, Introduzione, testo critico, interpretazione e commento. Papyrol. Florentiana X* (Firenze).

MARESCH, K. (1985), '203. Neue Komödie (Menander?)', in *Kölner Papyri* (*P. Köln*), Band 5: 1–21.

MASQUERAY, P. (1942) (ed.), *Sophocles II* (Budé, 2nd edn.; Paris). [*Les Limiers*: 225–50].

OHLERT, K. (1898), 'Zur antiken Räthselpoesie', *Philologus* 57: 596–602.

—— (1912), *Rätsel und Rätselspiele der alten Griechen* (Berlin).

PAGE, D. L. (1942) (ed.), *Greek Literary Papyri*, iii (*GLP*) (London).

PEARSON, A. C. (1917) (ed.), *The Fragments of Sophocles*, i (Cambridge).

PETRONE, G. (1995), 'Scene mimiche in Plauto', in Benz *et al.* (1995), 171–83.

PFEIFFER, R. (1938), 'Die Netzfischer des Aischylos und der Inachos des Sophokles. Zwei Satyrspiel-Funde', *Sitzungsber. der Bayerischen Akad. der Wiss., Philos.-hist. Abt.* Heft. 2: 3–22 = ' "Die Netzfischer" des Aischylos', in Seidensticker (1989), 58–77.

PÖHLMANN, E. (1989), 'Sucheszenen auf der attischen Bühne des 5. und 4. Jh.s. Zur Bühnentechnik der Eumeniden, des Aias, der Acharner und des Rhesos', in D. Werner (ed.), *Xenia, Festschrift Robert Werner zu seinem 65 Geburtstag dargebracht von Freunden, Kollegen und Schülern*, 41–61 (Konstanz Universitätsverl.).

RADT, S. (1977), *Tragicorum Graecorum Fragmenta* (*TGF*) iv (Göttingen). [*IXNEYTAI ΣATYPOI*: 274–308].

ROBERT, C. (1912), 'Aphoristische Bemerkungen zu Sophokles' *IXNEYTAI* ', *Hermes* 47: 536–61.

SANDBACH, F. H. (1990) (ed.), *Menandri Reliquiae Selectae* (2nd edn., Oxford).

SEAFORD, R. (1984) (ed.), *Euripides: Cyclops* (Oxford).

SÉCHAN, L. (1930), *La Danse grecque antique* (Paris).

SEGAL, E. (1987), *Roman Laughter: The Comedy of Plautus* (2nd edn.; Cambridge, Mass.).

SEIDENSTICKER, B. (1979), 'Das Satyrspiel', in G. A. Seeck (ed.), *Das griechische Drama, Grundriss der Literaturgeschichten nach Gattungen*, 204–57 (*Wissenschaftliche Buchgesellschaft*, Darmstadt) = Seidensticker (1989), 332–61 (abgedruckt 1979: 231–47, 247–55).

—— (1989) (ed.), *Satyrspiel* (*Wege der Forschung* 579; Darmstadt).

SIEGMANN, E. (1941), *Untersuchungen zu Sophokles' Ichneutai* (*Hamburger Arbeiten zur Altertumswiss.* 3; Hamburg).

SLATER, N. W. (1985), *Plautus in Performance: The Theatre of the Mind* (Princeton).

SNELL, B. (1928), *Aischylos und das Handeln im Drama* (*Philologus Supplementband* 20, Heft 1; Leipzig).

SPRANGER, P. P. (1984), *Historische Untersuchungen zu den Sklavenfiguren des Plautus und Terenz* (*Abh. Acad. Mainz* 1960; 2nd edn. Stuttgart).

STÄRK, E. (1989), *Die Menaechi des Plautus und kein griechisches Original* (*ScriptOralia* 11, *Reihe A: Altertumswiss. Reihe* 1; Tübingen).

STEFFEN, V. (1960) (ed.), *ΣΟΦΟΚΛΕΟΥΣ IXNEYTAI* (*Academia scientiarum Polona*; Warsaw).

—— (1965), 'Der Hilferuf in den Netzfischern des Aischylos und sein Fortleben im griechischen Drama', *Eos* 55: 38–43.

SÜSS, W. (1935), 'Zur Cistellaria des Plautus', *RhM* 84: 161–87.

—— (1938), 'Nochmals zur Cistellaria des Plautus', *RhM* 87: 97–141.

SUTTON, D. F. (1980), *The Greek Satyr Play* (Meisenheim am Glan).

SUTTON, D. F. (1985), 'The Satyr Play', in *The Cambridge History of Classical Literature: Greek Literature*, 94–102 (Cambridge).

TAPLIN, O. (1977), *The Stagecraft of Aeschylus: The Dramatic Use of Exits and Entrances in Greek Tragedy* (Oxford).

TUDEER, L. O. TH. (1916), *De vocabulis quibus Sophocles in Ichneutis fabula satyrica usus est* (*Ann. Acad. scient. Fenn.*, ser. B., 14/4; Helsingfors).

USSHER, R. G. (1974), 'Sophocles' *Ichneutai* as a Satyr-play', *Hermathena* 118: 130–8.

VOLLGRAFF, G. (1914), 'Ad Sophoclis Indagatores' (I), *Mnem.* 42: 81–90.

WALKER, R. J. (1919) (ed.), *The Ichneutae of Sophocles* (London).

WALTON, F. R. (1935), 'A Problem in the *Ichneutae* of Sophocles', *HSPh* 46: 167–89.

WEBSTER, T. B. L. (1970), *Studies in Later Greek Comedy* (2nd edn.; Manchester).

—— (1974), *An Introduction to Menander* (Manchester).

WEHRLI, F. (1936), *Motivstudien zur griechischen Komödie* (Zürich and Leipzig).

WILAMOWITZ-MOELLENDORFF, U. VON (1912), ' "Die Spürhunde" des Sophokles', *Neue Jahrbücher für das klassische Altertum* 29: 453–64 = *Kleine Schriften*, i. 353–67 (Berlin, 1935) = Seidensticker (1989), 93–108.

ZAGAGI, N. (1980), *Tradition and Originality in Plautus: Studies of the Amatory Motifs in Plautine Comedy* (*Hypomnemata* 62: Göttingen).

—— (1990), Review of Stärk 1989 in *JRS* 80: 202–3.

—— (1994), *The Comedy of Menander: Convention, Variation and Originality* (Duckworth).

—— (1995), 'The Impromptu Element in Plautus in the Light of the Evidence of New Comedy', in Benz *et al.* (1995), 71–86.

ZIMMERMANN, B. (1995), 'Pantomimische Elemente in den Komödien des Plautus', in Benz *et al.* (1995), 193–204.

11

Sophocles at Rome

LEOFRANC HOLFORD-STREVENS

When an artist from another age whom we admire has been admired by others before us, it is easy to suppose that their grounds of admiration were the same as ours; even when this is not so the fact may be overlooked, as when we complacently record Aristotle's admiration for the *Oedipus Tyrannus* without observing that the play is treated on the footing of a detective story, or that his second favourite play is the *Iphigenia in Tauris*, considered as a thriller and never reconciled with the Philosopher's own definition of the tragic. The Victorians, whose thoughts and feelings still govern us by default in the absence of conscious rejection, admired Shakespeare as a creator of rounded and individual characters; the classically minded Dr Johnson subordinated his appreciation of the characters as persons to his understanding of their dramatic function and the general insights they afford into human types and natures.[1] What, then, did the Romans admire in Sophocles?

[1] These are continually emphasized in his own comments: e.g. on *LLL* v. iii (in modern editions v. 2. 69–72), 'These [the Princess's] are observations worthy of a man who has surveyed human nature with the closest attention' (Johnson 1968: vii. 281). Even his famous apostrophe at the end of 2 *Henry IV* to 'Falstaff unimitated, unimitable Falstaff' concludes: 'The moral to be drawn from this representation is, that no man is more dangerous than he that with a will to corrupt, hath the power to please; and that neither wit nor honesty ought to think themselves safe with such a companion when they see *Henry* seduced by *Falstaff*' (ibid. 523–4). Of Orestes' last words to Aegisthus (S. *El.* 1505–7), Lloyd-Jones and Wilson (1990: 77) write: 'Most modern readers find these lines intolerably flat'; the emphatic κτείνειν at the beginning of 1507 is anything but flat, and these verses bestow the merit of action in support of a general principle on what would otherwise have been mere vendetta—particularly in a play so devoid of overt political reference (see Griffin, Ch. 5), whatever other ages could read into it (see Hall, Ch. 12). Nicephorus Basilaces, *Progymn.* 26 Pignani = *Rhet. Gr.* i. 461–6 Walz, praises these lines for extending the moral lesson from the specific crime of adultery to wrongdoing in

Praise of a writer, however welcome as a sign of an age's taste, is of no further help to the literary historian unless it reveals the basis of approval. The epigrammatist Statyllius, or rather Statilius, Flaccus, who at least bears a Roman name, and whose epigram on the boy who fell through the ice of the Hebrus appears to have been imitated by Germanicus,[2] writes (*AP* 9. 98 = Flaccus v, *GP* vv. 3821–6):

> Οἰδίποδες δισσοί σε καὶ Ἠλέκτρη βαρύμηνις,
> καὶ δείπνοις ἐλαθεὶς Ἀτρέος Ἥλιος,
> ἄλλα τε πουλυπαθέσσι Σοφόκλεες ἀμφὶ τυράννοις
> ἄξια τῆς Βρομίου βύβλα χοροιτυπίης
> ταγὸν ἐπὶ τραγικοῖο κατήνεσσαν θιάσοιο,
> αὐτοῖς ἡρώων φθεγξάμενον στόμασι.

Sophocles certainly wrote on the myth of Thyestes and Atreus; fr. 738 would prove specific allusion to the retrogradation of the sun if it needed to be proved. Unfortunately, it is difficult to extract from this text the specific virtues attributed to our poet, other than that his language is fit for heroes.[3]

Of course, one cannot expect detailed exposition in an epigram:[4] but even when Quintilian, while refusing to decide the relative merits of Sophocles and Euripides at large, declares that for rhetorical training the latter wins hands down, we learn, a comment on language apart, only what Sophocles is not (*Institutiones oratoriae* 10. 1. 67–8):

sed longe clarius inlustrauerunt hoc opus Sophocles atque Euripides, quorum in dispari dicendi uia uter sit poeta melior inter plurimos

general; for all the differences between Comnenian Constantinople and sub-Periclean Athens, he has at least as much right to be heard as any modern.

[2] *AP* 7. 542 = Flaccus IV, *GP* vv. 3813–20; Germanicus, *PML* iv. 103, no. 111 Bährens (but cf. Paul. Diac. *MGH Poet. Lat. Aevi Carol.* i. 50). There is a later Greek poem on this theme: Philip XXXVII, *GP* 2879–86. The Latin version was often ascribed to the Dictator; in Decembrio 1462: 165ᵛ–172ʳ = 1540: 124ᵛ–129ʳ, a papal diplomat and would-be humanist from Aragon who asserts that it is his favourite epigram is mercilessly exposed by Leonello d'Este and his learned courtiers as a bluffer who mistakes not only the author but the river, imagining it to be the Ebro.

[3] πουλυπαθέσσι, of course, denotes the many things that the rulers undergo, not (despite βαρύμηνις) the great passions that Sophocles portrays.

[4] Cf. Dioscorides *AP* 7. 37. 9–10 = HE XXII 1605–6: εἴτε σοι Ἀντιγόνην εἰπεῖν φίλον οὐκ ἂν ἁμάρτοις, | εἴτε καὶ Ἠλέκτραν· ἀμφότεραι γὰρ ἄκρον. This tells us that *Antigone* and *Electra* are the tops, but not why.

quaeritur. idque ego sane, quoniam ad praesentem materiam nihil pertinet, iniudicatum relinquo. illud quidem nemo non fateatur necesse est, iis qui se ad agendum comparant utiliorem longe fore Euripiden. namque is et sermone (quod ipsum reprehendunt quibus grauitas et coturnus et sonus Sophocli uidetur esse sublimior) magis accedit oratorio generi, et sententiis densus, et in iis quae a sapientibus tradita sunt paene ipsis par, et in dicendo et respondendo cuilibet eorum qui fuerunt in foro diserti comparandus, in adfectibus uero cum omnibus mirus, tum in iis qui miseratione constant facile praecipuus.

EARLY LATIN TRAGEDY

The relations between the Greek tragedies known to us in whole or part and the fragments of their early Latin counterparts are obscure and conjectural; to take but one example, Scaliger's notion that Ennius' *Aiax* was based on Sophocles' play has still not been conclusively refuted, though there is no obvious match in the fragments and Ennius, unlike Pacuvius and Accius, shows no other interest in Sophocles.[5] Even worse is our case when neither the putative model nor the putative imitation survives intact: both Sophocles and Pacuvius wrote a *Chryses*, but the former has been suspected of being satyric, and the latter appears to incorporate philosophical matter from Euripides' *Chrysippus*.[6]

If the tragic outlook is the recognition that the gods govern the world in their own interest and not in ours, and that those whose ἀρεταί raise them above the common mass of mankind are likely to be brought low, then it is incompatible with Christianity, at least so long as the worst that may befall the chief character is death, as in the French drama, and not, as in a noble Spanish play,[7] damnation; if Shakespeare is a true tragic poet, that is because his Christianity is paganism in a surplice. But it is also incompatible with Roman values, in which the individual is defined by his service to the City, and the gods' dealings with City and individual depend on the correctness of City's and individual's dealings with them; those who found this view too simplistic even when dressed up in the Stoic language of Providence would deny that the gods took any interest

---

[5] Cf. Jocelyn 1967: 177–9.

[6] Pacuvius 83–93 R², cf. Eur. fr. 839 N².

[7] Tirso de Molina (?), *El condenado por desconfiado*.

in human affairs at all. If we possessed even a single early tragedy whole, we could better understand what Romans expected of the genre; as it is, any attempt to consider the question risks becoming mere guesswork.

However, in one instance the σύγκρισις between Sophocles and Pacuvius has been conducted for us by Cicero, who reports (*Tusc.* 2. 48–50) that Pacuvius, in his *Niptra* (256–69 Ribbeck² = 305–17 D'Anna), modified his model by making Ulysses less of a crybaby;[8] even so he is rebuked by his attendants, and ultimately pulls himself together to depart this life with a maxim worthy of a scoutmaster. I cite the passage at length because it illustrates a theme we shall find in other Roman adaptations of our poet: a compulsion to make him conform to the self-conscious *virtus* of the *mos maiorum* or of Stoicism.

Non nimis in Niptris ille sapientissimus Graeciae saucius lamentatur in uulnere vel modice potius:

> VL. Pedetemptim ac sedato nisu
> ne succussu arripiat maior
> dolor . . .

Pacuvius hoc melior quam Sophocles—apud illum enim perquam flebiliter Vlixes lamentatur in uulnere; tamen huic leniter gementi illi ipsi, qui ferunt saucium, personae grauitatem intuentes non dubitant dicere:

> CH. Tu quoque Vlixes, quamquam grauiter
> cernimus ictum, nimis paene animo es
> molli, qui consuetus in armis
> aeuom agere . . .

Intelligit poeta prudens ferendi doloris consuetudinem esse non contemnendam magistram. Atque ille non immoderate magno in dolore:

> VL. Retinete, tenete! opprimit ulcus:
> nudate! heu miserum me, excrucior!

Incipit labi; deinde ilico desinit:

> operite, abscedite iamiam.
> mittite, nam attractatu et quassu
> saeuom amplificatis dolorem.

Videsne ut obmutuerit non sedatus corporis, sed castigatus animi dolor? Itaque in extremis Niptris alios quoque obiurgat idque moriens:

> conqueri fortunam advorsam, non lamentari decet:
> id uiri est officium: fletus muliebri ingenio additus.

---

[8] Cf. Leo 1913: 229: 'Gewiß hat Pacuvius das allzulaute Jammern (wie in Philoktet und Trachinierinnen) des Helden unwürdig gefunden und den Ausdruck der ganzen Szene gemäßigt.'

Huius animi pars illa mollior rationi sic paruit, ut seuero imperatori miles pudens.

Unfortunately, our surviving fragments of Νίπτρα ἢ 'Οδυσσεὺς Ἀκανθοπλήξ do not show any weeping on Odysseus' part, womanly or not. Greeks were just as well aware as Romans that men ought not to show weakness, but what counted as weakness differed,[9] except for a Plato, or perhaps at Sparta.

Willy Morel noted the resemblance between a passage in Accius' *Meleager*, in which the rejoicings over the slain boar are described in the narrative verses (444–5 Ribbeck[2] = 433–4 Warmington = 505–6 Dangel)

> gaudent, currunt, celebrant, herbam conferunt, donant, tenent;
> pro se quisque cum corona clarum conestat caput,

and one in Sophocles' play, in which a similar action is called for in lyric (fr. 402 Pearson–Radt), στεφάνοισι κρᾶτα καταμπυκοῖς, which he promptly emended to the third person, καταμπυκοῖ, in order to make a closer match.[10] Admission of the resemblance, however, does not license private dramaturgy that should seek to reconstruct the plays on the basis of each other. This warning must apply even when the relation is not disputed: though fifty verses of Accius' *Eurysaces* are preserved, we are at a stand for knowing only one word of the Sophoclean model (ἀδόξαστον, fr. 223 P–R). Similarly, although Accius' *Tereus* is confidently supposed to be based on Sophocles, rather than on Philocles, both Sophocles' and Accius' plays are fragmentary, and the fragments do not overlap. We may observe that Accius does not seem to have made the play so blood-and-thunderous as *Atreus*, but whether this was due only to Accius' greater maturity,[11] or reflected a difference in the originals, is impossible to determine.

Philocteta, of which we know more than most, may draw on all three of the great tragedians' plays; even Theodectes has been

---

[9] Jasper Griffin recalls the proverb ἀγαθοὶ δ' ἀριδάκρυες ἄνδρες (Zenobius 1.14).

[10] Morel 1927: 638: 'Die Übereinstimmung ist wörtlich, nur muß man bei Soph. καταμπυκοῖ schreiben. Auch möchte ich mit Pearson umstellen καταμπυκοῖ στεφάν. κρ. Die falsche Verbalform erklärt sich denn ungezwungen als Dittographie. Besonderer Beachtung verdient es, wie der Römer die z-[*sic*]Alliteration beibehält, die der bei Sophokles fand, ja sie noch überbietet.' What was regarded as mandatory ('nur muß man') by Morel is not so regarded by Radt or Lloyd-Jones.

[11] So Leo 1913: 399 n. 3, citing Gellius 13. 2.

invoked, of whose play we know only (*TrGF* 1, 72 F 5b) that Philoctetes, bitten in the hand and not the foot (which must have impeded the use of his bow) did his best to resist his agonies in order to elude Neoptolemus,[12] but could not hold out indefinitely and bade those present to cut off his hand. This does not entirely accord with Accius' portrayal of a screaming Philoctetes, at least as reported by Cicero, though in principle there could be a difference between his normal conduct and a special effort made for a particular purpose.

In the case of Accius' *Antigona*, relation to Sophocles is not in dispute; in particular the verses (142–3 R = 93–4 W = 581–2 D)

> iam iam neque di regunt
> neque profecto deum supremus rex res curat hominibus

can hardly not represent the despairing cry of Sophocles' heroine (922–3)

> τί χρή με τὴν δύστηνον ἐς θεοὺς ἔτι
> βλέπειν;

albeit expressed as a surrender to the Epicurean philosophy of Ennius' *Telamo*.[13] Three centuries of intellectual development are not to be swept away. However, it was of this play that Otto Ribbeck wrote in the pure tones of nineteenth-century Germany:

Vielleicht zeigte keine der altrömischen Tragödien schärfer den Unterschied zwischen der Vollendung eines griechischen Kunstwerks und dem Ungeschick barbarischer Verdolmetschung. Es gereicht zwar dem Gefühl des Accius für echte Poesie zur Ehre dass er ein Kleinod der attischen Bühne wie die Antigone des Sophokles seinen Landsleuten nicht vorenthalten mochte. Dass er sich aber nicht beschied seinem unvergleichlichen Muster soweit schlicht nachzugehen als seine mangelhafte Kunst erlaubte, sondern es wagte Aenderungen sogar in der Oekonomie vorzunehmen, das zeigt, dass ihm das feinere Verständniss und die schuldige Ehrfurcht vor seinem Meister abging.[14]

---

[12] Or 'Neoptolemus and his search-party', as Aspasius' τοὺς περὶ τὸν Νεοπτόλεμον may also be understood; see Radt 1980: 47–56. This has a bearing on the composition of the chorus: islanders as in Aeschylus and Euripides, or sailors as in Sophocles and Accius?

[13] Vv. 270–1 + 265 Jocelyn, rightly combined as *Trag.* 269–71 by Ribbeck: Ego deum genus esse semper dixi et dicam caelitum, | Sed eos non curare opinor quid agat humanum genus: | Nam si curent, bene bonis sit, male malis, quod nunc abest.

[14] Ribbeck 1875: 483–4.

None of us is allowed to talk like that, except when complaining that a film is a travesty of a novel; but while we may find it easier than Ribbeck to forgive Accius his adaptations of Sophocles' plot, we shall find it harder than he did to say exactly what they were.

In one fragment the drowsy watch is aroused with the words (140–1 R = 91–2 W = 579–80 D):

> Heus uigiles properate, expergite
> pectora tarda sopore, exsurgite!

Ribbeck, to general agreement, supposes that the scene is set on the battlefield, on the morning after the defeat of Polynices' army, when Antigone has already conducted the first burial.[15] It takes little knowledge of Roman manners to understand that the liveliness of barked orders would be far more appropriate to tragic decorum as understood by Accius and his audience than Sophocles' semi-comic watchman-messenger; as more than one scholar has reminded us, Roman poetry, like Roman society, was far less ready than Greek to relax its formality.[16] Creon (it becomes ever clearer as the play progresses) is a tyrant, not the champion of the *polis* that Hegel conceived and Anouilh drew;[17] yet he allows the guard to witter away about his φροντίδων ἐπιστάσεις in a manner that few consuls of the Roman people would have tolerated for an instant;[18] even Anouilh's well-meaning public servant cuts in sooner. This speech, I suggest, must have shocked Accius as the Porter in *Macbeth* shocks the modern heirs of the Romans.[19]

It is presumably Ismene who says to Antigone (136–7 R = 88–9 W = 577–8 D):

---

[15] Ibid. 484.

[16] Cf. Griffin 1984: 193–4; and see Goldberg 1995: 68–70, 138–9.

[17] Nevertheless, some (but not all) modern scholars argue that his decree was not as outrageous in itself, by Athenian standards, as a previous generation supposed; and a certain return of sympathy in his direction can be detected in the Mediterranean world, where Creon can be considered as representing the modern state, Antigone the archaic and unenlightened village.

[18] And those who did would be suspect as currying favour with their soldiers in pursuit of political ambition.

[19] 'The translator of my first book was, naturally, an *anglista*, so, having made my acquaintance, she tried out on me her theory, which was that all the comic elements in *Macbeth* ("Knock, knock, knock . . .") were patently an intrusion, the work of a different hand. Eliminate them, and you would have the pure tragedy that Shakespeare wrote. Tragedy is tragedy, and is dignified, while comedy is comedy: the pure element cannot mingle with the low' (Whitfield 1988: 37).

quanto magis te istimodi esse intellego,
tanto, Antigona, magis me par est tibi consulere et parcere.

This is a different tone from Sophocles' Ismene, who can only fear for her sister (οἴμοι, ταλαίνης ὡς ὑπερδέδοικά σου),[20] without claiming any right to take counsel for her. Did Accius, in a society where upper-class women were somewhat more self-assertive than at Athens, find the Ismene of Sophocles' πρόλογος a little too insipid for Roman taste,[21] and make her seek to hold back her headstrong sister by deeds as well as words?[22]

Yet in one respect Accius must have followed Sophocles: in making Antigone's rebellion the justified defiance of a tyrant, or in Latin a *rex*, and not, as some moderns would have it, a challenge to the *polis* in the name of higher morality. Such an anti-democratic interpretation traduces Sophocles, who indicates that this decree is the will of one man, painted in tyrannical colours, and determined to uphold it even in the face of public opinion;[23] at Rome, only the

[20] Sconocchia (1972) compares instead vv. 49–68, where Ismene gives of her wisdom; but the protective tone is still absent.

[21] In turn Ribbeck (1875: 485) complains: 'Ismene nahm den überlegenen Ton einer älteren Schwester an: statt jener reizenden, beschiedenen Scheu eines eng jungfräulichen Wesens hatte sie etwas Altkluges, Nüchternes.' Wilamowitz missed 'die liebenswürdige Ismene' at the end of Sophocles' play; see Eduard Fraenkel ap. Lloyd-Jones 1972: 215 n. 3 = 1990: 403 n. 3. When the norms of female behaviour are more restrictive than those for men, it may seem worthwhile to give the abnormal woman a normal foil: Ismene beside Antigone, Chrysothemis beside Electra. Depending on the nature of the unconventionality, readers, particularly male readers, may prefer the foil; see Hall, pp. 288 ff., and cf. Nabokov (1964: ii. 280–1) on the eclipse, in Soviet fiction, of the dreamy, idealistic Tatiana type by the 'noisily cheerful' Olga: 'she is the one who straightens things out at the factory, discovers sabotage, makes speeches, and radiates perfect health.' On the other hand, of the two widowed *ianitrices*, Ruth and Orpah, who in tradition become sisters with King Eglon for their father, Orpah, who in the Bible goes back to her mother and plays no further part in the story, was said in Midrash and Talmud to have been raped by a hundred men and a dog, given birth to the four giants Saph, Madon, Goliath, and Ishbi-benob, and been killed by Abishai b. Zeruiah when she tried to hinder his rescue of King David from the last-named.

[22] Verse 135 R = 87 W = 576 D 'quid agis? perturbas rem omnem ac resupinas, soror' is usually taken as Ismene's protest at Antigone's recklessness; but it might also be Antigone's rebuke of Ismene's interference. However, the perverse ingenuity of D'Antò (1980: 252–3), who identifies the speaker as Polynices' widow Argeia, is knocked on the head by Aricò (1978: 209).

[23] Having prescribed death by stoning for anyone who should violate his decree, Creon instead has Antigone immured; after Haemon's report, he could not be sure that the stones would fly in the right direction.

blackest portrayal of Creon could have lost him the sympathy of an audience by whose ancestors the Horatius who killed his sister for mourning her Alban fiancé had been acquitted in a *iudicium populi.*

If Cicero presents Sophocles in *De officiis* 1. 144 as the object of Pericles' rebuke for noticing a handsome boy, or at *De senectute* 47 for his relief, in old age, at being past such concerns, this shows merely that he was a subject for anecdote, as a great man of the past; but the poet meant a great deal to Cicero, despite one characteristic reservation. In the *Tusculan Disputations* (2. 20–2), most of Heracles' long speech in *Trachiniae* (vv. 1045–1111) is translated to make the point that even he *dolore frangebatur*; but whereas Heracles' lament at his downfall is rendered with reasonable fidelity, the sudden access of pain in vv. 1081–9 is reduced to the adverb *nunc*; the uncontrollable cries of woe that burst through the iambic trimeters are levelled out.

αἰαῖ, ὦ τάλας,   1081*a*
αἰαῖ.   1081*b*
ἔθαλψέ μ' ἄτης σπασμὸς ἀρτίως ὅδ' αὖ,
διῆξε πλευρῶν, οὐδ' ἀγύμναστόν μ' ἐᾶν
ἔοικεν ἡ τάλαινα διάβορος νόσος.
ὦναξ Ἀΐδη, δέξαι μ',   1085
ὦ Διὸς ἀκτίς, παῖσον.
ἔνσεισον, ὦναξ, ἐγκατάσκηψον βέλος,
πάτερ, κεραυνοῦ. δαίνυται γὰρ αὖ πάλιν,
ἤνθηκεν, ἐξώρμηκεν.

        tuque caelestum sator
iace obsecro in me uim coruscam fulminis;
nunc, nunc dolorum anxiferi torquent uertices,
nunc serpit ardor.

Had Cicero felt able to reproduce his original in this respect, he would have made his point more strongly; but Roman decorum forbade.

In the third book of the same dialogue (§71), Cicero presents a translation of fr. 576R (fr. 35 Bl):

τοὺς δ' ἂν μεγίστους καὶ σοφωτάτους φρενί
τοιούσδ' ἴδοις ἂν οἷός ἐστι νῦν ὅδε,
καλῶς κακῶς πράσσοντι συμπαραινέσαι·
ὅταν δὲ δαίμων ἀνδρὸς εὐτυχοῦς τὸ πρίν
πλάστιγγ' ἐρείσηι τοῦ βίου παλίντροπον,
τὰ πολλὰ φροῦδα καὶ καλῶς εἰρημένα.

πλάστιγγ' Ellendt, Lobeck: μάστιγ' codd. Stobaei, quod nonnulli Ciceronem
legisse credunt

Cicero has been extolling self-control; but:

Contra dicuntur haec: quis tam demens, ut sua uoluntate maereat? natura
adfert dolorem, cui quidem Crantor, inquiunt, uester cedendum putat.
premit enim atque instat nec resisti potest. Itaque Oileus ille apud
Sophoclem, qui Telamonem antea de Aiacis morte consolatus esset, is,
cum audiuisset de suo, fractus est; de cuius commutata mente sic dicit:

> Nec uero tanta praeditus sapientia
> quisquam est qui aliorum aerumnam dictis adleuans
> non idem, cum fortuna mutata impetum
> conuertat, clade subita frangatur sua,
> ut illa ad alios dicta et praecepta excidant.

Haec cum disputant hoc student efficere, naturae obsisti nullo modo posse:
et tamen fatentur grauiores aegritudines suscipi quam natura cogat. quae
est igitur amentia? ut nos quoque idem ab illis requiramus.

Cicero first makes Sophocles say what in Greek he does not, that no
one is above such backsliding, and then rebukes him once again as
the exponent of unrestrained emotion. George Eliot claimed the
influence of Sophocles 'in the delineation of the great primitive
emotions';[24] the Romans saw the same quality in him, but were less
sure that they approved. Contrast the five citations of Euripides in

[24] 'I asked her how Sophocles had influenced her:—(we had been talking about
him, and she had said that she first came to know him through a small book of
mine);—and her answer certainly startled me. Probably all people,—or most who
have any inner life at all—sometimes write down things meant for no eye but their
own. Long ago I was putting down in this way some things that had been passing
through my mind about Sophocles, and this among the rest,—that George Eliot was
the modern dramatist (in the large sense) most like him, and that he had told upon
her work probably *in the outlining of the first emotions.* Her answer to my question
was—"in the delineation of the great primitive emotions". *Verbally* this was an
accident; but hardly in substance. Of course I did not tell her. But was it not
curious?' (Jebb 1907: 155–6: to C[aroline] L[ane] S[lemmer], whom he later
married, 27 May 1873).

the *Tusculans*,[25] always for sound moral arguments that teach us to take the sorrows of the world for granted.

Lamentation, however, is not the only context in which Sophocles appears; it is clear that Cicero recognizes him as a great poet, not only because everyone says so (*De oratore* 3. 27) or because of the anecdote concerning the *Oedipus Coloneus* (*De senectute* 22),[26] or because in the first book of the dialogue *De finibus bonorum et malorum* he sets against the Greek poet's *Electra*, however admirably written, the poor translation by Atilius to be read on patriotic grounds (1. 5 'A quibus tantum dissentio ut cum Sophocles uel optime scripserit Electram, tamen male conuersam Atili mihi legendam putem'), but from a reference to *Coloneus* in the fifth book of that same dialogue in which Cicero makes his brother Quintus support Piso's assertion that places recall to mind the great men with whom they are associated by citing his own experience at Colonus (§3):

Tum Quintus Est plane Piso ut dicis inquit, nam me ipsum huc modo uenientem conuertebat ad sese Coloneus iste locus, cuius incola Sophocles ob oculos uersabatur. quem scis quam admirer quamque eo delecter. me quidem ad altiorem memoriam Oedipodis huc uenientis et illo mollissimo carmine quaenam essent ipsa haec loca requirentis species quaedam commouit, inaniter scilicet, sed commouit tamen.

Not only for modern readers, but for Plutarch (*Mor.* 785 E), or whoever was his source for the anecdote about the δίκη παρανοίας brought against Sophocles by his sons, the most enrapturing passage of the play is the stasimon εὐίππου ξένε τᾶσδε χώρας (668–93). However, Quintus' *carmen* cannot be Plutarch's μέλος, since Oedipus is not asking where he is. The word *carmen*, indeed, has no necessary connection with music, nor need it be an entire work: at *De senectute* 16 and *Pro Caelio* 18 it indicates a specific passage from a longer entity, respectively App. Claudius' speech in Ennius' *Annales* against making peace with Pyrrhus, and the Nurse's speech at the beginning of his *Medea*.[27] In our present passage we must interpret it of Oedipus' speech to Antigone, likewise the beginning

[25] *Tusc.* 1. 115; 3. 39, 59, 67; 4. 63.

[26] Cf. Powell ad loc., and esp. Lefkowitz (1981: 84–5), deriving the story from Oedipus' cursing of Polynices.

[27] Cf. Tac. *A.* 15. 70. 1, referring to Lucan 3. 635–46, and Gellius 17. 10. 8–9, referring to Pindar, *Pyth.* 1. 21–6 (Holford-Strevens 1988: 172 n. 50).

of the play; but what of *mollis*? Like most everyday words pressed into the service of literary criticism, it is not free from ambiguity:[28] it sometimes indicates the *genus tenue*,[29] sometimes a diction pleasing to the ear,[30] sometimes a style or rhythm that the speaker wishes to disparage as feeble or unmanly.[31] This last sense is not to the point, but the diction of Oedipus' opening speech may reasonably be described as unpretentious within the range of tragic diction, and as smoothly flowing in its σύνθεσις ὀνομάτων: liquids abound, especially nu, which in the first four lines, even allowing for maximum assimilation (which in Sophocles' day was normally reflected in the spelling), occurs no fewer than seventeen times, and except where final nasals are concerned, there are no clusters of consonants between words that could not begin a syllable.[32]

> Τέκνον τυφλοῦ γέροντος Ἀντιγόνη, τίνας
> χώρους ἀφίγμεθ' ἢ τίνων ἀνδρῶν πόλιν;
> τίς τὸν πλανήτην Οἰδίπουν καθ' ἡμέραν
> τὴν νῦν σπανιστοῖς δέξεται δωρήμασιν;

Few of us, I think, would unprompted have singled out this passage for commendation above any other in the play, however sensitive we may be to its beauties when they are pointed out and indeed to the contrast between the shambling beggar Oedipus who enters the action and the fearsomely heroic Oedipus who leaves it. The warning expressed at the beginning of this study is thus reinforced.

However suspicious we may be of Q. Cicero's purported opinions, when in *De diuinatione* 1. 17 he praises his brother's poetry, and in *De legibus* 3. 34–7 adopts the extreme right-wing position that Cicero would rather not endorse in his own name, his interest

---

[28] See Ernesti 1797: 257–8, and for μαλακός Ernesti 1795: 204.

[29] Cf. *Orator* 64. Velleius Paterculus even informs us that Hesiod was 'mollissima dulcedine carminum memorabilis' (1. 7. 1). In this sense it corresponds to ἀφελής; cf. Ernesti, *Lex. tech. Gr. Rh.* 51–2.

[30] e.g. *Rhet. Herenn.* 3. 20, 23–4, Cic. *Brut.* 274, cf. *Orator* 52, μαλακός D.H. *Comp.* 22. 35 Aujac–Lebel, ii. 110. 3 Usener–Rademacher, *Ep. Pomp.* 6. 9, ii. 247. 8 U.–R.).

[31] Cic. *Orat.* 3. 41 (cf. *Off.* 1. 128), Quint. 11. 3. 32. At D.H. *Lys.* 19 (i. 31. 21–2) Lysias' lack of a high emotional register is expressed as περὶ δὲ τὰ πάθη μαλακώτερός ἐστιν.

[32] For this consideration see Dionysius of Halicarnassus, *Comp.* 22–3; but the presence of the nasal groups would move this passage closer to the temperate style for which Sophocles is commended at 24. 5. In v. 4 σ + δ = ζ.

in tragic poetry is not to be denied; he himself wrote a tragedy on the theme of Erigone (*Q. fr.* 3. 1. 13), and knocked off four others in sixteen days (3. 5. 7). On the other hand, in Marcus' rebuke, 'Συνδείπνους Σοφοκλέους, quamquam a te actam fabellam uideo esse festiue, nullo modo probaui' (*Epp. Q. fr.* 2. 16. 3), the reference is not to a translation but to some incident in Caesar's camp[33]—either a dinner to which Quintus had not been invited, or an altogether too boisterous one to which he had—putting Marcus in mind of a satyr-play, as it appears to have been, set amongst the heroic Achaeans, in which one character throws a full chamber-pot at another's head (fr. 565 R).[34] Such things were not to Marcus' taste; but he knew his Sophocles well enough to find an apposite allusion.[35] There was a similar passage in Aeschylus (fr. 180R),[36] the prince of satyr-playwrights,[37] if satyric these texts were; but Cicero knew him less well.

Cicero's complaint that Sophoclean characters do not bear up against misfortune as bravely as they should will provoke some mirth amongst those familiar with his own accomplishments in that respect; he has been fortunate that his philosophical writings have been read without regard to their author or their context.[38] Nevertheless, that and his unease at lapses in decorum were no mere personal quirks.

---

[33] For this use of author and title cf. Plaut. *Rud.* 86 'non uentus fuit, uerum Alcumena Euripidi'; in English one hears 'It's Dante's *Inferno* out there.'

[34] Soph. fr. 565 Radt: ἀλλ' ἀμφὶ θυμῶι τὴν κάκοσμον οὐράνην | ἔρριψεν οὐδ' ἥμαρτε· περὶ δ' ἐμῷ κάρᾳ | κατάγνυται τὸ τεῦχος οὐ μύρου πνέον· | ἐδειματούμην δ' οὐ φίλης ὀσμῆς ὕπο.

[35] Bücheler emended *actam* to *factam*; Shackleton Bailey approves in his *editio maior*. But is that the way to say 'translated'? It is no answer to cite Plaut. *Capt.* 1029, which merely proves, had anyone doubted it, that *facio* may be used of writing a play.

[36] Ὀστολόγοι, fr. 180 Radt: ὅδ' ἐστὶν ὅς ποτ' ἀμφ' ἐμοὶ βέλος | γελωτοποιόν, τὴν κάκοσμον οὐράνην | ἔρριψεν οὐδ' ἥμαρτε· περὶ δ' ἐμῷ κάρᾳ | πληγεῖσ' ἐναυάγησεν ὀστρακουμένη, | χωρὶς μυρηρῶν τευχέων πνέουσ' ἐμοί.

[37] T125a–b = D.L. 2. 133, Paus. 2. 13. 6.

[38] The politics of *De officiis* were overtaken by events even in the brief remainder of their author's lifetime; but that did not impair the status of 'Tully's Offices' as timeless wisdom. Sallust and Seneca were no less fortunate.

AUGUSTAN POETRY

The relation between Vergil and Sophocles deserves a detailed study in itself.[39] His use of *Ajax* has often been noticed: when Aeneas adjures Ascanius (*Aen.* 12. 435–6):

> Disce, puer, virtutem ex me verumque laborem,
> fortunam ex aliis,

commentators recall Ajax' words to Eurysaces (*Ajax* 550–1):

> ὦ παῖ, γένοιο πατρὸς εὐτυχέστερος,
> τὰ δ' ἄλλ' ὁμοῖος· καὶ γένοι' ἂν οὐ κακός.

To be sure Aeneas, unlike Ajax, is not about to die; but this same conception is inverted in the case of Mezentius, *contemptor divom* like Ajax in his pride,[40] and his son Lausus, worthy of a better sire, whose death restores him to his moral sense. We are used to the comparison of *Ajax* 924

> ὦ δύσμορ' Αἴας, οἷος ὢν οὕτως ἔχεις

with *Aen.* 2. 274–5

> ei mihi qualis erat, quantum mutatus ab illo
> Hectore qui . . .

though the thought was not unique.[41] *Aen.* 4. 317–18 'fuit aut tibi quicquam dulce meum' has been compared with *Aj.* 521 τερπνὸν εἴ τί που πάθοι, and (more loosely) Dido's *Trugrede* with Ajax', problematic as the latter is.

Vergil's penchant for combining more than one source in a single phrase is not confined to his dealings with Ennius and Lucretius. At *Aen.* 1. 630

> non ignara mali miseris succurrere disco

---

[39] For Vergil's borrowings from tragedy see, in antiquity, Macr. *Sat.* 5. 18. 21–19. 24 (Sophocles fr. 534 at 5. 18. 8–11); in our own day König (1970), a work made available to me by the kindness of Dr Carmen Muñoz of the Departemento de Filología Griega y Latina, Facultad de Filología, Universidad de Sevilla.

[40] Horsfall 1995: 184–5.

[41] Cf. Thuc. 7. 75. 6 ἀπὸ οἵας λαμπρότητος καὶ αὐχήματος τοῦ πρώτου ἐς οἵαν τελευτὴν καὶ ταπεινότητα ἀφῖκτο.

scholars have noted that the language recalls Meleager CII (*AP* 12. 70). 4 = *HE* 4537 οἶδα παθὼν ἐλεεῖν and the thought Soph. *OC* 562–4

> ὃς οἶδά γ᾽ αὐτὸς ὡς ἐπαιδεύθην ξένος,
> ὥσπερ σύ, χὼς εἷς πλεῖστ᾽ ἀνὴρ ἐπὶ ξένης
> ἤθλησα κινδυνεύματ᾽ ἐν τὠμῷ κάρᾳ.

But *non ignara mali* echoes *Ant.* 1191

> κακῶν γὰρ οὐκ ἄπειρος οὖσ᾽ ἀκούσομαι.

In observing this, I am anticipated not by Heyne or Conington or any modern, but by the admirable Juan Luis de la Cerda,[42] who also cited *Od.* 12. 208, ὦ φίλοι, οὐ γάρ πώ τι κακῶν ἀδαήμονές ἐσμεν— the verse translated at 1. 198 'o socii—neque enim ignari sumus ante malorum', Dido's echo of which underlines the similarity between the wanderers. Dido's last speech owes something to Deianira as well as to Alcestis;[43] which does not mean that Vergil always took the texts he imitated and combined from books in front of him on a writing-desk like a scholar, but rather that, having read or seen on stage a number of tragic female deaths or other striking scenes, he composed a new one out of his recollection, no doubt aided but not governed by passages copied out into notebooks or even rereading of originals. One must also allow that he may have been stimulated by something that left no visible trace in his verses, and yet played its catalytic part in their composition.[44] Source-criticism is far from an exact science, even where purveyors of fact

---

[42] In his edition of *Aen.* 1–6 (Lyon, 1612), 116.

[43] See König 1970: 204–25; but I do not understand why the resemblance between 'dulces exuviae . . . accipite' (*Aen.* 4. 651–2) and Deianira's ὦ λέχη τε καὶ νυμφεῖ᾽ ἐμὰ . . . δέξασθ᾽ (*Trach.* 920–2) should be dismissed as an accident because Dido does not address the bed (König 1970: 377 n. 22).

[44] On 3 Feb. 1888 Theodor Fontane wrote to Georg Friedlaender asking for some place-names in the Riesengebirge to help him with his ballad 'Annemarie'; on the 6th he wrote again, thanking Friedlaender and stating that despite the excitement caused by Bismarck's 'Wir Deutsche' speech, 'setzte ich mich doch hin und schrieb unter dem Eindruck von "Heiden-Tilke" und "Hexentreppe" die Ballade nieder, in der natürlich nichts von Heiden-Tilke und Hexentreppe vorkommt, wie das immer der Fall zu sein pflegt. Man braucht die Namen-Anregung und das Bewußtsein, daß ein bestimmtes Quantum von Sachlichem neben einem liegt — und aus diesem Besitz-Bewußtsein heraus producirt man dann. Wie oft habe ich schon gehört: "aber Sie scheinen es nicht gebraucht zu haben." Falsch. Ich habe es d o c h gebraucht. Es spukt nur hinter der Scene' (Fontane 1954: 86–7, nos. 91–2).

are concerned, let alone for creative writers, and least of all for those whose minds transcend the ways of prose.[45] It is in spirit, not merely letter, that it is right to speak of 'Dido's markedly Sophoclean suicide'.

Specific borrowing, indeed, is less important than overall resemblance: the two parts are alike in their bursting the bounds of their respective languages and in their outlook on the world, their ability to see both the necessity of an outcome and its cost. The division among commentators on Vergil between imperialists and anti-imperialists matches that in Sophoclean scholarship between pietists and hero-worshippers,[46] for Vergil shares Sophocles' empathy with both sides in a conflict even as Ovid shares Euripides' forensic skill in putting their case.[47] Common to the two poets, moreover, is their ability to confront us, not with examination questions in abstract morality, but with the realities of human conduct. The defeated Turnus expects death at Aeneas' hands, and requests only that his corpse be restored to his kindred; Aeneas is about to take pity until he is overcome by battle-rage at the sight of Pallas' baldric, and kills him. It is disputed whether the conduct appropriate to a Homeric hero or a Turnus is good enough for the model of *pietas* Aeneas— who at this point is no longer the plaster saint that some modern readers have complained of but fully human; but which of us can be confident of doing otherwise in those circumstances? Even so,

[45] Great poet and master of language that Callimachus was, were his text preserved as well as Vergil's there are few if any difficulties that could not be solved with access to the Alexandrian library; but not even total knowledge of Vergil's reading would suffice to do the same for him.

[46] For these terms see Winnington-Ingram 1980: 303, and for the question ibid. 304–29.

[47] Moderns are far too much inclined to suppose that if you are on one side you close your eyes and your mind to its faults: either 'our side' is right, and therefore we do not wish to hear about the unpleasant things done in our name, or if we do pay attention to them we conclude that 'our side' is not right. This has been made worse by the fashion for subversive reading, in which the author is made to mean the opposite of what he appears to say. But the ancients are much readier to allow that the other side has a case but we are on our own side. When Tacitus puts biting denunciations of Roman imperialism into the mouths of a Caratacus or a Calgacus, we are inclined to suppose that Tacitus too disapproves; yet imperial coins, which were not produced by critics of the government, can complacently depict a conquered nation as a weeping woman; and the speech of the Gaul Critognatos presented by Caesar 'propter eius singularem ac nefariam crudelitatem' (*BG* 7. 77. 2) has matter to thrill the death-before-slavery school of anti-imperialists, all composed by the great imperialist himself.

Electra has become unnatural in her grief and longing for revenge; how else could she have endured, if she had too much spirit for Chrysothemis' meek submissiveness? When Orestes has struck their mother, Electra bids him strike twice as hard, if he has the strength; not very sweet-natured, but can we, or can we not, demand any other reaction from a person thirsting for revenge but relying on someone else to achieve it, at the moment when at last it is being achieved? In these things, it may be, the reading of Sophocles enabled Vergil to become what he was;[48] but he had read Euripides as well as Sophocles,[49] and for all that is tragic in the *Aeneid* the primary story is not.

Ovid could find in *Trachiniae* Achelous' shape-changes as well as the fate of Deianira and Hercules, but Sophocles, as Palmer observed, was not his only source.[50] Likewise, when he tells the tale of Tereus and the Athenian sisters, he admixes motifs from Euripides to generate 'an episode neither wholly Sophoclean nor Euripidean, but utterly Ovidian'.[51] What the eighth of his *Heroides* owes to Sophocles' *Hermione* we cannot tell; but the debt is in all probability no greater, and possibly somewhat less, than Shakespeare's to his prose sources.[52] No one will look for a Sophoclean spirit in him;[53] if he has returned to credit from his Victorian disfavour, it is not because we have followed the Middle Ages in their moral interpretations of his works, but because we have grown out of the demand for high seriousness.

A different kind of borrowing, of sound as well as sense, appears in Horace's Leuconoe ode, when the waves beat against the rocks in winter (*Carmina* 1. 11. 5–6)

> quae nunc oppositis debilitat pumicibus mare
> Tyrrhenum

---

[48] Suggestive is Knight 1949: 30–1. Hard-headed scholars are not always kind to that book, but hard-headed scholarship, without literary feeling, falls further short of understanding Vergil than almost any other ancient author, a fact of which it seems uncomfortably aware.

[49] König (1970: 250) finds an 'Affinität zu Euripides' contrasted with 'Vernach-lässigung von Sophokles und Aischylos' (257); but Euripides was so much the tragedian κατ' ἐξοχήν that predominant use of him was only to be expected.

[50] 'The *Trachiniae* is followed, but not closely': Palmer 1898: 359.

[51] Curley 1997: 320; see Larmour 1991.

[52] Louis C. Purser ap. Palmer 1898: p. xvi.

[53] To be sure tragedy is *Sophocleus . . . cothurnus* at *Am.* 1. 15. 15 as at Verg. *Buc.* 8. 10, but metre claims its due.

The sequence of choriambic words recalls the Colonean chorus' description of Oedipus buffeted, like itself, by the miseries of old age (*Oedipus Coloneus* 1240–1)

πάντοθεν βόρειος ὥς τις ἀκτά
κυματοπλὴξ χειμερία κλονεῖται.

THE SILVER AGE, AND BEYOND

The reputation of *Oedipus Coloneus* is yet again confirmed by Valerius Maximus 8. 7 ('de studio et industria'), ext. 12:

Sophocles quoque gloriosum cum rerum natura certamen habuit, tam benigne mirifica illi opera sua exhibendo quam illa operibus eius tempora liberaliter subministrando. prope enim centesimum annum attigit, sub ipsum transitum ad mortem Oedipode ἐπὶ Κολωνῶι scripto, qua sola fabula omnium eiusdem studi poetarum praeripere gloriam potuit. Idque ignotum esse posteris filius Sophoclis Iophon noluit, sepulcro patris quae retuli insculpendo.

If Valerius is as consistent with himself as he is in suppressing all mention of the lawsuit, it will be that play at whose one-vote victory Sophocles, in extreme old age, expired for joy (9. 12. ext. 5); in another version the play was *Antigone*,[54] perhaps supposed to be last because its plot is set later than the other Theban plays, and ascribed on a black day in Greek scholarship to Iophon.[55]

The elder Pliny has Sophocles buried by 'King'[56] Lysander at the command of Dionysus, who called him his favourite (*Naturalis historia* 7. 109):

Sophoclem tragici cothurni principem defunctum sepelire Liber Pater iussit, obsidentibus moenia Lacedaemoniis, Lysandro eorum rege in

---

[54] *Vita* 14.

[55] Scholia Londinensia in *Scholia in Dionysii Thracis Artem Grammaticam*, pp. 471–2 Hilberg: οὐ γὰρ κρίνει εἰ καλῶς γέγραπται ἢ οὔ [in itself a controversial view], ἀλλ᾽ ἢ νόθα ἢ γνήσια· πολλὰ γὰρ νοθευόμενά ἐστιν, ὡς ἡ Σοφοκλέους Ἀντιγόνη—λέγεται γὰρ εἶναι Ἰοφῶντος τοῦ Σοφοκλέους υἱοῦ—Ὁμήρου τὰ Κυπριακὰ καὶ ὁ Μαργίτης, Ἀράτου τὰ Θυτικὰ καὶ τὰ Περὶ ὄρνεων, Ἡσιόδου ἡ Ἀσπίς.

[56] The same error recurs in Popper 1966: i. 184, apparently unnoticed by the book's many enemies. To be sure Latin authors call more than one man *rex* who was never βασιλεύς: Periander frequently, Epaminondas at Ampelius 32. 4 (where *rex Thebarum Graecos pugnando uindicauit* would make the sense less bad: Holford-Strevens 1995: 602).

quiete saepius admonito ut pateretur humari delicias suas. requisiuit rex, qui supremum diem Athenis obissent, nec difficulter ex his quem deus significasset intellexit pacemque funeri dedit.

Chronology refutes, but the story suits Pliny's admiration for his poetry and his life, even if his prosaic mind could not abide the poet's assertion that amber is created from the tears of guinea-fowl east of India mourning for Meleager; having rebuked other Greeks who talked nonsense on the subject he continues (37. 40–1):

Super omnes est Sophocles poeta tragicus, quod equidem miror, cum tanta grauitas ei cothurni sit, praeterea uitae fama alias principi loco genito Athenis et rebus gestis et exercitu ducto. hic ultra Indiam fieri dixit e lacrimis meleagridum auium Meleagrum deflentium [fr. 830a R]. quod credidisse eum aut sperasse aliis persuaderi posse quis non miretur? quamue peritiam tam imperitam posse reperiri, quae auium ploratus annuos credat lacrimasue tam grandes, auesue quae a Graecia, ubi Meleager periit, ploratum adierint Indos? quid ergo? non multa aeque fabulosa produnt poetae? sed hoc in ea re, quae cotidie inuehatur atque abundet ac mendacium coarguat, serio quemquam dixisse summa hominum contemptio est et intoleranda mendaciorum inpunitas.

Pliny's quotations from the tragic poets no doubt come from his sources; very little attention is paid to their works in imperial Latin literature. Even Seneca, in his prose, is no exception to this neglect, nor Statius, who in his epicedion for his father (*Siluae* 5. 3) retails at length the Greek poetry learnt under his guidance, from Homer and Hesiod to Lycophron and Corinna: no dramatic poet is mentioned, though both the tragic and the comic poets are collectively bidden to weep for him along with Pietas, Iustitia, Facundia, Pallas, the Muses, epic and lyric poets, and the Seven Sages, since he embraced them all in his mind.

At a more advanced level, some people must have continued to read the tragedians, as Seneca tragicus and Quintilian show: but the implication that the tragedians were not at the heart of the syllabus is borne out by their neglect in the Roman literature of the second century. Fronto ignores them; Apuleius merely recounts the anecdote of the lawsuit (*Apol.* 37. 1 Vallette); even Marcus, writing in Greek, though he credits tragedy with improving our endurance of misfortune, cites nothing but *sententiae* detached from their context such as we find in Stobaeus. The same is largely true of Gellius: moreover, when he claims to be surprised that Plato in the

Theaetetus (or rather Plato in the *Republic* and Pseudo-Plato in the *Theages*) should ascribe to Euripides a verse that 'we have read' (*legimus*) in Sophocles, he is parading as his own discovery a fact well enough known to the Greeks; the remark that Sophocles was born before Euripides is evidently intended to prove that if Euripides did use this verse, yet Sophocles had used it first, an argument that would have solved all those embrangled disputes concerning the two *Electras* (13. 19. 2). The chapter is obviously taken, not necessarily without mediation, from the work of Greek scholars who had noted such echoes.[57] Gellius' other quotation (12. 11. 6) is the paraenetic fragment 301, ostensibly cited by the moral preacher Peregrinus Proteus and certainly used by Clement of Alexandria and Stobaeus; Sophocles is called *prudentissimus poetarum*, since he is being cited for practical wisdom.

It is also Gellius who tells us (6. 5) the famous story, not without import for the theory of acting,[58] that the actor Polus, playing Electra,[59] carried his own son's ashes in the urn supposedly containing those of Orestes. Having stated that Polus had to carry an urn 'quasi cum Oresti ossibus', he does not leave it at that, but summarizes the relevant portion of the plot: 'Ita compositum fabulae argumentum est, ut ueluti fratris reliquias ferens Electra comploret commisereaturque interitum eius existimatum.' Here we must regret that we lack Gellius' source: one would wish to know, first whether it was Greek or Latin, second whether Gellius could derive or infer the details of the action from it without having read the play, and third whether it stated the facts in the didactic fashion we find in §6 or incorporated them into the running narrative.

In the next century the learned Terentianus Maurus shows

---

[57] See Holford-Strevens 1988: 173, but the interpretation of 'legimus' as present (ibid. n. 55) is too kind.

[58] Whether the actor should become one with the character, or remain at sufficient distance to pull a face at other cast members in the middle of the most heart-rending speech, when turned by the action away from the audience, is a matter of debate to which no definitive answer can be given. Brecht (1957: 211) makes Helene Weigel ask 'Vielleicht war sein [Polus'] Sohn ein Schurke. Er mag trotzdem leiden, aber warum soll ich es?'; he is misled into fathering the anecdote on Cicero (ibid. 210) by the initial reference to *De oratore* 2. 189 in Gottsched's note on Horace, *AP* 102–3 (1751: 21), where Polus becomes 'ein römischer Komödiant' (= 'actor', not necessarily comic) and achieved the Horatian effect: 'Und da war kein Mensch auf dem Platze, der sich der Thränen hätte enthalten können.'

[59] Not 'the *Electra* of Sophocles' (Rolfe). Gottsched understood correctly: 'Polus . . . sollte die Elektra vorstellen, die ihren Bruder beweinet.'

knowledge of a play, as distinct from a tag; it is albeit from that general favourite, Euripides' *Orestes*.[60] Ausonius hopes that his grandson will revive his memory of 'soccos aulaeaque regum' (*Protrepticus* 54), and may (or may not) have derived Ajax' bitterness against 'pravus Atrides' (*Epitaphia* 3. 3) from Sophocles; but at the school whose bilingual curriculum was transcribed 502 years ago by Conrad Celtes only comedy is mentioned.[61]

IMPERIAL TRAGEDY

A study of Sophocles at Rome is exempt from the modern critics' otherwise justified demand that Seneca's plays be judged as independent works. The relation of plays in the Senecan corpus to known Greek plays of the same theme or title is not uniform, but is not always as distant as in the case of *Agamemnon*. Nevertheless, although the opening of *Phoenissae* seems to show the first scene of *Coloneus* transposed from Athens to Thebes and from human tenderness to posturing rhodomontade, and although Sophocles as well as Euripides has been found in his *Phaedra*,[62] I shall concentrate on the manifest instances, *Oedipus* and *Hercules Oetaeus*, beginning with the former as being of unquestioned authenticity.[63]

In Sophocles, an Oedipus who enjoys his own and his people's confidence asks why the citizens are praying to the gods and petitioning himself: the priest describes the plague, about which the monarch knows already, but the audience does not. Seneca, as if finding all this improbable, makes an Oedipus who already believes

---

[60] See Ter. Maur. 1960–4, on *Or.* 1369–72; note too the quotation at 963 (from *Or.* 1287).

[61] See Dionisotti 1982: 122.

[62] Zwierlein 1987: 54–68; his discussion of Sophocles' play, 'deren potentiellen Einfluß auf Senecas Phaedra manche Forscher sehr hoch veranschlagen' (p. 54), ends with admirable caution 'Damit genug der Spekulationen: Vielleicht dürfen wir mit aller Vorsicht, resümierend, soviel feststellen, daß es Indizien gibt, wonach eine von den beiden euripideischen Stücken im Handlungsverlauf deutlich unterschiedene Phaedra-Tragödie existierte, und daß diese erschlossene Tragödie mit jener des Sophokles identisch sein, oder Züge der sophokleischen aufgenommen haben könnte' (p. 68).

[63] On this play and its relation to Sophocles see too Töchterle 1994: 9–22 ('Quellen und eigene Gestaltung'); Boyle 1997: 92–102.

himself to be the plague-bringer, though for escaping rather than for
fulfilling Fate's decree, describe the pestilence, and pray in despair
not that it may end, but that he may not be the last to die: then
abandoning even that hope, he tells himself to flee, 'uel ad parentes',
which is Jocasta's cue to bid him be a man, missing the point
entirely.

Sophocles' Oedipus has already sent Creon to Delphi: he returns
with the apparently good news that the plague will cease if Laius'
murderer is punished, and relates what little is known of the case,
this being new to Oedipus. The prologos thus ends with an
optimism that the chorus somewhat lowers. In Seneca, Oedipus
closes the first scene by saying:

> Una iam superest salus,
> si quam salutis Phoebus ostendat uiam, (108–9)

the subjunctive of improbable contingency: but it is not till after the
chorus has piled on the agony that we learn of Creon's mission. So
far, that is the nearest we have come to suspense, as opposed to a
sense of fate: but Creon's report, which had seemed like good news
in Sophocles, strengthens the unwholesomeness in Seneca.

There comes now a clear echo: asked why no one had taken any
steps to hunt down Laius' murderer, Creon in both plays replies that
the matter was overtaken by the Sphinx.[64] The answer is not entirely
convincing, if one stops to think as Aristotle did,[65] since it does not
explain why Oedipus was not told how the throne has become
vacant. In Sophocles the audience has already been lulled into
acquiescence by nine consecutive two-line questions with two-line
answers before the awkward moment arrives;

> Οι. κακὸν δὲ ποῖον ἐμποδὼν τυραννίδος
> οὕτω πεσούσης εἶργε τοῦτ᾽ ἐξειδέναι;
> Κρ. ἡ ποικιλῳδὸς Σφὶγξ τὸ πρὸς ποσὶ σκοπεῖν 130
> μεθέντας ἡμᾶς τἀφανῆ προσήγετο.

Whereupon Oedipus diverts attention by commending both Phoebus and the Thebans for the diligence that in fact only Phoebus had
shown on Laius' behalf, assuring his subjects that he has his own
interest to look after and will therefore be zealous in his investiga-
tions:

[64] Contrast Soph. *OT* 566–7, omitted by Seneca.
[65] *Poetics* 1454[b]7, 1460[a]30.

ὑπὲρ γὰρ οὐχὶ τῶν ἀπωτέρω φίλων
ἀλλ᾽ αὐτὸς αὑτοῦ τοῦτ᾽ ἀποσκεδῶ μύσος.
ὅστις γὰρ ἦν ἐκεῖνον ὁ κτανὼν τάχ᾽ ἂν
κἄμ᾽ ἂν τοιαύτῃ χειρὶ τιμωρεῖν θέλοι.   140
κείνῳ προσαρκῶν οὖν ἐμαυτὸν ὠφελῶ.

Seneca, with a reading public to consider, glides past the difficulty as
swiftly as possible: his Oedipus, concerned with the past only as it
affects the present—including his own interest, but generalized to
the common interest of kings[66]—turns his attention away from
Creon's answer to the needs of the moment:

OE. Quod facere monitu caelitum iussus paro,
       functi cineribus regis hoc decuit dari,   240
       ne sancta quisquam sceptra uiolaret dolo.
       regi tuenda maxime regum salus:
       quaerit peremptum nemo quem incolumem timet.
CR. Curam perempti maior excussit timor.
OE. Pium prohibuit ullus officium metus?   245
CR. Prohibent nefandi carminis tristes minae.
OE. Nunc expietur numinum imperio scelus.

The proclamation, which in Sophocles extends to misprision, is
confined by Seneca to the murder itself.[67] This concentration is
made possible by the recasting of the Tiresias scene. In Sophocles,
the seer hesitates to speak until the tyrant accuses him of having
been a party to the crime; thus provoked, Teiresias tells him that he,
Oedipus, is the murderer he seeks, to which the infuriated ruler
replies with aspersions on the seer's professional integrity and
unwarranted accusations that he and Creon are conspiring to
depose him; after perplexed comment from the Chorus, Creon
himself appears, in order to find out what Oedipus has being saying;

---

[66] Claudius had executed Gaius' murderers (Suet. *Div. Claud.* 11. 1, Dio 60. 3. 4).

[67] It also takes the form of a curse, which in the Greek play only the spurious lines
246–51 do, though Seneca no doubt found them in his text. Erbse (1993: 70–1),
defending this curse against the Oxford editors' deletion, misunderstands my
objection to them ap. Lloyd-Jones and Wilson 1990: 86: κακὸς κακῶς is not
incompatible with elevated language, but suits only a personal imprecation, not
an act of state. Teucer at *Aj.* 1175–9, 1389–92, Philoctetes at *Phil.* 1368–9, do indeed
not speak colloquially (at p. 70 n. 28 I am said to list these passages 'aber als Belege
für die Alltäglichkeit des Ausdrucks'), but they speak only for themselves; if anyone
was likely to use it in the city's name it was Creon in *Antigone*, but he does not. In
any case, the style of 248 displeases as a whole.

an altercation ensues, in which Creon is threatened with execution, till Jocasta intervenes to restore peace. Seneca, indulging that Claudian taste for the gruesome which made his fortune in the second halves of the sixteenth and the twentieth centuries, first presents a Tiresias scene, in which the prophet's daughter Manto reports alarming, and quite unstageable, prodigies, while Oedipus watches in silence before asking what they mean and, on being told that only Laius' ghost can explain them, sending Creon to undertake the task; then, after an ode to Bacchus ordered by Tiresias, a Creon scene follows, in which reluctance to speak yields to compliance under duress that gives rise to the imputation of treason. This latter scene occupies the place of Sophocles' ἀγών between Oedipus and Creon; the motif of a report from the second man in the kingdom recalls the Greek poet's πρόλογος, but the structure is closer to his Tiresias scene. Yet there are differences: whereas in Sophocles Oedipus lays stress on the interests of the city—as indeed the Creon of the *Antigone* does—in Seneca he is a holder of *imperium* compelling the obedience that is his due:

> Imperia soluit qui tacet iussus loqui.

Since Seneca was writing under a monarchy, the difference in emphasis seems less important than the fact that his Oedipus keeps his temper better than Sophocles'. Creon tells his story, with much assistance from the sixth book of the *Aeneid*; Oedipus, believing that he is the son of Polybus and Merope, and therefore cannot be guilty of the crimes alleged, deduces quite rationally that Creon's report must be a lie, for which political ambition is the obvious cause. Sophocles' Oedipus might have argued on the same lines; instead he has flown into a rage. To be sure, ll. 703–4

> Odia qui nimium timet
> regnare nescit: regna custodit metus

have a distinct ring of *oderint dum metuant*, words spoken by a tyrant, mentioned more than once in Seneca's philosophical works,[68] and often cited by the mad, or at least unstable, Caligula;[69] but even when speaking like a tyrant, the Senecan Oedipus retains

---

[68] *De ira* 1. 20. 4; *De clementia* 1. 12. 4, 2. 2. 2.
[69] Suet. *Calig.* 30. 1.

his dignity: no raving, but cold command, and for imprisonment, not death.

Sophocles' Jocasta assures Oedipus that divination is a fraud, only to give Oedipus the clue that he may very well be Laius' murderer after all; in Seneca this is replaced with a short dialogue, initiated by Oedipus, who on thinking the matter over has begun to suspect as much himself. This leads directly to the entry of the Old Man of Corinth, who discharges the function of Sophocles' Messenger, followed by Phorbas, who supplies the final link; from Oedipus' 'Curas reuoluit animus' to Phorbas' 'Coniuge est genitus tua' is barely a hundred lines, as if Sophocles were staged by the Reduced Shakespeare Company.[70] His wonderful character of Jocasta, taught by experience to reject conventional beliefs that justify themselves after all, and desperate to stave off the looming disaster—surely this is her tragedy as well as Oedipus'—is whittled down almost to nothingness; and whereas in Sophocles she has plainly recognized the truth while Oedipus has not, in Seneca it is Oedipus who has guessed it, and conducts his inquiries simply to confirm it. Did Seneca consider that for a renowned problem-solver the Sophoclean Oedipus is incredibly obtuse, with his talk of being Fortune's child? If so, he has broached that Latin path of prosaic rationality down which Corneille travelled to a bad play and Voltaire to a worse.

It is no surprise that Seneca should adopt gory moments from the Outmessenger's description of Oedipus' self-blinding and make them even gorier: if Sophocles' Oedipus raises his eyes the better to assail them, Seneca makes them agents in their own destruction:

> τοιαῦτ' ἐφυμνῶν πολλάκις τε κοὐχ ἅπαξ   1275
> ἤρασσ' ἐπαίρων βλέφαρα, φοινίαι δ' ὁμοῦ
> γλῆναι γένει' ἔτεγγον, οὐδ' ἀνίεσαν.

> manus in ora torsit. at contra truces   962
> oculi steterunt et suam intenti manum
> ultro insecuntur, uulneri occurrunt suo.

The next two lines of the Greek text have been conjecturally deleted as interpolations by that successor to the *magistellus Byzantinus* as the incarnation of bad taste, the fourth-century ham actor.[71] Be that

---

[70] I know that not all have judged so; but I speak as I find.

[71] West (1978: 121), describes these 'clumsy and tasteless lines' as 'an obvious interpolation in the interest of goriness', comparing *Ajax* 918–19, 'Nauck's condemnation of which should not have been allowed to fall into oblivion'. Unlike our

as it may (and one is in any case corrupt), for Seneca those verses were Sophocles'; he read them, and found them to serve his purpose:

> φόνου μυδώσας σταγόνας, ἀλλ' ὁμοῦ μέλας   1278
> ὄμβρος †χαλάζης αἵματος† ἐτέγγετο.

> rigat ora foedus imber et lacerum caput   978
> largum reuulsis sanguinem uenis uomit.

Nevertheless, he has altered Sophocles' account by postponing Jocasta's suicide, which in his model was the event that turned Oedipus' cry of anguish (1183),

> ὦ φῶς, τελευταῖόν σε προσβλέψαιμι νῦν

from metaphorical wish to literal reality. Seneca's Oedipus needs no such outside stimulus; and he neither begs assistance in his departure from the chorus nor accepts persuasion from a noble Creon; he makes his own way off. If not exactly a sage, he is at least a Stoic in being beholden to none.

I cannot love this play; if that is because I love Sophocles too well, it is not a fault I care to mend. Differences of plot apart, I find the style inferior; this is no doubt a matter of taste, but one final example shall justify or condemn. Oedipus' apostrophe ἰὼ Κιθαιρών became a stock quotation, appearing at Epictetus 1. 24. 16 as a type for the fall of the great that characterizes tragedy, and in the emperor Marcus 11. 6. 2 as inculcating the lesson that even those in that condition can bear their evils; all this is well and good, but who would have remembered the passage had not audience and readers been moved, not merely instructed, by a pathos that in its simplicity of thought flies like an arrow to its mark?

> ἰὼ Κιθαιρών, τί μ' ἐδέχου; τί μ' οὐ λαβών   1391
> ἔκτεινας εὐθύς, ὡς ἔδειξα μήποτε
> ἐμαυτὸν ἀνθρώποισιν ἔνθεν ἦ γεγώς;

Seneca's Oedipus too invokes Cithaeron, but only in the messenger's report, and there is no pathos, only rhodomontade that at best

passage, however, these verses are linguistically unimpeachable; they also describe what the audience could not see. Nauck's condemnation is ignored by Lloyd-Jones and Wilson in their OCT, and by Lloyd-Jones in his Loeb edition, but West's deletion of *OT* 1278–9 is accepted; for supporting arguments and partial retraction see respectively Lloyd-Jones and Wilson 1990: 109–10, 1997: 63–4.

leaves the untroubled reader patting the author on his back for cleverness:

> ipse tu scelerum capax,   930
> sacer Cithaeron, uel feras in me tuis
> emitte siluis, mitte uel rabidos canes—
> nunc redde Agauen.

Still, admirers of *Schicksalstragödie* may think better of this play; nor is it without power in its concentration. In this it forms a contrast to the longest tragedy by far in the Senecan corpus, *Hercules Oetaeus*. This was first declared spurious by Daniel Heinsius,[72] whose arguments convinced Bentley.[73] Now Heinsius also rejected *Phoenissae*,[74] and assigned four other plays to M. Annaeus; but however we regard him as a critic of authenticity, his judgements on merit were delivered with the authority of a playwright in the Senecan manner who could admire the supernatural scenes in *Oedipus*,[75] find the choruses of *Thyestes* divine,[76] and even prefer *Troades* to its Euripidean original.[77] If, then, I find

---

[72] Heinsius 1621: 335–48. In my quotations I have eliminated compendia and ligatures, and corrected trivial misprints, but otherwise retained the original spelling and punctuation. These 'Animadversiones et Notae' are a revision of those in Heinsius 1611: 483-584 (on this play 566–84); the long passage 'Caeterum . . . secat' was added in 1621.

[73] 'Of the Four Passages, yet behind, which he [the Hon. Charles Boyle] cites as out of *Seneca*, no fewer than three are taken out of *Hercules Oetaeus*, which is not a play of *Seneca*'s, as the Learned *Daniel Heinsius* has prov'd fourscore Years ago': Bentley 1883: 184.

[74] Note esp. his comment (1611: 518 = 1621: '303' [304]) 'Caeterum vt Aeschylus et Sophocles Pythagoricos vbique fere profitentur: ita videas declamatores istos e decretis Stoicorum ducere colores.'

[75] Heinsius 1611: 536 = 1621: 314: 'Noster Episodia quae addidit, cum tam accurate ignem et viscera describit, vt e sacris hausisse ea libris videatur, tum prolixa illa νεκυίας ex Homero delineatio, ita pulchra sunt, vt quanvis habeant vernile et ambitiosum aliquid, potius in hoc laudanda tamen, quam in isto requirenda videantur.'

[76] Heinsius 1611: 507 = 1621: 297, 'Chori sunt divini.'

[77] Heinsius 1621: 317–18 (not in 1611): 'Non ausim Graecam vllo modo, sive dispositionem spectes, sive πάθος, sive gravitatem et augustum pondus sententiarum, cum ista conferre. Etiam in Choris noster vincit, quos ex paucis Graeci verbis, et quae sparsim leguntur, fecit alios et plane divinos. Apud Graecum vno loco illa invenerat [Eur. *Tro.* 187–90]. Alio, illa [1096–9]. Et paulo post nonnulla similia. Ex quibus praeclarum illum fecit, *Quae vocat sedes habitanda captas* [Sen. *Tro.* 814]. Et ex duobus versibus [Eur. *Tro.* 608–9] coelestem illum, *Dulce moerenti populus dolentum* [Sen. *Tro.* 1009].'

my adverse comments on *Hercules Oetaeus* anticipated by Heinsius, I claim acquittal on any charge, either of being prejudiced against a work already passing for spurious, or of failure to appreciate the ways of Silver authors.[78] Since Heinsius' general comments may be less familiar or even accessible to readers than more recent studies,[79] I cite them at large in the Appendix.

Of course, no one will suppose that a critic who wrote nearly four hundred years ago has spoken the last word on the subject; Heinsius' comments would certainly provoke the disagreement of Robin Nisbet, who has added to the resemblances between this and the undisputed plays a parallel with *Trachiniae* that he finds Senecan:[80]

> πολλὴν μὲν ὕλην τῆς βαθυρρίζου δρυός   1195
> κείραντα, πολλὸν δ᾽ ἀρσέν᾽ ἐκτεμόνθ᾽ ὁμοῦ
> ἄγριον ἔλαιον, σῶμα τοὐμὸν ἐμβαλεῖν . . .
>
> stat uasta late quercus et Phoebum uetat
> ultraque totos porrigit ramos nemus;   1625
> gemit illa multo uulnere impresso minax
> frangitque cuneos, resilit incussus chalybs
> uulnusque ferrum patitur et rigidum est parum.

The masculinity of the Sophoclean olive is transmuted to an equation between the oak and Hercules; in v. 1196 Nisbet detects hints at emasculation, remarking reasonably that 'even those who reject a double meaning here may grant that the Silver Age would have suspected one', and adducing a similar conceit at *Phaedra* 1099

> medium per inguen stipite ingesto tenet,

---

[78] E. Phillips Barker, in the first edition of the *Oxford Classical Dictionary* (p. 828) describes the *HO* as 'long, dull, and psychologically incredible'; the comment (retained over other signatures in the second edition, p. 977) is undermined in context by his assertion (not retained) that 'In the tragedies, too, we meet no product or promise of a balanced artist-mind, but the primitive thought-forms, rough-hewn idols, and nightmares risen out of a tortured egoist's unconscious mind.' Nevertheless it is true, as is its replacement in the third edition (p. 97): 'a pagan passion-play whose derivative language and overextended action suggest rather an imitator than Seneca himself.'

[79] See Zwierlein 1986: 313–43 and literature there cited. In defence of authenticity see Rozelaar 1985: 1367–91—but he even accepts *Octauia* (Rozelaar 1976: 598–607)—and Nisbet 1987 = 1995: 202–12.

[80] Nisbet 1987: 245 = 1995: 204–5.

where 'one suspects a bizarre caricature of Priapus'.[81] Stoic poets are notorious for their filthy minds, but if the author of *HO* did indeed understand Sophocles as Nisbet he so inverted him as to make the oak emasculate the axe, 'rigidum est parum'. One would certainly not put such things past a Silver poet, but since if the playwright was not Seneca he was unquestionably Seneca's ape, they can hardly prove authenticity.

Although the plot is taken from *Trachiniae*, the play begins very differently: gone are Deianira's loving and anxious wait, the deception whose unmasking warned us that Heracles' conduct had not been free from reproach, and the patience, exceeding what Greeks expected of a wife, that will undo both Heracles and Deianira herself when she seeks to win back her husband's love instead of demanding that he expel his mistress from the matrimonial home. The hero, whom in Sophocles we do not even see till v. 972, speaks the first lines, complaining it is high time his *uirtus* got him into heaven; the chorus and Iole lament the fall of Oechalia without suggesting it was a crime; but Deianira rages like Congreve's woman scorned. In the Greek poet, naive as she may be to believe Nessus, she patently intends her husband no harm, even though the black-galled poison of the Lernaean hydra had tainted the Centaur's blood:

> ἐὰν γὰρ ἀμφίθρεπτον αἷμα τῶν ἐμῶν   572
> σφαγῶν ἐνέγκῃ χερσίν, ᾗ μελάγχολος
> ἔβαψεν ἰός, θρέμμα Λερναίας ὕδρας, . . .

μελάγχολος . . . ἰὸς (*uirus*) Dobree: μελαγχόλους . . . ἰοὺς (*sagittas*) codd.

In the imitator the *tabes* (520, 527) is a *malum* (524) with a *uis dira* (578). Even the appeal to Cupid, called *horridus* (550), is distinctly sinister. If Hercules is a rational man aware of his divine qualities, Deianira is a passionate woman who to hear her talk has decidedly hellish capacities.

Nevertheless, it is no more than talk; once the harm is done she avers, and others accept, that she never meant it. When the poison first reveals its deadly power by destroying the dyecloth, she is just as afraid as in Sophocles, albeit the well-observed simile from daily life[82] has yielded place to an incoherent congeries of incompatible

---

[81] Ibid. 247 = 207.
[82] Naturally the Latin poet cannot mention anything so lowly as a saw.

comparisons that do not illustrate but obfuscate the comparandum.[83]

> εἴσω δ' ἀποστείχουσα δέρκομαι φάτιν
> ἄφραστον, ἀξύμβλητον ἀνθρώπω μαθεῖν.
> τὸ γὰρ κάταγμα τυγχάνω ῥίψασά πως   695
> {τῆς οἰός, ὧι προὔχριον, ἐς μέσην φλόγα}[84]
> ἀκτῖν' ἐς ἡλιῶτιν· ὡς δ' ἐθάλπετο,
> ῥεῖ πᾶν ἄδηλον καὶ κατέψηκται χθονί,
> μορφῆι μάλιστ' εἰκαστὸν ὥστε πρίονος
> ἐκβρώμαθ' ἂν βλέψειας ἐν τομῆι ξύλου.   700

> et forte, nulla nube respersus iubar,
> laxabat ardens feruidum Titan diem
> (uix ora solui patitur etiamnunc timor):
> medios in ignes solis et claram facem   725
> quo tincta fuerat palla uestisque illita,
> abiectus horret uillus et Phoebi coma
> tepefactus arsit (uix queo monstrum eloqui).
> niues ut Eurus soluit aut tepidus Notus,
> quas uere primo lucidus perdit Mimas,   730
> utque euolutos frangit Ionio salo
> opposita fluctus Leucas et lassus tumor
> in litore ipso spumat, aut caelestibus
> aspersa tepidis tura laxantur focis,
> sic languet omne uellus et perdit comas.   735

Hyllus now enters to describe the fatal event; there are sharp differences between the two plays. In Sophocles, both Hyllus and Heracles are fully aware that Deianira is to blame, and duly blame her; in the Latin play, although Hyllus speaks of 'your garment' ('ueste tunc fulgens tua', 788), neither he nor Hercules makes the connection. In the one he speaks as Heracles' son, albeit as the son of the finest man on earth, whose like Deianira will not see again (811–12); in the other he is concerned for the whole world's loss ('commune terris omnibus pateris malum'), for himself not till

---

[83] For a similar confusion in the Nurse's first speech see Friedrich 1954: 52–60; Rozelaar's defence (1985: 1353–61) requires *exilit* (v. 242) to mean *stat iam iam exultura* (that it means 'leaps up' not 'leaps out', cf. Friedrich 1954: 55 'auffährt', Rozelaar 1985: 1353 'aufspringt' makes no difference, *pace* Nisbet 1987: 249 n. 38 = 1995: 209 n. 38). Rozelaar, moreover, curiously takes vv. 233–6 to mean that Iole as well as Deianira is raging.

[84] Dobree was right to delete this verse, but the Roman poet had read it; see *HO* 726.

1426. In the former play, Heracles' first reaction is to turn on Lichas in anger and kill him in rage, by throwing him against a rock; in the latter he cries out and weeps, but Lichas has already died of terror when Hercules reaches him, giving the hero time to reflect that his being the cause of Lichas' death is a *clades* besides Lichas' being the cause of his (814–15). After discarding the corpse, he declares that madness has not taken away his wits: the evil is far worse, that he wishes to rage against himself (823–5). This means trying to tear off the adhesive shirt; but beneath the icing of Silver paradox one detects the Stoic unable to control his immediate reaction to φαντασίαι, but free to withhold his συγκατάθεσις from them by rational judgement of what is evil and what is not.[85] Whether this ethical substructure improves the play we need not here consider, but there is no question of his begging his son to kill him as in Sophocles; the weakness that Hyllus relates is purely physical.

Sophocles' Deianira does not dispel Hyllus' assumption that she intended to kill her husband, but departs to commit suicide; only then, when fetched by the nurse too late to save her, does he realize that ἄκουσα πρὸς τοῦ θηρὸς ἔρξειεν τάδε (935). The Latin poet makes her stay to rant about the best-merited mode of her death even as earlier about that most condign for Hercules; the contrast between reason and passion is portrayed anew. Both the nurse and Hyllus try to dissuade her, on the grounds that she is not at fault: 'haut est nocens quicumque non sponte est nocens' says the one (886), 'error a culpa uacat' the other (983). This reasoning does not convince her; she runs off to kill herself, and Hyllus to restrain her, having canvassed the conflicting claims of *pietas*.[86]

In comes the dying demigod, in Sophocles borne by others fast asleep with a doctor-like Old Man in attendance, in the Roman play on his own two feet. He is not exactly calm, bidding Jupiter bury him beneath the ruins of the world he will no longer be able to protect, but it is the consequence of his death, not the immediacy of his pain, that moves him; as the Chorus comments,

> Viden ut laudis conscia uirtus   1207
> non Lethaeos horreat amnes?

---

[85] See Gellius 19. 1, cf. Sen. *Ep.* 113. 18.

[86] Compare Jocasta's equally fruitless consolation 'Fati ista culpa est: nemo fit fato nocens' (*Oed.* 1019).

His long speech, interrupted by comments from the Chorus, adapts themes from the Sophoclean ῥῆσις, though not his appeal to Hyllus to bring out his mother that he may punish her. Instead, as Heinsius complains, while engaged on the disagreeable business of tearing himself limb from limb he delivers over three hundred verses full of such stuff as hardly an idle school-declaimer would have spouted. He describes the spread of the poison almost as if he himself were the doctor describing the progress of a patient's disease:

> Eheu, quis intus scorpius, quis feruida
> plaga reuulsus cancer infixus meas
> urit medullas? sanguinis quondam capax   1220
> tumidi uigor pulmonis arentes fibras
> distendit, ardet felle siccato iecur
> totumque lentus sanguinem auexit uapor.
> primam cutem consumpsit, hic aditum nefas
> in membra fecit, abstulit pestis latus,   1225
> exedit artus penitus et totas malum
> hausit medullas: ossibus uacuis sedet;
> nec ossa durant ipsa, sed compagibus
> discussa ruptis mole conlapsa fluunt,
> defecit ingens corpus et pesti satis   1230
> Herculea non sunt membra—pro, quantum est malum
> quod esse uastum fateor, o dirum nefas!

Only in these last words does he react, and even then it is with a second-order reaction commenting on a proposition that the facts have wrung from him. He is ashamed to weep (1265–77), as he was in Sophocles (1070–5); but now the fit strikes that makes him wish for instant death. We have seen how Sophocles' verses were watered down by Cicero; but all this poet gives us is (1277–8):

> urit ecce iterum fibras,
> incaluit ardor: unde nunc fulmen mihi?

The Sophoclean Heracles had sought a last meeting with his mother, but she was away in Tiryns; she was rightly left out, remarks Heinsius, for what could she say? In the Latin play she arrives unbidden: she completely fails to understand, telling Hercules not to cry and not to die; perhaps he has not been poisoned, but is simply worn out from his labours. In England she would make him a nice cup of tea. Only now does he sleep; Hyllus enters to announce his mother's death in three words, 'nurus Tonantis occidit', belatedly blaming her for his father's ruin.

> Pro lux acerba, pro capax scelerum dies!
> nurus Tonantis occidit, natus iacet,   1420
> nepos supersum; scelere materno hic perit,[87]
> fraude illa capta est.

Hercules awakes from a vision of his heavenly afterlife, and in his half-conscious state raves of killing Deianira; on learning she is dead, as in *Trachiniae* he recalls the prophecy of death at a dead man's hands and bids Hyllus arrange his funeral and marry Iole. In the Greek play the youth shows reluctance in both cases, but this is Rome; there is no question of his not obeying his father, even to save the poet some embarrassment: whereas Sophocles could let Heracles spare Hyllus the actual lighting of the fire, relying on the audience to know that Philoctetes would perform the task—

> Υλ. καὶ πῶς ὑπαίθων σῶμ' ἂν ἰώμην τὸ σόν;   1210
> Ηρ. ἀλλ' εἰ φοβῆι πρὸς τοῦτο, τἆλλά γ' εἰργάσαι.

—in the Roman play he must without explanation address his command not to Hyllus but to Philoctetes, who turns up from nowhere in the text:

> tu, genus Poeantium,   1485
> hoc triste nobis, iuuenis, officium appara:
> Herculea totum flamma succendat diem.

Having done so, however, Philoctetes can now report on that happy ending which Sophocles had suppressed because it would trivialize the hero's sufferings, but which here is the moment that Hercules has been waiting for, when he will finally take his rightful place in heaven.[88] At one moment, indeed, he declares that Jupiter's hand will be forced:

---

[87] 'Materno' = 'my mother's', not 'his own mother's', but said without guile in Alcmene's presence it is dramaturgically inept.

[88] The fire on Mt. Oeta made Heracles divine, by consuming his human element and releasing the divine, as at *HO* 1966–8; so Ovid, *Metamorphoses* 9. 250–3, 262–5; Lucian, *Hermotimus*, 7; note too the allusion at Plautus, *Rudens* 767, cf. Housman 1918: 163 = 1972: iii. 960–1. Other writers simply record that he was immortalized by the fire (DS 4. 38. 5, [Apollod.] *Bibl.* 2. 7. 7, Hyg. *Fab.* 36, Min. Fel. *Oct.* 22. 7).

> nube discussa diem
> pande, ut deorum coetus ardentem Herculem
> spectet; licet tu sidera et mundum neges
> ultro, pater, cogere.   1710

The language as well as the theme is taken from *Hercules furens* 961–9, where it suited the raving Hercules:

> en ultro uocat
> omnis deorum coetus et laxat fores,
> una uetante. recipis et reseras polum?
> an contumacis ianuam mundi traho?
> dubitatur etiam? uincla Saturno exuam   965
> contraque patris impii regnum impotens
> auum resoluam; bella Titanes parent,
> me duce furentes; saxa cum siluis feram
> rapiamque dextra plena Centauris iuga.

A similar discourse will suit Marlowe's Tamburlaine,[89] who until this moment has turned poetic exaggeration into fact (*II Tamburlaine*, v. ii. 46–63):[90]

> *Techelles* and the rest, come take your swords,
> And threaten him whose hand afflicts my soul,
> Come let vs march against the powers of heauen,
> And set blacke streamers in the firmament,
> To signifie the slaughter of the Gods.   50
> Ah friends, what shal I doe? I cannot stand,
> Come carie me to war against the Gods,
> That thus inuie the health of *Tamburlaine*.
> THERIDAMAS. Ah good my Lord, leaue these impatient words,
> Which ad much danger to your malladie.   55
> TAMBURLAINE. Why shal I sit and languish in this paine?
> No, strike the drums, and in reuenge of this,
> Come let vs chardge our speares and pierce his breast,
> Whose shoulders beare the Axis of the world,

---

[89] Cf. Boyle 1997: 169–70.

[90] Throughout the two *Tamburlaine* plays we find such passages as *I Tamb*. I. ii. 209–12:

> THER. Not *Hermes* Prolocutor to the Gods,
>   Could vse perswasions more patheticall.
> TAM. Nor are *Apollos* Oracles more true,
>   Then thou shalt find my vaunts substantiall.   ['Then' = 'than']

These expressions are to be understood, within the theatre, as no more than the truth; the plays are infused with the spirit of *plus ultra*.

That if I perish, heauen and earth may fade. 60
Theridamas, haste to the court of *Ioue*,
Will him to send *Apollo* hether straight,
To cure me, or Ile fetch him downe my selfe.

The end of our play, as we shall see, suggests that a like extravagance is intended here. Yet Hercules' next verses imply a purely moral compulsion: this ordeal will establish his worthiness to be a god:

> si uoces dolor 1710
> abstulerit ullas, pande tunc Stygios lacus
> et redde fatis; approba natum prius:
> ut dignus astris uidear, hic faciet dies.
> leue est quod actum est; Herculem hic, genitor, dies
> inueniet aut damnabit.

It would be dangerous to insist that the narrative of Hercules' apotheosis on Oeta must have been inspired by that of Oedipus' heroization at Colonus; but at all events it is clear enough to the reader that this *is* an apotheosis, though not to Alcmene, who, having already let the side down by weeping, now enters to show that she still doesn't get it; considering the characters of Deianira and Alcmene, the pair of them all feeling and no brains, I commend this play to feminist critics as a model of misogyny. However, her obtuseness is required dramaturgically so that the poet may let Hercules appear *ex machina* to announce that his *uirtus* has been rewarded; the chorus, which ends this play and *Octauia* but no other in the corpus, duly points the moral, 'Renowned virtue is never borne to the shades of Styx', and so on and so forth.

> Numquam Stygias fertur ad umbras
> inclita uirtus: uiuite fortes
> nec Lethaeos saeua per amnes 1985*a*
> uos fata trahent, 1985*b*
> sed cum summas exiget horas
> consumpta dies,
> iter ad superos gloria pandet.

And if the final invocation of a Hercules who surpasses his father is, as is urged on behalf of authenticity, a marker put down by Seneca himself for posthumous vengeance against Nero,[91] then the great

---

[91] Nisbet 1987: 250 = 1995: 211.

philosopher was no longer himself, but was Pseudo-Seneca no less than the imitator to whom the sceptics ascribe the play:

> Sed tu, domitor magne ferarum
> orbisque simul pacator, ades: 1990
> nunc quoque nostras aspice terras,
> et si qua nouo belua uultu
> quatiet populos terrore graui,
> tu fulminibus frange trisulcis:
> fortius ipso genitore tuo   1995
> fulmina mitte.

For all its glaring faults the work may appeal to those who, acknowledging with Schiller's Narbonne that justice exists only on the stage,[92] are all the more determined to see it there. If Hercules had occasionally let the pain of poison get the better of his *uirtus*, he puts such lapses behind him by his unflinching endurance of the self-chosen pain of fire; he might almost be a Christian atoning for his sins by bravely facing martyrdom.

We do not expect such moral simplicity from Sophocles; and therein lies our lesson, not only from this play, but from Romans' responses to our poet overall. They were not insensitive to the beauty of his language, and could find plenty in him that was to their taste; but there is a moral realism in his human portraiture that some found disturbing. From what these Romans did, no less than what they said, we have ascertained the things they did not admire in Sophocles, and perhaps have recognized all the more keenly that we do.

APPENDIX: Daniel Heinsius on *Heracles Oetaeus*

[335] Tragoedia, quam ex Sophoclis Trachinijs adumbrauit autor. Chorus primus est Oechalidum captiuarum: reliqui Trachiniarum. Scene Sophoclis est Trachine. Hercules enim ex Euboea advehitur. Hic, primo scena in Euboea statuitur. Vnde Hercules ad Cenaeum promontorium pergit. Haec enim dicit προλογίζων,

---

[92] The curtain-line of *Der Parasit*: 'die Gerechtigkeit ist nur auf der Bühne'. Not found in the model, Louis-Benoît Picard's *Médiocre et rampant, ou le moyen de parvenir*.

—*vos pecus rapite ocyus*
Qua templa tollens ara Cenaei Iovis
Austro timendum spectat Euboicum mare.   [101–3]

Sed et sequens chorus est ibidem. Ibi enim ista habes:

Stamus nunc patriae moenibus, heic locus
Et sylvis dabitur.   [122–3]

Item paulo post:

Ad Trachina vocor, saxa rigentia,
Et dumeta iugis horrida torridis,
Vix gratum pecori montivago nemus.   [135–7]

Reliqua Trachine fiunt: nisi quae δι' ἐπαγγελίας narrantur. Ἀνοικονομησία summa est. Hyllus ex Euboea venit in Thessaliam, Trachina vsque; et quae Herculi sacrificanti in Cenaeo promontorio evenerint, refert. Cum in ipso constitutionis principio, nondum sacrificaret, ac ne in loco quidem esset Hercules. Cogita iam, quantum sit iter ex Euboea Trachina vsque, quae sub Oeta est. Sed praeclare nos ludit. Nam cum Herculem in Euboeam primo posuerit, tamen in Oeta comburit, et tribus tantum versibus advectum [336] fuisse indicat.[93] Quod quidem iter semel vt conficiatur, triplo majore opus est tempore, quam Tragoediae est ambitus. Ideoque multum refert, qualem tibi fabulam sumas. Quaedam enim ipse Sophocles evadere non potuit. Quippe aliud est vitium τῆς ὕλης quod est in subiecto: aliud peccatum poetae, quod in constitutione est. Apud Graecum, semel in dolore Herculi tribuitur ῥῆσις prolixa: cujus divinitas omnem poeticum conatum excedit. Idque non nisi in fine. Hic Iovis ille filius, membra dum dilaniat sua, trecentos et amplius versus declamat. Et in occupatione tam molesta, multa dicit quae vix ociosus declamator in schola effunderet. Graeci oratio, tota est frugalis, sobria, casta, et quae ne levissimam quidem περιεργίας suspicionem admittit. Hic non modo plurima redundant, sed et saepe repetuntur. Sensus praesertim vsque ad nauseam. Deianirae à Graeco mores tribuuntur matronales. Hic perpetuo furit. Itaque cum saepe mortem marito esset minata, post tot minas, amoris remedium mittit. Postea nuncio accepto, plane dissimilis est sui: graviora enim optaverat. Et tamen mortem sibi infert. Ergo nota τὸ ἀνώμαλον τοῦ ἤθους, quod Euripides quoque in Iphigenia in Aulide manifeste commisit. Sicut supremus doctor Aristoteles vere observat.[94] Caeterum hoc non est ferendum, quod tale ἦθος tribuit Deianirae, quo τὸ πάθος vniversi dramatos evertitur. Nam dum furit, inter alia haec illi excidunt,

---

[93] vv. 839–41: 'Nunc puppis illum litore Euboico refert | Austerque lenis pondus Herculeum rapit; | destituit animus membra, nox oculos premit.'

[94] *Poet.* 1454[a]31–3.

Maximum fieri scelus, [330]
Et ipsa fateor: sed dolor fieri iubet.

Ac deinde fatetur, se de morte mariti cogitare:

—quid stupes segnis furor?
Scelus occupandum est. perge dum fervet manus. [435: *perage* Peiper]
NVT. Perimes maritum?
DE. Pellicis certe meae.

Deinde fatetur, vestem quam mittit, malum esse.

Altrix, fatebor: Nessus est autor mali. [491]

Quanto apud Graecum divinius. Primo enim negat se irasci viro posse, sed dolere iniuriam ab ipso sibi factam, quod in aedes, quasi donum aliquod, pellicem sibi [337] miserit, secundo iterum testatur, detestari se non tantum omne scelus sed et scelestos:

Κακὰς δὲ τόλμας μήτ᾽ ἐπισταίμην ἐγώ, [582]
Μήτ᾽ ἐκμάθοιμι, τάς τε τολμώσας στυγῶ.

Tertio, postquam misit, pauet, trepidat, pallet, ne quid se indignum fecerit. Digna igitur commiseratione, et cum luget et cum moritur. Alter vero dat operam, vt commiseratione Deianira frustraretur, ipse in Tragoedia excideret. Nam aut omnia falsa sunt, quae sub initium dicuntur Ethicorum tertij, aut nemo dignus est commiseratione qui et sponte et libenter improbe agit. Cum hanc nullae actiones moveant, praeter improbas, quae proprio cum damno fiant. καὶ γὰρ τὰς μὲν ἑκουσίως γινομένας ἀγαθὰς ἐπαινοῦμεν, τὰς δὲ ἑκουσίως πονηρὰς ψέγομεν· τὰς δὲ ἀκουσίως πονηρὰς οὐ ψέγομεν, ἀλλὰ συγγνώμης ἀξιοῦμεν, τὰς δὲ ἀκουσίως καὶ ἐπὶ βλάβῃ τῶν ποιούντων γινομένας, ἐλέου ἀξίας ἡγούμεθα, ait praeclarus ibi autor.[95] Iam ex machina dissolvit drama, in qua nulla est ἀμηχανία. Nihil enim opus erat matris causa apparere Herculem, cum per se soluta esset actio. Et hanc partem non desumpsit e Trachiniis, in qua ante mortem Hercules quaecunque agenda sunt absolvit, sed e Philoctete eiusdem. In qua plane ad machinam eundum erat, cum non posset ope humana flecti Philoctetes. Ideo apparet ille, et hunc nodum secat. Alcmenae personam optime omisit Graecus. Nam quae verba digna inveniri poterant? Hic

---

[95] i.e. the unknown paraphrast whose work Heinsius had edited first as *Aristotelis Ethicorum Nicomacheorum Paraphrasis* (Leiden, 1607; this passage in Greek i. 72, in Latin ii. 88), then as *Andronici Rhodii Ethicorum Nicomacheorum Paraphrasis* (Leiden, 1617; this passage pp. 119–20), and Gustav Heylbut re-edited as *Heliodori Prusensis in ethica Nicomachea paraphrasis* (CCAG 19/2; Berlin 1889; this passage p. 41, ll. 19–22). This fictitious compatriot of Dio was foisted on the text by Constantine Palaeocappa (Cohn 1889); the text itself existed by 26 Nov. AM 6875 = AD 1386, when the monk Joasaph, formerly the emperor John VI, paid to have it copied.

vbique sublimitatem quaesivit. Et vix drama invenias, quod aeque assurgeret, nisi tumeret. Passim tamen multa occurrunt, quae sublimitatis φαντασίαν habent. Neque raro sententiae, nihil minus quam humiles, affectatione acuminis exarescunt. Sermo arguit, longe post reliquas scriptam, quae in corpore isto extant. Multa ἰδιωτικὰ, indigna Seneca vtroque,[96] et nihil minus quam Latina, occurrunt, sicut infra prolixe probamus.

REFERENCES

Aricò, Giuseppe (1987), 'Analecta Scaenica', *Filologia e forme letterarie: studi offerti a Francesco Della Corte*, 5 vols. (Urbino), i. 201–12.

Bentley, Richard (1883), *Dissertations upon the Epistles of Phalaris, Themistocles, Socrates, Euripides, and the Fables of Æsop*, ed. Wilhelm Wagner (London).

Boyle, A. J. (1997), *Tragic Seneca: An Essay in the Theatrical Tradition* (London).

Brecht, Berthold (1957), *Schriften zum Theater: Über eine nicht-aristotelische Dramatik*, ed. Siegfried Unseld (Frankfurt am Main).

Cohn, Leopold (1889), 'Heliodorus von Prusa, eine Erfindung Paläokappas', *BPhW* 9/45: (9 Nov.): 1419–20.

Curley, Daniel (1997), 'Ovid, *Met.* 6. 640: A Dialogue between Mother and Son', *CQ²* 47: 320–2.

D'Antò, Vincenzo (1980), *L. Accio: i frammenti delle tragedie* (Lecce).

Decembrio, Angelo (1462), *De politia litteraria* = MS Biblioteca Apostolica Vaticana, Vat. lat. 1794.

——(1540), *De politia litteraria* (Augsburg).

Dionisotti, A. C. (1982), 'From Ausonius' Schooldays? A Schoolbook and its Relatives', *JRS* 72: 83–12.

Erbse, Hartmut (1993), 'Sophokles über die geistige Blindheit des Menschen', *ICS* 18: 5–71.

Ernesti, J. Chr. Theoph. [= G.] (1795), *Lexicon technologiae Graecorum rhetoricae* (Leipzig).

——(1797), *Lexicon technologiae Latinorum rhetoricae* (Leipzig).

Fontane, Theodor (1954), *Briefe an Georg Friedlaender*, ed. Kurt Schreinert (Heidelberg).

Friedrich, Wolf H. (1954), 'Sprache und Stil des Hercules Oetaeus', *Hermes* 82: 51–84.

Goldberg, Sander (1995), *Epic in Republican Rome* (New York).

Gottsched, J. C., *Versuch einer critischen Dichtkunst*, 4th edn. (Leipzig).

[96] Heinsius assigned only *Medea*, *Troades*, and *Phaedra* to Lucius, *Thyestes*, *Oedipus*, *Agamemnon*, and *Hercules furens* to Marcus, and the other plays to unknown poets.

GRIFFIN, JASPER (1984), 'Augustus and the Poets: "Caesar qui cogere posset"', in Fergus Millar and Erich Segal (eds.), *Caesar Augustus: Seven Aspects* (Oxford), 189–218.

HEINSIUS, DANIEL (1611), 'Danielis Heinsii in L. et M. Annaei Senecae ac reliquorum quae extant tragoedias animadversiones et notae', in *L. Annaei Senecae et aliorum tragoediae serio emendatae, cum Iosephi Scaligeri, nunc primum ex autographo auctoris editis, et Danielis Heinsii Animadversionibus et Notis* (Leiden, 1611), pp. 483–584.

—— (1621), 'Animadversiones et Notae; Emendatiores et auctiores denuo editae', in *L. Annaeus Seneca, Tragicus*, ed. Petrus Scriverius (Leiden), 277–348 of second sequence.

HOLFORD-STREVENS, LEOFRANC (1988), *Aulus Gellius* (London).

—— (1995), review of *L. Ampelius: Aide-mémoire (Liber memorialis)*, ed. Marie-Pierre Arnaud-Lindet (Paris, 1993), in *Gnomon*, 67: 600–4.

HORSFALL, NICHOLAS (1995), *A Companion to the Study of Virgil* (Leiden).

HOUSMAN, A. E. (1918), 'Jests of Plautus, Cicero, and Trimalchio', *CR* 32: 162–4.

—— (1972), *Classical Papers*, ed. J. Diggle and F. R. D. Goodyear, 3 vols. (Cambridge).

JEBB, R. C. (1907), *Life and Letters of Sir Richard Claverhouse Jebb, O.M., Litt.D., by his wife Caroline Jebb* (Cambridge).

JOCELYN, H. D. (1967), *The Tragedies of Ennius* (Cambridge).

JOHNSON, SAMUEL (1968), *The Yale Edition of the Works of Samuel Johnson*, vii–viii: *Johnson on Shakespeare*, ed. Arthur Sherbo (New Haven).

KNIGHT, W. F. JACKSON (1949), *Roman Vergil*, 2nd edn. (London).

KÖNIG, ANNEMARIE (1970), *Die Aeneis und die griechische Tragödie: Studien zur imitatio-Technik Vergils* (Inaugural-Dissertation, Freie Universität Berlin).

LARMOUR, D. H. J. (1991), 'Tragic *Contaminatio* in Ovid's Metamorphoses: Procne and Medea; Philomela and Iphigeneia (6. 424–674); Scylla and Phaedra (8. 19–151)', *ICS* 15: 131–41.

LEFKOWITZ, MARY R. (1981), *The Lives of the Greek Poets* (London).

LEO, FRIEDRICH (1913), *Geschichte der römischen Literatur* (Berlin).

LLOYD-JONES, HUGH (1972), 'Tycho von Wilamowitz-Moellendorff on the Dramatic Technique of Sophocles', *CQ*² 22: 214–28.

—— (1990*a*), *Greek Epic, Lyric, and Tragedy* (Oxford).

—— and WILSON, N. G. (1990): *Sophoclea: Studies on the Text of Sophocles* (Oxford).

—— —— (1997), *Sophocles: Second Thoughts* (Hypomnemata, 100: Göttingen).

MOREL, WILLY (1927), 'Zu griechischen Dichtern und zu Xenophon', *PhW* 47: 636–8.

NABOKOV, VLADIMIR (1964), *Pushkin: Eugene Onegin*, 4 vols. (Princeton and London).

NISBET, R. G. M. (1987), 'The Oak and the Axe: Symbolism in Seneca, *Hercules Oetaeus* 1618 ff.', in *Homo Viator: Classical Essays for John Bramble*, ed. Michael Whitby, Philip Hardie, and Mary Whitby (Bristol), 243–51.

—— (1995), *Collected Papers on Latin Literature*, ed. S. J. Harrison (Oxford).

PALMER, ARTHUR (1898), *P. Ovidi Nasonis Heroides* (Oxford; repr. Hildesheim, 1967).

POPPER, K. R. (1966), *The Open Society and its Enemies*, 5th edn., 2 vols. (London).

RADT, S. L. (1980), 'Noch einmal Aischylos, Niobe Fr. 162 N^2 (278 M.)', *ZPE* 38: 47–58.

RIBBECK, OTTO (1875), *Die römische Tragödie im Zeitalter der Republik* (Leipzig).

ROZELAAR, MARC (1976), *Seneca: Eine Gesamtdarstellung* (Amsterdam).

—— (1985), 'Neue Studien zur Tragödie "Hercules Oetaeus"', *ANRW* II 32. 2. 1348–1419.

SCONOCCHIA, SERGIO (1972), 'L'*Antigona* di Accio e l'*Antigone* di Sofocle', *RFIC*² 100: 277–82.

TÖCHTERLE, KARLHEINZ (1994), *Lucius Annaeus Seneca, Oedipus: Kommentar mit Einleitung, Text und Übersetzung* (Wissenschaftliche Kommentare zu griechischen und lateinischen Schriftstellern; Heidelberg).

WEST, M. L. (1978), 'Tragica II', *BICS* 25: 106–22.

WHITFIELD, J. H. (1988), '*Momus* and the Language of Irony', in Peter Hainsworth *et al.* (eds.), *The Languages of Literature in Renaissance Italy* (Oxford), 31–43.

WINNINGTON-INGRAM, R. P. (1980), *Sophocles: An Interpretation* (Cambridge).

ZWIERLEIN, OTTO (1986), *Kritischer Kommentar zu den Tragödien Senecas* (AAWM 1986, no. 6; Mainz).

—— (1987), *Senecas Phaedra und ihre Vorbilder* (AAWM 1987, no. 5; Mainz).

12

Sophocles' *Electra* in Britain

EDITH HALL

I. INTRODUCTION

In February 1992 the basketball pitch in Templemore Sport Stadium in Londonderry was covered over. On this space the Irish actress Fiona Shaw led the Royal Shakespeare Company in Deborah Warner's production of Sophocles' *Electra*. The set suggested the confinement of a mental hospital. Shaw's black shift and close-cropped hair brought new meanings to Electra's psychological disturbance. Her androgynous, athletic body was 'transformed into an instrument for expressing terrible, primitive emotions of grief, hatred and the desire for revenge'.[1]

During the week of the performances nine people, mostly Catholics, were gunned down in revenge for the murder of eight Protestant building workers a few days previously. The production had toured internationally, but no audience had ever identified with it like the people of Northern Ireland. One woman said Electra reminded her 'of Mrs Kelly whose son was killed on Bloody Sunday and how they would find her several years afterwards lying on his grave in the cemetery with the earth smeared on her face'.[2] Chrysothemis reminded another spectator of the relatives of the hunger strikers, who had urged them to accept defeat.[3] This audience found in Sophocles' play a devastating reflection of their

I am indebted to Jasper Griffin, Oliver Taplin, and especially Fiona Macintosh for helpful comments on this article.

[1] Holland (1992: 52). There is a striking photograph of Shaw as Electra on the cover of Macintosh (1994).
[2] Holland (1992). See also Shaw (1996: 160).
[3] See Shaw (1996: 160).

own community's experience of reciprocal violence. Yet Fiona Shaw is only one in a long line of Sophoclean Electras who have caught the British imagination outside academe. This article seeks to tell their story.

The tale begins, appropriately, in the hall of Christ Church, Oxford. There Thomas Goffe's *The Tragedie of Orestes* was performed between 1609 and 1619.[4] Goffe, a scholar at Christ Church, wrote several plays for performance by the college's students, most with Turkish settings.[5] Christ Church had enjoyed theatricals since at least as early as 1548, a tradition which had reached its zenith in 1592 under William Gager.[6] Nor was this the first time that Sophocles had informed the academic stages of England: there is evidence for performances at Cambridge of *Philoctetes* in Latin around the middle of the sixteenth century, a Latin *Ajax Flagellifer* in 1564, and Thomas Watson's Latin translation of *Antigone* (published 1581) in about 1583.[7] But Goffe's English tragedy is a free composition in the vernacular, influenced by the plays popular on the public stages of London. It is a bloodthirsty revenge tragedy, boasting the on-stage murder of Agamemnon and a disgusting climax which makes the imminent Puritans' Ordinance of September 1642, forbidding the acting of all stage plays, seem positively desirable.

Orestes stabs the infant son of Ægystus and Clytemnestra, squirts their faces with his blood, makes them drink it, and finally stabs them. Most surviving characters, including Electra, stab themselves in the final act. The play also features mad scenes by Orestes and Cassandra, a spectacular necromancy with Agamemnon's bones, his murder recapitulated in a dumb show, and three musical numbers including a lullaby and a song about the Argonauts. The language is vigorous and elaborately metaphorical; the many clever puns assume a good knowledge of the Greek and Latin Classics.[8]

The prologue to *The Tragedie of Orestes*, 'spoken by the Authour himselfe', declares that Euripides is the source:

---

[4] Goffe (1633).

[5] Bradley (1908).

[6] Hiscock (1946: 164, 174).

[7] Moore Smith (1923: 102, 107); Smith (1987: 216–17, 224).

[8] For example, Pylades asks Orestes (v. v), 'Still harping on thy mother?', to which Orestes responds, 'Harping, no, | Let *Orpheus* harp: O, I, she was, she was | A very, very Harpie.'

We heere present for to revive a tale,
Which once in Athens great Eurypedes [*sic*]
In better phrase at such a meeting told
The learn'd Athenians with much applause.

The action of the fifth act does begin at the same point as Euripides' *Orestes*: Ægystus and Clytemnestra are dead, and Orestes is repudiated by Tyndareus. But the play also uses other sources, including Seneca's *Agamemnon* and *Thyestes*, which lies behind Ægystus' drinking of his own son's blood (IV. viii). Moreover, the play owes as much to Jacobean revenge tragedy, especially *Hamlet*, as to its ancient archetypes. Orestes is exhorted by the ghost of his father, Pylades is a Greek Horatio, and Ægystus is similar to Claudius.[9]

Yet Sophocles' *Electra* was also used. This play had first begun to make some impression upon the imagination of English-speaking lands in the sixteenth century, with the circulation of the 1548 Latin translation of *Ajax*, *Antigone*, and *Electra* by the Dutchman George Rotaller, subsequently reissued by Stephanus in 1567.[10] *Electra* was thus one of the more familiar plays of the Renaissance. Goffe has drawn upon it in the messenger's false account of Orestes' death (II. v), the despair of Electra in response to it, Clytemnestra's cooler reaction, the (albeit highly truncated) recognition scene (IV. v), and in the notion that Clytemnestra and Ægystus have a child, which occurs only in the Sophoclean version of the story. The play also asks its audience to remember a performance of Sophocles' *Electra* in antiquity. When Orestes has handed the skull of his father to the witch Canidia, he invokes Aulus Gellius' story about the fourth-century actor Polus playing Electra. Gellius, writing in the second century CE, reported that Polus filled the theatre with real living grief and lamentations, by utilizing an urn containing the ashes of his own dead son (6.5).[11] Goffe's Orestes reflects (III. v),

---

[9] Smith (1987: 231–4); see Kerrigan (1996: 182).

[10] Sheppard (1927: 128).

[11] Aulus Gellius (6. 5. 7: 'Igitur Polus lugubri habitu Electrae indutus ossa atque urnam e sepulcro tulit filii et quasi Oresti amplexus opplevit omnia non simulacris neque imitamentis, sed luctu atque lamentis veris et spirantibus.' This anecdote does not necessitate close familiarity with *Electra* amongst Gellius' readership: Holford-Strevens (1988: 173) thinks that Aulus Gellius' recapitulation of the plot in 6. 5. 6 implies that his public 'could not be expected to have read the play'.

> There was a player once upon a stage,
> Who striving to present a dreery passion,
> Brought out the urne of his late buried sonne,
> It might the more affect him, and draw teares.

Orestes contrasts Polus' feigned grief with his own 'real' bereavement.

Although Electra features in Goffe's tragedy, her part is insignificant. This was a slight improvement on John Pikeryng's Elizabethan *Horestes* (performed by 1567), the first revenge tragedy to be written in Renaissance England, exploring the relationship of the English Crown to Scotland.[12] Electra had been altogether excluded from Pikeryng's plot, which draws on medieval versions of the tale. It will become apparent that Electra herself, rather than Orestes, only began to be fully appreciated with the rise of the women's movement.[13]

II. ELECTRA IN POLITICS

Goffe also wrote a drama, *The Careless Shepherdess*, performed in the Caroline court under the auspices of the French Queen of England, Henrietta Maria.[14] Her theatricals were indissoluble in the Puritan mind from the ceremonial display of her Roman Catholic religion. Goffe's anarchic play on the Orestes theme, requiring young men to impersonate females, would also have infuriated the Puritans, and it was they who were attacked in the earliest known English translation of *Electra* (1649).

Lines from Atilius' *Electra* had been sung at Julius Caesar's funeral games, 'to rouse pity and indignation at his death'.[15] In 1649 the death which prompted a use of Sophocles' *Electra* was that of

[12] Pikeryng (1567), reprinted in Axton (1982: 94–138). The author was probably Sir John Puckering, Lord Keeper under Elizabeth 1.

[13] Electra appeared in Thomas Heywood's synoptic dramatic overview of the Trojan war and its aftermath in Agamemnon's family, published in 1632, but even here her spoken contribution is confined to two short comments on Orestes' betrothal to Hermione: see *The Second Part of the Iron Age*, first published London 1632, in Heywood (1874: 355–431), at 398–9.

[14] Veevers (1989), 50.

[15] 'Cantata sunt quaedam ad miserationem et invidiam caedis eius accommodata', Suet. *Vit. Caes.* 1. 84. 2. Lines from Pacuvius' *Contest for the Arms* were also sung on this occasion.

Charles I, executed on 30 January. The author was the royalist Christopher Wase, whose translation was addressed to the Princess Elizabeth, Charles' second daughter, a prisoner of the Parliamentarians since the Civil War had begun in her seventh year. She was now imprisoned in Carisbrooke Castle on the Isle of Wight. This *Electra* (Fig. 1) offered Elizabeth a heroine from classical mythology with whom to identify, just as the plays of the Caroline court had often provided models of women performing generous actions for the sake of their country and menfolk, drawn from ancient Greek romances or from Greek and Roman history.[16]

Wase's royalist sympathies lost him his fellowship of King's College, Cambridge. In the dedication to *Electra* he inveighs against censorship and the Puritans' closure of the theatres:

Playes are the Mirrours wherein Mens actions are reflected to their own view. Which, perhaps, is the true cause, that some, privy to the Uglinesse of their own guilt, have issued out Warrants, for the breaking of all those Looking-glasses.

Wase further explains to Elizabeth that his translation is a 'dim Chrystall' which can reflect for her 'some Lines and Shadows of that Pietie to your deceased Father'.[17]

The volume contains four further dedications by sympathizers. The first reassures Elizabeth that 'Foreign Princes' crowd to support her, and that she will one day become a mother to Kings who will avenge her father. This poem concludes with a wish that the play reaches her in prison, and is not confiscated:

> If that it passe the Guard, and die not there
> For Foreign Spy, or Charles'es Messenger.[18]

The writer of the next, anonymous dedication draws an explicit parallel between Sophocles' Aegisthus and Cromwell, saying that the book makes Cromwell's followers in London fear that their '*Egist*' will fall. A fourth dedication elaborates the allegory:

[16] Veevers (1989), 68, 205.

[17] Wase (1649: 2–3). The book claims to have been printed in The Hague, but a librarian at the Bodleian has noted on the title-page that the typeface mans that it was 'almost certainly printed in London'. The falsified place of publication was probably designed to protect the author against prosecution.

[18] Wase (1649: 4).

FIG. 1 Christopher Wase's royalist translation of Sophocles' *Electra*, dedicated to Charles I's teenage daughter Elizabeth, and printed in 1649 after the execution of the King. Frontispiece and title page. Photo reproduced by courtesy of the Bodleian Library.

Me thinks this were a perfect Prophecie,
But that there wants still the Catastrophe:
Here guilt with guilt is parallel'd; the rime
Of vengeance too may be compleat in time.
Our *Agamemnon*'s dead, *Electra* grieves,
The only hope is that *Orestes* lives.

The current situation is thus conceived as a real-life reenactment of Sophocles' 'prophetic' tragedy, except that its vengeful ending has not yet been performed.

The final dedication remarks that Elizabeth has been reduced to second-hand servants' clothes by her captor Cromwell. Wase has brought her new clothes constructed by his wit, since

'twas ordered that she be array'd
In the cast gown of some stale Chamber-maid.

Stories about the mistreatment of Elizabeth had underlined the parallel between her and Electra. In the Bodleian's copy of this book an antique hand has reported a tradition that the 'infamous Regicides' forced the princess to become apprentice to a glover.

Wase and his collaborators have laboured to explain the significance of the allegory to their dedicatee. If the volume was not primarily intended for her eyes, but to circulate illegally as propaganda for the royal family, then it makes every attempt to disguise itself as a book for a poorly educated teenage girl. Wase describes the plot of the tragedy in these resonant terms:

The Tyrannical usurpation of the Mycenian Kingdome . . . the Destruction of the Conspiratours, the Enthroning of *Orestes*, with the Deliverance of the Royal Family.

Sophocles' tragedy, of course, does not depict Orestes' accession to the throne; indeed, it is unusual precisely because the murder of Aegisthus is not confirmed to the audience. Wase's royalist fantasies are transparently superimposed onto Sophocles' plot.

The translation itself is in English so robust that Wase must stand accused of insensitivity towards his dedicatee. He has slightly adapted the language used to describe the actual murder of Agamemnon in order to bring home the parallel with Charles I. The chorus remember the blow struck in the chamber,

> Where with the broad steel-faced Cleaver
> The Royall Temples they dissever,
> Treason was the Privy-Counsellor.[19]

Later the same action is couched yet more savagely, describing the 'Poll-ax Razor-edg'd' which decapitated the 'Sovereigne', and even adding a pictorial diagram of a hatchet![20]

Wase repeatedly underlines the parallel with the contemporary situation. Orestes' last words ring out like a defiant speech from the Civil War:

> 'Twere fit this Martiall law did still prevail
> That who so durst transgress the statutes pale,
> Might streight be kild, for villains soon would fail.[21]

This extraordinary book appends two additional poems. Prince Charles went to Jersey from Paris in September 1649, and thence to Scotland,[22] which dates this volume to the latter part of the year. *The Return* expresses joy that Elizabeth's brother 'on our Isles appears' and is planning how to regain the throne; *The Restauration* imagines the release of Elizabeth, and the country liberated from draining taxes and 'constrained Rites' in church. Alas for poor Elizabeth! Unlike Electra she did not survive to see her brother again or her father avenged. She died, at the age of 14, on 8 September the following year (1650).

But Wase lived to publish a Latin poem celebrating the Restoration in 1660,[23] when the theatres were reopened. The Restoration heralded a new era in British scholarship on Greek tragedy, beginning with Bentley at the end of the seventeenth century and ending in about 1825 with the deaths of Dobree and Elmsley.[24] Thomas Stanley's edition of Aeschylus (1663) was followed in 1668 by an unnamed edition of Sophocles at Cambridge in 1668, and thereafter by Thomas Johnson's much better edition of *Ajax* and *Electra* (Oxford 1705) and *Antigone* and *Trachiniae* (Oxford 1708), the third instalment appearing in 1746.[25] Johnson's was the standard edition of Sophocles for eighteenth-century England, and indeed internationally until Brunck's. Although he was a drunkard

---

[19] Wase (1649: 8). [20] Ibid. 19. [21] Ibid. 57.
[22] Bone (1972: 234). [23] Marchant (1909). [24] Clarke (1945: 1–2).
[25] Ingram (1966: 18–20).

who suffered gaol for debt, Johnson's edition was competent enough.[26]

Yet Electra met her first widespread audience in England with the appearance of André Dacier's French translation in 1693, an attractive volume including the *Oedipus Tyrannus* and *Electra*.[27] Dacier's book inspired the first popular English translations of *Electra*, two of which appeared in 1714. One, which is anonymous, was dedicated to Lord Halifax. It is in simple prose, and the translator claims to 'have aim'd at following the *Greek* original the nearest I can; at leaving no Word unexpress'd.'[28] In comparison, Lewis Theobald's poetic version is impressive. After Chrysothemis' first exit the chorus reflect (Soph. *El.* 473–83),

> Or my prophetick Soul mistakes,
> Or I in hope from Reason err;
> Or vengeance swift advances makes,
> Upon the Conscience-haunted Murtherer.
> Daughter she comes; she comes away
> With Pow'r and Justice in Array;
> I'm strong in hope, the boding Dream,
> The Herald of her aweful Terrors came.
> The King's Resentments shall not cease,
> Nor shall he bury Wrongs but in redress.[29]

Theobald's version, decorated with a powerful engraving illustration of Aegisthus' discovery of Clytemnestra's corpse, engraved by the Huguenot refugee Luc du Guernier (Fig. 2), was the most read *Electra* in England for fifty years. It was admired by Richard Porson.[30] But it never saw the stage, despite a misunderstanding to the contrary (see below).

Neoclassical adaptations of heroine-dominated Euripidean tragedies were moderately popular at this time, but no attempts were made to stage an adaptation of Sophocles' *Electra* until 1762. There are several reasons for this. One is the absence of a Senecan version of Electra's story. There were Roman tragedies on the theme,

[26] Clarke (1945: 59–60).
[27] Dacier (1693).
[28] [Anon.] (1714: p. iv). See e.g. the translation of *El.* 1058–62, 'Why behold we those very wise Birds above, taking care of their Parents who have begot and bred them up, and why don't we do the same?' (p. 39).
[29] Theobald (1714).
[30] Buchanan-Jones (1966: 424 n. 1).

FIG. 2. Orestes reveals the corpse of Clytemnestra to Aegisthus in the frontispiece to Lewis Theobald's 1714 translation of Sophocles' *Electra*. Engraving by the Huguenot refugee Luc du Guernier. Photo reproduced by courtesy of the Bodleian Library.

including the *Electra* of Cicero's brother Quintus, written when, bored with military duty in Gaul and Britain, he wrote four tragedies, including an *Electra*, in sixteen days;[31] other candidates might have included the *Electra* of Atilius, the *Aegisthus* of Livius, and the *Agamemnonidae, Aegisthus*, and *Clytemnestra* of Accius, but none of these survived.[32] Another reason for the reluctance of eighteenth-century tragedians to attempt adaptations of *Electra* is its unshrinking presentation of feminine aggression. Contemporary audiences had similar difficulties with Euripides' *Medea*, who was totally unacceptable unless the crime of infanticide was either deleted altogether, or ameliorated by an exculpatory fit of madness, as in Richard Glover's adaptation of 1767.[33] But in the case of Sophocles' *Electra*, the tragedy's long-standing association with the cause of the Stuart kings is probably more significant.

After the Glorious Revolution, most playwrights publicly espoused anti-Jacobite sentiments. John Dennis argued at the end of the seventeenth century that drama helped to keep people 'from frequenting Jacobite Conventicles, and contributing to our non-swearing Parsons . . . for as long as the enemies of the State are diverted by publick Spectacles' they will not have time or energy to listen to seditious preachers.[34] The theatre was often turned into a political battleground by audiences who perceived allegories every-where. The first performance of Addison's *Cato* in 1713 witnessed a political fray, both Whig and Tory claiming Cato for their own. Theobald described the politicization of the spectators acutely in 1717:

Party and Private Sentiments have so great a Prevalence, that the chief View with them is to wrest an innocent Author to their own Construction, and form to themselves an Idea of Faction from Passages . . . a War of *Whig* and *Tory* is carried on by way of *Clap* and *Hiss* upon the meaning of a single Sentence, that, unless prophetically, could never have any Relation to Modern Occurrences.[35]

It is hardly surprising that the first known attempt to stage a version of *Electra*, the archetypal regicide tragedy, ran into trouble. In 1762

---

[31] Cicero wrote to Quintus from Tusculanum at the end of October, 54 BCE, asking him to send his recently composed tragedies *Electra, The Trojan Woman*, and *Erigona* (*Ep. ad Quint. Frat.* 3. 5. 7).

[32] Jocelyn (1967: 284).   [33] See further Hall (1999*a*).

[34] Dennis (1698: 66–7).

[35] *The Censor*, 25 May 1717, quoted in Gray (1931: 24–5).

an adaptation of Sophocles' *Electra* by the merchant and playwright William Shirley was refused a licence altogether.[36]

Shirley published his play in 1765, prefixing an address 'To the Reader'. He claims that he began to write it in 1744, but had laid it aside on receiving first tidings of the Jacobite rebellion in 1745, 'from an apprehension that the subject, which he had casually chosen, might be considered as invidious and offensive'. Garrick of Drury Lane had much later turned the play down, but in 1762 Mr Beard, the manager of Covent Garden, had commissioned from Shirley a theatrical compliment on the birth of George III's first son, to consist of the tragedy and a masque, *The Birth of Hercules*. The plays went into rehearsal at the end of November, and copies were sent to the Lord Chamberlain to procure the necessary licences. The masque was approved, but the tragedy received a notice of refusal, writes Shirley, 'to the very great surprise of all persons who had ever seen it'. He protested to the Lord Chamberlain that the play 'was no other than the ELECTRA of SOPHOCLES, adapted to the English stage' and that no 'malignant intention' could be imputed to him.[37]

Shirley professes awareness that his play might have been taken for a pro-Jacobite text in 1745, when the only candidate for an analogue of Orestes was the Young Pretender. Scholars have understandably assumed that it was the association of *Electra* with the Stuarts (underpinning Wase's translation) which led to the censorship of the play in 1762.[38] But Shirley, far from being a Jacobite, was an ardent Whig. In 1759 he had published an attack on the legal system in Portugal in which he detailed abuses of power under the Stuart kings of England, and condemned the 'evil-disposed' James II. Against him the Britons, 'in defence of their Liberty . . . honourably took up arms, and gloriously secured their own rights, and those of their posterities, by the resolute expulsion of him and his male-issue'.[39] Moreover, Shirley seems to have been obsessively opposed to censorship; in this pamphlet he cites Charles II's persecution of the possessor of a manuscript.[40] In a satirical poem published in 1762 he fulminated against all those who 'dare in chains to bind | The bold productions of the Poet's mind', and lamented that

---

[36] Shirley (1765).
[37] Ibid. 'To the Reader'.
[38] Conolly (1976: 73–4), Macintosh (1995: 58–9).
[39] Shirley (1759: 69).
[40] Ibid. 8–9.

> In vain, alas! deceiv'd BRITANNIA boasts,
> That heav'n-born freedom guards her chalky coasts.[41]

It was in the same year that Shirley rewrote *Electra* as a denunciation of the then Prime Minister, John Stuart, third Earl of Bute, and his influence over the Royal Family. It is not surprising that Greek tragedy was invoked when the Whig aristocracy was under pressure. Greek had become fashionable in Whig circles; both Pitt and Charles James Fox were fine Greek scholars.[42]

George III had come to the throne in 1760 and had begun an onslaught onto the old Corps of the Whig party. He was encouraged by his favourite, intimate, and former tutor Lord Bute, who had waited in the wings for many years as the head of the heir apparent's shadow-cabinet. The Prime Minister Pitt, 'the Great Commoner' who had appealed to a popular constituency beyond the landed and parliamentary classes, resigned in October 1761, followed by Newcastle in May 1762. Much to George III's delight, Lord Bute became Prime Minister.

Bute's tenure of office was one of the most turbulent periods in British political history. The King's quarrel with the Whig leadership created a charged political atmosphere which galvanized rich and poor alike, and was expressed in political theatres which developed allusive techniques of commentary.[43] By June 1762 John Wilkes, champion of individual liberties, had begun his attacks on Bute in the weekly periodical *North Briton*, which took its name from Bute (who as a Scot was a Briton from the North). Wilkes was particularly supported by the members of the merchant classes, like William Shirley.[44] The temperature rose exponentially, until Wilkes was finally arrested in 1763. At the time when Shirley's *Electra* was put into rehearsal, and refused a licence, Bute had just been mobbed with such ferocity at the opening of parliament (5 November 1762) that he was lucky to escape with his life.[45]

Whig propaganda presented Bute as totally unaccountable, thereby threatening the balance of the constitution. It also targeted

[41] Shirley (1762: 32–3).

[42] Clarke (1945: 7).

[43] For example, Samuel Foote's *Mayor of Garret*, which attacked Bute. See Brewer (1979–80: 16–21). I am grateful to Jo Innes for bibliographical suggestions and other invaluable advice on the political climate of 1762.

[44] Brewer (1979–80: 15).

[45] Coats (1975: 30).

his friendship with George III's mother Augusta. Hundreds of cartoons attacked the alleged sexual liaison almost as soon as George III ascended the throne, purveying the image of a petticoat government under Scottish influence.[46] The jackboot (i.e. John Bute) and petticoat (the Princess) were burned in every riot.[47] Bute was labelled 'the Thane', the bestower of posts and pensions to hordes of hungry Scots. He was depicted as a Francophile Jacobite and the enemy of Liberty and the Magna Charta.[48] He was compared with Macbeth, with Rizzio (murdered lover of Mary Queen of Scots) and with Sejanus. The Princess Dowager was portrayed as the Queen in *Hamlet*, directing Bute to pour poison into her sleeping son's ear, or as Isabella, Queen of Edward II, who had murdered her husband and ruled with her lover Roger Mortimer.[49] Shirley was trying to add Aegisthus and Clytemnestra to this list. The arrival of the new baby son to the King in 1762 had supplied an analogue for Orestes, since Hanoverian Kings were traditionally opposed by their disaffected sons.

Although many of the famous Sophoclean scenes—Electra's argument with her mother, the messenger speech, the laments over the urn, the recognition—are taken from Sophocles, Shirley's adaptation charges the ancient story with contemporary political meaning. Ægysthus' terrible tyranny is underscored throughout; the 'griev'd people of two kingdoms' suffer under his scourge.[50] Ægysthus is himself from Mycenae but wants to take over Argos, which in 1762 is a transparent expression of Englishmen's fears of a tidal wave of Scots taking over high office in England. Orestes' revenge is framed as a struggle for 'liberty' and 'freedom' against 'oppression' and the tyrant's 'ambition'. The relationship of Ægysthus to Clytemnestra is presented as that of an upstart underling to a queen whose favour he has won with 'feign'd observance and obsequious vows', and whom he now tyrannically dominates.[51]

The chief hope of the fallen Whigs was that the now ageing Duke of Newcastle would lead his cohorts back:[52] as 'the Old Corps man *par excellence*', he tried to form a coalition of Whig groups to oppose the Crown and Bute.[53] Shirley's play stresses that under

[46] George (1959: 122–3 and pl. 33).
[47] Coats (1975: 30).
[48] George (1959: 119–21).
[49] Ibid. 127.
[50] Shirley (1765: 2).
[51] Ibid. 23.
[52] Brewer (1976: 62).
[53] Ibid. 13.

Agamemnon Argos was a happy people. In the climactic third act, Orestes meets a 'band of loyal and intrepid nobles' of advancing years. He assures them that he will respect the old compact between King and people: 'The thrones of kings, I . . . are only firm | While fix'd on public use and approbation.' He pledges to restore to all his nobles to 'The full possession of your natural rights, | Those rights which none but tyrants e'er invade'.[54] But Shirley's most striking alteration is to make the people responsible for dethroning Ægysthus. The rioting populaces of both Mycenae and Argos take over the palace, under the leadership of the ageing nobles and Melisander (the equivalent of Sophocles' *paidagōgos*), and arrest the tyrant. Melisander tells Orestes (v. 9),

> The government and city
> Are in our hands. So total a revolt
> Was wonderful!—and worthy of the people
> O'er whom immortal Agamemnon reign'd.[55]

Shirley's *Electra* thus dramatizes a return to the old, fondly remembered compact between the deceased King George II (i.e. Agamemnon) and his people. The hope—and threat—expressed through the play was that the new baby Prince of Wales would one day join forces with the populace and displaced Whig leaders, to depose the tyrannical usurper Bute. Shirley may be telling a lie when he claims in his address 'To the Reader' that the published play has not been altered except 'by meer touches of the language'. But even in its published version, it is manifestly a vitriolic Whig attack on Bute's regime.

III. ELECTRA VISUALIZED

There is no reason to believe Shirley's protestations that he had been planning his *Electra* as early as 1745. He was probably prompted by the appearance of the first complete English verse translation of Sophocles. In 1759 Theobald's translations were finally superseded by those of Thomas Francklin. A product of Westminster and Trinity, Francklin became professor of Greek at Cambridge in 1750, when Jeremiah Markland—a much better scholar—refused

---

[54] Shirley (1765: 53–4).
[55] Ibid. 97.

to stand for the position.[56] Francklin was not a distinguished Hellenist, but these were the days when Lord Chesterfield could write to his son in 1748 recommending that he pursue a Greek professorship, since 'It is a very pretty sinecure, and requires very little knowledge . . . of that language.'[57]

Yet Francklin was a versatile eighteenth-century gentleman with a high profile in the cultural and theatrical life of London. He resigned his professorship in 1759 and transferred himself to the literary circles of the capital. He was a close friend of Johnson and Reynolds, preached famously at St Paul's, and became the first chaplain of the Royal Academy. His translations of Voltaire, Cicero, and Lucian were, in their day, well respected.[58] He produced two successful theatrical works, *The Earl of Warwick* and *Matilda*, in which the heroines, Margaret and Matilda respectively, are torn between conflicting duties like the Antigone 'of Francklin's obvious model'.[59]

Francklin's translation of Sophocles remained standard well into the nineteenth century. It is aimed at a readership including women. Francklin guides his feminine reader's responses: 'The ladies may observe the modesty of Tecmessa's behaviour; she answers [Ajax] only with a sigh.' There is even a long note discussing whether it is seemly for Chrysothemis, as a virgin princess, to walk fast.[60] Francklin also demands that his readers *visualize* the theatrical action, capping his praise of the last scene of *Electra* with the following admonition:

Let the English reader conceive those inimitable actors, Quin, Garrick, and Cibber in the part of Aegisthus, Orestes, and Electra, and from them form to himself some idea of the effect which such a catastrophe would have on a British audience.[61]

Although he had persuaded the star actors Henry Quin and David Garrick to subscribe to the edition, Francklin unsurprisingly failed to persuade them to stage Sophocles unadapted. But he did arrange performances of his version of Voltaire's *Oreste*, a tragedy based on *Electra* which had been successfully staged in France in 1750. The starring role went to Mary Ann Yates, recently applauded for her performance in Richard Glover's *Medea* at Drury Lane (1767).[62]

---

[56] Clarke (1945: 29–30).   [57] Dobrée (1932: iii. 1084, no. 1518).
[58] See Lynch (1953: 180–3).   [59] Ibid. 186.
[60] Francklin (1759: i. 24, 26 n.); see also pp. 127–8 n., 148 n.
[61] Ibid. i. 193–4.   [62] See further Hall (1999a).

Francklin's *Orestes* was not a hit when it appeared at Covent Garden on 13 March 1769, and yet critics admired Yates's performance. A spectator wrote that

for tone, and justness of elocution, for uninterrupted attention, for everything that was nervous, various, elegant, and true, in attitude and action, I never saw her equal but Garrick.[63]

In 1774 Mrs Yates tried to win the hearts of the Drury Lane theatre with the same tragedy, renamed *Electra*. The new Prologue and Epilogue by Garrick were 'greatly receiv'd with great applause', and the excellent set by Philippe de Loutherburg comprised 'perspective scenery of Argos, the Palace of Aegisthus, and the Tomb of Agamemnon', with costumes deemed both 'elegant and characteristic'.[64]

This emphasis on the visual recreation of ancient Greece is significant, because scene design was beginning to respond to the early publication of Greek monuments, in particular the first volume of James Stuart and Nicholas Revett's *The Antiquities of Athens* (1762). At the beginning of the eighteenth century scenery had not been individuated historically or geographically. But Garrick's engagement of de Loutherburg at last put topographical scenery before the British public.[65] The admired costume which Mrs Yates wore to play Electra also strove for authenticity. It daringly dispensed with the pannier, substituting an unadorned black drape; Yates's hair, although piled high, was partly left to fall over her shoulders. Mlle Clairon had introduced this very costume in the same role in Paris.[66] The novel visual appeal of the revamped tragedy ensured that it was more successful, but it was still held to suffer from an excess of declamation.

When the multi-volume series Bell's British Theatre published Francklin's *Electra*, it substituted Theobald's translation for Francklin's play (Fig. 3), thus thoroughly confusing historians of the

---

[63] Quoted in Highfill *et al.* (1973–93: xvi. 328). For less enthusiastic contemporary reactions to Yates's Electra, see Stone (1962: 1390–1).

[64] *Westminster Magazine* (Oct. 1774), quoted in Stone (1962: 1841). When Dr Samuel Parr staged *Oedipus Tyrannus* and *Trachiniae* at Stanmore School, in 1775 and 1776 respectively, he was lent costumes by Garrick, perhaps those designed for the Drury Lane *Electra* of 1774. See Hall (1997*a*: 60).

[65] Rosenfeld (1981: 33).

[66] Pentzelel (1967: 109–10).

FIG. 3. Mary Ann Yates as Electra lamenting over the urn she believes contains Orestes' ashes. Yates starred in an adaptation of Voltaire's *Oreste* by Thomas Francklin, which was performed at Covent Garden in 1769 and Drury Lane in 1774. The frontispiece and title page to the Bell's 1777 edition of Lewis Theobald's *Electra*, reproduced here, misleadingly suggest that Theobald's translation, rather than Francklin's adaptation, was the text actually performed. Photo reproduced by courtesy of the Bodleian Library.

British theatre.[67] The reason is a mystery. It may demonstrate the flexible approach of the eighteenth-century mind towards translation: both Theobald and Francklin's plays were notionally versions of Sophocles' *Electra*. But Francklin was probably trying to imply that the *Electra* which had met a lukewarm response was not by him but by his dead rival. Francklin had long attacked Theobald's translations (as had Pope) in order to maximize the market for his own: while still Professor at Cambridge he had concluded a poem with an appeal to the 'Genius of Greece' to inspire him with Sophocles' fire, and

> From hands profane defend his much lov'd name;
> From cruel Tibbald [i.e. Theobald] wrest his mangled fame   (209–10).

Francklin here appended a scornful note, declaring that 'Tibbald translated two or three plays of Sophocles, and threaten'd the public with more'.[68]

Francklin's tragedy brought Electra into the cultural limelight. It prompted Simonin Vallouis, a French dancer, to star with his wife in a 'Grand Tragic Ballet' *Oreste et Electre* at the King's Theatre in May 1775. Although its plot is not certain, there was definitely a role for Clytemnestra.[69] Francklin's *Electra* also had reverberations in the visual arts. The 1769 production inspired a beautiful miniature by Samuel Cotes, which circulated on fashionable prints from an engraving,[70] and in the 1770s Sophocles' tragedy became a popular theme in painting.

Francklin had taken the prudent step of dedicating his translation of Sophocles to the then Prince of Wales, and was later rewarded by being made the first chaplain of the Royal Academy and its Professor of Ancient History. One of the founding members was Benjamin West, an American, who was inspired by Francklin's translation of *Electra* to paint a picture entitled 'Ægistus, raising the veil, discovers the body of Clytemnestra. Francklin's Sophocles.' When exhibited in the Academy in 1780 it provoked an admiring reaction.[71] It was with pictures such as this that West established

---

[67] See e.g. Bevis (1988: 133, 268).

[68] Francklin (1754: 13 and n.).

[69] Guest (1972: 148); see also the article 'Simonin Vallouis' in Highfill *et al.* (1973–93: xv. 102–3).

[70] The engraving, by P. Dawe, is reproduced in Highfill *et al.* (1973–93: xvi. 335). The miniature is reproduced in Foskett (1972: pl. 62).

[71] See von Erffa and Stanley (1986: 260). The painting is now lost, but an

himself as the most advanced proponent in England of the neoclassical style, which used antiquity to provide illustrations of 'modes of behaviour that were to inspire devotion to ideals of self-sacrifice for the sake of justice, honor, duty, and country'.[72]

West may have selected this particular scene because Francklin, his fellow Academician, was by now working on his translation of Lucian. Perhaps he drew West's attention to a passage in *The Hall* where Lucian's narrator describes scenes painted in a hall (23). One is a 'righteous deed, for which the painter derived his model, I suppose, from Euripides or Sophocles' (although the scene seems to fit only Sophocles' *Electra*). Lucian's narrator describes this 'righteous deed' thus:

The two youthful comrades Pylades of Phocis and Orestes (supposed to be dead) have secretly entered the palace and are slaying Aegisthus. Clytemnestra is already slain and is stretched on a bed half-naked, and the whole household is stunned by the deed—some are shouting, apparently, and others casting about for a way of escape.

West's picture was perhaps an attempt to recreate the painting in this ancient *ekphrasis*. He was not the only early Academician interested in *Electra*. Angelica Kauffman, one of the two female founding members, painted a picture of Electra and Chrysothemis by 1786;[73] Fuseli, who mixed in the same circle, had in 1776 drawn a sketch entitled *Orestes und Pylades führen Ägisth von der vor den von Elektra enthüllten Leichnam der Klytämnestra*.[74]

Despite this flurry of interest in the 1770s and 1780s, Sophocles' *Electra*, in common with all Greek tragedy, retreated from the professional stage into the Romantics' closet until the 1820s. Yet *Electra* was certainly being studied. In around 1800 it was the only Greek tragedy on the syllabus at Magdalen College, Oxford.[75] The theatrical critic Westland Marston recalls declaiming Electra's role at a breaking-up-day event held by his school at the Theatre Royal, Grimsby a couple of decades later.[76] But *Electra* only became

excellent mezzotint copy by Valentine Green, associate engraver of the Royal Academy, has been preserved. See Whitman (1902: 4, 159).

[72] von Erffa and Stanley (1986: 41–2).
[73] Manners and Williamson (1976: 224).
[74] Schiff (1973: i.2: 87, no. 392). The picture is now in Dijon. Thanks to Catherine Steel for help on this.
[75] Hurdis (c. 1800: 2). See Clarke (1945: 34).
[76] Marston (1888: i. 3–4).

popular again with the Europe-wide revivification of interest in Sophocles inspired by the Greek uprising of 1821. In France the followers of Jacques-Louis David competed annually for the Prix de Rome by painting neoclassical scenes. Between 1801 and 1821 the prescription was always from the *Iliad*, ancient historians, the Old Testament, and Ovid, but suddenly in 1822 it was 'Oreste et Pylade', and in 1823 that familiar Sophoclean scene, 'Egisthe, croyant retrouver le corps d'Oreste mort, découvre celui de Clytemnestre'.[77] In England the Greek War of Independence had two simultaneous effects on the theatre; there were numerous plays set in contemporary Greece, for example C. E. Walker's *The Greeks and the Turks; or, the Intrepidity of a British Tar*, which enthralled audiences at the Coburg Theatre in the autumn of 1821.[78] But Greek tragedy was simultaneously revived, and instead of Euripides' female-focused dramas, which had been the sources for most of the eighteenth century's staged versions of Greek tragedy, it was Sophocles who was now resuscitated, in adaptations all emphasizing resistance to tyranny.

In April 1825 Covent Garden staged Peter Bayley's spectacular version of *Electra*, entitled *Orestes in Argos*. Bayley may have been prompted by reports of the tragic *Oreste* by Jean Marie Janin, performed at the Théâtre Français in Paris in June 1821 shortly after the Greek uprising.[79] The background of the War of Independence informs *Orestes in Argos* as it was to inform English tragedies on ancient Greek themes into the 1830s.[80] The prologue argues that an important function of drama at Athens was 'to spread by scenic arts the Patriot flame', and the epilogue makes an allusion to the 'suffering Greeks'.[81] The play emphasizes the role of the people of Argos in the uprising against the tyrant Ægisthus, and Arcas, the

---

[77] In subsequent years other Sophoclean scenes were chosen: *Antigone* in 1825, *Philoctetes* in 1838, and *Oedipus Tyrannus* in 1843, 1867, and 1871. See Harding (1979: 32, 91–4).

[78] Other theatrical pieces of this type included the anonymous *The Siege of Missolonghi*, played at Astley's Amphitheatre in 1826, H. Miller's *Britons at Navarino* (Coburg Theatre, 1827), and the anonymous *The Mufti's Tomb* (Astley's 1828).

[79] Frenzel (1962: 484).

[80] See Hall (1997*b*); Talfourd's stirring *The Athenian Captive* (performed at the Haymarket 1838, published in Thomas Talfourd 1844: 105–50), uses *Electra* extensively.

[81] The prologue and epilogue do not appear in the first published version (Bayley 1825*a*), or in any other edition. They are quoted from a manuscript in the British Library, Add. MS 42865 fos. 172, 173.

paidagōgos figure, is central to the 'revolt against the tyrant'.[82] Although Bayley's tragedy uses Alfieri, Voltaire, and Shirley, the major source is Sophocles' *Electra*. One of the reviewers even called Bayley a 'translator' of Sophocles, and compliments him for greater fidelity to the Greek than either Voltaire or Crebillon.[83]

The production was praised for Charles Kemble's performance as Orestes (Fig. 4) and for the effectiveness of the recognition scene,[84] but its primary interest lay in its visual impact. It was long customary to condemn the theatre of the earlier part of the nineteenth century, but recently there has been fuller appreciation of the important technological and scenic developments in this period, which laid the groundwork for the modern theatre. Considerable work went into the classical scenery for Bayley's play; Greek architecture had become popular by the 1820s, incorporating features from the latest archaeological discoveries.[85] Theatre designers strove for minute archaeological exactitude, displaying their understanding of the different Doric, Corinthian, and Ionic styles (Fig. 5).[86] The stage directions for the opening of the second act of Bayley's play required the representation of the tomb of Agamemnon, the palace of the Pelopidae, and 'Argos in the distance—not too remote', while Aegisthus' death scene required numerous pillars. It was set in 'A large court of the Palace, with colonnade, entrances to various apartments, baths etc.'[87]

Charles Kemble's brother John had paved the way for antiquarian set design in his Covent Garden *Coriolanus* of 1811, and Charles became a pioneer in historical costumes. Indeed, historians of theatre have traditionally dated the birth of modern costuming in Britain to the medieval realism of his 1823 production of *King John*, two years prior to *Orestes in Argos*.[88] Kemble's enthusiasm was fed by Thomas Hope's *Costumes of the Ancients* (London, 1809), a compendium of illustrations based on ancient paintings on the vases Hope collected. The edition of Bayley's play published in the popular series *Dolby's British Theatre* provided illustrations and descriptions of the costumes. Miss Lacy's Electra wore an austere 'slate-coloured cotton long dress, and drapery', while Kemble's Orestes sported a

[82] Bayley (1825a: 49).

[84] Ibid. 373.

[86] Ibid. 174–6.

[88] See Campbell (1918: 213–15).

[83] *The Drama* (1824–5), 372–3.

[85] Rosenfeld (1981: 150, 174–6).

[87] Bayley (1825a: 12).

FIG. 4. Charles Kemble in 'authentic' Greek costume as Orestes. Frontispiece to the edition of Peter Bayley's *Orestes in Argos* published by Dolby's British Theatre in 1825, the year the play was performed at Covent Garden. Photo reproduced by courtesy of the Bodleian Library.

DOLBY'S BRITISH THEATRE.

—

ORESTES IN ARGOS.

T. Jones, Del.   *White, Sculpt.*

> *Orestes.* Where lurks the murderous and sensual beast?
> Ha! art thou found!   Ye Gods, I thank you!—Die—
> Die—a thousand deaths in one!

ACT V.   SCENE 4.

FIG. 5. The scenery for the fifth act of Peter Bayley's *Orestes in Argos*. Engraving in the edition of Peter Bayley's *Orestes in Argos* published by Dolby's British Theatre in 1825, the year the play was performed at Covent Garden. Photo reproduced by courtesy of the Bodleian Library.

lilach-coloured fine cloth short tunic, emboidered with black around the bottom; black belt, with white embroidery; white hat worn on his back; white square robe, embroidered with lilach, the colour of the tunich; white sandals, flesh legs and arms.[89]

Those 'flesh legs and arms', implying authentic Greek semi-nakedness, were an innovative feature. One commentator recalled that

the first time I saw naked feet represented, (in silk fleshings, of course,) was in a Greek tragedy, 'Orestes', at Covent Garden Theatre, and many people disliked the appearance, although it should have reminded them of some of the finest statues in the world; but English taste was very squeamish.[90]

Yet for all its antiquarian glamour, Bayley's tragedy did not inspire imitations on the same theme in the serious theatre.

The next manifestation of Sophocles' *Electra* takes us into the bizarre world of the Victorian burlesque, the main medium through which British audiences had access to Greek tragedy in the mid-Victorian era, and the precursor of W. S. Gilbert's operettas. Parodies of serious literature were the staple of the burlesque theatre, and the elevated tone and strange conventions of Greek tragedy furnished ideal material.[91] Frank Talfourd's popular *Electra in a New Electric Light* was one of the Easter entertainments offered to London theatregoers in 1859. Talfourd, despite failing to graduate from Christ Church as a result of excessive debauchery, was a student of Classics in possession of a 'gay and brilliant intellect'.[92]

During the 1850s the electric carbon-arc, which delivered an unprecedentedly brilliant light, began to be installed in London theatres.[93] Talfourd's title refers to the first occasion on which the carbon-arc was used in a sustained manner in a British theatre, in Paul Taglioni's ballet *Electra* at Her Majesty's Theatre on 17 April 1849. The ballet was subtitled *The Lost Pleiade*, for Taglioni's electric Electra was unconnected with Sophocles: she was the Electra of ancient cosmology, the Pleiad and mother of Dardanus, whose frequent invisibility as a star is explained by her concealment of her eyes at the sight of the ruins of Troy (Ovid, *Fasti* 4. 31–2,

---

[89] Bayley (1825*b*: p. ix).   [90] Fitzball (1859: i. 69).

[91] See Hall (1999*b*).

[92] *The Athenaeum* no. 1794 (15 March 1862), 365.

[93] Rees (1978: 65, 68–9, 72–4), Bergman (1977: 178–80).

174, 177–8).[94] Taglioni's ballet culminated in Electra's ascent as a star, 'so brilliant and far-piercing' that it stunned the audience, completely eclipsing the effect of gas.[95] But despite this reference to a previous theatrical hit, Talfourd's new electrified Electra was indeed the Sophoclean heroine.

The burlesqued *Electra* was 'really a magnificent affair', as the *Illustrated London News* opined.[96] This review suggests considerable popular knowledge of Greek myth: 'The classical story is, we may take for granted, well known.' For much of Talfourd's play requires a rudimentary knowledge of Sophocles' tragedy in order to understand the jokes. The famous scenes are humorously recreated: Electra's dialogues with Chrysothemis, her conflict with her mother, the news that Orestes has died after falling from his curricle, the urn scene (comically substituting a tea-urn), and Electra's recognition of her brother. But love interests supplement the plot, along with a wrestling match, a balletic *divertissement*, and star musical turns including that staple of the popular theatre, the 'laughing song', delivered as a trio to the tune *Rose of Castile* by Ægisthus, Orestes, and Pylades.[97]

The scenery commissioned by the manager of the Haymarket, John Buckstone, outstripped all opposition: 'Palatial chambers, sacred groves, curtained galleries, city squares, banqueting halls, are all finely painted and admirably set.'[98] The costumes, according to the witty playbill, were 'derived from most Authentic sources'.[99] The stage directions to the eyecatching fifth act illustrate the updated classicism typical of the mid-Victorian Greek tragic burlesque:

The Stage is crowded with PEOPLE *engaged in various pursuits—Some are looking at the exhibition of a classical 'Punch and Judy' . . . others are engaged witnessing the performance of a Strolling Company of* ACTORS *on a Thespian cart.*[100]

[94] This Electra came to represent the sun, and had figured in the masque by Ben Jonson offered as King James I's 'Entertainment in passing to his Coronation' on 15 March 1603. She met him in the Strand, delivering a long speech beginning 'The long laments I spent for ruin'd Troy | Are dried; and now mine eyes run teares of joy.' See Herford, Simpson, and Simpson (1941: viii. 107).

[95] Rees (1978: 67); Guest (1972: 139, 143 n. 3, 159).

[96] *Illustrated London News* 34 (1859), 419 col. 2.

[97] Francis Talfourd (1859: 23–4).

[98] *Illustrated London News* 34 (1859), 419 col. 2.

[99] Reproduced in Francis Talfourd (1859: 1–5).   [100] Ibid. 29–30.

This play-within-a-play is symptomatic of the burlesque stage's tendency to provide a self-conscious commentary upon the very genre which it is subverting. When Nemesis rises in the final scene, she delivers a lecture on ancient theatrical practice.

> I really cannot tell if all of you
> Recall the old Greek rule of stage propriety—
> Which was—the audience having had satiety
> Of crime displayed and vengeance on it willed,
> Upon the stage the actors were *not* killed,
> But by some fanciful poetic means
> Were decently disposed of—off the scenes.[101]

The middle- and lower-class audience, even if it knew nothing about Greek tragedy at the beginning of Talfourd's *Electra*, certainly knew something by its end.

It is paradoxical that the theatre of burlesque warmed to the heroines of Sophoclean tragedy more than any previous English-language drama. Electra, played by Miss E. Weekes, is central to this play, just as Alcestis had dominated Talfourd's other burlesque of Greek tragedy, *Alcestis* (Strand Theatre, 1850).[102] The burlesque theatre relished transvestism, and three other appealing young women played Chrysothemis, Orestes, and Pylades. 'This constellation of beauty and vivacity . . . could not fail of extraordinary effect'.[103] But the burlesque actresses needed to be more than pretty faces. The play involves a breathtaking acceleration of punning lines. When Electra enters in scene 1, '*her hair dishevelled, her dress torn and disarranged, shoes unsandaled and down at heel*', she begins to lament,

> Another day has passed, and yet another
> Brings with its light no tidings of my brother.[104]

Remarking self-consciously that she resembles a 'classic heroine', she turns to the subject of her unkempt hair in a manner only the industrial revolution can illuminate:

---

[101] Ibid. 34.
[102] Francis Talfourd (1850).
[103] *Illustrated London News* 34 (1859), 419 col. 2.
[104] Francis Talfourd (1859: 11). Francis was the son of the tragedian Thomas Talfourd (see n. 80 above).

> These locks of gold, when servants on me waited,
> Used to be carefully *electra-plaited*,
> Now all dis-*sheffield* down my shoulders flow.[105]

Electra is not prominent because a deeper understanding of our tragic heroine had developed. Talfourd's uncritical adoption of the burlesque genre's stereotypical caricature of the henpecking wife in his characterization of Clytemnestra suggests that he was no feminist.[106] But in Weekes he had an actress of virtuoso verbal agility, and it was her skill in singing, dancing, and delivering the fast-falling puns beneath the electric carbon-arc which his audience prized.

IV. ELECTRA READ BY WOMEN

The tragic potential of Sophocles' *Electra* reached its lowest ebb in the Victorian theatre of burlesque, but a new wind was blowing in the form of the movement for the emancipation of women. It was only as women began to study the play in earnest that the characters of Electra and her conflicts with her mother and sister began to strike chords of recognition, dislodging from centre stage the politicized battle between Orestes and Aegisthus. With a few significant exceptions, the characters of all three women had previously been thoroughly sweetened, and made secondary to the men's struggle over the throne.

The most popular book about ancient drama in the eighteenth century was the Jesuit Pierre Brumoy's *Le Théâtre des Grecs* (1730), which appeared in an English translation by Charlotte Lennox in 1759, and included a translation of *Electra*.[107] Brumoy was perturbed by the sentiments expressed by Electra and her mother in their bitter confrontation, to the extent that he departed significantly from the Greek in what is otherwise a faithful translation.[108]

---

[105] Francis Talfourd (1859: 12).

[106] In a forthcoming study, Fiona Macintosh is, however, to argue that issues connected with the rise of the New Woman are explored in mid-Victorian classical burlesque.

[107] Lennox (1759). Three of Brumoy's 'Discourses' in vol. i were translated by the Earl of Corke and Orrery.

[108] 'This whole scene, between the mother and daughter, is so much in the Greek manners, that no art is capable of rendering it exactly, and yet agreeable to us. I was

Electra's harshness and unbecoming behaviour—of which she is herself painfully aware (see 221–2, 307–8, 616–17)—repelled most eighteenth-century gentlemen. The unintelligent Paul Hiffernan was outraged in 1770 by the murder of Clytemnestra in Sophocles. It is one of the theatrical crimes by 'such monsters that degrade the whole human system', because it is encouraged by a woman.[109]

Electra's character seemed too masculine: Coleridge invoked it to support his view that 'the Greeks, except perhaps for Homer, seem to have had no way of making their women interesting, but by unsexing them'.[110] Even Shirley had turned Clytemnestra into a victim of her lover's ambition, and toned down Electra's vindictiveness, replacing it with a devotion to the liberation of her fatherland.[111] Francklin had shaped both Clytemnestra and Electra to fit eighteenth-century notions of ideal femininity: their difficult confrontation is muted, and his Electra regrets the murder.[112] Similarly, a reviewer of Bayley's play praises the characterization of Clytemnestra as a lamenting penitent instead of 'the ravening she-wolf who has murdered her own husband and was divested of all natural affection for her own offspring—the *Lady Macbeth* of the Greek stage'.[113]

We now are disappointed by the pusillanimity of these writers' reactions to Sophocles' magnificent women. There were, however, two brave exceptions. In 1714 Theobald had seen the importance which Sophocles attached to Electra, rather than her brother Orestes.[114] Theobald argues that the play's power lies in the multiple emotions Electra expresses:

she is equally Wonderful, in her strong and implacable Resentments against her Father's Murtherers; in her Impatience for Orestes to come and revenge him; in her excessive Sorrows for her Brother's supposed Disaster; in her Transports, when she comes to know he is living; and in her Zeal, for the performance of his Revenge.[115]

Shelley agreed, for Electra stands behind the Beatrice in his tragedy *The Cenci*, written in 1819 shortly before he drowned with a copy of

apprehensive that a too close translation would rob it of all its beauty.' Brumoy translated by Lennox (1759: i. 119 n.).

[109] Hiffernan (1770: ii. 57).   [110] Raysor (1936: 37).
[111] Shirley (1765: 4, 10, 23–4, 98).   [112] Francklin (1762).
[113] *The Drama* 7 (1824–5), 372–3.   [114] Theobald (1714: 69).
[115] Ibid. 70.

Sophocles in his pocket. Beatrice is driven by her father's incestuous impulses to plot his death, with the support of Bernardo (the brother to whom she is intensely attached), and her mother-in-law. In the Preface to this play Shelley talks about the incest theme in Sophocles' *Oedipus Tyrannus*, but also suggestively describes his heroine as 'thwarted from her nature by the necessity of circumstances and opinion' and perverted by 'revenge and retaliation'.[116] When the assassins cannot bring themselves to kill her father, Beatrice exhorts them in language echoing Electra's encouragement of her brother's violence.[117] Other reminiscences of *Electra* include Beatrice's concern over her dishevelled hair.[118] Shelley wisely remarks that if Beatrice had suppressed her vengeful instincts she would have been a better person, 'but she would never have been a tragic character'.[119]

When Angelica Kauffman had painted *Electra*, she had unusually chosen not the final scene of the play, but the two sisters conversing. Sophocles' *Electra* only came into her own when other women contemplated her in the nineteenth century. This era produced a new interest in female subjectivity going beyond hackneyed expressions of maternal and conjugal devotion. Female authors have been attracted to the emotional (rather than political) potential of this play, notably Sylvia Plath, in whose *Electra on Azalea Path*, written after she visited her father's grave, she sees herself as an actor who borrows 'the stilts of an old tragedy'.[120] Much earlier, Elizabeth Barrett Browning had compared the emotional response of France to the corpse of Napoleon with Electra's emotion on receiving Orestes' ashes; elsewhere she likened her depression before a reunion with her lover to Electra's 'sepulchral urn'.[121] Barrett is also remembering the Sophoclean Electra to whom Propertius' poetic persona refers: he compares his joy at a reconciliation with Cynthia with the joy of Electra, 'when she saw Orestes was safe, over whose feigned ashes she had wept a sister's tears as she clasped them' (2. 14. 5–6).[122]

---

[116] Shelley (1934: 276).   [117] Ibid. 314.
[118] Sheppard (1927: 179–80).   [119] Shelley (1934: 276).
[120] *Electra on Azalea Path*, line 33. The poem is published in Plath (1981: 116–17). See Bremer (1992).
[121] *Crowned and Buried*, stanzas 19–20; *Sonnets from the Portuguese*, stanza 5, in Barrett Browning (1994: 255, 219).
[122] 'Cuius falsa tenens fleverat ossa soror.' Another love elegist, Ovid, regarded Sophocles as one of the poets most admired by posterity (*Am.* 1. 15. 15).

The most important evidence for the distinctive contribution to be made by women to the understanding of *Electra* comes from Girton College in 1883, with the earliest attested production of Sophocles' play, unadapted, in the British Isles. There had been theatricals at this college as early as 1871, when the Mistress and the classical tutor were scandalized to see their pupils cavorting in male clothes at a rehearsal of Swinburne's *Atalanta in Calydon* and *Twelfth Night*. The performance was banned.[123] But by 1882 a more liberal ethos prevailed, and a Dramatic Club came into existence.[124] The decision to stage a Greek play was a response to the inauguration of the Cambridge Greek Play in 1882, with an all-male cast performing Sophocles' *Ajax*.[125] Now the Girtonian Janet Case took the lead in this alternative, female appropriation of Sophocles.[126]

The choice of play was determined by the strong roles for three women (Fig. 6), and the female identity of the chorus. An excited review in the national press announced that it was 'the first time that a Greek drama was acted by women', and there is no evidence that this assertion was false.[127] The early choices of plays for performances by the men at Cambridge shows a corresponding desire to select plays without demanding *female* roles (*Ajax* in 1882, *Birds* in 1883). When *Eumenides* was chosen in 1885, Janet Case's renowned realization of Electra won her the part of Athena,[128] but no other women acted in the Cambridge Greek play in the nineteenth century. In Oxford, conversely, the pathbreaking Balliol *Agamemnon* of 1880 had been performed entirely by men. But this had worried Jowett, who as Vice-Chancellor proscribed male impersonation of women in OUDS performances. Jane Ellen Harrison, who had studied Classics at Cambridge but was now an

---

[123] Bradbrook (1969: 43–4).

[124] Megson and Lindsay (1961): 39).

[125] On these early university productions of Greek tragedy see Macintosh (1997).

[126] See Easterling (1999). I am grateful to Miss Alison Duke, former tutor in Classics at Girton, and Mrs Kate Penny, the college archivist, for their invaluable help on the Girton *Elektra*. It is interesting to find *Electra* inspiring a tragedy written by a woman, which was published in the same year as the Girton production. Although she also uses the *Oresteia*, several Sophoclean scenes, in particular the messenger speech, are included in 'Ross Neil' (1883), esp. pp. 227–9.

[127] *Illustrated London News* 83 (1883), 527 col. 2.

[128] Easterling (1999: n. 10); Stephen (1920: 55).

Fig. 6. Janet Case as Elektra speaks to Chrusothemis in the 1883 all-female production of Sophocles' *Elektra*, in ancient Greek, at Girton College, Cambridge. Chrusothemis' dress was sea-green. Photo originally published by J. E. Biss, a local Cambridge photographer, and here reproduced by courtesy of Girton College Archives.

independent scholar in her thirties, was therefore offered the role of Alcestis at Oxford in 1887.[129]

The preparation for the Girton *Elektra* under Ethel Sargant were intensive. Tennis was forgotten, and frantic dress-making meant that 'Liddell and Scott gave way to sewing-machines'.[130] The organizers 'consulted authorities in the British Museum in order to ensure the correctness of the dresses and stage accessories', while Ethel Sargant's sister researched the scenery design in the libraries of Paris. The play was performed in the gymnasium, hung with subdued draperies. The set (Fig. 7) included a *thymele*, garlanded with bay-leaves, the palace of Agamemnon, a street of Mukenai in the background, and the famous Lion Gate, through which the ten *choreutai* entered, dressed in white, singing as they 'walked rhythmically in gracefully tangled evolutions'.[131]

Case's performance was superb.[132] Klutaimnestra, clad in yellow, came over as a 'haughty, overbearing shrew',[133] and the exit of Aigisthos (Miss Wallas, a Mathematics student) 'was the exit of a dastard'.[134] Appreciative members of the audience came from Newnham College, where a special lecture on *Elektra*, open to all members of the university, was delivered by the learned Miss Black; sketches appeared in both the local and the national press, making the front page of the weekly periodical *The Graphic* (Fig. 8).[135] The music was adapted from Mendelssohn's version of Sophocles' *Antigone*, played on the pianoforte.

The Girton *Elektra* had consequences. Other women's educational establishments began to enact Greek plays, and *Electra* was instantly included in their performance repertoire. The redoubtable Elsie Fogerty published an acting edition of the play in translation, a

[129] In an undated letter to Evelyn Abbott, the New College don W. Courtney recorded Jowett's Deuteronomic stipulations 'that the ladies' parts should be played by ladies and that no undergraduate should disguise himself in women's attire' (Jowett Collection, Balliol College Library). Thanks to Penny Bulloch for advice on this.

[130] *The Girton Review* 6 (Dec. 1883), 1, 3.

[131] *Illustrated London News* 83 (1883), 527.

[132] Ibid.

[133] Ibid.

[134] *The Girton Review* 6 (Dec. 1883), 3–5.

[135] No. 732 (8 Dec. 1883). The engraving was from a sketch by Miss F. R. Gray of Hampstead. Antique females were the headline news of the week: the cover is shared with an engraving of views of the newly discovered palace of the Vestal Virgins in Rome.

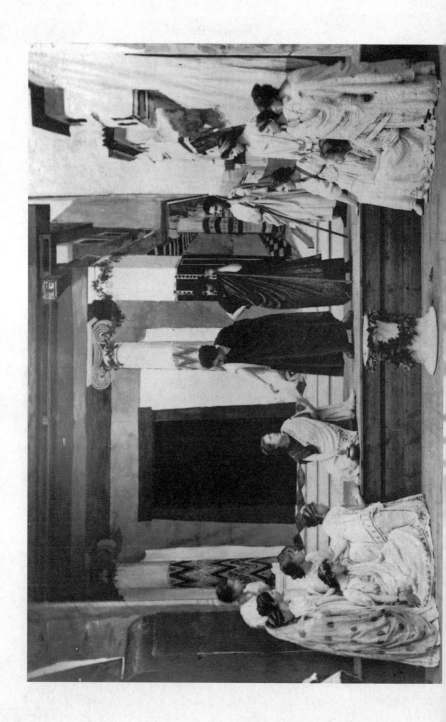

THE PERFORMANCE OF THE "ELECTRA" OF SOPHOCLES BY LADIES AT GIRTON COLLEGE, NEAR CAMBRIDGE

FIG. 8. Miss L. Morris enters as Klutaimnestra in the 1883 all-female production of Sophocles' *Elektra*, in ancient Greek, at Girton College, Cambridge. Klutaimnestra's dress was yellow. The illustration, copied from a sketch by Miss F. R. Gray of Hampstead, appeared on the cover of *The Graphic* no. 732 (8 December 1883). Photo reproduced by courtesy of the Bodleian Library.

FIG. 7. Elektra, with the urn, speaks to Orestes in the 1883 all-female production of Sophocles' *Elektra*, in ancient Greek, at Girton College, Cambridge. The set, inspired by the ruins of Mycenae, was designed and painted by Mary Sargant. Photo originally published by J. E. Bliss, a local Cambridge photographer, reproduced here by courtesy of Girton College Archives.

sequel to her *Antigone* for girls (1903), in the series 'Standard Plays for Amateur Performance'.[136] Moreover, Janet Case taught Virginia Woolf her Greek. When Woolf wrote Case's obituary in *The Times* (22 July 1937), she said Case had made Greek drama 'supremely desirable'.[137] Case's enthusiasm for *Electra* surely informed Virginia Woolf's wonderful essay 'On not knowing Greek', for it is Sophocles' *Electra* which Woolf chose to make the foundation of her case. In *Electra* she finds

the quality that first strikes us in Greek literature, the lightning-quick, sneering, out-of-doors manner . . . Queens and Princesses in this very tragedy by Sophocles stand at the door bandying words like village women, with a tendency, as one might expect, to rejoice in language, to split phrases into slices, to be intent on verbal victory.[138]

The agonistic, rhetorical power of the altercations between Electra, her sister, and her mother here discover a critic who can really appreciate them.

Woolf perceptively argues that Electra has been drawn as a character by 'little turns and twists of the dialogue' and by comments on her neglected appearance. These indicate 'something suffering in her, outraged and stimulated to its utmost stretch of capacity'. But Woolf does not feel the need to condemn Clytemnestra, for she 'is no unmitigated villainess'; Woolf cites her famous words, 'there is a strange power in motherhood' (*El.* 770).[139] Perhaps Woolf, so conscious of her female predecessors, was thinking of George Eliot's ironic use of the line in *Janet's Repentance*, the third scene of her *Scenes of Clerical Life*.[140]

For Woolf, Sophocles' women come alive across the centuries. The effort to 'get back' to the Greeks is justified, because

the stable, the permanent, the original human being is to be found there. Violent emotions are needed to rouse him [*sic*] into action, but when thus stirred by death, by betrayal, by some other primitive calamity, Antigone and Ajax and Electra behave in the way in which we should behave thus struck down; the way in which everybody has always behaved . . . These are the originals . . . of the human species.[141]

---

[136] Fogerty (1914: 1903).
[137] Quoted in Easterling (1999).
[138] Woolf (1975: 41). Hearty thanks to Peggy Reynolds for help with Woolf.
[139] Woolf (1975: 43–5).
[140] Ch. 13. Eliot actually quotes the Greek: see Jenkyns (1980: 114).
[141] Woolf (1975: 44).

Sophocles' heroines have here finally come into their own. Not only are their strident characters positively appreciated as examples of feminine characterization, but they are at last allowed to symbolize universal *human*kind.

Electra has also been appropriated to specifically female concerns. She was a symbol of womanly self-sacrifice in a popular American novel by the Texan Augusta Evans, *Macaria: or, Altars of Sacrifice*. The English edition, published in the same year as the Girton *Elektra*, enjoyed a wide circulation. Electra is an orphaned painter from New Orleans. She supports the confederate cause in the Civil War, and loses the man she loves. In the final chapter she completes her allegorical painting on the war, *The Modern Macaria*, which is ultimately inspired by Euripides' *Heraclidae* and depicts the suffering of the bereaved women of the confederacy. Together with her friend Irene, she sets up a School of Design for women, to alleviate the plight of the huge numbers of women whom defeat has thrown on their own resources. This offers a proto-feminist ending to a novel in which the Sophoclean Electra's emotional deprivation and passionate attachment to a defeated cause have been transplanted to a recent political situation.[142]

The Girton *Elektra* was imitated in America in 1889, when the American Academy of Dramatic Arts staged it at the New York Lyceum. The music was composed by Laura Sedgwick Collins.[143] Electra's feminist manifestations in America would indeed require a separate study: the play served explicitly suffragist concerns in 1923, when Henry Lister's *Clytemnestra* was performed by the 'La Boheme' club of San Francisco. This tragedy argues that Clytemnestra (despite killing her husband) and her daughters were, fundamentally, innocent victims of male aggression. It culminates with a rewriting of Sophocles' *Electra* in which Orestes is an unpleasant patriarch. He claims to his mother 'I am a man, who has more right than you I . . . to be the master of this house'. In the preface Lister wrote

The modern enfranchisement of women has . . . placed the sexes on an equal basis. In making Clytemnestra the heroine instead of villain of the play the author asks the world, newly awakened to the rights of women, whether Clytemnestra was guilty or not guilty.[144]

[142] Evans (1883: 109, 374–5).   [143] Brown (1903: iii. 591).
[144] Lister (1923: 51, 52, 8). This volume contains striking photographs of the leading actresses in costume.

V. CONCLUSION

Sophocles' *Electra* has not been the most performed of Greek tragedies on the British stage in the twentieth century, partly because of the huge impact made by Richard Strauss's operatic version of Hugo von Hofmannsthal's searing, sexually charged *Elektra*, first stunning London in 1910.[145] Gordon Craig designed a wonderful set for the Sophoclean *Electra* which he published in 1913, but the potential of a crypto-republican *Electra* at the Abbey Theatre, Dublin, in collaboration with Yeats, was alas never realized.[146] The tragedy has been performed in Britain by touring Greek actresses,[147] but few British women have attempted the role except for Peggy Ashcroft. She appeared in an Old Vic production by Michel St Denis (who had directed Olivier as Oedipus) in March 1951, in J. T. Sheppard's translation.[148]

Although performed shortly after the end of World War II, the production had no specific political reference, focusing instead on Electra's tortured psyche. This was to be Peggy Ashcroft's sole performance in a Greek tragedy. Kenneth Tynan applauded her 'unsuspected vocal strength and variety . . . spanning some amazing arpeggios'.[149] According to *Punch* she offered 'a haunting revelation of suffering. Miss Ashcroft can tear the heart out of you with a whisper'. The *New Statesman and Nation* was even more impressed: 'She drives her way through the part with an energy and resolution, and even a hardness . . . The assault on our feeling is just about as direct as it could possibly be.'[150] Ashcroft maintained that she learned more from Electra than from any other role; Electra put steel into her famous Portia, and inspired her revolutionary realization of Shakespeare's Cleopatra as a Greek (rather than Egyptian) Queen of ruthless cruelty and protean volatility.[151] But

---

[145] On which see Ewans (1984) and Bremer (1994). At a conference in Reading in 1995 Simon Goldhill delivered a fascinating paper (as yet unpublished) on the nervous British reaction to Strauss's *Electra*.

[146] Craig (1913: 34).

[147] Elsa Vergi, for example, stunned the 1966 Edinburgh festival in *Electra* in modern Greek, with the Piraikon Theatre from Athens. Bruce (1975: 153) recalls that her performance was imbued 'with such power that it was almost impossible to believe that we did not know the language'.

[148] Rowell (1993: 137, 142–3).   [149] Quoted in Findlater (1983: 30).

[150] These reviews are quoted in Tanitch (1987: no. 68).

[151] Findlater (1983: 31).

few actresses have dared challenge the memory of Ashcroft's performance, except for Fiona Shaw and even more recently Zoe Wanamaker, who in 1997 starred in an acclaimed Chichester Festival production (later transferred to the Donmar Warehouse), set in war-torn Bosnia (Fig. 9).

Sophocles' Electra has had some interesting experiences in

FIG. 9. Zoe Wanamaker as Electra in Sophocles' *Electra* in 1997, a Chichester Festival production directed by David Leveaux which later transferred to the Donmar Warehouse. The translation was by Frank McGuinness and the designer was Johan Engels. Photo reproduced by courtesy of Ivan Kyncl.

Britain. She has been impersonated by men, played by an all-female cast, and has appeared at Covent Garden, Drury Lane, and the Haymarket. She has been painted, engraved, sung, danced, burlesqued, censored, electrified, and declaimed in Grimsby. She has been refashioned for audiences ranging from royalty to the lowest class of spectators of the mid-Victorian popular theatre. She has been associated in British imagination with violence in Bosnia, Londonderry, the American Civil War, the Greek War of Independence, and riots in Georgian England. She has been a passionate Royalist, an ardent Whig, a witty romantic lead, a monster who degrades her sex, and a proto-feminist.

This quest has introduced us to people from Scotland and Ireland as well as England: let us conclude with a manifestation of *Electra* in Wales. On 5 and 6 July 1933 it was performed in Mrs Bertie Perkins' garden in Sketty Green by the Swansea Little Theatre.[152] An unremarkable event in the annals of Sophoclean reception, certainly. But it gave rise to a remarkable poem, for one of the active members of the company was Dylan Thomas. The production inspired him to write a beautiful poem, worth quoting in full because of all the spectators of *Electra* we have met, Thomas comes closest to responding not to Electra's morals, politics, or position on gender, but on the effect of her poetry in performance.[153]

Dylan Thomas, 'Greek play in a garden', from Daniel Jones (ed.), *Dylan Thomas: The Poems* (London 1971), pp. 56–7.

> A woman wails her dead among the trees,
> Under the green roof grieves the living;
> The living sun laments the dying skies,
> Lamenting falls. Pity Electra's loving
>
> Of all Orestes' continent of pride
> Dust in the little country of an urn,
> Of Agamemnon and his kingly blood
> That cries along her veins. No sun or moon
>
> Shall lamp the raven darkness of her face,
> And no Aegean wind cool her cracked heart;
> There are no seacaves deeper than her eyes;
> Day treads the trees and she the cavernous night.

---

[152] See Maud (1965: 315); Rolph (1956: 69–70); *Herald of Wales* 15 July 1933, p. 1. Many thanks to Chris Collard for information about the Swansea production.
[153] Jones (1971: 56–7).

Among the trees the language of the dead
Sounds, rich with life, out of a painted mask;
The queen is slain; Orestes' hands drip blood;
And women talk of horror to the dusk.

There can be few tears left: Electra wept
A country's tears and voiced a world's despair
At flesh that perishes and blood that's spilt
And love that goes down like a flower.

Pity the living who are lost, alone;
The dead in Hades have their host of friends,
The dead queen walketh with Mycenae's king
Through Hades' groves and the Eternal Lands.

Pity Electra loveless, she whose grief
Drowns and is drowned, who utters to the stars
Her syllables, and to the gods her love;
Pity the poor unpitied who are strange with tears.

Among the garden trees a pigeon calls,
And knows no woe that these sad players mouth
Of evil oracles and funeral ills;
A pigeon calls and women talk of death.

REFERENCES

[ANON.] (1714), *Electra, a Tragedy: Translated from the Greek of Sophocles* (London.

AXTON, MARIE (1982) (ed.), *Three Tudor Classical Interludes* (Cambridge).

BARRETT BROWNING, ELIZABETH (1994), *The Works of Elizabeth Barrett Browning*, Wordsworth edition (Ware, Herts).

BAYLEY, PETER (1825*a*), *Orestes in Argos* (London).

——(1825*b*), *Orestes in Argos*, in *Dolby's British Theatre* vol. xii (London).

BERMAN, GÖSTA M. (1977), *Lighting in the Theatre* (Stockholm and Totowa, NJ).

BEVIS, RICHARD (1988), *English Drama: Restoration and Eighteenth Century* (Harlow).

BONE, QUENTIN (1972), *Henrietta Maria* (London).

BRADBROOK, M. C. (1969), *'That Infidel Place': A Short History of Girton College 1869–1969* (London).

BRADLEY, E. T. (1908), pseudonym of Mrs A. Murray Smith, 'Goffe or Gough, Thomas', *Dictionary of National Biography* (London), viii. 70–1.

BREMER, JAN MAARTEN (1992), 'Three Approaches to Sylvia Plath's *Electra on Azalea Path*', *Neophilologus* 76: 305–16.

—— (1994), 'A Daughter Fatally Blocked: von Hofmannsthal's *Elektra*', in Henk Hillenaar and Walter Schönau (eds.), *Fathers and Mothers in Literature* (Amsterdam and Atlanta, Ga.), 113–21.

BREWER, JOHN (1976), *Party Ideology and Popular Politics at the Accession of George III* (Cambridge).

—— (1979–80), 'Theater and Counter-Theater in Georgian politics', *Radical History Review* 22: 7–40.

BROWN, T. ALLSTON (1903), *A History of the New York Stage* (New York).

BRUCE, GEORGE (1975), *Festival of the North* (London).

BUCHANAN-JONES, JOHN (1966) (ed.), *The Remains of Thomas Hearne (Reliquiæ Hernianæ), Being Extracts from his MS Diaries, Compiled by Dr. John Bliss* (London and Fontwell).

CAMPBELL, LILY B. (1918), 'A History of Costuming on the English Stage between 1660 and 1823', *University of Wisconsin Studies in Language and Literature* 2: 187–223.

COATS, ALICE M. (1975), *Lord Bute: An Illustrated Life of John Stuart, Third Earl of Bute* (Princes Risborough).

CLARKE, M. L. (1945), *Greek Studies in England 1700–1830* (Cambridge).

CONOLLY, L. W. (1976), *The Censorship of English Drama 1738–1824* (San Marino).

CRAIG, EDWARD GORDON (1913), *Towards a New Theatre* (London and Toronto).

DACIER, ANDRÉ (1693), *Tragédies grecques de Sophocle traduites en Francois [sic] avec des notes Critiques, et un Examen de chaque pièce selon les règles du Théâtre* (Paris 1693).

DENNIS, JOHN (1698), *The Usefulness of the Stage to the Happiness of Mankind. To Government, and To Religion. Occasioned by a Late Book written by Jeremy Collier M.A.* (London).

DOBRÉE, BONAMY (1932) (ed.), *The Letters of Philip Dormer Stanhope, 4th Earl of Chesterfield* (London).

EASTERLING, PATRICIA (1999), 'The Early Years of the Cambridge Greek Play: 1882–1912', in Christopher Stray (ed.), *Classics at Cambridge* (a forthcoming supplement to *PCPS*, Cambridge).

EVANS, AUGUSTA J. (1883), *Macaria; or, Altars of Sacrifice* (London).

EWANS, MICHAEL (1984), 'Elektra: Sophokles, von Hofmannsthal, Strauss', *Ramus* 13: 135–54.

FINDLATER, RICHARD (1983), *These Our Actors* (London).

FITZBALL, EDWARD (1859), *Thirty-Five Years of a Dramatic Author's Life* (London).

FOGERTY, ELSIE (1903), *The Antigone of Sophocles: Adapted and Arranged for Amateur Performance in Girls' Schools* (London).

——(1914), *Sophocles' Electra: Acting Edition* (London).

FOSKETT, DAPHNE (1972), *A Dictionary of British Miniature Painters* (London).

FRANCKLIN, THOMAS (1754), *Translation: A Poem* (2nd edn., first published 1753; London).

——(1759), *The Tragedies of Sophocles, from the Greek* (London).

——(1762), *Orestes a Tragedy*, in *The Works of M. De Voltaire. Translated from the French by Dr. Smollett and Others* (London, 1761–5), xiv. 22–118.

FRENZEL, ELIZABETH (1962), *Stoffe der Weltliteratur* (Stuttgart).

GEORGE, M. DOROTHY (1959), *English Political Caricature to 1792* (Oxford).

GOFFE, THOMAS (1633), *The Tragedy of Orestes, written by Thomas Goffe, Master of Arts, and Student of Christs Church in Oxford, and Acted by the Students of the Same House* (London).

GRAY, CHARLES HAROLD (1931), *Theatrical Criticism in London to 1795* (New York).

GUEST, IVOR (1972), *The Romantic Ballet in England* (2nd edn.; London and Nairobi).

HALL, EDITH (1997a), 'Greek plays in Georgian Reading', *G&R* 44: 59–81.

——(1997b), 'Talfourd's Ancient Greeks in the Theatre of Reform', *International Journal of the Classical Tradition* 4: 283–307.

——(1999a), 'Medea and British Legislation before the First World War', *G&R* 46.

——(1999b), '1845 and All That: Singing Greek Tragedy on the London Stage', in Michael Biddiss and Maria Wyke (eds.), *Uses and Abuses of Antiquity* (Peter Lang Publishers).

HARDING JAMES (1979), *Artistes Pompiers: French Academic Art in the 19th Century* (London).

HERFORD, C. H., SIMPSON, PERCY, and SIMPSON, EVELYN (1941) (eds.), *Ben Jonson* (Oxford).

HEYWOOD, THOMAS (1874), *The Dramatic Works of Thomas Heywood*, iii (London).

HIFFERNAN, PAUL (1770), *Dramatic Genius in Five Books* (London).

HIGHFILL, PHILIP A., BURNIM, KALMAN A., and LANGHAM, EDWARD A. (1973–93), *A Bibliographical Dictionary of Actors, Actresses, Musicians, Dancers, Managers and Other Stage Personnel in London, 1660–1800* (Carbondale and Edwardsville).

HISCOCK, W. G. (1946), *A Christ Church Miscellany* (Oxford).

HOLFORD-STREVENS, LEOFRANC (1988), *Aulus Gellius* (London).

HOLLAND, MARY (1992), 'Heart of Darkness brought Home to Derry', *Observer* 23 Feb.: 52.

HURDIS, JAMES (*c*.1800), *A Word or Two in Vindication of the University of Oxford and of Magdalen College in Particular, from the Posthumous Aspersions of Mr. Gibbon* (Bishopstone).

INGRAM, WILLIAM HENRY (1966), 'Greek Drama and the Augustan Stage: Dennis, Theobald, Thomson' (Diss. Pennsylvania).

JENKYNS, RICHARD (1980), *The Victorians and Ancient Greece* (Oxford).

JOCELYN, H. D. (1967) (ed.), *The Tragedies of Ennius* (Cambridge).

JONES, DANIEL (1971) (ed.), *Dylan Thomas: The Poems* (London).

KERRIGAN, JOHN (1996), *Revenge Tragedy* (Oxford).

LENNOX, CHARLOTTE (1759), *The Greek Theatre of Father Brumoy* (London).

LISTER, HENRY B. (1923), *Clytemnestra* (Washington, DC).

LYNCH, JAMES (1953), *Box, Pit and Gallery: Stage and Society in Johnson's London* (Berkeley and Los Angeles).

MACINTOSH, FIONA (1994), *Dying Acts: Death in Ancient Greek and Irish Tragic Drama* (Cork).

—— (1995), 'Under the Blue Pencil: Greek Tragedy and the British Censor', *Dialogos* 2: 54–70.

—— (1997), 'Tragedy in Performance: Nineteenth and Twentieth Century Productions', in Patricia Easterling (ed.), *The Cambridge Companion to Greek Tragedy* (Cambridge), 284–323.

MANNERS, Lady VICTORIA, and WILLIAMSON, Dr. G. C. (1976), *Angelica Kauffman, R.A.: Her Life and Work* (New York).

MARCHANT, E. C. (1909), 'Christopher Wase', *Dictionary of National Biography* (London), xx, 896–7.

MARSTON, WESTLAND (1888), *Our Recent Actors* (London).

MAUD, RALPH (1965) (ed.), *Poet in the Making: The Notebooks of Dylan Thomas* (London).

MEGSON, B., and LINDSAY, J. (1961), *Girton College 1869–1959: An Informal History* (Cambridge).

MOORE SMITH, G. C. (1923), *College Plays Performed in the University of Cambridge* (Cambridge).

'NEIL, ROSS' [Augusta Webster] (1883), *Orestes*, in *Andrea the Painter* (London), 181–238.

PENTZELL, RAYMOND (1967), 'New Dress'd in the Ancient Manner: The Rise of Historical Realism in Costuming the Serious Drama of England and France in the Eighteenth Century' (Diss. Yale).

PIKERYNG, JOHN (1567), *A Newe Enterlude of Vice conteyning the History of Horestes with the cruell revengment of his Fathers death upon his one naturall Mother* (London).

PLATH, SYLVIA (1981), *Collected Poems*, ed. Ted Hughes (London).

RAYSOR, THOMAS MIDDLETON (1936) (ed.), *Coleridge's Miscellaneous Criticism* (London).

REES, TERENCE (1978), *Theatre Lighting in the Age of Gas* (London).

ROLPH, J. ALEXANDER (1956), *Dylan Thomas: A Bibliography* (London and New York).

ROSENFELD, SYBIL (1981), *Georgian Scene Painters and Scene Painting* (Cambridge).

ROWELL, GEORGE (1993), *The Old Vic Theatre: A History* (Cambridge).

SCHIFF, GERT (1973), *Johann Heinrich Füssli 1741–1825* (Zurich and Munich).

SHAW, FIONA (1996), 'Electra Speechless', in Francis M. Dunn (ed.), *Sophocles' 'Electra' in Performance* (Stuttgart), 131–57.

SHELLEY, PERCY BYSSHE (1934), *The Cenci*, in Thomas Hutchinson (ed.), *The Complete Poetical Works of Percy Bysshe Shelley* (Oxford, London, New York, and Toronto), 274–337.

SHEPPARD, J. T. (1927), *Aeschylus and Sophocles: Their Work and Influence* (New York).

SHIRLEY, WILLIAM (1759), *Observations on a Pamplet lately Published, entitled, The Genuine and Legal Sentence Pronounced by the High Court of Judicature of Portugal upon the Conspirators against the Life of his Most Faithful Majesty* (London).

——(1762), *The Rosciad of C_v__nt G__rd__n* (London).

——(1765), *Electra, a Tragedy; and the Birth of Hercules, a Masque* (London).

SMITH, BRUCE R. (1987), *Ancient Scripts and Modern Experience on the English Stage 1500–1700* (Princeton).

STEPHEN, Lady (1920), 'Girton College, an Historical Sketch', *The Girton Review: Jubilee Number* (Cambridge), 50–63.

STONE, GEORGE WINCHESTER (1962) (ed.), *The London Stage 1660–1880*, IV. iii (Carbondale).

TALFOURD, FRANCIS (1850), *Alcestis; the Original Strong-Minded Woman: A Classical Burlesque in one Act* (Oxford and London).

——(1859), *Electra in a New Electric Light: An Entirely New and Original Extravaganza in One Act* (Lacy's Acting Edition, London).

TALFOURD, THOMAS (1844), *Tragedies* (London).

TANITCH, ROBERT (1987), *Ashcroft* (London, Melbourne, Auckland, and Johannesburg).

THEOBALD, LEWIS (1714), *Electra: A Tragedy. Translated from Sophocles, with Notes* (London).

VEEVERS, ERICA (1989), *Images of Love and Religion: Queen Henrietta Maria and Court Entertainments* (Cambridge).

VON ERFFA, HELMUT, and STANLEY, ALLEN (1986), *The Paintings of Benjamin West* (New Haven and London).

WASE, CHRISTOPHER (1649), *The Electra of Sophocles: Presented to Her Highnesse the Lady Elizabeth: With an Epilogue Shewing the Parallel in two Poems, The Return, and The Restauration. By C.W.* (The Hague).

WHITMAN, ALFRED (1902), *Valentine Green* (London).

WOOLF, VIRGINIA (1975), 'On not Knowing Greek', in *The Common Reader* (first published, 1925; London).

13

'A Crazy Enterprise':
German Translators of Sophocles,
from Opitz to Boeckh

RICHARD STONEMAN

Kindly spirits have long since fled from here. Two knights in dented armour lie in the dust beside a soot-blackened industrial hoist. Iron girders encircle a ruined factory, flames belch from metal casks. The human beings in this post-war rubbish dump declaim, screaming and stuttering, into the void; they lacerate and humiliate each other uncomprehendingly to death. In the highest row of the theatre the schoolchildren are scarcely disturbed by the surrounding racket. Any videotape could offer them something more exciting. At most they whisper more quietly, whenever their teacher leans over to admonish them. But of the tragedy *Antigone*, which is being performed below them in the dark and difficult translation of Friedrich

The literature on German literary classicism is considerable. The following general studies (most of which are not specifically cited in the notes) are particularly relevant to the subject of this paper. E. Behler, *German Romantic Literary Theory* (Cambridge, 1995); id., *Friedrich Schlegel* (Rowohlt Monographien, 1966); W. Benjamin, *The Origin of German Tragic Drama*, tr. J. Osborne (London and New York, 1977); E. M. Butler, *The Tyranny of Greece over Germany* (Cambridge, 1935); H. Cancik, *Nietzsche und die Antike* (Stuttgart and Weimar, 1995); H. Flashar, *Inszenierung der Antike* (Munich, 1991); F. J. Lamport, *German Classical Drama* (Cambridge, 1990); M. Marshall, *Hölderlin and the German Neo-hellenic Movement* (Oxford, 1923); Gabriele Schmoll May, *Tradition im Umbruch: Zur Sophokles-Rezeption im deutschen Vormärz* (New York, 1989); K. Reinhardt, 'Hölderlin und Sophokles', *Tradition und Geist* (Göttingen, 1960), 381–97; W. Schadewaldt, 'Antike Tragödie auf der modernen Bühne', *Hellas und Hesperien* (Stuttgart, 1960), 543–70; id., 'Hölderlins Übersetzung des Sophokles', ibid. 767–824; M. S. Silk and J. P. Stern, *Nietzsche on Tragedy* (Cambridge, 1981); G. Steiner, *Antigones* (Oxford, 1984); H. Trevelyan, *Goethe and the Greeks* (Cambridge, 1941; reissued with introduction by H. Lloyd-Jones, 1981).

Hölderlin, they gather at most that antiquity had something to do with self-destruction, the madness of war and the darkness of male power.[1]

This is the opening paragraph of an article which recently appeared in the German magazine, *Der Spiegel*, about the decline of classics and classical education in Germany. The article provoked considerable, and partly justified, outrage among classicists by its negative view of the current state of the subject; but I quote this passage, not because of its contemptuous view of some types of modern theatre production, but because the classical tradition is, almost unthinkingly, represented for a German readership by *this* play, by *this* author, and in the translation of Hölderlin.

Translation of Greek authors came late to Germany, and translation from classical languages never made itself as central to literary practice in Germany as it did in England; yet Hölderlin's Sophocles has acquired the status of a classic in its own right. What I want to explore in this chapter is the way in which the enterprise of translation meshed with that of literary creation, as well as that of scholarship, in the two centuries when German was coming into its own as a literary language. What were translators of Greek tragedy, and specifically of Sophocles, trying to achieve? Why did they choose the plays they did? How should we judge their work? I shall start with the earliest translators, but shall stop with the translation of *Antigone* by August Boeckh, which he completed in 1841. I choose this closing point because that is the moment at which the literary handling of Greek tragedy, and its scholarly study, begin to diverge in Germany; the two enterprises cease to be interwoven, and the great works of art and drama influenced or inspired by Greek tragedy—one thinks of Wagner's *Ring* cycle, or the plays of Gerhart Hauptmann on classical themes, or later those

---

[1] *Der Spiegel* 17 (1997), 216. 'Gute Geister sind hier längst entflohen. Zwei zerbeulte Ritterfiguren liegen im Staub neben einem russgeschwärzten Fabriklift. Eisenträger umrahmen eine industrielle Ruine, aus Blechtonnen lodern Brände. Die Menschen in dieser Nachkriegs-Müllhalde deklamieren schreiend und stammelnd ins Leere; verständnislos demütigen und schinden sie einander bis zum Tod. // Im obersten Rang des Theaters lassen sich die Schüler vom Untergangslärm kaum stören. Jedes Videospiel würde ihnen Aufregenderes bieten. Höchstens tuscheln sie gedämpfter, sobald der Lehrer sich mahnend herüberbeugt. Doch von der Tragödie 'Antigone', die unten in der schweren, dunklen Übersetzung Friedrich Hölderlins über die Bühne geht, erfahren sie bestenfalls, dass Antike etwas mit Selbstzerstörung, Kriegswahn und männlichem Machtdünkel zu tun haben muss.' This and all following translations from German are my own unless otherwise noted.

of Hofmannsthal—are carried out in independence of a scholarly engagement with the ancient text. Several of the authors I shall be discussing—including Johann Elias Schlegel, Hölderlin, and Boeckh himself—worked on their translations as part of a scholarly and even philosophical enterprise of understanding.

Let us begin by considering some contemporary views of what translation of the classics might be for. One of the earliest and most forcefully expressed discussions of this topic is a letter by Frederick the Great of Prussia, addressed to his minister Hertzberg in 1780. It was originally written in French, and was titled, not altogether cheeringly, 'On German literature; on the shortcomings one may object to in it; the causes of the same and the means to improve them'.[2] The king begins with praises of Greek art and language, and goes on to discuss the reasons why Greek writers have found so few imitators in German. He bemoans the fact that Greek and Latin are known only to a few scholars, and suggests that an energetic programme of translation would have a beneficial effect on the German language. Part of his concern here is that German is an unsatisfactory medium for any kind of literature, because the range of dialects is so wide that, for example, a Swabian cannot be understood in Hamburg; but he is also suggesting that the act of translation, or of reading translations, has a beneficial effect on style. 'Were the good writers of antiquity and our neighbours once translated, I should recommend reading them as a necessary and highly important matter.'[3]

An argument of this kind is one rather familiar in the history of translation in England: Alexander Tytler, in his *On the Principles of Translation* of 1790,[4] writes on his opening page 'In the works of Quinctilian, of Cicero, and of the Younger Pliny, we find many passages which prove that these authors have made translation their peculiar study; and, conscious themselves of its utility, they have strongly recommended the practice of it, as essential towards the

---

[2] Friedrich II, *Über die deutsche Literatur; die Mängel, die man ihr vorwerfen kann; die Ursachen derselben und die Mittel, sie zu verbessern*. Reprinted in Steinmetz (1985: 60–99); the passage referred to is on p. 60. The German translation by the Prussian diplomat Christoph Wilhelm von Dohm was prepared at the request of the king himself.

[3] Ibid. 79. 'Wären die gute Schriftsteller der Alten und Nachbarn einmal überstezt, so würde ich ihre Lektüre als eine notwendige und höchst wichtige Sache empfehlen.'

[4] Tytler (1790: 1).

formation both of a good writer and an accomplished orator.' The craze for translation in the English seventeenth century was a major influence on the development of poetry in that century; but, as James Sutherland has pointed out, we find at that period scarcely any sense of translation as having a historical function; it is, in effect, simply a type of rhetorical *inventio*.[5]

Frederick the Great, we shortly find, has strong views as to how these improvements to the German language shall be effected. For a start, something has to be done to prevent the further corruption of German taste by the appalling plays (*die abscheulichen Stücke*) of Shakespeare, which have already been translated into German.[6] Not only do these plays not observe the unities, but they allow the mixing of classes on stage: kings and gravediggers may appear in conversation! Frederick's second recommendation is the imposition of a national or core curriculum on all professors and philosophers: 'In my view, one should prescribe to every professor precisely the rules which he is to follow in his lectures.'[7] He proceeds to do so; the rules include the detail that the professor must denigrate the philosophy of Epicurus, defend Galileo, and say nothing at all about Locke. This is somewhat by the by to the project of translation, but I mention it as an indication of the unlikelihood of Frederick's recommendations being adopted in detail. In fact the practice of translation gathered momentum from this time onwards.

Many German writers exhibited a more historical outlook in their approach to translation. Nietzsche remarks (in *Die fröhliche Wissenschaft*[8]) 'One can estimate the degree of historical sense that a period possesses from the way in which it makes translations and attempts to incorporate past times and books.' His example is the remoteness of the Roman world portrayed in the dramas of Corneille from the actual Roman world, and it is evident from what he says that, for him, historicism is a virtue in a translator. That view was current already at the beginning of the Romantic period, when Friedrich Schlegel wrote his essay, *Über das Studium der griechischen Poesie*. Criticizing Voss's translation of Homer, he writes,

---

[5] Sutherland (1969: 409 f.).
[6] Friedrich II, in Steinmetz (1985: 81).
[7] Ibid. 83–4. 'Nach meiner Idee müsste man also jedem Professor genau die Regeln vorschreiben, die er bei seinen Vorlesungen zu befolgen hätte.'
[8] Nietzsche (1969: ii. 91, para. 83).

Voss's translation of Homer is a shining example of how truly and successfully the language of the Greek poets can be imitated in German. His ideal is, by general agreement, the product of mature reflection and superb execution. But woe to the imitator of the Greeks, who lets himself be led astray by the great translators! If he does not know how to separate the Objective Spirit from the Local Form, where they are most deeply melded, he is lost . . . In particular details [the work of Johannes Müller] breathes through and through an authentic sense of the ancients; but as a whole it still collapses into manneredness, because, alongside the classical spirit, the ancient individuality is also affected.[9]

Twenty pages later, he writes again,

The French, like the English and Italians, are now absolutely lacking in objective theory, and in genuine knowledge of ancient poetry. Even to find the right path, which would lead them on to the road, they would have to come to school with the Germans. A thing to which they are hardly likely to steel themselves!

In Germany, and only in Germany, aesthetics and the study of the Greeks have reached a height which must have as a natural consequence a complete transformation of the art of poetry and of taste.[10]

Two of the most thoughtful discussions of translation appeared in 1793 and 1813 respectively: the first is Wilhelm von Humboldt's essay *Über das Studium des Altertums, und des griechischen insbesondere*, and the second is Friedrich Schleiermacher's essay *Über die verschiedenen Methoden des Übersetzens*.[11] Humboldt argues that

---

[9] Schlegel (1982: 272–3): 'Vossens Übersetzung des Homer ist ein glänzender Beweis, wie treu und glücklich die Sprache der griechischen Dichter im Deutschen nachgebildet werden kann. Sein Ideal ist unstreitig so reiflich überlegt, als vollkommen ausgeführt. Aber wehe dem Nachahmer der Griechen, der sich durch den grossen Übersetzer verführen liesse! Wenn er hier, wo sie am innigsten verschmolzen sind, den objektiven Geist von der lokalen Form nicht zu scheiden weiss, so ist er verloren . . . Im Einzelnen atmet das Werk durch und durch echten Sinn der Alten: im Ganzen aber verfällt es dennoch wieder ins Manirirte, weil neben dem klassischen Geist auch die antike Individualität affektiert ist.'

[10] Ibid. 293–4: 'Ohnehin fehlt es den Franzosen wie den Engländern und Italiänern . . . an objektiver Theorie, und an ächter Kenntnis der antiken Poesie. Um nur auf die Spur zu kommen, wie sie den Weg dahin finden könnten, wuŕden sie bei den Deutschen in die Schule gehn müssen. Eine Sache, zu der sie sich wohl schwerlich entschliessen werden! // In Deutschland, und nur in Deutschland hat die Ästhetik und das Studium der Griechen eine Höhe erreicht, welche eine gänzliche Umbildung der Dichtkunst und des Geschmacks notwendig zur Folge haben muss.'

[11] Wilhelm von Humboldt, 'Über das Studium des Altertums, und des

translations may be designed for three kinds of person: (1) for those who cannot read the original; (2) for those who can read the original, as a help to understanding; and (3) for those who can read the original, as an interim measure before they embark on intensive study. His valuation of these three purposes is interesting. The first he regards as the least important and satisfactory; it requires *Anpassung*, adaptation to the needs of the reader, and hence lack of fidelity. The second is important, but not the best method of understanding a text: it does require fidelity to the letter of the original. The third is the most important because it may tempt the reader to turn to the original; this sort of translation requires fidelity to the spirit of the original, as well as to its 'clothing', by which he means that the translator should as far as possible reproduce the diction and metre of the original. Humboldt, like Schlegel, regards Greek literature as being of unique value and excellence, and insists that one should study all aspects of the Greeks. Again, his argument is for an essentially historical translation.

Schleiermacher's work is of a very different character. A philosophical study of the process of translation, it effectively concludes that real translation is quite impossible. It is, he says, a 'crazy enterprise' (ein thörichtes Unternehmen').[12] His primary reasons are (1) the fact that words in different languages are never exact synonyms, and (2) the fact that one cannot think outside one's own language, or even perhaps think in the same way as a member of another class who uses the same language. He dismisses the usual justifications of translation: paraphrase gets around the irrationality of language, but does it by a mechanical process of adding *Zeichen* (signifiers?) until a kind of mathematical equivalence is reached; imitation (*Nachbild*) preserves the individuality (*Einerleiheit*) of the work, but destroys its identity. It aims to make a similar impression, but not to 'bring the two languages together'. These two activities are the border outposts of translation; real translation must effect a rapprochement of the author and the reader, and this can be done either by bringing the reader to the author, or by bringing the author to the reader. The first aims to create a replacement for the original, to write as the author would have written, if he knew German. This can only be done by scholars immersed in the original

griechischen insbesondere', in Humboldt (1969: 1–24 = Nippel 1993:33–56); Friedrich Schleiermacher (1838: 207–45); also in Störig (1969).

[12] Schleiermacher (1838: 216).

culture, and they will be unable to convey their own depth of understanding, and will mock at all translations. The second is to write in the way that you know the original author (his example is Tacitus) would have written, if he were a German. This, however, is quite unattainable because language is not a mechanism, and if Tacitus wrote as a German, he would no longer be Tacitus. QED. As a release from complete aporia, Schleiermacher concludes by stating that only the first method—writing as an author would have written if he knew German—is remotely allowable. As Walter Benjamin put it in a similar conclusion to his discussion of translation,[13] it is not that the Greek text must become German, but that the German language must become Greek.

I have gone into some detail about these theoretical approaches to translation from classical authors because they bear very directly on what the translators of Sophocles were trying to do. The growth of a historical sense about Greek tragedy and Greek culture in general, of Greek otherness, and a philosophical concern about the nature of the act and processes involved in bringing Sophocles into another language, are both central to the practice of the translators. It is time to turn to the first of our authors, Martin Opitz.

Opitz (1597–1639) is a kind of founding father of German literature. Born in Silesia, he moved in 1620 to Holland to avoid the disturbances of war. Here he became acquainted with the humanist Daniel Heinsius and studied with him, as did his younger contemporary Andreas Gryphius. In this circle Opitz and Gryphius will come to know the great Dutch poet Joost van den Vondel (1587–1679). Though ten years older than Opitz, Vondel lived until 1679, forty years after Opitz's death from plague. Opitz did not live to see the publication of the earliest of Vondel's translations from Sophocles, his *Electra* of 1639, but I wonder whether it was something in the atmosphere surrounding Heinsius that led both authors to try their hand at translations of Greek plays. Vondel later translated the *Oedipus Tyrannus* and the *Trachiniae*, as well as plays of Euripides and works of Ovid and other classical authors. Opitz translated Seneca's *Trojan Women* in 1625, the year after the appearance of his little book, *Von der deutschen Poeterey*. This book says frustratingly little about the theory of literature, and nothing at all about translation as such, being mainly concerned

---

[13] Walter Benjamin, 'The Task of the Translator', in Benjamin (1970: 69–82); the reference is to 80 f.

with the rhetorical selection of topics, correct diction, prosody and rhyme. The book concludes with a programme for his own literary activity in German:

We follow that to which God and Nature lead us, and we hope to be assured that respectable people will express favour and love towards us, for the service we seek to do to our fatherland. But to those who despise this divine science, that they may not go home empty, we wish, in the tragedies we shall in future write, to give them those persons who, in the chorus, have to howl and wail at the narration of disasters; so they can then bewail at length their own coarseness and lack of understanding.[14]

This rather obscure sentence does not promise well for a profound understanding of the nature of Greek tragedy, and the one such translation Opitz produced, is *Antigone* of 1636, bears out one's anxiety. It is a work born before its time, and though it is accurate in linguistic terms and competent in its versification (the dialogue is in Alexandrines, the chorus in shorter ballad lines), it does not, I think, convey much of the character of the original. His translation of the first strophe of the chorus πολλὰ τὰ δεινά, shows his limitations, not least in the choice of the feeble *List*, 'cunning', for that most imponderable of opening phrases.[15]

> List ist gar bey vielen Dingen,
> Menschen Witz behält den Preis,
> Dann er kühnlich sich zu schwingen
> In dem Wiederwinde weiss
> Über die beschaumten Wellen,
> Und die Schiffahrt anzustellen.
> Auch der Götter Werck, die Erde,
> Die stets währt und nie erliegt,
> Dass er Früchte von ihr kriegt,

[14] Opitz (1970: 71): 'Wir folgen dem | an welches vns Gott vnd die natur leitet | vnd auss dieser zueversicht hoffen wir | es werde vns vornemer leute gunst vnd liebe | welche wir | nebenst dem gemüte vnserem Vaterlande zue dienen | einig hierdurch suchen | nicht mangeln. Den verächtern aber dieser göttlichen wissenschafft | damit sie nicht gantz leer ausgehen | wollen wir inn den Tragedien so wir künfftig schreiben möchten die Personen derer geben | welche in dem Chore nach erzehlung trawriger sachen weinen vnd heulen mussen: da sie sich denn vber jhren vnverstand vnd grobheit nach der lenge beklagen mögen.'

[15] Dr Holford-Strevens has pointed out to me in discussion that in Middle High German 'List' is more than the modern 'cunning', and means rather 'the skill of a craftsman'; perhaps this meaning lingered into early modern German.

Lässt er durch die Schlacht der Pferde
Jährlich nimmer ungepflügt.

The run of the style is very similar to that of Vondel in his Dutch translation, which uses Alexandrines for the dialogue and a similar ballad metre for the choruses: Vondel's translation of a famous line from the *Oedipus* (896), τί δεῖ με χορεύειν, is if anything even more inept: 'Wat lust het my ten rey te gaen?' which I take to mean 'Why should I want to go to the dance?'

It was hard for Opitz to penetrate deeply into the character of Greek tragedy because in the foreground of his vision was the German *Trauerspiel*, a genre superficially similar but actually very different, and in which he was himself active. Walter Benjamin describes his work in this genre: 'For Opitz it is not the conflict with God and Fate, the representation of a primordial past, which is the key to a living sense of national community, but the confirmation of princely virtues, the depiction of princely vices, the insight into diplomacy and the manipulation of all the political schemes, which makes the monarch the main character in the *Trauerspiel*.'[16] His translation of *Antigone* thus conveys the superficial sense, but completely bypasses the inner meaning of the work: in Humboldt's terms it is of his first type, it adapts itself to his audience but is not faithful to his original; in Schleiermacher's terms it is nowhere at all!

The next Sophocles translation does not appear for another hundred years: this is the *Electra* of Johann Elias Schlegel, written in the 1740s but not published until the posthumous appearance of his collected works. Schlegel (an uncle of the famous brothers Schlegel) works in a very different literary ambience from Opitz. The dominance of the *Trauerspiel* on the German stage has been replaced by an enthusiasm for the French classical theatre of Corneille and Racine. The theory of drama is largely derived, as it was for the French dramatists, from Scaliger's presentation of the *Poetics* of Aristotle, with the result that the question of the unities is in the forefront. German literary theory was currently dominated by Johann Christoph Gottsched (1700–66), who saw himself as a successor to Opitz in the remodelling of the German language; his efforts to reform the theatre were based on an unblinking adherence to the French model, and his doctrines became tiresomely prescriptivist.

[16] Benjamin (1977: 62).

Schlegel's translation of *Electra* was undertaken at the behest of Gottsched, 'who wished to add to the *Poetics* of Aristotle, which he had decided to edit, as an aid to elucidation, one of the most famous Greek tragedies in a German translation.'[17] However, the work was done at a time when Gottsched's reputation was already fading as a result of the attacks of the Swiss critics J. J. Bodmer and J. J. Breitinger, and consequently the translation was never given its final polish for publication. Gottsched had become a figure of fun by the next decade, when Lessing ridiculed him in his Seventeenth Letter on Literature,[18] and J. E. Schlegel called his style 'niedrig, kriechend und pöbelhaft' ('low, creeping, and vulgar').[19] But the categories in which he discussed literature did not become outmoded for a good deal longer. Though the French theatre ceased to dominate German stages, Lessing, in his long exchange of letters with C. F. Nicolai and Moses Mendelssohn,[20] continued to debate the poetic theory of Aristotle in terms of the unities, and worried endlessly at the precise way in which tragedy should arouse fear and pity, what precisely those terms meant, and how the effect could be replicated in the modern theatre.

Schlegel's translation is quite a scholarly piece of work. This passage is from the third stasimon (1058–68).

> Ist der Vogel, der mit Speise
> Dem zur Nahrung sich beschwert,
> Der ihn selbst gezeugt, genährt,
> Denn für uns vergebens weise?
> Menschen folgen andere Bahn.
> Doch wo Jupiter noch blitzet,
> Und im Himmel Themis sitzet;
> Ist es nicht umsonst gethan.
> Auf! dring in des Todes Höhlen!
> Dieses Hauses Schmach und Fall
> Den Atriden zu erzählen;
> Töne dein betrubter Schall!

Stylistically it sticks to the alexandrine metre for dialogue, ballad metre for choruses; but it is accompanied by copious notes which

---

[17] J. E. Schlegel, *Electra*, preface. On Gottsched's attitude to Greek tragedy, cf. Bünemann (1928: 21). On Schlegel in general, Wilkinson (1995).

[18] G. E. Lessing, Seventeenth Letter, 16 February 1759, in Lessing (1973: v. 70–3).

[19] Rentsch (1890).

[20] Lessing (1973: iv: 155–227).

explain and justify the translation and consider difficulties of interpretation. His note on his translation of the first strophe[21] is probably incorrect (it seems more likely that the first lines refer, not to Ismene's disloyalty to Electra, but to her disloyalty to her dead father), but Schlegel has observed that there is an issue to be discussed, and he has accompanied is verse translation with a prose version to make clear his understanding of the lines. This is Humboldt's second type of translation—to aid those who can read the original—and in Schleiermacher's terms it counts, I think, as paraphrase—one of the border outposts of translation.

Schlegel's *Electra* is the first harbinger of the explosion of German translation from Greek (and other languages) in the second half of the eighteenth century.[22] It would seem that a tradition had been established, Frederick's prayers had been answered, and German literature was embarking on a new phase.

I think that is probably true, and that this flurry of translation did have a profound effect on literature; but it is interesting that some of the greatest poets absorbed the classical influence from these translations without actually translating anything themselves. Neither Schiller nor Goethe, central though classical literature, including tragedy, was to their poetic practice, undertook translations of Greek poetry (Goethe translated one scene of the *Bacchae* late in life, accompanied by caustic comments about how 'the poor

---

[21] 'Nach dem Griechischen wäre, wie mire es scheint, diese Stelle so zu übersetzen: Was sehen wir die verständigen Vögel in der Höhe an, welche sorgfältig denenjenigen Speise schaffen, von denen sie hervorgebracht sind, und bey denen sie Hülfe gefunden haben, und thun doch nicht eben so? So weit bezieht sich die Betrachtung des Chors auf den vorhergehenden Streit der Elektra mit ihrer Schwester. Das folgende aber zielt auf Agamemnons Ermordung.'

[22] Translations from English were also popular: Bodmer (the attacker of Gottsched) had translated *Paradise Lost* in 1732, and there also appeared translations of *Robinson Crusoe*, numerous Scots ballads (by Herder, 1773), and the first complete Shakespeare, by Christoph Martin Wieland (1762–6), which was the version that so enraged Frederick the Great. The doyen of translators from the classical languages was Johann Heinrich Voss (1751–1826), whose *Odyssey* appeared in 1781, and his *Iliad* in 1793. He also translated Virgil's *Georgics* (1789), Ovid's *Metamorphoses* (1798), the works of Horace (1806), of Aristophanes (1821) and of Propertius (1830), as well as Shakespeare (1818–29). Around this time Schleiermacher also made his translation of the works of Plato (a particularly tough nut for a philosophical translation), but the only attempt on Greek tragedy was made by C. F. Tobler, at Weimar in 1781, and the versions of Aeschylus and Euripides were not published. (See Flashar 1991: 54.)

herrings' who don't know Greek can't appreciate it).[23] It seems quite
out of the blue that Hölderlin's translations of Sophocles appeared,
in the last years of his sanity, in 1799–1804.

Hölderlin's poetry, and not least his Sophocles translations, have
attracted an enormous amount of scholarly discussion, to the point
where the matter has become an industry. This is all the more
impressive as the translations were received by contemporaries as
the work of a lunatic. The younger Voss wrote to a friend: 'What do
you say to Hölderlin's Sophocles? Is the man mad (*rasend*) or is he
just pretending to be? Is his Sophocles just a satire on bad
translators? Recently I spent the evening with Schiller at Goethe's
home and entertained them both with it. Do read the fourth chorus
of the Antigone—you should have seen how Schiller laughed.'[24]

It is not clear whether these great poets were more amused by the
mannered syntax of the German or the apparent unreliability of the
translation: I guess the former, unless they were reading line-for-
line. The inaccuracy of Hölderlin's translations has become a
byword, and there is a good example already in the first strophe
of the chorus Voss mentions, Ἔρως ἀνίκατε μάχαν. For lines 787–90

καί σ' οὔτ' ἀθανάτων φύξιμος οὐδείς
οὔθ' ἀμερίων σέ γ' ἀν-
θρώπων, ὁ δ' ἔχων μέμηνεν,

Hölderlin has

Fast auch Unsterblicher Herz zerbricht
Dir und entschlafender Menschen, und es[25] ist,
Wers an sich hat, nicht bei sich.

Almost also heart of Immortals breaks against you, and of men who are
falling asleep, and it is, for whoever has it in himself, not in his right mind.

Well, it is possible to see what caused Voss and his friends so much
mirth and confusion; none the less, Hölderlin's translations have, as
I noted at the outset, become classics in their own right, often being
performed in a tidied-up version by Martin Walser.[26] It has become

[23] See Trevelyan (1941: 268).
[24] Quoted in W. Schadewaldt 'Einleitung zur Antigone', in Schadewaldt (1960:
268); cf. Constantine (1988: 271).
[25] The sense is somewhat improved by reading *er*, as Professor Nesselrath pointed
out to me in discussion. It would be valuable to see the translations edited by a
scholar intimate with the Greek source as well as with Hölderlin's manuscripts.
[26] Walser and Selge (1969: 27).

a commonplace to say that there is a howler in virtually every line of the translations; and yet their poetic quality, and their intensity, is regularly acknowledged. I want to spend a little time on Hölderlin's Sophocles, because it seems to represent an extreme case of the questions raised by the idea of translation at all. Most scholars who have studied Hölderlin's Sophocles, as well as his brief and hermetic notes on the plays and his understanding of them, have found that something intensely serious is going on beneath the surface.

Friedrich Hölderlin, born in Swabia, had received a standard German classical education in boarding schools at Denkendorf and Maulbronn, and at the theological seminary in Tübingen. As soon as he began to write poetry his themes combined an attempt to rescue a traditional Christian piety with a desire to recreate the world of the Greek gods in Germany; this, allied with a revolutionary fervour stimulated by the French Revolution, made for a complex intellectual mixture. His love affair with the young woman whose husband had employed him as a tutor, and its unhappy ending, further troubled his enthusiastic spirit, and by the age of 32 his mind was seriously disturbed. In 1807, at the age of 37, he was entrusted to the care of a carpenter in Tübingen, and spent the rest of his life in an upper room in the carpenter's house. That life lasted another thirty-six years, in which he wrote no poetry, or only the simplest ditties.

The translations of Sophocles (and of Pindar) date from the time when his madness was incipient, and were published in volume form in 1804. Apart from *Hyperion* and some poems that appeared in periodicals, they are the only works that were published in his lifetime. At a time when his mental energy was not sufficient for sustained literary work, the translations became a kind of exploration of literary form, of Greek religion, of his own psyche; the notes to *Oedipus* and *Antigone* make very clear that he reads the tragedies as, in some way, a commentary on his own affliction. Even the passage quoted above, with its reference to 'broken hearts', more violent than anything in the original, seems to echo his own experience. Are we looking here at a case of Schleiermacher's second model of translation: this is how Sophocles would have written if he had been Hölderlin? The question bears thinking about, not least as a test case for Schleiermacher's theory.

We should begin by looking at some of the practical details of Hölderlin's version. First, his Greek was clearly not that of a scholar, though he had had a regular classical education with many hours of Greek per week. Wolfgang Schadewaldt's indispensable study of the translations[27] lists many of his venial and worse errors: he mistakes μέν for μή, διά for Δία, ὄμβρος for ὄλβος, for example. Furthermore, he had a bad edition of Sophocles. The one he owned was a copy of the Frankfurt edition of 1555: it is usually called the Juntina, but Jochen Schmidt[28] has correctly described it as the Braubach edition published in Frankfurt. There is a copy of this edition in the Bodleian; one of its most striking features is the inadequate colometry of the choruses. See for example *Antigone* 1137 ff., where this edition has

> τὰν ἐκ πασᾶν τιμᾶς
> ὑπερτάταν πολέων
> ματρὶ σὺν κεραυνίᾳ
> καί νυν ὡς βιαίας
> ἔχεται πάνδημος πόλις
> ἐπὶ νόσῳ μολεῖν
> καθαρσίῳ ποδὶ Παρνησίαν
> ὑπὲρ κλιτὺν ἢ στονόεντα
> πορθμόν . . .

Compare this with the edition of Brunck, first published in 1816:

> τὰν ἐκ πασᾶν
> τιμᾶς ὑπερτάταν πολέων
> ματρὶ σὺν κεραυνίᾳ.
> καί νυν, ὡς βιαίας
> πάνδημος ἔχεται πόλις
> ἐπὶ νόσου, μολεῖν ποδὶ
> καθαρσίῳ Παρνησίαν
> ὑπὲρ κλιτύν, ἢ
> στονόεντα πορθμόν . . .

It is notable that Hölderlin made no attempt to reproduce Greek metres: the iambic parts of the plays are done into blank verse, but the choruses are in free verse, without strophic responsion. It seems that Hölderlin did not even know about metre—a point in which Boeckh's translation, being based on Gottfried Hermann's epoch-making text, represents a great advance.

[27] W. Schadewaldt, 'Hölderlins Übersetzung des Sophokles', in Schadewaldt (1960).

[28] Schmidt (1994-5).

Linguistic points may also be observed in this chorus, notably the strange case of the Naxian maidens. In 1148 ff. Brunck's (and earlier) texts have

> παῖ Διὸς γένεθλον
> προφάνηθι Ναξίαις
> Θυίασιν ἄμα περιπόλοις

while modern texts incorporate Bergk's excellent correction

> προφάνηθ᾽ ὦναξ.

It was not then to be avoided that Hölderlin would translate

> Sohn, Zevs Geburt!
> Werd offenbar! mit den Naxischen
> Zugleich, den wachenden Thyaden, die wahnsinnig
> Dir Chor singen, dem jauchzenden Herrn.

The point is not perhaps an important one in itself, but it needs to be borne in mind that Hölderlin was at the mercy of the text before him. More interesting from the point of view of translation method is his practice—visible in this passage—of adhering closely to Greek word order, repeating adjectives with articles in asyndeton. Another example is *Ant.* 1284-5

> ἰὼ δυσκάθαρτος Ἀΐδου λιμήν,
> τί μ᾽ ἄρα τί μ᾽ ὀλέκεις;

where Hölderlin's Creon exclaims

> Io! Io! du schmutziger Hafen
> Der Unterwelt! Was? mich nun? was? verderbest du mich?

Not only does Hölderlin try to reproduce the sequence of words exactly; there is also a very interesting howler here. 'Schmutzig' 'dirty' is Hölderlin's translation of δυσκάθαρτος, 'unappeasable'. While this is certainly, in one sense, a simple 'mistake', it also has reverberations with Hölderlin's theory of what tragedy was about. The same can be said of one of the famous of all his mistranslations, of the line (*Ant.* 450)

> οὐ γάρ τί μοι Ζεὺς ἦν ὁ κηρύξας τάδε

which becomes

> Darum. *Mein* Zevs berichtete mirs nicht.

Hölderlin's theory of tragedy is expounded in the brief and obscure notes to the translations, and it has been well elucidated by Jochen Schmidt in an article (see n. 28) which represents some developments of the exhaustive discussion by Schadewaldt. Hölderlin's idea of tragedy has nothing to do with tragic flaw, he never mentions fear and pity, he is not interested in character, the unities, or the dominance of plot. His is a philosophical interpretation of tragedy. His notes to Oedipus present the play, not as the unfolding of a linear tale, but as the achieving of a balance: 'Das Gesetz, das Kalkul, die Art, wie, ein Empfindungssystem, der ganze Mensch, als unter dem Einflusse des Elements sich entwickelt . . . ist im tragischen mehr Gleichgewicht, als reine Aufeinanderfolge.' Each play, he says, is divided by a caesura in which the hero 'steps into the path of fate', 'is removed into another world and snatched into the eccentric sphere of the dead'. ('Er tritt ein in den Gang des Schicksals . . . die [ihn] in eine andere Welt entrückt und in die exzentrische Sphäre der Toten reisst'.)

These are dark words, but they need to be considered alongside Hölderlin's polarity of the *aorgisch* and the *organisch*, by which he means something like what Nietzsche meant by Apolline and Dionysiac. (Just to be confusing, Hölderlin's *aorgisch*, his world of chaos and the irrational, is the territory of Apollo, while Dionysus is a kind of gentle Christ-like figure in his thought.) For Hölderlin, the hero is *zornig*, 'raging', and the action of a tragedy consists in a hero (Oedipus or Antigone) pitting himself, not against a human rival (this is not the dialectical view of Antigone espoused by his contemporary and college friend Hegel), but against the god who is waiting to 'snatch him into another realm'. The tragic denouement is an epiphany of the god.

The terror of this view of Greek tragedy becomes clear when we realize that Hölderlin, who throughout his poetic career had striven to create a union of Greek religion with the Christianity he had been brought up in, has decided that the gods are only to be met through an experience of this kind of pain. Furthermore, he saw his own madness as an onslaught of the gods: in a letter of November 1802 to Böhlendorff he writes 'Apollo hat mich geschlagen'. The notes to Oedipus make it even more plain that he sees the tragedy as a kind of commentary on his own condition: Oedipus' crime is his desire to know, he is engaged in a 'crazed search for consciousness' (das narrischwilde Nachsuchen nach einem Bewusstsein).[29]

[See opposite page for n. 29]

Let us look in the light of this at one of the most magnificent pieces of poetry in Antigone, both in Greek and in German, Antigone's lament, especially 823 ff., the lines beginning

> ἤκουσα δὴ λυγροτάταν ὀλέσθαι
> τὰν Φρυγίαν ξέναν
> Ταντάλου Σιπύλῳ πρὸς ἄ-
> κρῳ, τὰν κισσὸς ὡς ἀτενὴς
> πετραία βλάστα δάμασεν,
> καί νιν ὄμβροι τακομέναν,
> ὡς φάτις ἀνδρῶν,
> χιών τ᾽ οὐδαμὰ λείπει
> τέγγει δ᾽ ὑπ᾽ ὀφρύσι παγ-
> κλαύτοις δειράδας· ᾷ με δαί-
> μων ὁμοιοτάταν κατευνάζει.

Bernard Böschenstein[30] has analysed Hölderlin's translation of this stanza to show how far it diverges from the original Greek, not this time through a lack of competence in Greek, but because Hölderlin was using the lines to say something of his own. ξέναν is translated as 'lebensreich', λυγροτάταν as 'der Wüste gleich'. In terms of Hölderlin's view of the elemental powers, Niobe starts as 'full of life' a representative of the 'aorgisch', who as a result of her conflict with the god becomes desert-like, sterile, 'organic'. Antigone's 'raging' insistence on her duty brings her to a destructive (aorgisch) encounter with the god ('mein Zevs') which leads her to her death in the tomb, sterile and desert-like—or, in terms of the later passage, 'dirty Hades'. Böschenstein concludes: 'Alle zumal in den Chorliedern der Antigonä hervortretenden Abweichungen der Hölderlinischen Übersetzung folgen der an diesem einen, extremen Beispiel vorgeführten programmatischen Tendenz, Antigones Schicksal als die Strafe für eine unzulässige Vereinigung mit der Gottheit aufzufassen, hinter der eine eigene analoge Erfahrung steht, die zuletzt gleichfalls in eine für den Geist tödliche Strafe mündet, nämlich in das Dürrwerden der ursprünglichen üppigen Fruchtbarkeit' (59).

Hölderlin himself regarded this passage as the finest passage in the play: 'Der erhabene Spott, so fern heiliger Wahnsinn höchste

---

[29] Hölderlin (1969: ii. 733). Cf. the later passage, 'Zuletzt herrscht in den Reden vorzüglich das geisteskranke Fragen nach einem Bewusstsein' (ibid. 734).

[30] Böschenstein (1994–5).

menschliche Erscheinung, und hier mehr Seele als Sprache ist, übertrifft alle übrigen Auѕserungen.'[31] We should note too Antigone's response to the chorus's comment after this stanza, οἴμοι γελῶμαι. Hölderlin translates this as 'Weh! Närrisch machen sie mich' (Alas! they are making me mad). These plays are about Hölderlin's madness as much as they are about his—undoubtedly profound and considered—theory of tragedy and of Greek religion; and they are much more about this than they are about an historical attempt to bring the Greek world to the reader. It is difficult to place them in terms of Humboldt's categories of translation, but if, as I suggested, they do fit the most demanding of Schleiermacher's categories, that may explain why they have become classics of German literature in their own right, whatever their shortcomings as cribs.

My last example will be more briefly treated. In 1841 J. J. C. Donner was commissioned to provide a translation of *Antigone* for performance at the court of Friedrich Wilhelm IV in Berlin (it was followed in 1845 by *Oedipus at Colonus*). The translation was revised by August Boeckh and the music was provided by Felix Mendelssohn.[32] The most notable advance on previous methods of translation is its adherence to the original metres. The dialogue is done in Alexandrines, but the choruses are in accentual versions of the quantitative metres of the original. German poets had discovered the hexameter early, Klopstock being the first to use it, and Voss had employed it for his translations of Homer; in general German recreates the run of the hexameter better than any English attempt has ever done (the Elizabethan efforts are uncouth, but Tennyson scored some success with his Virgilian hexameters). Wilhelm von Humboldt used original metres in his translation of the *Agamemnon*, which appeared in 1816, remarking that German of all modern languages was the only one capable of reproducing the rhythm of the original.[33] It must be remembered that the colometry of many of the texts was quite bad in the eighteenth century (though there were better texts than the one Hölderlin owned to draw

[31] Hölderlin (1969: ii. 785).

[32] See Flashar (1991: 79–81). There are recordings of Mendelssohn's music by the Berliner Rundfunkchor conducted by Stefan Soltesz (Königshof: Capriccio 1993), serial nos. 10392 (*Antigonä*) and 10393 (*Ödipus*).

[33] Wilhelm von Humboldt, *Aeschylos' Agamemnon, metrisch übersetzt*, preface (in *Gesammelte Werke* 8), 136.

upon!). A further problem was the long persistence of the Reuch-
linian pronunciation of Greek in German education, which meant
that it was pronounced much as if it were modern Greek, with no
distinction of long and short syllables and with several of the vowels
sounding like 'i'. In the circumstances a deep understanding of
quantitative metres was in effect impossible.

Humboldt in preparing his *Agamemnon* had the advantage, as he
tells us, of long conversations with Gottfried Hermann, at that time
engaged on his epochal study of Greek metre (also published in
1816). His *Agamemnon* is based on Hermann's text and his
colometry is that of Hermann.

Donner in his translation of Antigone followed the same method.
This the first stasimon of *Antigone*, in Donner's version.

> Vieles Gewalt'ge lebt, und Nichts
> Ist gewaltiger als der Mensch.
> Denn selbst über die dunkele
> Meerflut zieht er, vom Süd umstürmt,
> Hinwandelnd zwischen den Wogen
> Die rings umtoste Bahn.
> Er müdet ab der Götter höchste,
> Gäa, die ewige, nie zu ermattende,
> Während die Pflüge sich wenden von Jahr zu Jahr,
> Wühlt sie durch der Rosse Kraft um.
>
> Flüchtiger Vögel leichter Schaar
> Und wildschwärmendes Volk im Wald,
> Auch die wimmelnde Brut der See
> Faħgt er listig umstellend ein
> Mit nezgeflochtenen Garnen,
> Der vielbegabte Mensch.
> Er zwingt mit schlauer Kunst des Landes
> Bergdurchwandelndes Wild, und den mähnigen
> Nacken umschirrt er dem Ross mit dem Joche rings,
> Wie dem freien Stier der Berghöh'n.

Boeckh revised this for his own publication (which did not appear
until 1884), and the booklet to the recorded version I have gives
slightly different wording again. But all three versions follow the
same metrical pattern. We know that Mendelssohn devoted a good
deal of time to the study of Greek metre when preparing his music,
and the example here (Fig. 1) shows that the setting does in fact
follow the rhythm of the Greek (though it is rather more difficult to

A *Punch* cartoon of an 1845 London performance of Sophocles' *Antigone* with choruses by Mendelssohn

discern through the medium of the quaint English translation of Donner's German).

Boeckh had thought a lot about the nature of Greek music too, and in his essay on Antigone[34] he remarks that the music of the κομμοί will have been 'passionate': 'leidenschaftliche Musik, bei den Gesängen der Antigone höchst wahrscheinlich mixolydische, einen herrlichen Gegensatz gegen die Dorische Ruhe der Anapästen des Chors'. Perhaps it was this reference (maybe in a programme note) which led to one of the rather numerous parodists who quickly responded to the performance presenting a newly discovered Sophoclean drama, Ariadne auf Naxos, 'with a chorus of guinea-pigs in the Mixolydian mode'.[35]

Mendelssohn's setting of the Antigone became very popular, and this became the standard version of the play for much of the nineteenth century. It was restaged frequently, including one season in Munich, where the translation was revised again by the great Munich philologist Friedrich Thiersch.[36] Antigone's lament was played at Mendelssohn's own funeral. But the music was not universally admired. Friedrich Hebbel called it 'as suitable to Sophocles as a waltz to a sermon', and Richard Wagner called it 'eine grobe künstlerische Notlüge' (a crude artistic white lie), and 'scheussliche Liedertafelmusik' (dreadful dinner-table music), commenting that Mendelssohn's scholarly attainment should have warned him off setting the play to music.[37]

Donner and Boeckh's translation represented, not so much a culmination, as there is hardly anything that could be called a tradition of Sophoclean translation before them, but a beginning. With the educational reforms of Wilhelm von Humboldt, the study of antiquity (not just of texts) became central to German education. Translations were made by scholars, or by poets; scholar and poet no longer interacted as they had done in the practice of John Elias Schlegel. Boeckh's translation, as one would expect of that great scholar, is the first of the historical translations of Sophocles (in Nietzsche's sense): it is a translation suitable for those who can read

[34] Boeckh (1824 and 1828); reprinted in his edition of Sophocles' *Antigone* (Leipzig, 1884).
[35] See the note in the booklet accompanying the CD, by H. C. Worbs, p. 11.
[36] Flashar (1991: 92 f.).
[37] For Hebbel, cf. the reference in n. 35. For the quotation from Wagner see Flashar (1991: 106).

the original to inspire them to go further (in Humboldt's terms); it is an exercise in writing as the author would have written had he known German (and *not* as if he had *been* a German, or Hölderlin), in Schleiermacher's terms. From here on the story of translation is the story of attempts to recreate an ancient original in terms that will not so much challenge a modern readership or audience, as be acceptable to them in their own terms.

Only Hölderlin represents an unflinching representation of strangeness, a work that positively struggles to be as alien and difficult as its original. If that gives it a continuing life as a work of German art (to borrow a phrase from *Die Meistersinger*), it does not necessarily make it acceptable to schoolchildren—or to journalists from *Der Spiegel*.

REFERENCES

BENJAMIN, W. (1970), *Illuminations* (London).
—— (1977), *Ursprung des deutschen Trauerspiels* (Frankfurt: Suhrkamp 1963): cited from the English translation by John Osborne, *The Origin of German Tragic Drama* (London and New York: Verso, 1977).
BOECKH, AUGUST (1824 and 1828), 'Über die Antigone des Sophokles', *Abh. d. Königl. Preuss. Akad. d. Wissenschaften*.
BÖSCHENSTEIN, BERNARD (1994–5), 'Göttliche Instanz und irdische Antwort in Hölderlins drei Übersetzungsmodellen', *Hölderlin Jahrbuch*, 47–63.
BÜNEMANN, H. (1928), *Elias Schlegel und Wieland als Bearbeiter antiker Tragödien* (Leipzig).
CONSTANTINE, D. (1988), *Hölderlin* (Oxford).
FLASHAR, H. (1991), *Inszenierung der Antike: das griechische Drama auf der Bühne der Neuzeit 1585–1990* (Munich: Beck).
HÖLDERLIN, FRIEDRICH (1969), *Werke und Briefe*, ed. F. Beissner and J. Schmidt (Frankfurt: Insel).
HUMBOLDT, W. VON (1969), *Werke in 5 Bänden, II: Schriften zur Altertumskunde und Aesthetik* (Darmstadt: Wissenschaftliche Buchgesellschaft).
LESSING, G. E. (1973), *Werke* (Munich: Hanser).
NIETZSCHE, FRIEDRICH (1969), *Werke*, ed. K. Schlechta (Munich: Hanser).
NIPPEL, WILFRIED (1993), *Über das Studium der alten Geschichte* (Munich: dtv).
OPITZ, MARTIN (1970), *Buch von der deutschen Poeterey* (1624), ed. C. Sommer (Stuttgart: Reclam).

RENTSCH, J. (1890), *J. E. Schlegel als Trauerspieldichter* (Leipzig).

SCHADEWALDT, WOLFGANG (1960), *Hellas und Hesperien* (Stuttgart).

SCHLEGEL, FRIEDRICH (1982), *Über das Studium der griechischen Poesie* (1795–97), ed. with introduction by Ernst Behler (Paderborn: Schöningh).

SCHLEIERMACHER, F. (1838), *Über die verschiedenen Methoden des Übersetzens*, in *Sämtliche Werke, dritte Abteilung: zur Philosophie, Zweiter Band* (Berlin: Reimer).

SCHMIDT, JOCHEN (1994–5), 'Tragödie und Tragödientheorie: Hölderlins Sophoklesdeutung', *Hölderlin Jahrbuch*, 64–82.

STEINMETZ, H. (1985) (ed.), *Friedrich II, König von Preussen, und die deutsche Literatur des 18. Jahrhunderts: Texte und Dokumente* (Stuttgart: Reclam).

STÖRIG, H. J. (1969) (ed.), *Das Problem des Übersetzens* (Darmstadt: Wissenschaftliche Buchgesellschaft).

SUTHERLAND, JAMES (1969), *English Literature of the Late Seventeenth Century* (Oxford).

TREVELYAN, H. (1941), *Goethe and the Greeks* (Cambridge; 2nd edn. 1981).

TYTLER, ALEXANDER FRASER (1790), *On the Principles of Translation* (Edinburgh).

WALSER, M, and SELGE, E. (1969), *Sophokles* Antigone, übersetzt von Friedrich Hölderlin, bearbeitet von Martin Walser und Edgar Selge (Frankfurt: Insel).

WILKINSON, E. M. (1995), *Johann Elias Schlegel: A German Pioneer in Aesthetics* (Oxford: Blackwell). ·

Index Locorum

General Index

DATE DUE

SEP 0 4 2003

DEMCO 38-297